AF361313

ILLNESS AND AUTHORITY

Disability in the Life and *Lives* of Francis of Assisi

DONNA TREMBINSKI

Illness and Authority

Disability in the Life and *Lives* of Francis of Assisi

UNIVERSITY OF TORONTO PRESS
Toronto Buffalo London

© University of Toronto Press 2020
Toronto Buffalo London
utorontopress.com
Printed in the U.S.A.

ISBN 978-1-4875-0741-1 (cloth)
ISBN 978-1-4875-3620-6 (EPUB)
ISBN 978-1-4875-3619-0 (PDF)

Library and Archives Canada Cataloguing in Publication

Title: Illness and authority : disability in the life and lives of Francis
of Assisi / Donna Trembinski.
Names: Trembinski, Donna, 1974– author.
Description: Includes bibliographical references and index.
Identifiers: Canadiana (print) 20200285998 | Canadiana (ebook)
20200286153 | ISBN 9781487507411 (cloth) | ISBN 9781487536206 (EPUB) |
ISBN 9781487536190 (PDF)
Subjects: LCSH: Francis, of Assisi, Saint, 1182–1226 – Health. | LCSH:
Christian saints – Italy – Assisi – Biography. | LCGFT: Biographies.
Classification: LCC BX4700.F6 T74 2020 | DDC 271/.302 – dc23

This book has been published with the help of a grant from the Federation
for the Humanities and Social Sciences, through the Awards to Scholarly
Publications Program, using funds provided by the Social Sciences and
Humanities Research Council of Canada.

University of Toronto Press acknowledges the financial assistance to its
publishing program of the Canada Council for the Arts and the Ontario Arts
Council, an agency of the Government of Ontario.

For Michael and Clara

Contents

Acknowledgments

Illness and Authority was almost ten years in the making, and it could not have been done without the support of many, many people. First and foremost, it is safe to say that this book would not have existed had my daughter Clara not come into the world in 2010. She refocussed my life and changed my goals and, yes, even my research projects. My partner Michael also provided unwavering support, from proofreading chapters to organizing playdates when I was working. My extended family, my parents Don and Chris, my sister Carrie, my aunt Carole, and my in-laws Don, Jean, Chris, and Margaret also provided immense support, cheerleading, and not a little bit of guilt about not being done yet! Finally, Denise DeCoste, whose role in our lives defies category, helped me, in more ways that I can count, find the time to finish this book.

Academic colleagues and friends were also sources of inspiration and support. Since early school days, Drs. Isabelle Cochelin, Joe Goering, and Bernice Kaczynski have provided continual guidance on academic life and writing. I am also particularly blessed to have had a cohort of wonderful medievalists with whom I trained at the University of Toronto; I still often turn to them for answers and advice.

The community of scholars at my current institution, St. Francis Xavier University, who supported this research project in spite of the fact that it was about the "wrong" St. Francis, also deserve special thanks – especially, but not only, Dr. Robert Zecker in the Department of History, Dr. Christina Holmes of the Health Program, Dr. Sharon Gregory in the Department of Art History, and Drs. Robert Kennedy and Ron Charles in the Department of Religious Studies. The Department of History's administrative assistant, Joanne Bouchard, also enabled me in many ways to finish this project, from helping me figure out the new photocopier to witnessing contracts. Finally, I could not have finished this project without the support of the staff of the Research Services Group and the Angus L. MacDonald Library and at St.FX, especially its inter-library loans specialist, Angela Hagar, who was amazing at finding the books I needed and coaxing libraries to lend them to me. This work would also not have been possible without the support of research funds from St. Francis Xavier's University Council for Research, the University Travel Fund, and especially the Father Edo Gatto Chair in Christian Studies Research Fund. That the book manuscript received a grant from the SSHRC-funded Aid to Scholarly Publications, which allowed it to be published in a timely manner, was the icing on the cake.

More than colleagues but friends, Drs. Cory Rushton and Rhonda Semple heard me vent about difficulties in writing and research, and helped to keep the process of completing this book on track. I think they are probably happier than I am that this book is done.

Over the years I have presented work related to this book, and received valuable feedback, in many different venues, from the Feminist Hive for Research at St.FX to the World of St. Francis of Assisi Conference held in Siena in 2015. I presented parts of this so often to colleagues at the Atlantic Medieval Association and the Canadian Society of Medievalists that I am sure that members groaned when they saw another talk about St. Francis – but they never complained (to me at least). Always, the questions and comments on those talks helped to move this project forward; for instance, a particularly astute and pointed question by Dr. Elizabeth Edwards inspired me to write an entire section of this book.

Many other colleagues read and critiqued parts of this draft, including Dr. Marc Cels, Dr. Mairi Cowan, Dr. Mary Dzon, Anne Laughlin, Dr. Cory Rushton, Dr. Bert Roest, Dr. Rhonda Semple, Alec Foran, and Dayna Smockum. I would also like to thank the two anonymous reviewers for their helpful comments and Suzanne Rancourt of UTP, who helped shepherd this book through to completion.

A final thank you goes to the students I have had over the years, first at the University of Toronto, then Queen's University, and now St. Francis Xavier University. Thank you for geeking out with me as I talk and teach about what I love. I hope you've learned at least a little something, because I have learned so much from you.

Abbreviations

AC	*Assisi Compilation*
AP	*Anonymi Perusini* or *Anonymous of Perugia*
AVR	*Acts of Blessed Francis in the Rieti Valley* or *Actus beati Francisci in Valle Reatini*
FA:ED	*Francis of Assisi: Early Documents*
FAS	*Francis of Assisi: Scripta*
FF	*Fontes Franciscani*
LM	Bonaventure, *Legenda maior*
LTS	*Legenda trium sociorum* or *Legend of the Three Companions*
MGH	*Monumenta Germaniae Historica*
MOPH	*Monumenta Ordinis Fratrum Praedicatorum Historica*
PL	*Patrologia Latina*
RB	Francis of Assisi, *Regula bullata*
RNB	Francis of Assisi, *Regula non bullata*
TdeM	Thomas of Celano, *Tractatus de miraculis* or *Treatise on Miracles*
VB	Thomas of Celano, *Vita brevior* or *The Life of Our Blessed Father Francis*
VP	Thomas of Celano, *Vita prima*
VS	Thomas of Celano, *Vita secunda* or *Remembrance of the Desire of a Soul*

ILLNESS AND AUTHORITY

Disability in the Life and *Lives* of Francis of Assisi

Introduction

Francis of Assisi suffered frequent illnesses throughout his adult life. His vision was seriously impaired by his mid-thirties and he became so disabled as to be unable to walk by the end of his life.[1] Even for those well familiar with the story of the saint, this blunt summary of Francis' life may come as a surprise. Francis is far better known for his love of nature, his experiential devotional practices, and, of course, founding the Franciscan Order.

Born circa 1180, Francis was the son of a wealthy cloth merchant in Assisi. In his youth, the early *vitae* tell us, he was frivolous and light-hearted until he took up arms to fight for Assisi against the rival territory of Perugia. After this period of his life, in which he may have been held as a prisoner of war, Francis began to reconsider his life, turning to increasingly more serious contemplation of God. He left his family and his inheritance behind, devoting himself to the repair of local churches and to the care of lepers. Behind these actions was a desire to follow in the path of Christ and the apostles, in a life of poverty and itinerant preaching.

Francis' way of life soon attracted followers, and in 1209 he and his group travelled to Rome; there Pope Innocent III granted them licence to follow their chosen path of apostolic poverty. Thus the Franciscan Order was created. In those early years, Francis and his followers travelled and preached, drawing many to their new way of life. Francis himself travelled to Spain and Egypt, though he frequently turned back from other planned trips for a variety of reasons. He initially led the order himself, but by 1221 or so, the order had grown so large and so diverse that he no longer felt capable of leading it himself. He resigned as its leader, and though he did write a revised rule for the order circa 1223, he increasingly divorced himself from roles of leadership and spent more time in contemplation. At Christmas 1223 in the small town of Greccio, Francis reportedly created the first Christmas crèche, a scene emblematic of the personal piety Francis was so famous for, even during his own lifetime. In the early fall of 1224, Francis and a few of his close companions retreated to a hermitage on La Verna in the Apennine Mountains. There, in contemplation, he saw a vision of a seraph, who, as later tradition would have it, gifted Francis the wounds of Christ. Francis continued his contemplative life and still preached occasionally, but was increasingly worn out by his ascetic practices. In the fall of 1226, no longer able to walk, he asked to be returned to his home in Assisi. Shortly afterward, in late October, he died there in the company of his closest companions.

Like many saints of the period, Francis practised rigorous asceticism; it is well known that he suffered, sometimes tremendously, during his life. Academic discussions of his suffering, however, even by historians, remain few. Most studies of Francis focus on the saint's decision to embrace absolute poverty, his ascetic practices more generally, and, of course, his reception of the *stigmata*, the wounds he reportedly carried during the last two years of his life. Very few biographies, even recent ones, mention Francis' illnesses except in passing. In part, this is no doubt owing to the modern propensity for "disappearing" and invalidating bodies and individuals who exist outside the given parameters for "healthy," "whole," "normative," or "average."[2] As Lennard J. Davis wrote in 1995, "disability is the bodily state that dare not speak its name in professional circles."[3] In the same work, Davis argued that, as with analyses of race, class, and gender, one could only begin to interrogate and challenge normalized categories of difference (for instance ablebodied and disabled) by recognizing them as socially constructed and specifically tied to historical moments and developments, and, above all, changeable.[4] Since Davis wrote his work, scholarly interest in disability studies has grown remarkably, but it is still in its relative infancy, especially in the discipline of history.

Even within the field of medieval disability studies, Francis' illnesses have been largely bypassed by scholars. Of course, in the Middle Ages ascetic suffering was expected of holy people and the passive acceptance of illness was expected as well. The multitude of works on the importance of bodily suffering to religious devotion, especially for women in the High Middle Ages, attests to this.[5] However, an impairment that incapacitated individuals to the point that they were unable to function in expected ways was problematic in medieval contexts, just as it can be in modern ones. People then, as now, were often valued according to their ability to produce and contribute to the economy.[6] For women using suffering as a tool to engage in mystical devotion, lack of active participation in economic life was not especially concerning, but for Francis of Assisi, who had largely practised an active devotion by preaching and begging publicly until he was too infirm to continue, this was more problematic. It is for this reason, perhaps, that scholars speak of the Franciscan way of life as a new form of devotion, as one which combined an active life with experiential, emotive, and more contemplative devotion.[7]

Whatever the reasons for scholarly disregard of Francis' illnesses on the part of historians, that they did disregard them is not in question. In the last one hundred years, more than a dozen works have described Francis' illnesses and attempted to diagnose them. Nearly all of them were written by physicians, rather than historians, and, for the most part, their work has been passed over by scholars of Francis' life. Unlike medical scholars, most historians have tended not to focus on naming or categorizing Francis' illnesses. Indeed, many historians treat all of the saints' illnesses and infirmities, as they do the *stigmata*, as part and parcel of the hagiographic trope of *imitatio christi* found in many saints' *lives* written in the High Middle Ages. Francis' illnesses, if they are discussed at length at all, are regarded as the mechanism by which Francis was able to attain an even more perfect relationship with Christ. A survey of two of the most recent biographies of Francis in English will demonstrate this trend clearly: André Vauchez' *Francis of Assisi: The Life and Afterlife of a Medieval Saint*, published in French in 2009,[8] and translated into English by Michael Cusato and published in 2012;[9] and Augustine Thompson's *Francis of Assisi: A New Biography*, also published in 2012.[10]

André Vauchez' biography of Francis spends little time discussing the saint's illnesses, even those he suffered in the last two years of his life. For Vauchez, none of Francis' illnesses or impairments are important facets of his life story. The first mention of Francis' illnesses occurs during his discussion of Francis' withdrawal from his position as leader of the Franciscan movement at a general chapter most commonly dated to September of 1220.[11] Vauchez writes: "To justify this unexpected decision … [Francis] pointed to the state of his health."[12] Yet Vauchez does not accept this rationale, provided by reports of Francis' own speech, writing:

> [Francis] had indeed come back sick from the East, where he had, it seems, contracted trachoma, which was eventually to make him virtually blind, and malaria, which raked him with violent pains of the spleen and liver. But the real reason for his unexpected withdrawal was probably his desire to avoid putting himself into conflict with the papacy or with those friars who were calling for a more precise definition of the order.[13]

Thus, for Vauchez, Francis' failing health masked the true reason for the saint's formal withdrawal from the leadership of the order. Indeed, Vauchez argues that Francis' withdrawal from leadership was a calculated move – while removing himself from a position of power, Francis preserved for himself a higher authority, one based on his devout spirituality rather than his position as founder.[14] Vauchez acknowledges that Francis' illnesses took a turn for the worse by 1224, but even then, he maintains that the primary reason for the illnesses was not physiological but rather emotional and mental distress over the direction the order was taking under new leadership. The suffering he felt as a result of this unease became nagging, only further "aggravated by problems of health."[15] Even at this late date, for Vauchez, Francis' suffering was primarily caused by psychological worry. The state of Francis' health in the last two years of his life take up less than a page in Vauchez' biography[16] and, in describing the saint's death, Vauchez twice uses the medieval hagiographic convention of "giving up his spirit"[17] rather than describing the physical reality of the saint's passing. Certainly, in Vauchez' work, the illnesses and impairments the saint experienced are not at all central to the telling of his life.

Only slightly better in this regard is Augustine Thompson's biography of Francis, published in 2012. In Thompson's view, Francis had always been unsuited to the leadership and administrative roles that the founding of an order as immediately popular as the Friars Minor required. It is this reality, along with recognition that he was a poor leader, that plagued Francis' interaction with his order throughout his life. Little mention is made of the role of illness in the saint's life, and certainly Thompson does not believe his illness impacted the saint's ability to lead – he was already unsuited to the task before he became seriously ill. For Thompson, Francis' perception of his own incompetencies, not his impairments, led to his withdrawal from that leadership role, likely in the fall of 1220.[18] Francis' illnesses and infirmities, constant throughout his converted life and especially problematic after his return from Egypt in 1219, are a far distant reason for Francis' withdrawal, in Thompson's estimation. Thompson describes the fevers and encroaching blindness Francis experienced after 1219 as resulting in "unstable health." He argues that the fevers Francis complained about, as recalled by his early companions, were perhaps "a bout of the malaria that he had contracted in Egypt," but he immediately notes that for Francis "the torment was above all spiritual."[19]

Thompson also denies that Francis' illnesses or infirmities played a role in the so-called Chapter of the Mats, which probably occurred in 1221. At this chapter, Francis reportedly sat on the floor at the feet of his vicar Elias of Cortona, who presided over the meeting. When Francis wanted to address the crowd, he did it through Elias, speaking into his vicar's ear. Elias then relayed the message to the whole of the chapter. Jordan of Giano, a probable early witness to the chapter, notes in his *Chronicle* that Francis did this because he was too ill to address the crowd himself,[20] yet Thompson dismisses this as unlikely, believing it was the saint's humility that was the source of his actions.[21] Thompson does concede that Francis' illness became much more severe in the last two years of his life,[22] but here, too, the illnesses were a part of his larger struggle with humility. In Thompson's view, "illness intensified Francis' interior struggle to combine total submission to others with his status as the moral exemplar for the brothers."[23] To provide a specific example, Thompson writes that near the end of his life, Francis was "nearly blind and hardly able to eat" and could only eat "specially prepared food, but when the brothers went to the trouble of preparing it, he refused to eat it."[24] Thompson also notes that the future saint struggled "with the temptation to use his power harshly"[25] and only accepted medical treatment on the insistence of his vicar.[26] However, Thompson does not believe that Francis' *stigmata* were caused in any way by his various illnesses; indeed, he suggests that "[m]iraculous or not, the form of the marks is difficult to square with some natural cause,"[27] just as "[i]t is difficult to imagine a fraud or psychologically induced condition that would take such an unusual shape as fleshy nail heads." To summarize, according to Thompson, Francis' illnesses and infirmities play a minor role in the saint's life until the last two years, when, he suggests, they became so severe they resulted in the saint's steady physical decline. The *stigmata*, however, were not a product of these illnesses.

Even the recently published *Cambridge Companion to Francis of Assisi* minimizes Francis' experience of impairment. There is no chapter of the book dedicated to exploring the impact of Francis' infirmities, and none of the chapters mention the saint's illnesses other than in passing. Like Vauchez' recent biography of Francis, Michael Cusato's essay about Francis and his movement suggests that although Francis was ill with malaria at the time of his decision to step down as the leader of the order, this was not the primary motivating factor in the decision. Rather, his resignation came about because Francis was unable to reconcile the different visions individuals within the order had for it. Cusato writes that "[s]tunned by the clashing visions contending within the fraternity and overwhelmed by what he might have to do to bring the order back to its original way of life, Francis chose instead to resign as minister."[28] Cusato acknowledges that "the last days of Francis were difficult ones filled with physical pain and suffering,"[29] but concentrates on the saint's ability to overcome that suffering to compose the *Canticle of the*

Creatures.[30] In describing Francis' death, Cusato also falls back on traditional hagiographic language, writing that the saint "surrendered his spirit back to God, from whom he had come forth and to whom he now returned to praise for ever."[31]

Only two other essays in the *Cambridge Companion* allude to Francis' suffering and these only in passing. Michael Blastic's essay about the early hagiographies of Francis notes that Thomas of Celano had to place the reception of the *stigmata* in the chronology of Francis' life, since Elias of Cortona's encyclical letter did not mention when the saint received the wounds of Christ.[32] Thomas placed the event later in Francis' life, during his retreat at La Verna, at a time when, according to Blastic, the saint already "suffered physically in addition to his own spiritual and emotional distress with regard to the order."[33] Steven McMichael notes in passing that most of Francis' writings date from after 1220 and were thus "influenced by his state of disillusionment and sickness."[34] Note that both authors place physical suffering alongside, and perhaps subordinate to, Francis' emotional turmoil.

Historians of disability fare little better in recognizing the reality of Francis' illnesses and infirmities. The most surprising example can be found in Henri-Jacques Stiker's *A History of Disability*. While Stiker notes that Francis transformed medieval ideas about poverty, making individuals and groups previously marginalized newly deserving of admiration, he does not comment at all on Francis' own myriad impairments. Unintentionally ironic, Stiker ends his discussion of Francis' influence on the acceptance of poverty as a positive virtue by stating "[i]t may be remarked that in the course of the inquiry into St. Francis, I seem to have lost sight of the truly disabled."[35] Stiker certainly has, for from the very moment of his conversion, Francis was plagued by various infirmities. Angela Montford's work, which describes the medical practices of mendicant friars in the thirteenth century, does not spend much time describing Francis' illnesses, mentioning only his reception of cautery for his eye disease and his care of lepers.[36] Even Irina Metzler, whose pioneering study of disability in the Middle Ages opened the now rich and growing field of medieval disability studies, discusses Francis only as a saint who heals the sick and infirm, not as an infirm individual himself.[37]

Framework and Methodology

This book is an attempt to provide a corrective lens to the seemingly common view that Francis' illnesses and infirmities did not matter during the course of his life except in so far as his devotional practices and spirituality were concerned. As with other frameworks that the methodologies of social history have brought to bear (for instance those that highlight constructed cultural narratives of race and gender), looking at the texts of Francis' life through the new lens of disability theory allows for different insights into how the meaning of the saint's life and early hagiographies might be interpreted. It insists that the illnesses and impairments Francis suffered throughout his entire adult life be recentred in the history of his life. It also allows for a more nuanced understanding of the tensions that developed between a holy man who needed his health and strength to guide his new and wildly popular order, and the living saint who increasingly withdrew himself from such duties to live a more contemplative life. It also allows attentive readers to see how Francis' earliest hagiographers struggled to speak coherently about Francis' ailments and their impact on his secular and even spiritual life.

The application of the theories and methodologies of disability studies to the discipline of history is still in its relative infancy.[38] In 2012, medievalist Julie Singer outlined four models used by students of historical disability.[39] In part because no single model of disability fits all experiences of non-normate bodies, even for a single individual in a single place and time, models of disability used by scholars have multiplied.[40] The most commonly used today is the so-called medical model, because it is effective in demonstrating how languages of disability are constructed around the experiences of particular impairments in modern contexts. In this medical model, impairments are medicalized as bodily experiences that are detrimental to full participation in life and society, and that can be ameliorated by medical intervention.[41] This model might be a reasonable one to apply to some individuals who experienced impairment in the Middle Ages. For instance, Giles Le Muisit, a French abbot of the fourteenth century, had his eyesight restored with cataract surgery.[42] However, some evidence from the Middle Ages does not support the idea of the desirability of medical intervention to mitigate or cure impairments. It does, however, support the desirability of holy and divine intervention. As Edward Wheatley has argued, while medicine is the basis of modern narratives surrounding impairment, medieval narratives of the same had their origin in Catholic theology.[43] In the modern medical model, an impairment is framed as the absence of full health; in the medieval religious model, it is the absence of divine grace that is most often narratively linked to impairment. In this latter context a cure may come with greater faith and trust in God.

While it is important to remember that not every impairment was automatically and unthinkingly linked to a sinful existence, the ethos

of medieval Europe encouraged such linkages at a general if not individual level. Yet, the links between sin and illness were not monolithi-
cally accepted.[44] Medieval theologians argued that the fall of mankind
had brought every kind of suffering, including illness, into the world,
and preachers in the High Middle Ages ensured this message was cir-
culated. Sermons and hagiographies at that time taught that patient
endurance of suffering and affliction would be rewarded in the afterlife and that prayer and belief in God could bring relief in the form of
miraculous healing. Canon law, too, enforced the connection between
cure of illness and cure of the soul. A new canon issued at Lateran IV
in 1215 insisted that people see physicians only after they had seen a
priest since people who have been confessed may respond better to the
physicians' medicine, as "after the cause ceases, so the effect stops."[45]
This canon implies that some people were seeking the advice of physicians instead of praying for a cure. Thus, in the High Middle Ages,
when Francis lived, we appear to have a pluralist approach to illness
and medicine. On the one hand, health practitioners of all kinds were
consulted regularly, especially if individuals could afford it, and, on the
other, the sheer number of healing miracles which occurred at shrines
suggests cures were very often sought through divine intervention. In
many cases ill or impaired individuals sought a variety of medical and
divine interventions.

Other models that have been used to discuss historical experiences
of impairment include the social model of disability, which differenti-
ates between physiological impairment and the socially imposed barriers to agency that theorists categorize as disabilities. Disabilities in this
respect are constructed by the cultures in which impaired individuals reside. As Irina Metzler has argued, the application of the social
model of disability to medieval Europe might lead to the finding that,
although impaired people existed in medieval Europe, a community
of disabled persons did not.[46] She noted that no umbrella term encom-
passing people with different impairments, such as the English word
"disabled," existed in Latin or in any vernacular of the time.[47] Yet, it
seems clear, too, that people in the Middle Ages who suffered from
impairments did have their agency restricted in various ways. From
statutes forbidding blind individuals from entering various cities in
the Italian peninsula to the confinement of lepers to certain areas, the
restrictions medieval societies placed on people with known infirmities marked them as different. Though "disabled" as a category of people did not yet exist in medieval Europe, disabled people certainly did.
A caveat to the social model also exists. It reminds scholars that the
division between a person's physiological experience and their social

marginalization and/or lack of agency cannot necessarily be easily teased apart.[48] Julie Singer's transhuman model of disability makes the same point, while reminding scholars not to fall into the trap of using binary language. Instead disabilities might be placed on a spectrum, and not every impairment need be read as a disability in every culture.[49] This is certainly true of the Middle Ages, where impairment could be read as a sign of special grace.

Feminist disability studies can also highlight particular aspects of Francis' embodied experience as described in early *lives* of the saint. Feminist disability studies aim to combine the insights feminist theory has provided about how different cultures inflect the body with different meanings with findings from the newer field of disability studies. Like the social model of disability, feminist disability studies emphasizes that different cultures can present different meanings for similar impairments. In the words of Rosemarie Garland-Thomson, it sees the construction of disability, like the construction of race and gender, as an "exclusionary and oppressive system rather than as the natural and appropriate order of things."[50] Feminist disability studies, then, tries to understand how cultural narratives of disability impact cultural discussions and even personal experiences of the impaired embodied self.[51]

Scholars of feminist disability studies recognize the historic link between women and disabled bodies in Western culture.[52] This idea has its roots most clearly in the work of Aristotle, who argued that women's cooler and wetter complexions meant that they were passive, weaker, and generally inferior to hotter and drier men, who were more active by nature.[53] In *On the Generation of Animals*, Aristotle famously stated that "the female is, as it were, a mutilated male."[54] Aristotle's hierarchy of humours was adopted into the medical language of the Middle Ages through the work of Galen, though nowhere did Galen suggest outright, as Aristotle did, that females were imperfect males.[55] Nonetheless, the triumph of Aristotelianism within the universities in the thirteenth century ensured that, during the High Middle Ages, Aristotle's position shaped the medieval intellectual worldview.

But, if women were regarded as imperfect or impaired men, does it follow that impaired men were regarded as more feminine? This has been generally assumed, if not adequately theorized, by specialists of modern disability studies. For instance, Daniel J. Wilson has suggested that American survivors of the polio crisis in the 1950s were "unmanned," though he further argues that the experience was one of returning to childhood rather than of being feminized.[56] In her study of the eighteenth-century Parisian cloth merchant Jean-Denis Jameu, Catherine Kudlick suggests that Jameu's marriage was arranged in much the same way a daughter's marriage would be arranged (to someone of lesser stature), and that Jameu understood his position as a blind man to be similar to that of a woman.[57] It has been generally recognized that impaired men tend to renegotiate their masculinity, given societal responses to their impairments.[58]

Explicit examples of disabled men being regarded as feminized are rare in the medieval context. One literary example, from the century after Francis, might be found in Chaucer's Pardoner, who is described at length in the General Prologue. Chaucer describes the Pardoner's long blond hair, "yelow as wex" and arranged in an attractive style, and notes that the Pardoner did not have a beard, nor would he ever. The Pardoner's soft voice is also mentioned, and the narrator concludes his description by noting that the Pardoner "trowe he were a geldying or a mare."[59] Much ink has been spent on exploring how the Pardoner's sexuality and gender can be understood. The narrator's words, "I trowe he were a geldying or a mare," raise the possibility of castration, a condition which may have been constructed as a disability in the Middle Ages. Certainly it impacted readers' perceptions of the Pardoner's masculinity.[60] Elspeth Whitney's work on the Pardoner as a phlegmatic man allows an opening for constructing the Pardoner as "disabled," in terms of his possible castration, but also in terms of his humoral complexion.[61] As Whitney argues, a phlegmatic complexion, more than any other, would have suggested sexual ambiguity to medieval audiences.[62] As a person's role in sex acts was closely tied to perceptions of his or her gendered characteristics,[63] the possibility that Chaucer's Pardoner was regarded by his audience as an effeminate man must be acknowledged.[64] Although modern scholars are only beginning to explore this viewpoint, the Pardoner is one site where medieval notions of sexuality, sex, and gender further intersect with medieval perceptions of a disabled body. It is this nexus of disability, gender, and power that will be explored in the final chapters of the present study of St. Francis.

As this book will demonstrate, reading Francis' own writings, his early *vitae*, and early chronicles of the order through the lens of disability studies, and feminist disability studies in particular, allows for startlingly different conclusions about Francis' life than those presented by many scholars of Francis. Intended to offer a particular perspective to add to our growing knowledge about Francis, this book will argue the following: 1) that Francis suffered from various illnesses and infirmities throughout his converted life; 2) that those illnesses and impairments limited the secular power Francis was able to command over the early Franciscan Order and within the medieval church, and helped to create an environment in which he had to seek alternative ways to establish and retain authority in his order; 3) and that Francis' early biographers recognized that his illnesses and consequent lack of secular power within the order he had founded were of concern for the legacy of the saint and, to compensate, they employed different narrative strategies to demonstrate the saint's moral authority. To explore each of these arguments in detail, this book is divided into six chapters. Chapter 1 explores how Francis' various infirmities have been interpreted by scholars of the nineteenth and twentieth centuries, before ultimately concluding that the impossibility of knowing what modern physicians would have diagnosed Francis to be suffering from does not negate the reality of his infirmities in his own time. In fact, the specificity with which scholars addressed descriptions of Francis' symptoms can remind us to centre these symptoms on our explorations of Francis' life.

By carefully examining Francis' own writings and his earliest hagiographers' testimony about his life and illnesses, chapters 2 and 3 demonstrate in detail how central Francis' illnesses were throughout his life. Various episodes have been interpreted inaccurately by modern scholars and these have served to de-emphasize Francis' experience of impairment. Here, they are re-examined to demonstrate the everpresent reality of Francis' infirm body and the social consequences of his ailments. Chapter 4 explores the tensions Francis experienced as he navigated the expectations placed upon him as a leader of a newly established religious order and a holy man, even as he experienced periods of illness and suffered from ailments that sometimes seriously impacted his ability to lead. In particular, tensions between the need to care for his body in the face of his own perceptions of holy ascetic practices are examined. Francis' desire to refuse medical care and accept his ailments as God's will for him, and his order's insistence that he seek treatment, will also be explored for what they suggest about how Francis' ideal of obedience may have even denied him his own bodily autonomy. Chapter 5 examines how Francis' earliest hagiographers, from Thomas of Celano to Bonaventure, worked to disappear Francis' illnesses and infirmities by limiting discussions of them in various ways. From focusing on morals and object lessons rather than the infirmity itself, to disappearing doctors and pain, to diminishing the role that Francis' guardian played caring for his health, the saint's early hagiographers employed various narrative strategies that de-emphasized, or outright disappeared, many instances of his impairments and illnesses.

By way of a conclusion, chapter 6 explores how Francis established alternative modes of power for himself as he was increasingly denied formal mechanisms of authority within the order he had founded and within the larger structures of the Roman Catholic Church. It further demonstrates that Francis' Latin hagiographers framed his suffering as a way of demonstrating his nearness to Jesus, investing him with an unassailable moral authority derived from God's support, the proof of which was written on the saint's body itself. Indeed, the very wounds that denied Francis access to secular modes of power are those that allowed him to claim a very different kind of authority, one derived directly from God, and that could be used to challenge the more worldly authority of the church hierarchy. This section concludes speculatively, by questioning if Francis' disabilities, which denied him access to traditionally masculine modes of power within the Catholic Church while at the same time granting him greater moral authority owing to his suffering embodied state, allowed medieval hagiographers and modern scholars to read his more experiential mode of devotion as feminine.

Sources and the Franciscan Question

Fortunately for scholars who study Francis and the early Franciscan Order, there is an abundance of thirteenth- and early fourteenth-century sources that narrate the saint's life – some of which have been rediscovered only in the last decade. The survival rate of so many sources is, in one respect, surprising, for after Bonaventure wrote his *Legenda maior and Legenda minor* in the early 1260s, members of the order were asked to destroy all other earlier works. There was nothing particularly nefarious about this request. It was an attempt to create unity and meaning out of the many earlier formal and informal *lives* of Francis that already existed before 1260. It is our luck that the request was not vigorously carried out everywhere. The result is that, aside from Francis' own writings, there are some ten sources that include information about the saint that predate Bonaventure's attempt at writing a coherent and formulaic saint's *life*. As all of these sources have been discussed in depth elsewhere, I will include only a short introduction to each here. The sources are divided into three clear categories: works attributed to Francis himself; formal *lives* of Francis, written to tell and explain the significance of the saint's experience to Christians everywhere; and informal reminiscences of Francis' life, usually written in response to a call for such remembrances and often lacking the organizational and exegetical structure of the more formal *lives*.

Works Attributed to Francis

Francis claimed to be "ignorant and uneducated,"[65] yet a surprising number of works attributed to him have come down to us today. Only three are in the saint's own handwriting, but that we even have these is owing to the fact that the parchment pieces on which he wrote were treated with the devotion shown to relics. All three of these autographs are important, since they attest to the encroaching blindness Francis experienced in the final years of his life. Two of the three autographs, *The Praises of God* and a blessing he wrote to his close companion, Brother Leo, can be found on one parchment, called the *Assisi Chartula*, now housed as a relic at Sacro Convento in Assisi. Although contained on the same parchment, *The Praises of God* was likely written earlier than the blessing. The third autograph is a short letter also addressed to Brother Leo, likely written after the *Praises*, but before the blessing. All three texts almost certainly date from between 1224 and 1226, the last two years of Francis' life.[66]

Several other texts that have come down to us in various forms have also been attributed to Francis. The collection includes some eight letters (some in different redactions); songs, prayers, and praises; several different recensions of the so-called *Regula non bullata*, the unapproved, earliest version of the Franciscan *Rule*; and the *Regula bullata*, the *Rule* that was approved by Pope Honorius III and, of course, Francis' *Testament*.[67] In spite of difficulties in the lateness of witnesses of some of these texts, all are generally regarded as authentic and will be used as reasonably reliable representatives of Francis' thoughts, if mediated through secretaries and editors.

Formal Lives of Francis

The first official *life* of Francis was written by an early convert to Franciscanism, Thomas of Celano. Thomas was not a close friend or confidant of Francis; he had, in fact, spent the last years of Francis' life with the Franciscan mission in Teuton, the new German province established in 1221. He was *custos* or administrative superior for an area within the province from 1223 and seems to have spent most of the time until Francis' death there.[68] Sometime after Francis' death, Thomas travelled to Assisi, where, scholars suggest, he attended the saint's canonization.[69] While there he was commissioned to write the first official *life* of Francis which he completed shortly after the saint's canonization and perhaps as early as 1228. Between 1230 and 1240, Thomas wrote two other *lives* of Francis, the *Choir Legend*, which was a summarized version of the

Vita prima in a format suitable for use to celebrate the saint's feast, and a new version of Francis' *life*, the *Life of Our Blessed Father Francis*, sometimes now called the *Vita brevior*. The *Vita brevior* contains some material not found in the *Vita prima* and has only recently been discovered in its entirety.[70] Dalarun believes that *The Life of Our Blessed Father* and the *Vita prima* were sources for Julian of Speyer's short *life*, completed circa 1232, and Henry d'Avranches versified *life* of Francis, completed circa 1235.[71] The precise ways in which these early texts, all certainly written before 1240, intersect and connect are just beginning to be understood.

Another set of formal *lives* was composed in the 1240s, after the fifth minister general of the order, Crescentius of Iesu, sent out a call for any remembrances of Francis from the older members of the order, to be recorded for posterity. This new information was acquired between approximately 1244, when Crescentius' call went out, and 1247, and was used by Thomas of Celano to write two further *lives* of the saint – the *Remembrance of the Desire of a Soul*, sometimes referred to as the *Vita secunda*, and the *Treatise on Miracles*. Both were completed by 1250 at the latest, and incorporated some of the new material gathered as a result of Crescentius' call.[72] Divisions within the order occasionally present themselves in these later works by Thomas, especially in the *Remembrance*. In one especially poignant scene recalled in this text, Francis laments that his illness keeps him from attending the general chapter, saying that if he were not sick, he would travel to it and set his order to rights. "'Who are they,' [Francis] said, 'who stole my religion and my brothers from my hands! If I had gone to the general chapter, then I would have shown them what I might will.'"[73] Possibly because some of the early divisions within the order were apparent in the *Remembrance*, some Franciscans remained dissatisfied with the *lives* of Francis available to them. So, in 1260, under the leadership of Bonaventure as minister general, there was yet another call for a new official *life* of the saint.

The order's adoption of Bonaventure's *Legenda maior* and *Legenda minor* in the mid-1260s as the only *lives* of Francis to be used in the order from that point forward further illustrates the concerns and divisions sensed within earlier *lives* of the saint. Yet Bonaventure's *lives* of Francis changed the narrative remembrances of Francis dramatically, ensuring the fallible, human experiences of Francis were underplayed, and demonstrating the saint's sanctity more fully. In Bonaventure's *life*, more than any earlier formal *vita*, we see Francis, the saint, conforming to known and understood hagiographical tropes, and the jagged edges of Francis' actual lived experience smoothed out and tamed into a suitable story of holy devotion.

Informal Lives of Francis

Another reason Bonaventure's *lives* of Francis were adopted to the exclusion of all other *lives* occurred because of the confusion surrounding the saint owing to the many hagiographies available in the first decades after his death. Aside from the formal *lives* described above, there were several informal reminiscences circulating separately from the formal *lives*. Crescentius of Iesu's call for remembrances was answered, several times over, it seems.

For the purposes of reconstructing Francis' experience of disability and illness, and the social, religious, and political consequences of it, the most important informal source is the *Assisi Compilation*. The manuscript in which the *Assisi Compilation* is found – Perugia, Biblioteca Communale, MS 1046 – is late, having a *terminus ante quem* of 1310. Most scholars suggest the date of 1311 for this manuscript, but this dating must be somewhat suspect as it originates external to the manuscript itself, in a note by Ubertino da Casale that suggests he had in his possession, at that date, both Father Leo's original reminiscences and a copy of them in a different codex. Rosalind Brooke argues that it is this second codex from which the *Assisi Compilation* was copied.[74] A second problem with the *Assisi Compilation* as a source for Francis' life is the clear proto-Spiritual ethos with which many stories are infused. Although the formal split between Spirituals, who believed that Francis advocated absolute poverty for individual Francisans and the order as a whole, and Conventuals, who argued that the order as an organization could hold property, did not fully develop until the latter half of the thirteenth century, David Burr has suggested proto-Spiritual leanings can be found even in the later positions of some of Francis' earliest companions.[75] In *the Assisi Compilation*, some of the narratives appear to represent later Spiritual perceptions of how Francis ought to have reacted to certain events. If they do represent the true remembrances of Francis' closest companions, they reflect their dissatisfaction with the direction the order was taking in the 1240s, when they were asked to record their memories of the saint. The *Assisi Compilation* must be used with care, but, regardless of its uncertain and late date, the narratives included in it appear to represent earlier traditions about the saint, especially the last years of his life; for that reason, the *Assisi Compilation* needs to be taken seriously as an authentic source for Francis' life, perhaps the most authentic source not written by Francis himself.

Two other texts also contain stories and information that appear similar to much of that found in the *Assisi Compilation*, though they are arranged in a different and more thematic order. These are the two different surviving versions of the so-called *Mirror of Perfection*. Both versions have been edited and translated many times, but there is not much new that either version adds to the image of Francis in his later years, captured so clearly in the *Assisi Compilation*. As is shown in the section below, the relationships between the *Assisi Compilation* and different versions of the *Mirror of Perfection* are far from clear.

Another couple of documents that share material and served as source material for Thomas of Celano's *Remembrance* are the works generally titled *The Legend of the Three Companions* and the *Anonymous of Perugia*. At first glance, the *Legend of the Three Companions* appears to be an extremely important source for Francis' life. In all extant manuscripts, it is prefaced by a letter addressed to Crescentius of Iesu and signed by three of Francis' close companions, Brothers Leo, Angelo, and Rufinus. The letter states that the brothers are sending along a series of stories about Francis, not told in a linear narrative but as a series of unconnected reminiscences, drawn from their own experience and of others who were in or near his circle. Yet, the letter, always found at the beginning of the *Legend of the Three Companions*, does not match the thematically organized content of the *Legend of the Three Companions*, and so cannot refer to the text with which it is found.[76] Nonetheless, the *Legend* is an important source for Thomas of Celano's *Remembrance of the Desire of a Soul*.

Another unofficial source for the *Remembrance* is the now erroneously titled *Anonymous of Perugia*, which dates from approximately 1240. This work is now often ascribed to an early convert to the Franciscan brotherhood, John of Perugia. John's text provides little new about Francis himself, though he further contextualizes some narratives found in Thomas of Celano's *Vita prima*. The far greater contribution of the *Anonymous of Perugia*, however, is its new insights into the development of the order.

To this more or less universally accepted list of early sources about Francis' life, I have added one more not usually included. This is the *Acts of Blessed Francis in the Rieti Valley*. As I argue in detail below, this text, largely marginalized in mainstream Franciscan studies, appears to include reliable testimony about Francis' last years of life – testimony whose source could have been one of Francis' closest companions, Brother Angelo, mentioned in the letter that prefaces the *Legend of the Three Companions*.[77]

Aside from the various early *lives* of St. Francis, early chronicles of the order can also be useful in determining information about Francis. One of the earliest and perhaps most reliable accounts is Jordan of Giano's chronicle, probably written in 1262.[78] The account is more complete for the years after Francis' death, when John Parenti and especially Elias of Cortona were ministers general of the order, but is informative on many details of the earlier period as well.

The Vexed Franciscan Question

Any book that examines the early *lives* of Francis very quickly runs up against the Franciscan question, a debate that has vexed scholars for more than a century. Essentially the question is, Which of the many surviving early hagiographies of Francis described above, or which of the narratives within these early hagiographies, are the most likely to contain the most reliable information about Francis' life? It seems clear, now, that the earliest *life* of Francis, Thomas of Celano's *Vita prima*, is not necessarily the best in this regard. Thomas did not know Francis intimately and had spent the final years of Francis' life as a friar in Germany, far from where Francis centred his own ministry.[79] To be sure, Thomas used eyewitness accounts of many who knew Francis well – Elias of Cortona and Hugolino dei Conti di Segni (the future Pope Gregory IX), to name two important ones, and, as Jacques Dalarun has suggested, he also appears to have consulted with other independent witnesses who disagreed with these two major players.[80] Yet, for a glimpse of the conflicted and seemingly more human Francis, readers must turn to non-official *lives*, many of which can be conclusively linked back to the reminiscences of the first companions. As we have no autographs or manuscripts which can clearly be proven to be direct testimonies of the companions, much ink has been spilled attempting to determine which narratives in later manuscripts might reflect earlier traditions and stories. The many scholars who have spent time trying to determine the most reliable sources for Francis' life have used different methodologies, including codicological and paleographical examinations of surviving manuscripts and critical literary, linguistic, and philological analysis. Until the early 1980s, almost all efforts had been aimed at determining which manuscripts reflected the earliest and most reliable traditions of scholarship on Francis and combining these early narratives into hypothetical source texts. This strategy is similar to one in the field of New Testament Studies in which a theorized Q Gospel of Christ's sayings, thought to be a common source for the gospels of Matthew and Luke, has been reconstructed by scholars. In Franciscan studies, the result of this search for earlier, hypothetical documents is most clearly evident in the appendix of Théophile Desbonnets *From Intuition to Institution*, which, in its most complex discussion of the *stemma* of early Franciscan sources, posits four different conjectured texts of early reminiscences of Francis to explain the various sources for stories in later hagiographies and compilations.[81] Much effort has been expended trying to determine the contents of these hypothetical early documents.

Attempting to find the historical Francis even from hagiographical sources written by people close to the saint is fraught with difficulties, if not impossibilities. The most common method of deducing a historical account from hagiographic themes, tropes, and earlier examples is what Jacques Dalarun, borrowing a term from the field of geology, calls stratigraphy.[82] Using this method, the scholar begins with the oldest narrative of the account and attempts to unravel any additions or deletions made to the account as a result of particular perspectives and the vagaries of faulty memory. One can never reach absolute historical truth, but this method, practitioners assert, may come close to a possible approximation of a historical event. In Franciscan studies, a new methodology has gone beyond what simple stratigraphy can suggest, however, and it has borne much fruit. Raoul Manselli's *Nos qui cum eo fuimus*[83] argued that new and valuable information about Francis could be found by applying the methodologies of *formgeschichte* to early Franciscan texts. As in the hunt for the earliest narratives of Francis' life, the methodologies of *formgeschichte* were adopted from biblical criticism. The premise of *formgeschichte* is that it is possible to recover the near original form of oral traditions within written texts. This is done by examining each narrative in isolation from the text in which it is preserved, and studying the form or genre of that narrative. Once the type of narrative is determined, the text is examined to determine the use of that narrative, its *Sitz im Leben* (place in life) within its oral contexts. Possible adaptations of the tradition to suit the needs of the author and audience of the text in which it resides are also determined.[84] When additions to the narrative are discovered and set aside, the original oral tradition can thus be recovered.

Manselli's work argued that there were a number of stories shared across the unofficial biographies of Francis,[85] especially the unstructured reminiscences included in the *Assisi Compilation* (which Manselli calls the *Legend of Perugia*), and in the different versions of the *Mirror of Perfection* found in the Lemmens and Little manuscripts.[86] He further argued that each of these texts is from Umbria, which means their authors had access to early Franciscan documents,[87] and, as we have already noted above, it seems likely that all three are related to each other and the stories in them drawn from the writings of Brother Leo.[88] For this reason, some of the content of these later manuscripts must be regarded as more reliable than that in earlier texts. Particularly important in these later manuscripts are those introduced by an often-repeated formula, "nos qui cum eo fuimus" (we who were with him). In the three texts above, there are seventeen different passages that contain this formula.[89] Most of them are shared across two, or even three, of the texts, which suggests the stories have a shared source. As none of the passages with the formula occur in Thomas of Celano's *Vita prima*, it is likely that they came into circulation as the result of Crescentius of Iesu's request to the order, made in 1244, that remembrances of Francis and the early days of the order be forwarded to him. Further, Manselli argues that, as many of the passages marked with the formula deal with Francis' last days, they are likely the stories told by those friars who attended Francis during his final illnesses.[90] Manselli traces how those narratives were used in the texts themselves, and in other more formal hagiographies of Francis written after 1244, notably Celano's *Remembrance of the Desire of a Soul*. The core oral tradition, Manselli suggests, are the episodes themselves, episodes which often present Francis as unpredictable and even moody.[91] Later, more organized, works used these narratives, but attempted to bring out a higher meaning in the reported episode – to make these "teachable moments." Thomas of Celano, especially, is singled out by Manselli as repeatedly changing the meaning of episodes recorded by Francis' companions,[92] perhaps trying to minimize the potential for conflict between friars who had proto-Spiritual leanings and those who were more conventual. Bonaventure, too, as we will see, was eager to normalize the sometimes problematic Francis found in these earlier narratives.[93]

Manselli's work, revolutionary though it was, has come under some criticism since its publication. Rosalind Brooke has suggested, rightly I think, that Manselli's work isolated and privileged those stories marked with the formula "nos qui cum eo fuimus" from the rest of the narratives in the texts he studied. She argues that the authenticity of those stories does not necessarily negate the authenticity of other episodes thought to come from early, reliable sources, especially those stories that are sandwiched between or otherwise contextualize narratives marked with the formula.[94] Indeed, Brooke argues for the authenticity of many episodes included in the collections with which Manselli worked, especially for much of the *Assisi Compilation*.[95] More recently, Augustine Thompson has argued that recovering an authentic oral tradition from texts written after 1244 is impossible. The very "plasticity" of oral traditions means that the original *Sitz im Leben* is impossible to determine.[96] The *Assisi Compilation*, retained today in a manuscript written around 1311 (but containing older material), is, for Thompson, "powerful[ly] ideological," and even if it does present authentic remembrances, the views of the elderly brothers may have romanticized the past.[97] While care is needed in using the informal *lives* of Francis as sources of information about the saint's life, it seems rash to dismiss such sources entirely.

Keeping Manselli's work in mind, along with Brooke's criticism of it, this study will use a hierarchy of sources in presenting its arguments. Those works deemed the most reliable sources for Francis' life are those written by Francis himself. Particularly important among Francis' works are the *Regula non bullata* and the *Regula bullata*, and, of course, Francis' *Testament*. His letters, too, can give us insight into his life experiences.

Looking to the early hagiographies, I agree with Manselli that the unsystematized collections found in the *Assisi Compilation* and in the *Mirror of Perfection*, found in MS Little and in the *Speculum Lemmens*, suggest that these were private collections of stories created to remind readers about various episodes of Francis' life. Perhaps, as Manselli argues, these collections speak to disquiet about the increasing clericalization occurring within the order in the latter half of the thirteenth century and beginning of the fourteenth century.[98] In spite of possible ideological inclinations of these collections, they do all seem to include many recollections about Francis, and of events which occurred during his last days. Many include the kind of detail and treatment of the saint that suggests they are authentic remembrances of companions close to Francis. These narratives will be treated as among the most reliable records of Francis' life, with preference given to those included in the *Assisi Compilation*, probably the earliest of these non-systematic texts, copied perhaps circa 1311. Within these early collections, those episodes that contain the phrase "nos qui cum eo fuimus," and derivations thereof, will be given special attention, as they are likely reminiscences that were translated, perhaps initially in an oral form, from the recollections of Francis' companions.[99] However, in keeping with Brooke's warning not to deny the authority of other, non-authenticated texts, other narratives will be explored after their authenticity has been established as much as is possible.

The relative reliability of the more systematically organized texts is perhaps more difficult to assess. Although Thomas of Celano's *Vita prima* does not necessarily reflect the knowledge of a close companion of Francis, and was written as an official document to support Francis' canonization, it has the advantage of being the text written nearest to Francis' living days. Similarly, Celano's *Remembrance* and *Tractatus de miraculis*, both written and based on the call for remembrances of Francis made in 1244, also often reflect reliable early traditions. Written near the same time as Celano's *Remembrance*, the *Legend of the Three Companions* offers some new information about Francis, perhaps gleaned from the reminiscences of those who were acquainted with Francis and who recorded their stories in the wake of Crescentius' call. Less helpful to the primary goal of this book, but extremely helpful in understanding the development of governmental structures within the order, is the so-called *Anonymous of Perugia*, now thought to have been written by John of Perugia, a companion of Brother Giles, who himself was a close companion of Francis.[100] This short text was likely written between March 1240 and August 1241[101] and was certainly used by Thomas of Celano when composing the *Remembrance of the Desire of a Soul*.[102] It was also likely written before the *Legend of the Three Companions*, as that text is clearly responding to the *Anonymous of Perugia* in parts.[103] In the last decade yet another *life* of Francis has been found and attributed to Thomas of Celano. This one, the *Vita brevior*, unlike the other three, was not an authorized *life* of Francis; rather, it seems to have reflected the author's own position on the saint. Jacques Dalarun's recent study of this text has suggested it was composed before 1239 and perhaps even before 1232.[104] All of the formal and organized hagiographies of Francis discussed thus far date from before 1250, within two generations of Francis' death. These surely are the texts to be most trusted, even if all of them were written with particular ideological goals in mind. To these early and reasonably reliable sources that date before Bonaventure's official *lives*, I add one more that dates later, but may contain early reliable material about Francis.

The *Actus beati Francisci in valle Reatina* is a little-known text that was composed between 1279 and 1319.[105] As its title suggests, it was composed in Rieti, probably at Fonte Columbo, where Francis traditionally was said to have written the *Regula bullata* and where he was treated by doctors for his eye disease. Indeed, many episodes related in the text refer to Francis' illnesses, infirmities, and medical treatment, which is why the text is so valuable to the topic of this study. As its title suggests, the *Actus beati Francisci* deals specifically with the events of Francis' life that occurred in Rieti, though it also includes a biography of Angelus Tancredus, most often identified with the Brother Angelo who was a known close companion of Francis. The major sources for the *Actus* include Bonaventure's *Legenda maior* and the *Assisi Compilation*,[106] but Cadderi finds references to Bernard of Besse's *Book of Praises*, which was composed between 1279 and Bernard's likely death in 1283.[107] However, the *Actus* does contain some material that cannot be found in earlier extant sources,[108] and even when a related episode has a known earlier source (often such episodes come from the *Assisi Compilation*), the author of the *Actus* relates the story in a different way and occasionally adds details left unreported in the suspected source material. Cadderi tentatively posits that much of this new material was written by the unknown author himself, but also suggests that another work, now lost, might be a possible source for some of this new material.[109]

When Luke Wadding wrote his magisterial *Annales minorum*, he used a text he reported was written by Angelus Reatinus as a source for Francis' life. Wadding writes that Angelo's text was about the deeds of Francis which took place within the boundaries of Angelo's homeland, Rieti.[110] While the *terminus a quo* of 1279 for the *Actus* does not allow for Angelo being the author of the *Actus*, the seemingly similar subject matter of the *Actus* and the work attributed to Angelo by Wadding, along with the inclusion of a biography of Angelo in the *Actus*, suggests that the author of this text may have had a work by Angelo as one of his sources.[111] A final consideration that supports the authenticity of some of the episodes about Francis related in the *Actus* is that they are tagged with a line designed to demonstrate their authenticity. It is not "nos qui cum eo fuimus," as in the *Assisi Compilation* and the *Mirror of Perfection*, but rather "nos qui videmus" that attempts, at least, to demonstrate the eyewitness basis for episodes included in the text.[112] Thus, because of the subject matter, and because many of the episodes seem authentically early, I include the *Actus beati Francisci in valle Reatina* in the sources I scoured for evidence of Francis' illnesses and infirmities.

This is not the place to resolve the Franciscan Question definitively, if, indeed, it can ever be resolved. In prioritizing some earlier sources above others, I have made editorial choices based not only on the palaeographical and textual history of manuscripts but also on how reliable the information on Francis' illnesses and infirmities seemed to be in the descriptions within the text. This is sometimes difficult to judge, but, in general, if discussions of Francis' ailments took place in the context of narratives that focused on other points, or the ailments were not the point of the particular story, I deemed them more likely to be reliable. If descriptions of Francis' ailments were found in narratives authenticated by the eye-witness phrases "nos qui cum eo fuimus" or "nos qui videmus," I deemed them more reliable. If I found the discussion of disability in the source did not have a didactic message I deemed it more reliable. In total, more than one hundred different discussions of Francis' illnesses and infirmities in the early sources were examined in detail for what they said about his physical impairments and his own and others' responses to them.

Before exploring my own findings, however, I will begin, in the next chapter, with an examination of the various ways Francis' ailments have been diagnosed across history. Such an exploration drives home the idea that diagnoses based on descriptions in historical texts are difficult at best and misleading at worst. The sheer number of different diagnoses suggested demonstrates that we cannot know with certainty what exactly he suffered from. However, the very specificity of some of the diagnoses given, mostly by medical practitioners dabbling in historical diagnoses, is useful to historians, reminding us that whatever Francis suffered, his ailments and infirmities were serious and likely had serious consequences for the saint's own physical well-being and for his position in medieval society.

Chapter One

Francis Overdiagnosed
and Undiagnosed

No one who has studied the early biographies of Francis can doubt that the saint suffered. Like many other saints, Francis' conversion was prompted by an illness, a fever, which forced him to contemplate the direction of his life.[1] His illnesses also served other purposes within his hagiographies; they were reminders of the ephemeral nature of the flesh. Working within the narratives to impose periods of contemplation and revelation rather than active living, Francis' illnesses provided opportunities for the saint to practise and experience humility. Certainly, some of the discussions of Francis' various illnesses and infirmities had a role in constructing Francis' hagiography along normative medieval lines. Yet, many historians treat Francis' impairments and illnesses as *only* hagiographic tropes. But before Francis was a saint, he was a man who founded a fraternity, which then became an order of friars that numbered in the thousands, long before his death. There are clues in Francis' own writing and in the writings of the earliest and most reliable witnesses to his life that Francis' infirmities and illnesses did result in some difficulties in his own life, particularly with respect to his ability to administer his growing order and to continue his ministry as he wished.

Although one of the purposes of this book is to explore Francis' infirmities and impairments as depicted in writings of early Franciscans, I do not aim to produce a forensic diagnosis based on the symptoms he is described as presenting. Several scholars have attempted this more than one hundred years since Paul Sabatier reinvigorated Franciscan studies with the publication of his *Life of St. Francis of Assisi*.[2] Most often, the diagnoses given reflect more about the time in which the author was writing than Francis' own medical condition.[3] In more recent decades, such works have also explored Francis' psychological well-being, almost always from a modern diagnostic perspective. As with the diagnoses of physiological ailments, the psychological discussions of Francis are almost all reflective of new trends and findings in the field. A brief overview of the most important and influential studies that attempt to diagnose Francis demonstrate this clearly.

The first full-length study of Francis' illnesses was written in 1893, the same year that Sabatier published his biography of Francis. It was written by a French doctor, Albert Bournet, and was entitled *S. François d'Assise: Étude Sociale et Médicale*.[4] Relying on research conducted by Jean-Martin Charcot, Josef Breuer, and Sigmund Freud on hysteria in the 1880s, which explicitly linked the religious experience of mystics such as Francis of Assisi and Teresa of Avila to the pathological experience of hysteria,[5] Bournet tentatively suggested that although Francis certainly experienced physiological illnesses throughout his life, including dyspepsia and, perhaps, malaria, he also had the "principle etiological factors" of nervous exhaustion.[6] Yet, Bournet linked Francis' death to physiological disorders, the result of complications from a stomach ulcer and hepatitis,[7] which doctors in the late nineteenth century had just determined was a disease that was bloodborne.[8] Like many clinicians of his day, Bournet believed that Francis' *stigmata* had their origin in the psychological experiences of the saint; but while Freud and Breuer had argued that a stigmatized saint was a clear sign of an individual suffering from pathological hysteria,[9] Bournet was careful to argue that the psychological impulses that resulted in the presentation of the *stigmata* were not pathological.[10] Indeed, very few other scholars seemed willing to suggest that Francis was suffering a pathological psychosis. Only much later, in 1992, did clinical psychologist Nitza Yarom publish a book that suggested Francis' illnesses and even his *stigmata* could have been the result of conversion hysteria. In Yarom's book, Francis' illnesses were framed as the physiological manifestations of a psychological crisis of gender and sexual identity.[11] Even more recently, Lisa Cataldo has used the work of Heinz Kohut, who argued that narcissism need not necessarily always be pathological but could in fact be healthy, to argue that although Francis of Assisi experienced narcissism, through the therapeutic intervention derived from his spiritual encounters with God, Francis' potentially pathological narcissism was transformed into a healthier form.[12]

Most works that discuss Francis' emotional state, however, are reluctant to suggest the saint suffered from any form of psychosis. For instance, in response to Bournet, Lorenzo Gualino, an Italian physician best known for his work in the history of medicine, published a popular work about Francis' psychological and physiological constitution, entitled *L'Uomo d'Assisi* in 1927.[13] Clearly influenced by Sabatier's turn of the century work on Francis, the saint's life is romanticized; much of the first chapter is dedicated to refuting the notion that Francis suffered from anything resembling hysteria as defined by Charcot and others in the late nineteenth century. Indeed, Gualino specifically refutes claims made by Charcot that Francis of Assisi was an "undeniable hysteric."[14] Speaking more generally of saints who have ecstatic mystical visions, Gualino argues that the experiences of these saints do not fit the symptoms in others suffering from hysteria or epilepsy. However, he does recognize that some doctors might reclassify the experiences of the saints into symptoms that fall into known medical categories to better understand them.[15] Yet, seemingly speaking from a position of faith, Gualino argues that Francis' experience cannot be understood by the limited knowledge and language of "common pathology,"[16] for human knowledge and categories cannot capture experiences of the divine. Rather, Francis' rigorous ascetic life, his poor health, and especially his readiness for death allowed him to see God and truth more clearly than others. His visions were thus not the result of a psychological malady, but of his devotion to God.[17]

The idea that Francis' mysticism represented a healthy psychological state was reiterated in a 1991 study by Roberto Zavalloni, an Italian Franciscan and professor of psychology at the Antonianum. Grounding his argument within the framework of Augustinian theology, he suggested that Francis, as a sanctified individual, had managed to do what most of fallen humanity cannot: attain perfect psychological development – completeness as a human being. Since psychological and physiological development go hand in hand, Zavalloni argued that perfect maturity in all senses, psychological, physiological, and spiritual, comes when a body and mind are completely integrated.[18]

The most recent study of Francis' psychological state, Lino Temperini's *Francesco di Assisi: Cronistoria psicologia itinerario spirituale* was published in 2012.[19] It suggests that, although the saint suffered from depression after he was a prisoner of war to the time of his conversion, it was in this state that Francis was inspired to follow God. Francis' depressed psychological state thus worked to allow the saint to live the penitential, Christ-like life he so desired. Generally, Temperini argues that suffering for Francis was not only "cathartic and therapeutic" but also "inspirational and constructive."[20] His psychological state and any physical impairments he suffered only served as a useful restraint on his secular dreams and as an inspiration to his new religious life.[21]

Turning from the psychological, to the physiological, several studies have been published about Francis' health since the late nineteenth century. Two years after Bournet's largely psychological portrait of Francis, another physician, Théodore Cotelle, wrote another medical study.[22] Cotelle was adamant that he applied the impartiality of the science of medicine to his understanding of Francis' health and illness.[23] As with most work in this period, Cotelle was not concerned with using the most reliable of the early sources on Francis; he was far more interested in using what scant information he could find to to indicate symptoms and potential diagnoses. Cotelle suggests Francis' early fevers might have been caused by malaria,[24] but the rest of the saint's early illnesses he ascribes to "prolonged fasts and the austerity of his life,"[25] along with the intellectual exhaustion that came with founding a new way of penitential living.[26] As for Francis' deteriorating eyesight in the later years of the saint's life, Cotelle argues that it was the result of an eye infection of some sort. Since cauterization was used to treat local infections in the thirteenth century, Francis' eye disease must have demonstrated symptoms that affected the visible parts of the eye and thus constituted something that looked like an eye infection.[27] The last chapter of Cotelle's work is a very short discussion of the illnesses Francis suffered just before his death. Cotelle references Francis' probable experience of hepatitis[28] and stomach ailments,[29] but does not discuss them in depth. Similarly, he alludes to the saint's dropsy, which caused his limbs to swell.[30] Yet Cotelle cannot find a scientific explanation for the *stigmata*. He rejects several such possibilities: that Elias produced them on Francis' body after the saint died,[31] that a naturally occurring electrical force caused them,[32] that Francis suffered from hematidrosis, a rare condition that caused one to sweat blood,[33] that he had microhemorrhages on his hands and feet,[34] or that his psychological state caused the *stigmata* to appear.[35] He is thus forced to concede that science cannot explain how Francis received the *stigmata*. Cotelle never attempts a universalized diagnosis for Francis' illnesses, and, although he argues that his book is about science aiding faith, it is clear his faith allows him to set his scientific inquiry aside, especially in the last chapters.

Francis' issues with his eyes and the treatment he received for them have perhaps been given the most attention by scholars wishing to diagnose the saint's various ailments. In 1918, an ophthalmologist from Rome, Orestes Parisotti, wrote a treatise that tried to establish what caused Francis' eye disease and the near blindness that afflicted the saint in his later years.[36] In it, Parisotti concludes that Francis' blindness was not necessarily caused by whatever disease responsible for his head pain. Rather, he suggests that Francis had tuberculosis of the brain (tubercular meningitis), which caused painful inflammation of the iris and the ciliary body in the eye.[37] Francis' visit to a surgeon for cauterization was to cure his blindness, caused not by the disease that was causing such distress to his eyes, but by cataracts, which could have formed as a result of disease or invasive medical study of the eyes.[38]

A second attempt at diagnosing Francis' eye ailments was undertaken by a Swiss ophthalmologist, Josef Strebel. In the article, published in 1937, Strebel examined the various illnesses of Francis, but diagnosed his eye disease most thoroughly. He suggested Francis suffered from tuberculous iridocyclitis, an inflammation of the iris caused by tuberculosis. According to Strebel, Francis' eyesight was further compromised by glaucoma and cataracts.[39] Strebel's diagnosis was affirmed in 1991 by Rosario Zeppa, the director of the ocular department at the city hospital in Benevento. Zeppa noted that Francis' symptoms seem to confirm iridocyclitis rather than trachoma, and pointed to early images of St. Francis to confirm his theory.[40]

Outside of Europe, too, doctors were turning to the historical study of the past, including, of course, the life of Francis. In 1935, an American doctor, Edward F. Hartung, published a short article about Francis' illnesses.[41] With respect to Francis' near blindness, Hurting argued that Francis' eye disease was the "Egyptian eye sickness,"[42] a then common term for trachoma, used because many European soldiers suffered from it in the wake of Napoleon's Egyptian campaign.[43] Hartung's diagnoses are based on medical research taking place in the early part of the twentieth century. Although historians of medicine believe trachoma to be a very old disease, the late nineteenth century and early twentieth century saw advances made in the treatment of it. The bacterium that caused trachoma, *chlamydia trachomatis*, was known to exist by 1907, though the bacterium itself was not successfully isolated until 1957.[44] Hartung's diagnosis of trachoma contracted during Francis' visit to Egypt has been largely accepted by most modern scholars of Francis.

With respect to the regular fevers from which Hartung believed Francis suffered, he argued they were caused by quartan malaria, a type of malaria that results in fevers every 72 hours or so. He believed Francis had contracted malaria fairly early in his ministry, certainly by 1214,[45] Hartung further argued that a symptom of malaria, *purpura*, could account for the saint's apparent *stigmata*. Although not a common symptom of malaria, *purpura*, red or purple marks below the skin, sometimes raised, presenting especially on the hands and feet, caused by bleeding underneath the skin, can occur as a symptom.[46]

After Hartung's treatment, interest in Francis' illnesses waned for a time, until an Italian physician, Sante Ciancarelli, wrote a book entitled *Francesco di Pietro Bernardone: Malato et santo*,[47] published in 1972. The diagnoses provided by Ciancarelli are specific and detailed. Noting that Francis was ill from at least the time of his conversion to the mendicant life, Ciancarelli suggests that Francis was suffering from pulmonary tuberculosis as early as 1203.[48] For Ciancarelli, recurring tubercular infections account for many of the times Francis suffered illness, including the illness that preceded his conversion to religious life[49] and that which prevented him from travelling to Morocco in 1213.[50] With respect to Francis' eye ailment, Ciancarelli, like Hartung, suggests Francis developed a trachoma infection after his visit to Egypt in 1219.[51] This, in turn, caused glaucoma and the development of cataracts.[52] As a result of this eye infection, Francis began to experience more frequent fevers, his eyes frequently watered, and he became increasingly sensitive to light[53] – all symptoms described in the earliest hagiographies of the saint. As his symptoms worsened, Ciancarelli suggests, Francis was exhibiting the first signs of developing glaucoma.[54] The infection was debilitating and Ciancarelli argues that Francis became totally blind after a surgeon in Rieti cauterized his face in an invasive treatment for his eye infection.[55] Ciancarelli argues that at the end of his life, Francis' condition was complicated by trigeminal neuralgia[56] and gastric stenosis.[57] The most common symptom of trigeminal neuralgia is chronic, intense pain in the head, especially in the areas near the trigeminal nerve, a nerve that originates above the ears and has branches that travel towards the eyes, the nose, and the mouth. Gastric stenosis is most common in infants during their first year of life, but it can also affect adults. It is caused by a narrowing of the pylorus, preventing food from leaving the stomach and entering the intestines. The most common symptoms are vomiting and abdominal pain. Ciancarelli suggests Francis' stenosis was further complicated by an ulcer caused by his constant fasting, which resulted in a swollen belly and coughing up blood.[58]

Ciancarelli also provided a medical explanation for the *stigmata*, one that again, to some extent, linked to the work of Charcot. He argued that, although the mechanism through which this works is not well understood, stress as a result of stimuli like trauma or mental exhaustion (or even heat or cold) could produce lesions destructive to the skin that might resemble *stigmata*.[59] Ciancarelli also leaves room for God in his medical explanation, though, suggesting that God granted to Francis the ability to arrange the lesions caused by stress in whatever likeness he would[60] and, given that Francis had been contemplating the crucifixion, the wounds appeared as Christ's had.[61] Francis was practising a conscious and unconscious *imitatio christi*.

Ciancarelli's Italian study was soon followed by another one, written by historian Keith Haines and published in 1976. While Haines ultimately concluded that it was impossible to determine what illnesses Francis suffered, he nonetheless outlined an extensive differential diagnosis. He was the first to mention the possibility that the saint suffered from leprosy; he argued, however, that the symptoms the saint exhibited, at least according to the hagiographies, did not seem to indicate leprosy unless of the mildest sort.[62] He also suggests the possibility of brucellosis, a highly infectious disease caused by eating infected meat or drinking infected milk. The major symptoms of brucellosis are repetitive fevers, the swelling of various organs, especially the kidney and spleen, and chronic fatigue.[63] Haines also discusses tuberculosis, Hodgkin's disease, and ulcers as potential causes for Francis' symptoms, before going on to argue that the most likely cause was malaria. In terms of the deterioration of Francis' eyesight, Haines suggests, as many previous authors had, that it may have been trachoma. He also recognizes as possible Parisotti's diagnosis of glaucoma and further suggests that it could also have been a secondary symptom of brucellosis.[64] In spite of Haines' lengthy discussions of the various illnesses Francis may have had, the larger point of his conclusion is worth noting: that it was Francis' health that led him to withdraw from the community he began and that withdrawal had devastating consequences for the unity of the order, which Francis, had he been healthier and lived longer, may have been able to help smooth over.[65]

Haines' exploration of leprosy as a possible explanation for Francis' illnesses was taken up in 1987, when Joanne Schatzlein, a Franciscan nurse, and Daniel Sulmasy, a Franciscan doctor, wrote an article which argued that most of the symptoms Francis exhibited could have been caused by tuberculoid or cutaneous leprosy. Unlike the more common and widely known lepromatous form of leprosy, this form of leprosy does not necessarily result in the expected symptoms – thickened nerves and skin and generalized pain.[66] Rather, tuberculoid leprosy results in a few small sores on the skin, often flat or slightly raised, and usually red rather than the yellow or brown lesions usually associated with lepromatous leprosy. Schatzlein and Sulmasy suggest that even the skeleton of St. Francis, recovered in the first half of the nineteenth century, provided evidence for their diagnosis.

The burial and subsequent recovery of St. Francis' body are unusual and slightly mysterious. In 1230, fearing that Francis' body might be stolen by rival cities,[67] the minister general of the Franciscan Order, Elias of Cortona, had Francis' body, which had been resting at the church of San Giorgio in Assisi, secretly interred ahead of schedule in the newly built (though not yet complete) basilica dedicated to the saint. Moreover, so afraid was he of Francis' body being molested that Elias buried his body deep beneath the basilica, covering the metal cage that held Francis' body with a slab of marble, with three iron bars to hold the marble in place and a second slab of marble cemented to the walls.[68] Relic thieves were thus unable to steal pieces of Francis' body, but pilgrims could no longer gaze upon the saint as they had when he had been at San Giorgio. The location of Francis' burial was known for at least some generations after his translation, but slowly the knowledge of where precisely Francis' tomb was located was lost.[69] Francis' remains were recovered only after extensive excavations in the lower basilica, which occurred in the first two decades of the nineteenth century.[70] The skeleton recovered during these excavations was not complete. The skull, while present, was not in good condition, especially in the area of the lower jaw, which was present only in fragments. Only six teeth remained with the lower jaw[71] and only five of eight incisors remained.[72]

Schatzlein and Sulmasy suggest that the imperfect condition of the skull could be the result of leprosy, especially as leprosy can cause erosion in the lower jaw bone and the loss of upper incisors.[73] The poor survival rate of the phalangeal bones of both hands and feet (16 of 28 in the hands and 4 of 28 in the feet)[74] and the "tapered presentation" of the proximal phalange of Francis' right "pinky" finger also led Schatzlein and Sulmasy to argue that the saint suffered from leprosy.[75] They further suggested that Elias' protection of Francis makes it very unlikely bones were lost to pilfering relic hunters, and that the loss of bones must then necessarily reflect the state of health in which Francis died.[76] Schatzlein and Sulmasy also assert that the one disease that can account for all the symptoms Francis experienced in the six years before his death is tuberculoid leprosy.[77]

In recent years, there have been few lengthy attempts to further diagnose Francis' seeming myriad illnesses. This is owing to two trends. The first is increasing scepticism on the usefulness of diagnosing people of the past with modern diseases. This is especially the case in the area of psychiatry, where post-structuralist theorists such as Ian Hacking and Graham Richards have argued that cases of psychological disorders could only have occurred after they had been named and their symptoms enumerated. Thus, the language of the disorder, in some sense, creates and structures the experience of the disorder itself.[78] The second trend is the exponentially increasing use of scientific testing to determine, precisely, what disease a person, or rather, a person's skeleton, was carrying. Since the first successful extraction of DNA from the bacterium which causes tuberculosis from a skeleton from ancient Egypt occurred in 1993,[79] an increasingly large number of skeletons from ancient and medieval sites have had DNA from various pathogens successfully extracted and identified from them.[80] The success of this work has "revolutionized the field of palaeopathology."[81] Since, obviously, actually determining precisely what disease afflicted a person based on modern DNA testing is much more reliable than guessing based on symptoms described in texts from the period, this method has become the preferred one for determining diseases of the past.

As should be clear from the summary above, most of the diagnoses of Francis completed over the last hundred or so years were completed by physicians and other medical clinicians. Historians tend to shy away from applying modern diagnoses to historical figures. Of course, applying modern diagnoses to individuals of the past is always difficult. Very often there is no way to test these theories by examining a body, and the diagnosis itself is often regarded as anachronistic and unlikely to further our understanding of the experience of the sufferer in their own context.[82] Yet, this is not always the case. How would Francis' life be analysed differently if it were known he suffered from leprosy – as historians as diverse as Daniel Spoto and Chiara Frugoni[83] have taken up as if not true, as least possible – with all the fraught meaning that diagnosis carried in the Middle Ages? In this way, modern diagnoses are helpful, for they remind us that whatever Francis suffered, the illnesses he experienced were serious, and he suffered with severe symptoms for much of his life, especially after his return from Egypt circa 1220. A specific diagnosis of malaria or leprosy, or even glaucoma, reminds historians that there were social and political consequences for Francis in having such a disease, for although he was considered very holy, Francis was not a saint in 1220, nor did his closest companions believe him to be one. Indeed, for them, Francis was a man, a man who was very sick and could no longer carry out all the duties for which his position called. If modern diagnoses of Francis do no more than recall this reality, they are doing historians a service.

Thus, it seems that historians can learn something from the medical scholars who dissect Francis' illnesses so carefully. It is not that it is necessary to name and categorize Francis' illnesses or to quantify his symptoms, but rather the very centrality of Francis' illnesses in the work of medical scholars is something that should be noted by historians. By minimizing the impact of Francis' illness, historians limit their understanding of him because this perspective does not allow scholars to see beyond the regularized, aestheticized saint to the man beneath the narrative. For the purpose of this study, there is no need to name or categorize Francis' illnesses either in medieval or modern medical terminology. It is enough to prove that he clearly suffered serious symptoms from them throughout the entirety of his public life and to explore the consequences of his illnesses.

That Francis *was* ill and infirm throughout his converted life cannot be questioned in spite of the seeming reluctance of historians to grapple with this reality. As the next chapters demonstrate, the earliest and most reliable sources of Francis' life illustrate his illnesses and infirmities over and over again, not just in the last two years of his life, but throughout the entirety of it. They were always central to Francis' experience, both as a man and as a saint. Francis' own writings draw attention to his infirmities, as do those anecdotes which appear to have been written by his earliest companions. In summary, these early sources attest to the following:

1) In his youth, Francis served as a cavalryman in Assisi's militia in a battle against Perugia. During the battle, Francis was captured and imprisoned awaiting ransom. While in prison, Francis' health suffered.
2) After his conversion, Francis embarked on a trip to Morocco but stopped in Spain when he fell ill. The illness is unspecified, but of long duration.
3) In 1217, Francis suffered from another long illness or series of illnesses; the most commonly cited symptom of these in the sources is fever.
4) In 1219–1220, Francis began to experience constant pain in his eyes, the beginning of a very long eye illness, which was never cured in spite of numerous medical interventions.
5) Between 1220 and 1226, Francis' health continued to deteriorate; wounds which resembled the *stigmata* became apparent on his body and often wept blood. By 1225, Francis had become almost blind, various limbs and organs were swollen, and he occasionally vomited blood.

This list might well come as a surprise to many who study the life of St. Francis. But, as chapters 2 and 3 show, the early and most reliable sources of Francis' life bear it out. It is indisputable that Francis was ill and/or infirm for much of his adult life. Exploring the personal, social, and political effects of these sicknesses and infirmities is vital for a more complete understanding of the man from Assisi.

Chapter Two

Recentring Illness and Infirmity
in Francis' Lived Experience

Access to Francis' earliest years is limited in the sources, but the little information they afford of his family history is well known. Francis was the son of a wealthy textile merchant in Assisi, and his early life was one of relative ease. If we can trust the hagiographic trope just a little, Francis was frivolous and unfocused in his youth, and remained so until he was held for a time as a prisoner of war, having fought in a battle between his home town of Assisi and its neighbouring rival, Perugia.[1]

As the following pages will show, it seems likely that Francis became ill during his time in the Perugian prison and that he continued to feel ill effects as a result of his stay there for the rest of his life. There are repeated references to Francis' delicate nature in the early hagiographies, especially in the *Assisi Compilation*, and that delicate nature was not only apparent in the last years of his life, when the saint was clearly suffering, but also in the earliest years of his ministry. In the years between 1210 and 1219, when he left for Egypt, Francis experienced at least two different bouts of illness that forced him to rest for days, and held him back from completing a planned course of action. Francis' health was compromised even further during his trip to Egypt; there he likely contracted an eye infection that may have resulted in his loss of vision. Although he remained somewhat active in his ministry in the years after 1219, by around 1221 he had resigned from his leadership position in the order, citing illness as a reason for his withdrawal. By the time Francis had his famous vision of the seraph, his health was already precarious. In the years after the vision, between 1224 and 1226, the saint's health declined rapidly, until he was in the near constant care of doctors. Finally, in the last months of his life, he was completely bedridden, suffering from a multitude of symptoms from various illnesses that affected his eyes and internal organs.

By centring Francis' illnesses and infirmities in the story of his life, this book aims to highlight the realities of Francis' illnesses and the social and political consequences those illnesses had for Francis in the secular world in which he lived. By the mid-thirteenth century, it had become a common trope to suggest saints' earthly suffering – while engaging in ascetic practices or holy athleticism during long illnesses – ensured their place in heaven. Earthly suffering was presented as a kind of purgatory, providing redemption for sins, original and otherwise.

Francis' hagiographies include this common narrative. Yet, as the following pages show, it is possible to peel back the layers of religious and redemptive meaning the hagiographers assigned to discussions of Francis' suffering to recognize the saint's many illnesses and infirmities. These infirmities sometimes inhibited Francis' ability to act in the secular, masculine, ableist realms of the ecclesiastical hierarchy and political world which he inhabited. Further, it becomes clear that Francis' ailments were a source of anxiety, not only for the saint himself, but for those who were charged with his care and for the hagiographers who reworked Francis' deeds.

Francis' Ailments and Impairments in His Own Words and Writing

Perhaps the most reliable windows into Francis' life were those writings he left us himself. While much of the history of Francis' writings is open to debate – about original content, about the date when it was written, and about the reliability of the manuscript tradition – Francis left us three works written in his own hand. The evidence of the difficulty the physical act of writing caused Francis, much more than the content of the works themselves, demonstrates Francis diminishing eyesight, especially at the end of his life. Two other works, aside from his autographs, provide evidence of the saint's struggles with illnesses. Of these, the *Testament*, for which the authorship and manuscript tradition are reasonably sound and agreed upon, must be regarded as the most reliable. The other, possibly the earliest of all Francis' works considered here, a redaction of the *Letter to the Faithful*,[2] has caused much debate among scholars of Francis. It is problematic for us, too, since a sure date for the composition of the longer version would help with more precisely mapping Francis' experience of illness.

There are two versions of the *Letter to the Faithful*, one shorter and one longer. Scholars disagree on which version was written first, on when each version was written, to whom the letters were addressed, and even whether these texts should properly be considered letters as we understand them. The longer version of *Letter to the Faithful* has an early attestation, as it is included in the mid-thirteenth century collection of Franciscan materials now found in Assisi, Bibliotheca Communale, MS 338. Its inclusion in this collection demonstrates its authenticity. Further, while nearly fifty known manuscript copies of the longer version of the *Letter to the Faithful* are in existence, there is only one of the shorter version.[3] Yet the shorter version, too, has an early provenance, for the manuscript version of the shorter letter also dates from the mid-thirteenth century.[4] Both versions of the letter appear to have been redacted by a person or persons other than Francis, Or, perhaps more generously, the letter was cowritten by Francis and other, more learned, colleagues.[5] Thus, there is much uncertainty to navigate when using a text such as the *Letter to the Faithful* as a source.

For the project of writing a history of Francis' ailments and disabilities, the need to date the letter accurately is especially important. The idea that the letter is late, since it mentions Francis' illness and his inability to travel must be rejected, since, as will become clear through the course of this book, there were many periods in Francis' life when he was unable to travel, not just in the months before his death. And indeed, a version of the text was in all likelihood written circa 1220 or 1221, given similarities in phrasing between the *Letter* and the *Regula non bullata*, written at that time.[6] However, the still debated question of whether the shorter version of the letter preceded or succeeded the longer version is important to a discussion of Francis' illnesses, since only the longer version of the *Letter* contains Francis' account of his illness. Since this question has not been definitively answered in Franciscan scholarship,[7] the most that can be said is that sometime after 1220, Francis experienced an episode of illness that forced him to abandon plans to travel and visit the people to whom he addressed the longer version of the so-called *Letter to the Faithful*.

The longer redaction of the *Letter to the Faithful* also contains the most direct evidence of how Francis' ailments impacted his ability to lead. In it, Francis wrote that he could not come to see the recipients of the letter in person, the "Christian religious and lay men and women" to whom the letter was vaguely addressed, because his body was weak and infirm.[8] The letter clearly implies that Francis himself felt unable to carry out some of his duties, such as visiting fellow religious, owing to his illnesses. Historians of Francis should pause at this, for too often, as has been noted in the introduction, are Francis' ailments put aside as a likely reason for his withdrawal from leadership roles. But here is a clear indication that Francis felt he was held back from acts of leadership not by humility but by illness.

That Francis experienced infirmities is briefly reiterated in his *Testament*, written at the end of his life, in which he says that although he is "simple and infirm" he wishes to have a priest with whom he can say the offices.[9] It is tempting to read this phrase as a particular hagiographic trope – the saint suffering in this world to achieve glory in the next – but there is much evidence to substantiate the claim that at the time when Francis wrote the *Testament* he was quite ill and experiencing impairments in his eyes and the rest of his body. In fact, Francis' struggle with his failing eyesight is literally written out in the three extant autographs of his work.

Francis left only three small parchments of his own writing, and these were preserved as relics by his close companion, Brother Leo. Leo kept the autographs with him for many years after Francis' death, surrendering them to the Poor Clares of San Damiano either in 1257, when he handed over a breviary used by Francis, or in 1270, just before his death.[10] One, the so-called *Assisi Chartula*, is a small, double-sided parchment, written in Francis' hand on both sides. It is now kept as a relic of Francis, held at Sacro Convento in Assisi. On one side, Francis wrote *The Praises of God*; on the other, he wrote and illustrated a blessing to Brother Leo. The text of the *Praises* is faded, likely because Brother Leo kept the parchment folded, and the *Praises* were on the outside with the *Blessing* folded on the interior side, probably to protect it.[11] Despite its less than perfect condition, which makes the text of the *Praises* difficult to read, it is possible to see that the lines of the *Praises* are relatively even and well spaced. The letters, formed carefully and in a simple hand, based in a Carolingian, but perhaps more closely related to an Umbrian, book hand,[12] are easy to read for the most part. The writing is laboured and halting,[13] as if the scribe were unused to writing, but the letters are generally well formed. There are, however, noticeable corrections to the spelling and grammar of the texts.[14]

Although on the same piece of parchment, the *Praises* and the *Blessing* were not written at the same time. They were written with different pens,[15] and there is a noticeable difference in the way the letters and words were formed in the *Blessing* from the way they were formed in the *Praises*. A short note written by Brother Leo, tells us that Francis wrote both sides of the *Assisi Chartula*, the *Praises* and the *Blessing to Brother Leo*, at La Verna, two years before his death, after he had experienced his vision of the seraph and, according to tradition, received the *stigmata*.[16] Langeli argues that the *Blessing*, although often dated slightly later, has smoother penstrokes and more regularly formed letters than the *Praises*.[17] The most noticeable disparity between the two texts is that the letters of the *Blessing*, although formed in the same way as the letters used to write the *Praises* and presumed by most scholars to be by the same hand, are approximately one-third larger than the letters in the *Praises*.[18]

The third autograph is a letter to Brother Leo, now preserved at the cathedral in Spoleto. Experts often date this letter to 1225, but possibly as late as the spring or summer of 1226.[19] In the letter, Francis returns to a discussion with Leo they had had while they were together. Francis suggests to Leo that he need not[20] come to him for further counsel on that issue; rather Leo should follow in the Lord's footsteps and in his poverty in whatever way seems best to him.[21] In his in-depth study of the manuscript, Langeli suggests that the last four lines of the letter have been added after the letter was originally finished. The final four lines are even more cramped than the rest of the letter, and a careful examination of the letter revealed that the space had previously contained a tau that was erased to make room for the extra lines.[22] As Langeli notes, Bonaventure's *Legenda maior* mentions in passing that Francis generally signed his letters with the mark of the tau.[23] If the *Legenda maior* is correct in this (and that is a rather large "if," the *Legenda maior* is late, and not necessarily trustworthy), then such a finding would suggest that Francis did indeed add the last four lines of the letter at a different time. That the pen also looks different in the last four lines also supports this hypothesis. Francis' formation of letters throughout this text was careful, and, at times, almost laboured, especially in the last four lines.[24] Langeli suggests the writing in the letter is more "broken and difficult" than it is on either side of the *Assisi Chartula*, and even a cursory examination of the autographs bears this out.[25]

Francis' careful formation of the letters (along with the spelling and grammatical mistakes found in the texts) is most often linked to his lack of training in scribal practices rather than his eye impairment. One need only compare Francis' writing to Leo's careful book hand (gothic textualis) on the *Blessing to Brother Leo* to note the clear differences in writing styles. Leo's is a careful, well-trained book hand, Francis' is clearly not.[26] Although some perceived difficulties in Francis' writing can be attributed to early, rather poor transcriptions of Francis' autographs,[27] since Langeli's reconstruction, scholars of the autographs have put much of these concerns to rest. The consensus remains that Francis was not fluent in Latin, nor was he a practised scribe.[28] Yet the careful and deliberate formation of letters might not be wholly due to a lack of education or practice. This might as easily reflect an increasing inability to clearly see the words being formed on the parchment in front of him. Jean-Baptiste Auberger notes that, in the *Blessing for Brother Leo*, the margins are uneven, as are the spaces between the lines.

The length of lines is irregular. As Auberger writes, "there is no explanation for this unless we recall that Francis was nearly blind."[29]

Further evidence for Francis' growing inability to see can be found in the flow of the letters on the page. The alignment of letters and words in both the *Blessing* and the *Letter* are uneven, however the letter contains many more breaks or unnecessary spaces between the letters of words than does the *Blessing*. In the first line of the *Letter*, there is a break in the middle of Francis' own name; it is written as "francis sco." The word "oportet" is similarly broke up as "opor tet" in line 7. "Melius" in line 10 is broken up into three sections as "me li us." In contrast, on other lines, there is no spacing at all, even between words, as is the case in lines 6 and 15 (the original end of the letter). This is altogether different from the flow of words in the *Blessing*, where, for the most part at least, Francis' words are spaced correctly and, as is especially the case in the blessing to the right of the tau, the words "dominus bene te dicat" appear to be deliberately and carefully placed.[30] One could argue, of course, that the comparison of the handwriting of the *Blessing* to that of the *Letter* is unhelpful, for one was written carefully with extra attention paid to the formation of the blessing and the other was a quick note jotted to a friend and colleague. This is true, but the shaky and laboured formation of the letters in the *Letter to Brother Leo* suggest that Francis wrote the letters slowly, deliberately, and carefully, as he would have had to do if his eyesight had become impaired. No, the mistakes in Francis' writing are not attributable to the rapidity with which he jotted his note. Rather, the letter provides clear evidence that Francis' eyesight had deteriorated in between the time he wrote the *Blessing* and the *Letter*,[31] though few scholars have argued as much.[32]

There are mistakes and corrections in all three texts. While the *Praises* is faded and extremely difficult to read, it is clear enough to see that several spelling and grammatical errors are present.[33] In line 4, Francis used the siglum "dnus" instead of the more regularly used "dmus" as an abbreviation for *dominus*. In line 6, however, he uses the correct form. In line 7, a superscript *h* has been added to the word "umilitas." Langeli suggests that this correction was "undoubtedly" done "in the hand of Brother Leo."[34] In line 8, Langeli notes the presence of two letters which do not seem to fit the way Francis formed his letters, and so were perhaps added by someone other than Francis, but the poor state of the text does not allow for speculation beyond that.[35]

In the *Blessing*, there are two major changes. First, the initial minuscule *b* with which it originally began has been corrected to a majuscule *B*, probably by Brother Leo.[36] A second correction occurs at line 4, where the word "at" has been corrected to "ad". Langeli argues that this correction was completed by someone well trained as a scribe, since that the correction is subtle and, untrained as Francis was, he did not have the skills to perform the correction as adeptly as it was done.[37]

It is, however, in the *Letter to Brother Leo* where the most errors and corrections can be found. There are erasures, often without replacement in lines 4, 7, 11, and 17. In line 4, an *e* is erased and then apparently replaced by Francis in his own hand. A second *e* appears to have been erased later in the line. Several letters at the beginning of line 7 were erased without replacement. In line 11 a couple of letters in the middle of the word "videre" were erased without replacement, and in line 17 there is an erasure over which the word "aliam" has been written.[38] One word, "tibi," was added in a superscript at line 11. There is some debate about whether this correction was done by Francis or Leo, but Langeli argues that the formation of the *t* is "unworthy of Leo," and so the correction must have been done by Francis' own hand.[39]

Another sort of error found in the *Letter to Brother Leo* is the misspelling of words, as in line 4, in which "disimus" was written instead of "dixmus." This error appears to have been corrected.[40] Non-standard abbreviations were also sometimes used, as in line 7, when Francis used an incorrect abbreviation for "propter." This, too, was later corrected by Leo.[41] Lastly, Francis' letter includes several words which are spelled in an unusual way. Unsurprisingly, the letter *h* is often dropped in words, as in line 5, in which "hoc" is spelled "oc"; an *h* was added, probably in Leo's hand, slightly above the beginning of the word.[42] Additionally, as in the *Blessing*, Brother Leo has corrected the minuscule *i* at the beginning of the letter after the address to a majuscule *I*.

That Francis left us only three short works in his own hand has sometimes been attributed to his use of scribes in the creation of his texts. There is some evidence for this in the *Testament*, where Francis notes that he "made written" ("feci scribi"), rather than "wrote" ("scrivi"), the Lord's direction for his first *Rule*.[43] Brother Leo, seems to have functioned as his scribe at times. It is perhaps for this reason that he emended Francis' *Blessing* and *Letter* addressed to him. Francis' use of scribes is also usually linked to the presumed poor state of Francis' education and his inability to write with ease, especially in Latin. Indeed, Carlo Paolazzi has speculated the *Testament*, at least, and perhaps, other earlier works, were dictated by Francis in his vernacular Umbrian dialect and translated into Latin by the assisting scribes.[44] Yet the *Vita prima* testifies that Francis "learned to read" ("didicerat legere") in the place he was first buried, the school in the parish church of San Giorgio in Assisi.[45] The curriculum at a parish school in that period would likely have consisted of learning to read and write Latin in a grammatically correct fashion, first and foremost.[46] Octavian Schmucki has argued that, based on grammatical and spelling errors in Francis' autographs, his time in school must have been limited,[47] and, there can be no doubt, Francis' grasp of Latin was less than perfect and his writing skills less than adept. As Jean-Francois Godet-Calogeras has noted, Francis appears not to have even understood the general form of writing texts and letters, as evidenced by the fact that in both the *Blessing* and the *Letter* the initial letter of each was originally written as a minuscule.[48]

However, some of the errors in the autographs are more easily attributable to the saint's visual impairment than his poor education. Thus, for instance, the double tall *s* in Francis(s)co in the first line of the *Letter* is perhaps not a simple spelling error, or an Italianism breaking through, but the error of a man who was visually impaired, who stopped mid-word (even if the word was his own name), forgot precisely where he had left off writing, and could not see clearly enough in that moment to determine his place visually. The large space between the two letters supports this hypothesis, as does the uneven placement of letters within the line. Similarly, the addition of Brother Leo's name in the *Blessing*, placed as it was across the tau with a smaller and slightly raised *o*, suggests an inability to see the placement of his letters on the page clearly.[49] Another such error could be the misspelling of the siglum for "propter" as *Pr* in line 7. The siglum was corrected, probably by Leo, but Francis himself correctly formed the abbreviation in line 17. This suggests that the error in line 7 could have been the result of Francis' losing his place while writing. A similar thing may have occurred in line 11, where Francis added in a superscript a siglum for "tibi" in his own hand, between the words "videtur" and "placere."[50] Finally, even the image Francis drew on his blessing suggests either an individual who lacked even rudimentary drawing skills or whose skills had been impacted by visual impairment. At the very least, Brother Leo seems to have felt the need to describe the image by adding another rubric below it which stated, "In a similar way, he made the sign of the tau with a head in his own hand."[51] As Chiari Frugoni has suggested, by rubricating the blessing, Brother Leo turned a piece of personal communication into a "public testimony of the veracity of the apparition of the seraph and the manifestation of the *stigmata*."[52] This is certainly true of the first and longest rubric. But what was the purpose of the rubric that describes the image on the page? Beyond the obviously important testimony to Francis' creation of the image, the purpose of the rubric appears to be describing the image – not the meaning of the image, the image itself. This suggests that the image was already so unclear that it needed a description and explanation.

The extent to which Francis could write while his eyesight became increasingly impaired is an open question, especially since we have only three autographs in the saint's hand, and those appear to date from near the end of his life. Francis learned to write with a basic, unadorned alphabet long before his eyesight became impaired. As long as he retained some vision he could and did continue to write. Blind individuals who had to rely on written communication in the Middle Ages most often relied on notaries and scribes, yet there is evidence that sometimes people with partial or total blindness continued to write in their own hand. This is demonstrated in the case of Enrico Dandolo (d. 1205), the much-revered doge of Venice who suffered head trauma sometime during the 1170s, an injury that slowly diminished his ability to see clearly. The doge continued to sign documents until sometime later in life.[53] After his impairment became so profound he could no longer see to read, Dandolo continued to do business with notaries.[54] Francis followed a similar trajectory at the end of his life, writing when he could and otherwise relying on scribes.

Francis' own writings, in both form and content, bear witness to the illnesses and infirmities the he experienced. By ignoring the existence of this evidence, we run the risk of making Francis' struggles with his eye impairment invisible and of misunderstanding or misconstruing the saint's life. Francis himself testifies to his infirmities in some of his writings. His extant autographs, if they are dated correctly, show a deterioration in his handwriting and in his ability to formulate Latin sentences in grammatically correct ways. All of this indicates that the saint was not only struggling with a deficiency in his Latin training but also with a visual impairment.

Brother Leo's Testimony in the Dedication of Francis' Breviary

Brother Leo's testimony on the *Blessing* has already been described above, but there is one other source, directly from Leo's hand, that also attests to Francis' illnesses and infirmities. This is seen in the dedication to Sister Benedetta that Leo wrote at the front of Francis' breviary when he gave it to the convent of the Clares, circa 1257. In the dedication, Leo discusses how Francis used the breviary:

> ... [in the] time of his health, [Francis] always wished to say the office, as is
> written in the *Rule*. And in the time of his infirmity, when he was not able
> to say it, he wished to hear it. And this continued, while he lived. He also
> had a text of the Gospel written, so that on that day when he was not able

to hear mass owing to his experience of infirmity or to any other manifest impediment, he had the Gospel read to him, that section which on that day was said in mass.[55]

There are several interesting pieces of information in this dedication. In the first place, Leo bluntly acknowledged that Francis cycled through periods of health and illness. He also clearly stated that these infirmities impacted Francis' usual routine of life and that the saint modified his daily habits as a result. Although Leo was not specific about what infirmities Francis suffered to cause him to change his routines, certain clues in the dedication indicate that one issue with which the saint struggled was visual impairment. Take, for instance, how Leo discusses Francis' ability to say the canonical hours. Unsurprisingly, the saint said the hours of the office daily when he could. However, Leo implies that there were times when Francis' infirmity ("infirmitas") stopped him from saying the hours. In those instances, Francis wished to *hear* the hours. While Francis' illness could have stopped him from speaking, it seems more likely that it was his inability to read the hours from the breviary in which Leo wrote these very words that stopped Francis from saying the hours as he normally would.

There are other places in the dedication where Leo emphasized hearing over seeing or reading. For instance, Leo noted that Francis had texts of the gospels written for him for those times when he could not hear mass due to his illnesses. Leo wrote that on those occasions, he had the gospel text used for the mass of that day read to him ("faciebat sibi legi evangelium quod eo die dicebatur in ecclesia in missa").[56] This awkward construction surely implies that Francis was not reading the gospel himself, but that his companions were reading it to him. When, a little later in the dedication, Leo wrote of the way Francis always kissed his copy of the gospels, he noted that this occurred whether "[Francis] had heard or read the gospel."[57] That hearing was privileged before seeing in the phrase suggests that, towards the end of his life, hearing the gospels, rather than reading them, was the norm for Francis. Thus, the hearing of the gospels, like the hearing of the canonical offices, was likely a reference to the consequences of Francis' blindness on his devotional practices.

A final reference to the saint's blindness appears to come from Francis himself. Leo quoted the saint, saying, "For he said, 'when I do not hear the mass, I adore the body of Christ with the eyes of my mind in prayer, just as I adore it when I see it in the mass.'"[58] Ostensibly Leo was describing Francis' chosen alternative to mass: devotional prayer. Yet the phrasing also allows a way for a visually impaired individual to adore the host, by seeing it in the mind's eye; a reminder that a physical impairment need not impede intellectual or emotional spiritual endeavours.

In spite of Francis' ability to adore the host in the absence of a priest saying mass, Leo was also at great pains in this dedication to show that the saint missed mass only when he had a clear and justifiable reason to do so. In demonstrating this, Leo used the somewhat legalistic terminology of "manifest impediments." Though the phase was uncommon when Leo used it in the mid-thirteenth century, it was at least used in southern France and northern Italy to mean a clear (and so justifiable) obstacle to an action, whether this be fulfilling a contract or going on a crusade. It is unclear what might constitute a "manifest impediment" to attending mass, as there were no universally accepted impediments to hearing mass at all. With the exception of lepers in non-leper communities, infirmities could keep a person from hearing mass only if they were too unwell to attend or to sit through it. No other "clear and justifiable reasons" were present in the writings about church law and practices at the time. Yet it is apparent that Leo wants his readers to understand that Francis missed hearing mass only when he had a valid reason to do so. This raises the question of whether Leo felt a need to defend Francis' absence from church services. This is a possible reading, given the emphasis Leo placed on justifying Francis' absences.

The earliest witnesses to Francis' life suggest the saint suffered from a variety of ailments. To be sure, evidence written by Francis himself is scant, but the material record of his writings suggests a man struggling to write clearly, not only because he was unschooled in the art of writing but because his eyesight was weak, and becoming weaker, when those short texts were written. Texts that can be directly linked to Brother Leo, Francis' close companion, are also scarce, but those we have allude to Francis' illnesses and infirmities. Indeed, Leo clearly stated that Francis had periods of both health and illness. During times of illness, Francis modified his daily routines to compensate for his ailment. As will become clear in the next chapter, these early references to Francis' illnesses by the saint himself and his close companion are bolstered by the earliest hagiographies written about the saint.

Chapter Three

Et licet infirmus fuisset semper: Testimonies of Illness in the Early *Lives* of Francis

A thorough study of early sources of Francis' life, in particular Thomas of Celano's suite of works, along with the *Legend of the Three Companions*, the *Assisi Compilation*, the *Legenda maior* of Bonaventure, and the anonymous *Acta Beati Francisci in valle Reatini*, suggests that Francis' experience of illness should not be something set aside or dealt with lightly by modern biographers.[1] Nor should discussions of Francis' illnesses be limited to the final two years of his life, thereby collapsing his supposed experience of the *stigmata* and his experience of infirmity. Indeed, a careful reading of early sources suggests that Francis' illnesses and infirmities cannot so easily be confined to the end of his life. Even after excluding references to the *stigmata* and obvious hagiographic tropes, as, for instance, when God promises that Francis will experience rewards in heaven due to his earthly suffering,[2] some 76 different discussions of Francis' illnesses and infirmities can be found in these early sources. Unsurprisingly, the work that summarizes the remembrances of Francis' close companions, the *Assisi Compilation*, contains the most references at 43, followed by Thomas of Celano's *Remembrance of the Desire of a Soul*, with 29. The earliest source, Thomas of Celano's so-called *Vita prima*, contains 19 different references to Francis' various sicknesses. The shorter texts prepared for use during feast day sermons, have far fewer references, with the *Legend for the Use of the Choir* containing six and the *Vita brevior* three. As the following pages will demonstrate, Bonaventure's *Legenda maior* contains many (25) of the narratives surrounding Francis' illnesses found in other, earlier, texts, but Bonaventure often changes them, either eliding the references to illnesses, omitting references to doctors and their care of Francis, or implying divine agency in Francis' illnesses when no such agency was proposed earlier. Indeed, Bonaventure's projection of Francis' illnesses is more contained and more oriented towards the idea that they were a kind of earthly purgatorial suffering rather than the messy and problematic reality of his lived experience, as earlier sources describe.

As in all studies of Francis, it is difficult to peel back the layers of hagiographical intent to find the kernels of historicity in early documents. It is also difficult to ascertain a strict chronology of various described events in Francis' life. Nonetheless, the essential outlines of Francis' medical history can be sketched from the sources. However, attempts to diagnose Francis' illnesses will be avoided here since, as chapter 2 has demonstrated, numerous such attempts by other scholars have yielded little consensus. In any case, a medieval or modern diagnosis is unnecessary to demonstrate the larger point – that Francis was both ill and infirm throughout his life. In this chapter, discussions of Francis' illnesses and infirmities are divided into five distinct periods, those that occurred 1) before or just after his conversion to religious life, roughly between the years 1202 and 1210; 2) during his most active time of ministry, between 1211 and 1218; 3) between his departure for Egypt in 1218 and his slow withdrawal from the leadership of the order by 1221 – it was in this period that his infirmities began to affect the way he lived his life and his willingness to continue his leadership roles within the Franciscan Order; 4) between his resignation and the beginning of his retreat to La Verna, roughly from late 1221 to the fall of 1224; and finally, 5) at the end of his life, from his descent from La Verna in October of 1224 to his death in early October 1226.

The medical history presented here will not focus on the *stigmata* or pain and infirmities the sources suggest might be to be caused directly by the *stigmata*. Francis' *stigmata* were first mentioned by Elias of Cortona, Francis' vicar general, in an encyclical to the order just after the saint had died.[3] By the time Thomas of Celano composed the *Vita prima*, circa 1228, Francis' reception of the *stigmata* had become part of the story told about the saint. While I agree with Frugoni, who suggests that the story of the *stigmata* came into being in the first instance to make some greater sense of the evidence of tremendous suffering Elias saw written on the saint's bruised and battered flesh at the end of the saint's life, in his encyclical Elias publicly declared that Francis carried the wounds of Christ on his body.[4] This was not a big leap on the part of Elias, as has been perceived in past work. Carolyn Muessig's recent work on the spirituality of the *stigmata* has outlined the development of the idea that clerics carried Christ's wounds on their bodies, an idea that dates from Jerome's fourth-century commentary on Galatians. For Jerome, such *stigmata* resulted from living an ascetic life or living through the tribulations of persecution and trial, as Paul himself had done.[5] Throughout the central Middle Ages, *stigmata* shifted from being a sign of imitating Paul to imitating the suffering of Christ himself.[6] By the time of the Gregorian reforms in the mid-eleventh century, *stigmata* had become associated with the signs of clerical investiture,[7] though Peter Damian, at least, also believed holy men and men who were not in orders could also attain the marks of Christ through devotion and ascetic acts.[8] Thus, as Muessig's work demonstrates, Elias of Cortona's description of Francis' signs of suffering as *stigmata* drew on a long tradition of stigmatic spirituality.

It is also clear that Francis' early hagiographers sincerely believed that his wounds were *stigmata*, and that the saint had received them through divine intervention. It seems unlikely, then, that the *stigmata*, understood to have been given to Francis as marks of divine favour, would have been seen by Francis' contemporaries as being an impediment to leadership in the same way that illnesses and infirmities they believed to be attributable to natural causes would have been.

Captivity and Conversion: 1202–1210

One of the first incidents of Francis' life that negatively impacted his health was his imprisonment as a captured war combatant in 1202. As the son of a merchant of Assisi, Francis was outfitted as a knight and was expected to fight when Assisi and its allies engaged in an on-again, off-again war with Perugia, beginning circa 1202. Francis was likely captured at the Battle of Collestrada.[9] He was imprisoned afterwards for between six months and one year. While he was probably housed with the nobles rather than the rank and file, the conditions of the prison would have been challenging. Many of his modern biographers suggest that the illness which led to his conversion to religious life began during his time as a prisoner of war in Perugia,[10] yet there is no evidence from the early Franciscan sources that this was actually the case. The *Legend of the Three Companions* and the *Remembrance of the Desire of a Soul* record that Francis was a prisoner of war, but that his sunny and happy disposition helped other prisoners deal with their sadness and depression.[11] Whether this is true or not, the *Legend* clearly separates the time between Francis' imprisonment and his experience of his first illness by "a few years,"[12] while the *Remembrance* does not allude to early illnesses the saint experienced as a result of his incarceration at all.

The rational for modern biographers arguing that Francis fell seriously ill while imprisoned in Perugia is two-pronged. First, there is the general consensus among historians of Francis, but not, it is important to note, among historians of prisons, that the conditions in medieval prisons were appalling. Thus, from Thomas of Celano's short discussion of "the squalor of prison,"[13] Vauchez suggests that Francis contracted "various illnesses that seriously weakened his health,"[14] and Thompson links the report in the *Vita prima* that Francis was "worn down by a long illness"[15] spanning his youth to his time in prison, arguing that by the time of his release from prison in Perugia, Francis' health was "severely damaged."[16] This link between Francis' imprisonment and his early illnesses seems to have had its origins in the research of Arnaldo Fortini. Published in 1959, Fortini's *Nova Vita di San Francesco* contextualized the story of Francis within the archival records of repositories in Umbria, at least as far as was possible. Fortini suggests that Francis fell ill during his imprisonment. With a novelistic flair for description, Fortini writes that after Francis had contracted an illness, he was "taken from the dark dank underground cell and put with the other sick prisoners ... [and his] fever rose. It would not disappear. Outside the bestial cries of the guards ordering silence rang out. The dying ones fell silent, exhausted. Night's shadow enveloped them."[17] While these images may evoke tremendous pathos and sympathy for Francis' predicament, there is not a shred of evidence in any source to support this description of events.

Somewhat more compelling evidence for Francis becoming ill in prison is presented in the next chapter of Fortini's book, where he argues that the continued war in Perugia might shed some light on the timeline of Francis' early life. Fortini states categorically that peace was not declared between Assisi and Perugia until 1209 or 1210.[18] Thus, if Francis were released from prison at the end of the war, he would not have been released before 1209. Yet, the *Legend of the Three Companions* records that Francis and his fellow prisoners were released and allowed to return to Assisi after only a year of captivity.[19] That text further reports that Francis travelled to Apulia "a few years later" out of a desire to live a military life.[20] Fortini argues that the person whose army Francis wished to join was Walter of Brienne, who had first led Francis to war against Perugia in 1202. While there is nothing to verify this in any early hagiographies or chronicles, Fortini's presumption makes a certain amount of sense. Taking it to be certain that Francis went to Apulia to join the ranks of Walter of Brienne's army, Fortini then argues that this trip must have occurred sometime before 1205, the year in which Walter died. Fortini claims, based on this scaffolding, that Francis must have been released from the prison in Perugia at least two years earlier, perhaps in 1203. Given that there was no peace between Assisi and Perugia in 1203, Francis must have been released from prison for another reason. Fortini suggests that this reason was that Francis was ill. There had been a long tradition in Perugia of allowing ill prisoners to be ransomed back to their families before a formal peace treaty between warring parties had been negotiated, and Fortini found a document that suggested a fraternity, the Congregatio et societas captiuorum alamatorum, accepted responsibility for prisoners of war who fell ill and arranged ransoms for their return.[21]

While the explanation of Francis falling ill in prison and being ransomed back to his family on account of his serious illness is plausible, evidence to support this reading is circumstantial at best. There is no definitive proof in the early *lives* of Francis that the lengthy illness he experienced as a youth before his conversion was a result of his time as a prisoner of war in Perugia. Indeed, we have evidence of precisely the opposite in the *Remembrance*. Thomas writes that Francis "laughed and mocked his chains," and seemed to his companions in prison mad for exulting in his predicament.[22] While this sounds like (and probably is) a hagiographic trope rather than a reliable narrative of how Francis experienced his time in prison,[23] it remains true that there is no clear link in the hagiographical record between Francis' imprisonment and the illness he experienced before his conversion to religious life. Recent research by Guy Geltner suggests that conditions in medieval prisons, especially in Italy, were generally "tolerable," though hardly pleasant.[24] The fact that prisoners were housed together, in less than salubrious conditions, meant that sickness could be a chronic problem.[25] In spite of this reality, sick wards were not established in Italian prisons until the late fourteenth century.[26]

All that can be said with certainty about this first sickness is that Francis experienced a long illness before his conversion. While this, too, is a hagiographic convention, the details about Francis' illness and recovery recorded in the *Vita prima* adds authenticity to the account. This long illness seems to have had serious impacts on his mobility, for the *Vita prima* records that "when he had enjoyed a respite from his illness and was supporting himself with a cane, he began to walk here and there through his house for the sake of recuperating his health."[27] Thomas' *Vita prima* does link Francis' illness to the beginning of his conversion, for the future saint "began to think on accustomed things," "having been worn down by a long illness."[28] Later *vitae* limit the details of Francis' early illness but clearly link it to his conversion.[29]

There is evidence in the early *lives* of Francis that his companions and others close to him believed that this early illness resulted in his having fragile health throughout the rest of his life. The *Assisi Compilation* reports baldly that "Francis was always sick, since he was a fragile and weakened man according to his nature even in the secular world, and, daily, up until the day of his death, he became sicker on account of this."[30] This account is reported in a narrative of the text that carries an authenticating phrase, a variation on the "nos qui cum eo fuimus."[31] As Manselli notes, for once, there is no debate about who was with him, as one of the three companions, Angelo Tancredi, is named as being present within the narrative.[32] He was clearly one of those who testified to the truth of this account.

Francis' regular bouts of illness are also demonstrated by the numerous discussions of his activities, which he does in both "times of illness and times of health."[33] Such statements happen most frequently in the *Assisi Compilation* and the *Remembrance*. Francis practised severe asceticism whether he was healthy or sick,[34] he rejected medicine and even food whether healthy or sick,[35] he engaged in charitable works whether healthy or sick.[36] The discussion of Francis doing things whether healthy or sick becomes a bit of a repetitive theme in sources on Francis' life, but its inclusion, especially in parts of the *Assisi Compilation*, which are authenticated by the phrase "nos qui cum eo fuimus,"[37] does imply that his close companions knew that there were times during Francis' life when he was not healthy. Indeed, chapter 79 of the *Assisi Compilation* suggests that he was always weak and infirm, and when he seemed healthy, it was an appearance of health only.[38]

There are further indications that Francis was inattentive to his physical well-being in the early years of his conversion, and that this inattention impacted his general health going forward. His earliest biography, Thomas of Celano's *Vita prima*, records that in the early days after his conversion to religious life, Francis was mocked by people who knew him from his previous secular life. They called the future saint demented and threw mud and stones at him. "For they recognized," Thomas goes on to say, "that he had altered his earlier habit and was truly consumed by the maceration of his body and so they thought that he acted as he did due to his weakened and deranged state."[39] The account of Francis' early, desperate ascetic acts and their impact on his body, along with the reactions of his former friends and acquaintances, is also recorded, virtually word for word in the *Legend of the Three Companions*.[40] By the time the report finds its way into the *Legenda maior* of St. Bonaventure, the discussion of Francis' emaciated state had been left aside, and the opinions of his former friends and neighbours about his illness are reported instead as insults slung at the saint by unnamed and unknown citizens. There is no room in Bonaventure's normalizing narrative of St. Francis for neighbours and former friends who believed the future saint was ruining his fragile health by overzealous asceticism, or for the possibility that Francis might have been acting irregularly owing to his extreme mistreatment of his body. Thus, Bonaventure writes, "When the citizens saw him, filthy in his face and changed in his mind, they thought that he had taken leave of his senses and insulted him with bawling voices as though he were insane and demented."[41]

Yet, it is clear in early *vitae* that Francis' new ascetic lifestyle, combined with the seemingly fragile state of his health, ensured that he sought out medical help and other forms of interventions from the earliest years of his conversion. In a story told in the *Assisi Compilation*, Francis was unable to tell his first brothers to go and beg for food. He was so pleased to have their company that he wanted to spare his new companions the shame of begging for food. Thus, Francis went out alone, begging for alms every day. "He tired his body out doing this, largely because he was a delicate man in the world, and weak according to his nature. On account of his excessive abstinence (from food) and the suffering he sustained, he became weaker from that very day he left secular life." However, recognizing that he "was not able to tolerate such labour" and that begging for alms was the life to which his companions had been called, Francis encouraged his brothers to go out and beg for alms, which they gladly did.[42] This story has a didactic quality in that it clearly demonstrates the need for all Franciscan brothers to be engaged in the practice of seeking out alms, and further demonstrates that Francis believed such a duty to be a central one of the order. Yet, in spite of the narrative's clear connection to the political goals of the stories of the *Assisi Compilation*, it does seem to provide credible evidence both that Francis' way of life was negatively impacting his health, and, somewhat surprisingly, that he sought out a way to minimize those negative consequences by asking for help.

A second example is even more clear-cut. The *Legend of the Three Companions* records that when Francis was taking his vision of fixing the church literally and working to restore San Damiano, perhaps as early as 1206, a priest recognized his delicate constitution and sought out special food for the saint.

Francis, who was so refined while he lived in his father's house, carried stones on his own shoulders, in the service of the Lord, afflicting himself in many ways. However, the aforementioned priest, although poor himself, thought that the work to which Francis surrendered himself so fervently out of compliance to the divine, was beyond [the capability] of that man. He procured something special for him for the purpose of nourishment, knowing that Francis had lived delicately in the world. Of course, as that man of God said in confession afterwards, he frequently used medical supplements and medicinal preparations and abstained from contrary foods.[43]

Although the translators of the *Legend* in *Francis of Assisi: Early Documents* suggest the priest bought delicacies and sweets for Francis, the better translation of this sentence alludes to a medical meaning. *Electuaria* has the most common meaning of medical pastilles or supplements. To be sure, they were often (but not always) sweet, but the primary purpose of *electuaria* was medicinal.[44] Because the medicines were usually suspended in sugar or honey, they were also expensive.[45] Confection is a false cognate for *confectio*, which more properly means a prepared mixture. By the High Middle Ages, the word had come to mean a mixture prepared for medicinal purposes, just as *confectionaris* had come to mean someone who mixed medicines, a pharmacist.[46] It was sometimes, though rarely, used as a synonym for electuary.[47] Similarly, it is not that Francis abstained from "disagreeable foods," as the translation in *Early Documents* suggests, it is that he abstained from those foods which were humorally contrary to his delicate complexion. That Francis felt a need to confess taking medicine and refusing some foods can be explained by his position on seeking out medicine for bodily concerns too quickly and by his dedication to the notion that, in living a mendicant life and following the traditions of the gospel, the poor man should eat whatever he is given in charity.

This report of Francis receiving medicine and following a particular regimen to maintain his health so early in his converted life was almost immediately perceived as problematic for inclusion in texts about the already sainted Francis. Although the story of the priest worrying over Francis' work was reworked into Thomas of Celano's *Remembrance of the Desire of a Soul*, the elements that suggest Francis' vulnerability and inability to follow his own teachings are elided. Thus, the *Remembrance* reports that while Francis was engaging in the physically taxing work of rebuilding the church of San Damiano, his very delicate constitution changed to that of a *rusticanus*, a country labourer who patiently bore his work. The priest who was attached to San Damiano "discerned that Francis was worn down from constant fatigue, [and] moved by piety, began to supply him daily with some of his own food, although it was not savoury, since he was a pauper." Even this, the Francis of the *Remembrance* turned into a teachable moment. Although Francis commended the priest's concern and embraced his piety, he told himself that he would not always find a priest to serve him and that this was not the sort of life that profited a person who claimed voluntary poverty.[48] Note that Francis' delicate constitution was not weakened; rather, he became a rough (but hardy) labourer. The care of the priest, rather than accepted as it was in the *Legend of the Three Companions*, spurs Francis to take up his life of apostolic poverty. Unsurprisingly this somewhat problematic story about Francis' health is not included at all in Bonaventure's normalizing *Legenda maior*.

Only one other account that suggests Francis' early health concerns need be mentioned. This incident does not recount an illness of Francis, but rather suggests that an observer believed Francis to be ill or in pain. As both the *Legend of the Three Companions* and the *Assisi Compilation* relate, a few years after Francis' conversion to religious life, he was walking near the church at Porziuncula, wailing and lamenting. A "spiritual man" saw Francis and thought he was suffering from some illness or pain" and asked him why he was crying. Francis, of course, answered that he wept for the passion of the Lord.[49] While this does not directly reference any illness or infirmity of Francis, it does suggest that both his appearance and behaviour could be read by people, even "spiritual" people, as indicative of illness rather than devotion.

In summary, information about Francis' early life and the first years of his conversion is not easy to find, yet the little evidence that can be gathered suggests Francis suffered a long illness before his conversion to religious life. This illness may have been caused by his imprisonment as a prisoner of war in Perugia, but there is no evidence in the earliest *lives* that supports this reading. There is, however, a surprising amount of evidence that suggests that Francis' general constitution was delicate from his conversion onward and, more surprisingly still, that he sometimes modified his ascetic practice in those early years to compensate for this delicate state. As is completely expected, later, more traditionally hagiographic *vitae* of Francis, especially Bonaventure's *Legenda maior*, diminish such references.

Negotiating Ministry and Illness: 1210–1219

There is not much more evidence of Francis' sick and fragile nature in the narratives that describe the second portion of his converted life than in the first but there is enough to suggest that illness was a chronic if not constant concern. Between 1210, when Francis and his early companions' way of life was confirmed by Pope Innocent III, and 1219, when Francis travelled to the Holy Land and Egypt, he suffered at least two distinct episodes of illness, one in Spain and a second in Assisi itself. Other experiences of illness occurred between these two major events. Already, as we will see, Francis' role as the leader of his order, and his ministry itself, were being compromised by his experience of illness.

The first lengthy illness the saint experienced after his conversion took place in either 1213 or 1214, while he was on what was to be a missionizing trip through Spain to Morocco. Francis and some of his companions left Assisi to travel through southern France and into Spain. While in Spain, Francis suffered a severe illness that forced him to abandon his plans. The episode is recorded in Thomas of Celano's *Vita prima*, the *Treatise on Miracles*, and Bonaventure's *Legenda maior*. Thomas does not include many details in the *Vita prima*, saying only that when Francis had reached Spain on his way to preach in Morocco, God "resisted [Francis] to his face. With an illness threatening lest he proceed further, God recalled him to the beginning point of his journey."[50] This narrative is repeated more or less exactly in Bonaventure's *Legenda maior* – Francis was overcome by a grave illness sent by God, who wished him to carry out deeds other than preaching in Morocco.[51] At first glance, Thomas of Celano's *Treatise on Miracles* appears to add detail to the story of Francis' illness in Spain. But a careful parsing of the text suggests that this illness Francis experienced may be one which occurred slightly later than the grave ailment that forced Francis to end his travels in Spain.

> While returning from Spain after he had not been able to set out to Morocco according to his vow, he incurred a very serious illness. Afflicted with weakness in extreme need, repulsed from the lodging of his host as a result of his rough appearance, he lost speech for three days. When he had finally recovered his strength, walking along the road with Brother Bernard, he said to him that he would eat something of a bird if he had one.[52]

There are several things to note about this short excerpt. The first is that this illness did not befall Francis *in* Spain, but rather when he was returning *from* Spain. This suggests that Thomas was recording a second illness, separate from that which convinced Francis that he could not travel to Morocco. Unlike the narrative of Francis' illness found in the *Vita prima* and the *Legenda maior*, this discussion records a particular symptom, the loss of Francis' ability to speak. Finally, unlike the other two sources, the *Treatise on Miracles* Francis suggests to a companion that he would eat "something of a bird," presumably to aid his recovery, if he had it. Miraculously, this plea for food was answered when a knight rode to them to offer them a "very good-looking bird," which Francis "received with joy."[53] Note that, here again, Francis accepted intervention to care for his ill body. This time however, that intervention was not explicitly medical.

Other incidents of illness in this part of Francis' life are not so easily datable to particular years between 1210 and 1219. The *Remembrance of the Desire of a Soul* recounts how Francis was once so worn out and weak from fasting that he was unable to reach his intended destination, Bevagna, a small town south of Assisi. Francis' companion sent word ahead to a "certain spiritual lady" that he was seeking some food and wine for Francis. She and her daughter came and delivered the food to Francis. The point of the story is not the saint's illness, rather it is his reluctance to show too much familiarity with women, even those women who were "devoted to God," as were this woman and her daughter. Perhaps for this reason, we can more readily trust the report that suggests Francis was fasting so rigorously he weakened his body and endangered his health.[54]

Francis also spent some time weathering an illness at the bishop's palace in Assisi. This occurred "in the time when no one was received into the life of the brothers without the licence of blessed Francis."[55] That Francis alone was receiving initiates places the date of this anecdote sometime before 1221, when Francis stepped down from any sort of leadership role, and also likely before 1219, when Francis left for Egypt, leaving two vicars to care for the order in his absence, one of whom, Matthew of Narni, was to receive brothers into the order.[56] This evidence for an early experience of sickness on Francis' part is believable in part because it is mentioned in passing while illustrating another point, a miracle demonstrating Francis' gift of prophecy. The aim of the narrative in the *Assisi Compilation* is to demonstrate how Francis denied entrance to his fledgling fraternity the son of a nobleman from Lucca, knowing his conversion to religious life was only superficial. In later accounts of this miracle, discussions of Francis' illnesses are withheld. Thus, the story of the nobleman's son's failed attempt to enter Francis' brotherhood is mentioned in the *Remembrance of the Desire of a Soul*,[57] but there is no mention of the saint's illness at all. It seems likely, then, that the unknown author(s) of the *Assisi Compilation* can be trusted in their suggestion that Francis was staying in the household of the bishop of Assisi because he was, in fact, suffering from an unspecified illness.

A second account in the *Assisi Compilation*, corroborated and expanded by the *Actus beatus Franciscus in valle Reatina*, describes another time when Francis was sick at the bishop's palace in Assisi. This account is generally dated to long after the account in AC 70; in fact, it is most often thought to have occurred in the final weeks of Francis' life.[58] However, a convincing argument can be made for placing this episode earlier, at a time much nearer to the episode outlined in the paragraph above. The *Assisi Compilation*'s report of this new miracle is quite short, noting that, "[a]t a certain time, while Francis remained very sick in the same palace [here the text refers to the Bishop of Assisi's palace mentioned in AC 70, just above], his brothers asked and encouraged him that he might eat something." Francis answered that he did not wish to eat anything, but if he had a particular kind of fish, a *squalo*, he might be able to eat a little. A miracle occurred, and someone came carrying a basket of three *squalo* and crab cakes sent from Father Gerard, a minister at Rieti.[59] Francis ate these and gave thanks to the Lord for the gift, noting that he appreciated these especially because such fish were not available in the area around Assisi in winter.[60] The bare account in the *Assisi Compilation* is fleshed out in the *Actus beatus Franciscus in valle Reatina*. In it, as in the *Assisi Compilation*, Francis' brothers urged him to eat, and he said he had no appetite, except that he might be able to eat a little of the fish called *squalo*. The narrator then adds, informationally, that the *squalo* is a white river fish, and that Francis also "willingly ate crab cakes," which were, he further helpfully provides, "cakes made up of the flesh and juice of crabs, with nuts and sweets."[61]

Although not explicitly stated in the text, medieval readers and auditors may have understood that the crab cakes also had humoral benefit for Francis. Nuts were regular ingredients in medicinal preparations, including the famed theriac, in the High Middle Ages.[62] Certainly, the nuts and sweets in the crab cakes were generally understood to be injecting much needed heat into Francis' sick body. The humoral qualities of crab (and most seafood) seems to have been debated in the premodern period. Some experts, like Galen, suggested that all fish and seafood was nutritious though difficult to digest. Others suggested that since seafood was cold and wet it had little nutritional value.[63] As *squalo* was a fish, it, like the crab in the crab cakes, was perhaps nutritionally suspect, so these foods may have been perceived as comfort foods, rather than as having any medicinal value.

As in the *Assisi Compilation*, the gift bearer in the *Actus beatus Francsicus* brought both *squalo* and crab cakes, and, as in the earlier text, Francis gave thanks to the Lord for taking care of his needs; he was especially appreciative of the gifts of things which were not available in Assisi in winter. What is startlingly different in the version in the *Actus*, however, is the end of the account, which states "[a]nd eating the aforesaid, [Francis] was restored to pristine health by divine virtue within a few days."[64] To my knowledge, the addition of the description of the *coppus*, or cake, and the end, which states that Francis recovered his health relatively quickly, are unique in the corpus of early works about the saint. And yet, there is no sound reason to deny the possible veracity of this account, especially if, as the editor of the *Actus beatus Franciscus* argues, a potential source for this text might be the now lost text by Angelo,[65] one of Francis' close companions, on the subject of the saint's deeds in the Rieti valley.[66] The additional material in the *Actus* is not intended to rationalize or to find the didactic meaning of the story, rather it provides greater detail – perhaps the crab cakes were a specialty of the region? In fact, they may well have been, for in another miracle account, a woman provides a meal of little crab cakes, among other items, when the brothers were in need.[67]

Based on the evidence found in the *Assisi Compilation* alone, the traditional dating of this episode to the last weeks of Francis' life must be called into question. The chronology of Francis' final months is fairly certain, and he seems to have been in Assisi in the late summer and early fall before he died there at the Porziuncula at the beginning of October 1226. In no way can this time of year be described as winter, yet Francis gives thanks in the narrative, particularly because he was brought fish that were not available in Assisi in winter. Further, the paragraph containing the discussion of Francis' gift of prophecy and this narrative are linked textually (this narrative references the location where Francis was staying, mentioned in the previous narrative) and thematically in terms of Francis' illness. Such connections between the two accounts suggest the possibility of a further temporal link between the stories. Finally, if it reflects an authentic early tradition about the narrative, the final sentence of the account in the *Actus beatus Franciscus* further cements the likelihood that this episode of sickness did not occur in Francis' final weeks, as Francis is described as recovering full health. Most likely these events occurred at the same time as noted in the previous narrative in the *Assisi Compilation*, when Francis was still personally receiving initiates into the order: so, before 1219.

One more event in Francis' life can be firmly dated to this earlier period of his illness in Assisi. The narrative is a common one, found in the *Vita prima*, elaborated on in the *Assisi Compilation* and even included in Bonaventure's *Legenda maior* with few changes. Thomas of Celano reports briefly that once, when Francis was seriously ill, he ate a bit of chicken, and then, upon recovering his heath, he insisted on doing penance and ordered a fellow brother to lead him around the city with a rope, yelling loudly that Francis was a "glutton who fattened himself with the flesh of a chicken."[68] In a similar account in the *Assisi Compilation*, Francis ate a little meat (*carnis*), rather than chicken. This is an important distinction, at least for those in medieval Europe, for there was, at the time, some debate about whether chicken should be categorized as meat, and thus forbidden in times of fasting by monastic rule and custom.[69] The narrator in the *Assisi Compilation* is also quick to point out that Francis was so ill "on account of his many and diverse and long illnesses that he was not able to eat" much of anything at all.[70] In this version, Francis did his penance even though it was winter and quite cold, and he was still ill with a recurring quartan fever.[71] The *Assisi Compilation* adds some information that allows us to date this episode more accurately than the account recorded in the *Vita prima*: the brother with whom Francis made his confession, and whom Francis ordered to lead him around by a rope around the neck, was Peter Catani.[72] This dates the episode to at least before Catani's death in March 1221,[73] and possibly to as early as before 1219, when Catani travelled with Francis to Egypt.[74]

As with the earliest part of Francis' converted life, there are few examples of Francis in sickness or distress that can be categorically placed during the period of his early ministry. However, the few examples we do have demonstrate that Francis had several different episodes of illness interspersed with other periods of relative health. This equilibrium was not seriously challenged until Francis travelled to the Holy Land and Egypt circa 1219, after which Francis began a constant struggle with his health that would last the rest of his life. Nonetheless it is clear that Francis' missionary activities were already sometimes being curtailed on account of illness, as, for example, during his early attempt to travel to Morocco.

Travel and Retreat from Leadership: 1219–1222

If the years before 1219 had sometimes challenged Francis' aims for his life as a missionary and his order, the years after were even more challenging. Organizational help within the order and a respite from serious illnesses allowed Francis to plan a trip to Egypt, which he undertook in 1219. He travelled with a wave of the Fifth Crusade on a mission to preach Christianity to the Muslims. Accounts suggest Francis was well received by the Muslim leaders with whom he interacted, though he had no success in converting them. During this trip, Francis contracted a severe eye disease. This year and this illness mark a turning point in Francis' already fragile health, for the malady slowly caused his eyesight to deteriorate to near blindness. Much of the discussion of Francis' eye ailment in his early hagiographies occurs in the discussions of his final years, especially between 1224 and 1226. Thus, for instance, Thomas of Celano suggests that Francis contracted his eye disease around the same time that he began to experience other ailments, circa 1224, after his vision of the seraph at La Verna and his reception of the *stigmata*.[75] However, there is good reason to believe that Francis contracted his eye disease earlier, during his time in Egypt. Aside from the reality that trachoma was a common occurrence in medieval Egypt, and had been since Pharaonic times,[76] the *Assisi Compilation* specifically notes that Francis contracted his eye disease in Egypt. This passage from the *Assisi Compilation* is particularly interesting in that it seems to imply that Francis suffered from serious illnesses long before his trip to Egypt, and that the eye disease he contracted on that trip simply exacerbated already present weaknesses.

> Although blessed Francis had had for a long time and had up until the day of his death, infirmities of the kidneys, spleen, and stomach, from that time at which he travelled to parts across the sea for the purpose of preaching to the Sultan of Babylon and Egypt, he also had had a great infirmity of the eye due to the great hardship from the exhausting nature of his journey, during which he experienced great heat both on the way there and returning.[77]

So exhausted was Francis after his trip to Egypt that, upon his return to Italy, he rode a donkey while travelling. The story of Francis riding a donkey and knowing that his travelling companion, Brother Leonard, believed that he himself should be riding, since his family was more noble than Francis' own, is a well-known one. Although the *Assisi Compilation* does not state when this incident occurred, nor does it name the brother in question, the *Remembrance of the Desire of a Soul* and Bonaventure's *Legenda maior* do. Both note that it was "during the time when he was returning from overseas."[78] Both texts note that this companion was also quite tired. However, if, in fact, the source text for both Thomas of Celano and Bonaventure is an earlier version of the story found in the *Assisi Compilation*, both later texts have changed the story slightly, for the story in the *Assisi Compilation*, unlike the others, suggests that Francis was riding the donkey not just because he was tired (as was Brother Leonard) but because he was a "weak man and ill."[79]

There is, then, some evidence that Francis' ill health was reasserting itself shortly after his return from Egypt, in late 1219 or early 1220. While many of the discussions of Francis' illnesses are dated to the end of his life, certainly after 1220 and often after 1224, I will suggest in the following pages that, like those describing Francis' experience of his eye impairment, many of these narratives need not be dated so late, and that Francis' health, always so fragile, deteriorated rapidly, not after 1224, as so many have argued, but after 1219.

To be sure, Francis' initial actions after his return from Egypt do not necessarily suggest that he was falling ill. He was travelling rapidly, gathering information about changes that had occurred within his order while he had been absent, and trying to return it to one aligned with his original vision. Jordan of Giano reports that, upon Francis' return from

Egypt, he successfully "reformed the order according to his own statutes."[80] This period after Francis' return to Italy was clearly one of high energy and emotion, as Francis sought to take control of his order back into his own hands and away from others who had different visions for it. And yet there are hints in the sources that all was not well with the saint, even at this point of his life.

Aside from the discussion of how Francis began to experience a disease which led to visual impairment in the *Assisi Compilation* noted above, there are three other events that suggest Francis might have been weak and ill from the time of his journey home from Egypt, and that his burst of activity in 1219 may have been one of his last truly energetic periods: 1) his so-called resignation from the leadership of the order; 2) his behaviour at the Chapter of the Mats; and 3) his request of the papacy for a protector of the order, just after his return from Egypt. Each is discussed in turn below.

Resignation

The first event is a complicated and much-discussed one – Francis' decision to step down as the head of his order.[81] Jordan of Giano's account of Francis' triumphant return from Egypt and his ability to reform the order in keeping with his own vision is at odds with Francis' decision, perhaps made less than six months after his return, to step down as the order's head. Much ink has been spilled trying to explain it. Most historians, following Bonaventure's quick discussion of Francis' decision to withdraw, argue that Francis' sense of humility encouraged his decision.[82] Bonaventure included his brief reference to Francis' resignation in his chapter about humility, saying that, "[t]herefore, ceding the office of general, he sought a guardian, to whose will he submitted on all things."[83] However, the perhaps more reliable source, the *Assisi Compilation*, suggests there was confusion about the reason Francis decided to give up his leadership position, even among those close to him. The *Assisi Compilation* gives three different accounts of Francis' resignation. The first account is also found in Thomas of Celano's *Remembrance of the Desire of a Soul*, and describes Francis' resignation as being motivated by humility.

> For the purpose of preserving the virtue of sacred humility, when a few years had passed after his conversion, he resigned the office of prelate at a certain chapter, among all the brothers of the religion, saying, "From this time forward, I am dead to you. But here is Brother Peter Catani, whom I and you shall all obey." And immediately bending down before that man, he promised reverence and obedience to him.[84]

The mention of Peter Catani allows us to date the resignation discussed to before March 1221, for Peter died in that month and was buried at the Porziuncula. However, this report may be less reliable than the other two accounts included in the *Assisi Compilation*, for several reasons. In the first place, this version of the resignation is found in both the *Assisi Compilation* and the *Remembrance of the Desire of a Soul*. Although it is clear that the texts have a common source, the incidence of exact phrasing of a narrative being shared between the two texts is relatively rare. That this resignation episode is told in an exact, word-for-word, repetition suggests to many scholars that the authors of the *Assisi Compilation* copied it exactly from the *Remembrance* when the *Assisi Compilation* was compiled or composed in the early fourteenth century. This possibility seems even more likely given that Francis' resignation is discussed twice more in the *Assisi Compilation* and in a different way.

The other two accounts in the *Assisi Compilation* report the saint's own words about the resignation itself and, more intriguingly, both use precisely the same phrase to describe the action of his resignation. Francis says "dimisi officium fratrum," a phrase that appears to have been used only in the context of explaining Francis' resignation (and nowhere else in medieval literature), but is found twice in the *Assisi Compilation* and its cognate texts.[85] This lends credence to the possibility that this phrase, given in Francis' own voice, is the way that Francis himself may have described his relinquishing of formal authority within the order. Finally, and perhaps most convincingly, one of the two later accounts in the *Assisi Compilation* occurs in the same section of the manuscript as a narrative authenticated by a statement of eye-witness testimony, "nos vero qui cum ipso fuimus," though it is important to note the authentication specifically refers to Francis' inclusion of regulations unpopular with prelates in his *Rule* and not to his discussion of the reasons for his resignation.[86]

These two accounts of Francis' resignation appear to be copies of source material requested by Crescentius of Iesu at the General Chapter of 1244 for the purpose of constructing a new life of Francis. Unlike the narrative found in AC 39, both of these other accounts link Francis' resignation to his illnesses, though the import of his sickness on his decision to resign differs in each. In the first, included in AC 106, Francis, lying ill, speaks with one of his companions, probably in the bishop's palace at Assisi.[87] Possibly reflecting the concerns of the proto-Spirituals, who seem to have recorded much of the material found in the *Assisi Compilation*, Francis' companion asks why Francis tolerates brothers who do not live his vision. Francis answers that when he was leading the order, everyone lived his vision. However, as the order grew, he realized some would turn away from his example. And so, as Francis explains in his own voice: "[b]ut since that time when I renounced and gave up that office of the brothers, I excused myself among the brothers at the general chapter, because I was not able to have care and concern for them on account of my infirmity."[88] Francis was then quick to reassure his companion that "if the brothers had walked and were walking in accord with [his] will, he would not have wished them to have had any other minister except [himself] until the day of [his] death."[89] Clearly there is some attempt by the author of this narrative to suggest that Francis' order had become something other than what Francis had envisioned for it. However, in the narrative Francis does not deny that he resigned his position of authority as a result of illness or infirmity. Rather the intent of this narrative is to render comprehensible his resignation and his perhaps then well-known comment that it was due to his illnesses and/or infirmities.

The third discussion of Francis' resignation in the *Assisi Compilation* does similar work, seemingly trying to explain Francis' resignation and what appears to be the well-known reason of illness given for it. The narrative reads:

> For often blessed Francis said to the brothers at chapters and also in *collatio* these words of his: "I have pledged and decided to observe the *Rule* of the brothers and all brothers are similarly obligated to [do] this themselves. For this reason, from that time I gave up the office of the brothers, finally, on account of my infirmities and for the greater advantage of my soul and of all the brothers. I am not bound to my brothers except to show a good example. For I learned this from the Lord and I find and know it in truth, since, even if my infirmity did not excuse me, the greatest aid I am able to devote to the religion of the brothers is that I daily be free to pray to the Lord for it, that he might govern, conserve, protect, and defend it."[90]

Again, there is no denial in the narrative that Francis gave up his leadership role because of his illness, though this is not the only reason suggested. In this explanation, the infirmities or illnesses were freeing, for they enabled the saint to devote more time to prayer. Yet the placement of the term *de cetero*, meaning "finally," is interesting, as it may imply that Francis had continued to lead his order while sick, and only resigned when his infirmities became too onerous. Thus, two independent testimonies that appear to be somewhat reliable in the *Assisi Compilation* suggest the saint himself had stated that he had resigned owing to illness. Perhaps we should take the discussion in Francis' own words at face value. He resigned because he was sick. He may also have been humble and/or overwhelmed by the fast-paced growth of his order or the direction the order was taking towards regularization, but the reason Francis himself cited, according to "those who were with him," was his failing health.

There is some corroborating evidence that suggests Francis was experiencing significant ill health near the time he stepped down. Upon his withdrawal from leadership, Francis asked for a guardian ("guardianus") who would guide him in all things and to whom Francis would owe absolute obedience. Most often in biographies of the saint, the guardian is presented as a spiritual guide for Francis, one who allows the saint to practise humility in his obedience. Yet, the role of the guardian as described in the hagiography indicates he was responsible for the saint's physical well-being as well as his spiritual needs.

The use of the word *guardian*, in Latin, *guardianus*, is unusual in and of itself. The term, which Francis himself uses to describe his overseer,[91] seems to have been used only sparingly before its adoption into the Franciscan administrative language. In the order today, as it meant soon after Francis' death, a guardian refers to a friar who is responsible for the spiritual care of a community.[92] Its primary meaning until that point, though, seems to have been a person who provides protection,[93] a surprising link for Francis and his hagiographers to make if Francis merely wished to obey his guardian as an act of humility.[94] Yet there is no doubt that at times Francis'guardian acted as a sort of protector, defending the saint's physical well-being from his attempts to destroy his already infirm body through severe ascetic practices. There are several examples which demonstrate this in the early *lives* of Francis. For instance, AC 81 and *Remembrance* 2.93.130 record how Francis' guardian requested that he sew a piece of fur into his tunic to protect his stomach and spleen from the cold during a time of illness. Francis agreed, but only if he was also allowed to sew fur on the outside of his tunic so as not to hide the steps he had taken to protect his health. Similarly, in a much-discussed episode from the *Assisi Compilation*, Francis' guardian had to be summoned to extinguish Francis' garments which had caught fire because he had been sitting too near the fireplace. A companion had frantically tried to encourage Francis to put out the fire burning next to his skin, but he would not; thus the companion ran to get Francis' guardian, who extinguished the fire against Francis' wishes.[95] The *Assisi Compilation* presents this episode as demonstrating Francis' love and respect for "Brother Fire," but it also demonstrates a guardian doing precisely what legal guardians or custodians of the Middle Ages in other contexts were supposed to do: protect the health and welfare of individuals who could not, or would not, take care of

themselves. Francis' guardian may well have protected Francis against
the sin of pride, and ensured the saint's humility, but part of his pur-
view, it seems, was to care for the saint's physical, as well as spiritual,
well-being.[96]

Francis' health, always somewhat frail, began to seriously fail after
his return from Egypt and the Holy Land in 1219 or 1220. Certainly,
Francis' resignation from his order should be seen in the context of his
increasing disabilities and illnesses. An understanding of Francis' failing health, especially his encroaching visual impairment, allows us to
see that his guardian may have fulfilled multiple purposes – caring for
the saint's physical well-being even as he ensured Francis' continued
humility.

Chapter of the Mats

Like so much about Francis' life, the so-called Chapter of the Mats has
been the subject of intense scrutiny and debate. Even the date of the
chapter is not certain. It apparently received its name from the fact that
so many brothers attended that huts had to be made to house them all.
Indeed, the Chapter of the Mats was likely one of the last chapters to
which every brother of the order was invited. The Chapter of the Mats
is mentioned in the *Assisi Compilation* and possibly in Jordan of Giano's
chronicle. However, the two accounts differ in details, especially concerning conflict within the order, and Jordan does not refer to the chapter as the Chapter of the Mats in his chronicle at all, saying instead that
at this chapter the brothers "lived, ate, and slept under the shade."[97] It
is thus possible, but unlikely, that the two sources are describing different chapters.

The *Assisi Compilation* notes that "at a general chapter ... called the
Chapter of the Mats,"[98] Hugolino and "some wise brothers" wished
Francis to adopt a monastic rule. Examples mentioned in the text refer
to the Benedictine, Augustinian, and Cistercian *Rules*. Francis refused.
Thompson has argued, correctly I think, that this story is a narrative
addition, and not based in historical fact.[99] The story more clearly represents the growing divisions between the factions that would eventually become the Spirituals and the Conventuals in the generations
after Francis' death. Here, as in other places, the author or authors of
the *Assisi Compilation* show their proto-Spiritual alliances.[100] However,
if there is a kernel of historical reality in the discussion of the Chapter of
the Mats described in AC 18, it is not necessarily the chapter described
in Jordan of Giano's *Chronicle*, for Jordan does not report any conflict
among the senior members of the order.

Jordan is correct in dating the creation of a Franciscan mission to Germany to the Chapter of 1221, and his description of that event and Francis' apparent illness at the same chapter are clearly linked.[101] Jordan notes that near the end of the chapter, "because Francis was quite weak," whatever he said was reported by Brother Elias. "Blessed Francis was seated at the feet of Brother Elias and tugged at his tunic to get his attention. Elias bent down to him to inquire what he wished; then, straightening himself, he would say 'Brothers, thus says the Brother,' signifying the blessed Francis."[102] Thompson[103] argues that in spite of Jordan's suggestion that Francis' illness required this arrangement, it was humility more than suffering that caused Francis to use Elias as his mouthpiece. Other scholars, like Fortini,[104] suggest Francis was, indeed, weak and ill by the end of the chapter. Yet, it is difficult to reconcile a weak and ill Francis, incapable of speaking to the members of the order, with the Francis who preached a sermon to three thousand friars, as Jordan reported he had, just a few days earlier. Fortini argues that Francis rallied his strength to preach in spite of his debilitating illness.[105] In his English translation of Jordan's *Chronicle*, Placid Hermann suggests that the discrepancy can be reconciled by realizing that Jordan collapsed his recollection of two distinct chapters, those of 1219 (when Francis did preach) and 1221 (when Francis was ill) into a constructed memory of one,[106] remembered more than forty years after the event. Yet Jordan is careful to distinguish what he knows from what he has heard, noting that "it is believed that Francis read the Gospel" at the mass that opened the general chapter,[107] while remarking that Francis did "preach to the brothers, having taken up the theme of Blessed be the Lord, My God, who trains my hand for battle."[108] The very specificity of this memory would seem to support its general accuracy. Jordan most often proves reliable in his reminiscences and is careful in delineating what he knows from eyewitness testimony and what he knows from hearsay, and so we must consider his claims plausible – that Jordan is describing the events of a single chapter at which Francis was well enough to preach at the beginning of the week-long chapter, but was ill by the end. Since it seems that the most easily datable events in Jordan's description of the chapter are linked by others to the chapter of 1221, this date seems a likely one for the Chapter of the Mats. Indeed, Jordan's oblique reference to "sleeping and eating under the stars" might reference the huts which were said to have housed the brothers at this chapter. Regardless of a precise date, sources indicate there was a general chapter at which Francis was so ill he was unable to speak loudly enough to be heard. Jordan of Giano, at least, clearly links this event to Francis' infirmities.

Adopting a Protector for the Order

It is well known that sometime after Francis' return from Egypt, Cardinal Hugolino dei Conti di Segni, the future Pope Gregory IX, took on a more official role as an intermediary between the papal curia and the growing Franciscan Order. Francis' *Testament* gives him the title of "Lord, Protector, and Corrector of the Whole Fraternity."[109] *The Legend of the Three Companions* reports that Francis had had the support of a friend of the Bishop of Assisi, Lord John of St. Paul, the cardinal bishop of Sabina, in his initial encounter with Pope Innocent III, when the way of life of Francis' early *religio* was approved, circa 1209 or 1210. This support was never officially sanctioned by the papacy, however, as the support of Cardinal Hugolino was. The sources generally agree that, in 1219 or 1220, Francis asked Pope Honorius III for someone to whom he could go with problems and concerns about the order instead of always going directly to the pope. Honorius agreed and asked him whom he would like appointed. Francis replied that Hugolino should have the position.

The *Vita prima* reports that Francis had met Hugolino in Florence, when he was planning to travel to France, sometime between 1210 and 1219 – probably circa 1217. There, impressed with Francis' piety, Hugolino offered Francis his help and protection, along with the advice not to leave his order without a leader as he travelled to France. He convinced Francis to turn back. It is perhaps the cardinal bishop's offer, along with the sound advice of not leaving his fledgling order, that encouraged Francis to look to Hugolino when it became clear he would need the support of someone in the papal curia to return his order to his own vision of a mendicant life of apostolic poverty.

Francis asked for a protector of the order freely and chose Hugolino for that role himself. Superficially, there is not much evidence that Francis asked for a cardinal protector of the order as a result of his illness; rather, it was a result of Francis wanting to apply pressure on his order to encourage reform by finding allies in the ecclesiastical hierarchy who supported his vision. However, Francis' request for a protector almost certainly came after his return from Egypt, though the date of the visit to Honorius is uncertain. Brooke gives a date of winter 1220,[110] but this date is problematic since the *Vita Prima* and *Legend of the Three Companions* explicitly state that Francis met with both Hugolino and Honorius in Rome.[111] Because of a conflict with the people of Rome, Honorius and his court were away from the city from July 1219 until late October 1220.[112] If the testimony of the *Legend of the Three Companions* is to be trusted, Francis' meeting with Honorius likely did not occur until the late fall of 1220 or the early winter of 1221 at the earliest, perhaps a full year after Francis had returned from Egypt.[113] This later date for the formal appointment of Hugolino as the protector of the order raises interesting questions about why and how Francis asked for Hugolino to become the lord cardinal protector of the order. If Francis did meet with Honorius in Rome, the earliest he could have done so was in late October or early November 1220 and possibly much later. Such a date would mean that Francis could have asked for Hugolino to become the lord cardinal protector after he had resigned from his leadership role within the order. Francis' resignation and Hugolino's adoption of the position are roughly contemporaneous, and thus could be related. Perhaps Francis formalized the association between the Franciscan Order and Hugolino as part of the process of creating an explicit organizational structure for the order he was leaving in the hands of other people. Choosing Hugolino for this role can thus be seen as one of the last acts of governance completed by the (or soon to be) former leader of the order.

By itself, this does not suggest that Francis asked formally for Hugolino as a protector for the order due to his increasing infirmities. Yet, further circumstantial evidence that links his request to his illness comes in the positioning of the episode in both the *Anonymous of Perugia* and the *Legend of the Three Companions*. In a tradition that is clearly common to both texts, the request for Hugolino occurs immediately before a discussion of Francis' reception of the *stigmata* and his death. Further, the *Legend of the Three Companions*, along with the *Remembrance of the Desire of a Soul*, suggests a causal link between Francis' weakened state and his request for Hugolino as the "pope" of the Franciscan Order. The *Legend* reports that Francis had had a vision which led him to "ask for the cardinal and entrust the order to the Roman Church."[114] In the vision, Francis saw a black hen with a dove's feet and so many chicks that the hen was unable to keep them all under her wings. Francis interpreted this vision to mean that he would have so many followers that he would not "be able to protect them with his own strength (*virtus*)."[115] The *Legend of Three Companions* then reports that, "a few years after the vision had passed," Francis went to Rome to visit Hugolino. While in Rome, he preached to the papal curia and afterwards entrusted his *religio* to the care of the curia. He then, as he had recognized he would do earlier, asked for Hugolino as a sort of protector prelate for the order.[116] The story is much the same in the *Remembrance*, and, indeed, the positioning of Hugolino as a protector of the order ends the first book of Thomas of Celano's text,[117] the final act of Francis as the leader of the order, before Thomas turns to a discussion, in Book II of the *Remembrance*, of the miracles Francis performed. While the link between Francis' vision of the black hen and the request for Hugolino as a protector of the order does not confirm that Francis sought out Hugolino's aid when he was becoming more ill and infirm, the discussion of Francis' strength (*virtus*) – a word which had both moral and medical resonances at the time – points to this possibility.

Most scholars of Francis argue that the saint's health deteriorated slowly between 1219 and 1224, with a rapid decline leading to death almost immediately after he is traditionally said to have received the *stigmata* in 1224. Yet a closer examination of the sources suggests that Francis' health, always a concern, was already steadily in decline by the end of 1219. Aside from the above discussions, other pieces of evidence from the early sources suggest he was not only suffering from an illness in his eyes shortly after his return to Italy in late 1219 or early 1220, but also from other illnesses, even as he arranged for the administrative future for his order.

Withdrawal and Contemplation: 1222–1224

It is well recognized in Franciscan scholarship that Francis was extremely ill by the end of 1224. However, even before he became so incapacitated, and before he experienced his vision on La Verna in the early fall of 1224, there are many indications – from his regular interactions with his newly appointed guardians to his slow withdrawal from public life – that the saint was suffering from a continued decline in his health.

The evidence for Francis' declining health is not abundant for this period, but one way it can be uncovered is by looking closely at the several stories about Francis' tunic found in the *Assisi Compilation*. Most of these narratives appear to take place while he was actively engaged in his ministry, that is to say, before the last two years of his life, when his infirmities and illnesses became so extreme he spent much of his time caring for his health. They are not reminiscences from the end of Francis' life. AC 90 records that Francis occasionally patched his old, battered tunic with new cloth on the inside to allieviate the symptoms of "his many illnesses."[118] The next chapter of the *Assisi Compilation*, AC 91, records that a poor man came to a hermitage at which Francis was staying, asking for some cloth. When the brothers could find none to give him, Francis secretly gave him a piece of his own. He had to be secretive because "he knew his guardian would forbid him."[119] And indeed, once his guardian discovered Francis' actions, he forbade him from giving away his tunic, "chiefly because it was very cold then and [Francis] was very sick and cold."[120] Of course, neither of these incidents is clearly dated, but the presence of the guardian in AC 91 places the incident after 1221, and before he became so infirm that walking would have been difficult, perhaps in late 1224.

The *Assisi Compilation*, especially, further suggests that Francis suffered various illnesses long before the final two years of his life. Twice, once in AC 77 and once again in AC 119, the unknown author(s) of the *Assisi Compilation* assert that Francis suffered "for a long time and would continue to suffer unto the day of his death" diseases of the liver, spleen, and stomach.[121] AC 119 attempts to define the time he suffered by stating "for many years (*multos annos*) Francis suffered the greatest infirmity of the stomach, spleen, and liver, as well as suffering an infirmity of the eyes."[122] The illnesses were so severe that the author(s) of the *Assisi Compilation* believed that they would necessitate rest during long periods of prayer by leaning against a wall, but were also quick to note that Francis never succumbed to this need. If we look solely at the activities of Francis' life between 1222 and 1224, we see that the saint was not always sick during this time. He was preaching in Bologna in 1222, when Thomas of Spoleto saw him and recorded his impressions of the saint's preaching and his appearance. Thomas' dating is fairly certain since his account is accompanied by a discussion of an earthquake that impacted Liguria, Emilia, and Venice.[123] The earthquake is attested to in some thirty-seven other sources, many of whom agree with Thomas on the date of that event, Christmas Day, 1222.[124] It seems unlikely that Thomas would have mistaken the year, given the importance and devastation of the earthquake.

The sources also support Francis of Assisi's retreat to a mountain in the early part of 1223. It was there that he wrote the *Rule* that would finally be approved by his order and the papacy,[125] though it has long been maintained that this second *Rule* represented a compromise of Francis' ideals. The mountain on which Francis wrote the *Rule* is traditionally given as Fonte Columbo, a hermitage in the Rieti valley,[126] but in the earliest texts, the location of Francis' retreat is not specifically named.[127] More certain is Francis' presence at Greccio during Christmas of 1223, with his creation of the Christmas crèche,[128] and his presence at La Verna in 1224.[129]

Although the evidence is not as abundant for the years after his withdrawal from leadership, there is a clear recognition across the sources that Francis was in a state of deteriorating health. The stories of his guardian insisting that Francis care for his weakened body in the cold, along with discussions of Francis' maladies of the stomach and spleen, attest to this. Yet, it is also clear that during this period Francis had times of relative health, which allowed him to travel, preach, and minister. These periods of health must have become infrequent by the fall of 1224, though, when Francis retreated to La Verna for rest and contemplation.

Unseeing Eyes and Broken Body: 1224–1226

Although suffering from various ailments and increasingly unable to see since 1219, Francis' health declined precipitously after the fall of 1224. At the behest of Hugolino and Elias, he began to see doctors, not one, but many, over a sustained period of time. He was treated by several surgeons and travelled by horse and donkey, and, at the very end, was carried from place to place in a litter. It is difficult to know precisely what happened in Francis' life after his famous vision of the seraph at La Verna in September 1224, but a reconstruction would surely include many visits to doctors and much time spent convalescing.

In spite of Francis' impairments, which will be discussed in detail below, many scholars suggest that Francis spent the winter and spring of 1225 preaching in Umbria and the Marches. In his biography of Francis, André Vauchez,[130] following the work of Paul Sabatier[131] and Walter Seton,[132] suggested that Francis undertook that preaching tour from November or December 1224 until February 1225. Other biographers, such as Fortini[133] and, more recently, Thompson,[134] argue that Francis could not have managed a preaching tour so late in his life. Careful analysis of the evidence used to support the claims of Sabatier and Vauchez indicates that, although Francis may have preached occasionally, calling his work in 1225 a "preaching tour" denies the reality of Francis' weakening condition. The evidence for the tour comes primarily from the *Vita prima*, which notes that after Francis received the *stigmata* he still "so valued the health of souls and he [so] thirsted for profit of those close to him that, although he was not able to walk on his own, he was carried around the lands by a donkey."[135] However, this description of Francis taking part in a "preaching tour" occurs within a much broader discussion of how Francis is failing physically. The entirety of the discussion is worth laying out in full.

> But since, according to the law of nature and the rule of human condition,
> it is necessary that exterior man be corrupted day by day, even as he is
> renewed inwardly, [Francis] that most precious instrument in which the
> treasure of heaven was hidden, began to shatter in all ways and to suffer
> the loss of all [his] strength. But since when a man has been consumed,
> then he will begin again; when he has finished, [then] he will start to work
> again, his spirit was more readily brought about in his infirm flesh. *Also,*

he so valued the health of souls and so thirsted for the profit of his neighbours that since he was not able to walk, he wandered through the lands carried on a donkey.

 The brothers frequently admonished him, suggesting to him with all the urgency of prayers, that he ought to revive his infirm and very debilitated body to whatever extent necessary with the help of doctors. But Francis, who merely wished to be freed and to be with Christ, with his noble spirit directed toward heaven, utterly refused to do this. But since he had not yet finished those things of Christ's passion which were absent in his flesh, although he carried [Christ's] *stigmata* in his body, he incurred a very serious infirmity of his eyes. In this way, God multiplied his compassion in him. And since that infirmity grew from day to day, and it seemed to increase [in severity] daily from neglect, Brother Elias, whom he had chosen in the place of a mother for himself, and had made a father of the other brothers, finally compelled [Francis] not to shrink back from medicine but to receive it in the name of the Son of God, through whom it was created, just as it was written: The Most High created medicine from the land and the prudent man will not abhor it. The holy father then cheerfully agreed [to seek treatment] and, with humility, he complied with the dictates of he who was advising him.[136]

There is much in this passage that calls for close examination. The tension between Francis' own desire not to seek medical attention for his infirmities will be discussed in the next part of the book, along with the seemingly shifting position of the church hierarchy on when medical interventions should be sought out. For now, however, it is enough to note that Thomas' point here is emphatically not that Francis engaged in a preaching tour. It is clear that Francis was extremely ill after his time at La Verna in the fall of 1224, and becoming more so – so much so that those travelling with him sought the intervention of his vicar to ensure that Francis accepted the care he needed. Yes, Thomas does say that Francis was so invested in the care of souls that, even when he could not walk, he travelled around by donkey to preach. And yes, the word used, *circuiret*, is suggestive of a circuitous path or a "tour." But the other words used to describe Francis' actions, along with the clear evidence of the poor state of his health suggest he was in no condition to travel far or preach widely. Francis preached to those closest to him, for he desired the profit of those most near to him ("lucra proximorum"). The word proximus cannot be applied easily to the whole of Umbria (let alone the marches), particularly when it refers to people rather than places, as it seems to here. By the fall of 1224, Francis was simply too sick to engage in a lengthy and geographically distant preaching tour. Indeed, Francis had precious little time to do anything other than attend to his chronically failing health in the last two years of his life.

The early source *lives* record some forty different incidents of Francis' illnesses and infirmities that can with certainty be dated to between the time he had his vision of the seraph at La Verna in September 1224 and his death in early October 1226. Many cannot be dated beyond this with much accuracy[137] but what does become clear is that during the last two years of Francis' life, he was locked in a struggle for survival. That struggle involved regular consultation with physicians, the intervention of at least one surgeon (but probably more), prolonged periods of rest and recuperation, near constant care given by his companions, and myriad special measures taken to protect his eyes and other parts of his body aggravated by illness. As Thomas of Celano reports (and the evidence discussed above demonstrates), the experience of illness was not new, but it increased in severity in the last two years of the saint's life. "Throughout the same course of time [the last two years of his life] [Francis'] body began to be attacked with various frailties more severe than those to which he was accustomed. He suffered frequent illnesses since he had completely chastised his body and driven it into servitude during so many preceding years."[138]

Early sources report that Francis was unable to walk for periods of time after 1224. At times Francis was so weakened he rode donkeys from place to place. Such instances are recorded in the *Vita prima*,[139] the *Assisi Compilation*,[140] the *Remembrance of the Desire of a Soul*,[141] the *Treatise on Miracles*,[142] and the *Legenda maior*.[143] Francis also regularly wore special clothing in deference to his deteriorating eyes and on account of other illnesses, both before and after the fall of 1224. As noted above, Francis wore fur on the inside of his tunic at times to help protect his ailing spleen and stomach from the cold. He also wore a wool cap, first to protect his eyes, which were becoming increasingly sensitive to the light, and then to hide the scars he received as a result of a cauterization undertaken to cure his eye disease. The *Vita prima*, for instance, reports that a *capitale* that Francis had used in his illness had worked so many miracles that it was even venerated by the king and queen of France.[144] The translators of *Francis of Assisi: Early Documents* translate *capitale*[145] as pillow, but it can also mean a headband, perhaps something worn to cover his sensitive eyes or the wounds left from his cauterization.[146] Certainly, he was wearing a cap by the time he fell ill at San Damiano in the late fall and early winter of 1224, for his eyes had become extremely photosensitive. By the time he descended from La Verna, too, he was relaxing the harsh discipline which he had applied to his body for much of his life. Even though Francis did not wish to receive medical treatment, his will was overruled and the necessary medicine was applied,[147] an experience Francis encountered several times in the last years of his life. Indeed, as will become clear, Francis seems to have finally privileged obedience to the Franciscan hierarchy over his ideal that medical interventions for illness and infirmities ought not to be too readily sought out.

The first of Francis' many enforced periods of rest and recuperation in the last two years of his life occurred shortly after he left La Verna. The *Assisi Compilation* notes that some two years before his death he was "already very ill, especially from the infirmity of his eyes" and remained in a little cell made of rushes at San Damiano.[148] The date is uncertain, but if the *Assisi Compilation* is correct, it may be, as Thompson suggests, that Francis left La Verna for San Damiano, already knowing he was in need of serious medical care.[149] At San Damiano, it appears that Francis had periods of relative health and, perhaps towards the end of his stay, had periods in which he was increasingly ill. Most scholars[150] agree that it is at this time that Francis composed the song variously known as the *Canticle of the Sun*, the *Praise of Creatures*, or the *Canticle of Creatures*, along with the *Canticle of Exhortation* for the cloistered women of San Damiano, also called *Audite Poverelle*.[151] The testimony of the *Assisi Compilation* supports this conclusion.[152] In the last two years of his life, as the saint's eyesight increasingly failed him, he more readily turned to music as an outlet for his devotion.

During his time at San Damiano, Francis also had occasion to reconcile the bishop of Assisi, Guido, and the podestà of Assisi, Oportulo di Bernardo. The political machinations are complicated and difficult to ascertain,[153] but Bishop Guido had felt compelled to excommunicate the podestà owing to his open support of the nobility in a conflict between different factions within Perugia. The papacy, who supported other factions, had insisted that Assisi not have, nor form, any new alliances with the Perugian nobility. In retaliation, Oportulo declared an economic blockade against the bishop's household. But Francis knew both men and both had supported his movement. Acting through his companions since he was incapable of visiting the men himself, Francis organized a meeting between the two.[154] The *Assisi Compilation* reports that Francis composed another verse for his *Canticle of the Sun*, this one about forgiveness, and asked two brothers to sing it for the bishop and the podestà. Due to Francis' intervention, the two reconciled. This story of this intervention in the *Assisi Compilation* carries the authenticating phrase, "nos qui cum fuimus Beato Francisco."[155]

Sometime during his stay at San Damiano, Francis' eye disease worsened and he experienced extreme photosensitivity for "fifty days and more." The *Assisi Compilation* records that he was unable to stand the light of day or even the light of the fire at night. He remained in the dark in the convent ("in domo") and in his cell, unable to rest or to sleep, which further exacerbated both "the serious infirmity of his eyes and his other infirmities."[156] So ill was he that Elias of Cortona, in his position as leader of the order, came to visit Francis and urged him to seek medical attention, especially for his eyes.[157] Thomas of Celano notes that after Francis agreed to receive medical attention "many ("plures")" approached to help with their remedies, but with the cure not found, he travelled to the city of Rieti, where there was said to be a very skilled man devoted to curing that infirmity."[158] Thus, seeking expert attention, Francis left San Damiano and was led on horseback to the hermitage of Fonte Columbo, near the city of Rieti, all the while wearing a *capuche*, with a cloth made of wool and linen sewn in to protect his eyes from the sun.[159]

It is likely in Rieti that Francis saw Hugolino, the cardinal protector of the order, who also admonished him to seek out medical attention. While the *Assisi Compilation* places this discussion at San Damiano, before Francis left for Rieti, the *Vita prima* suggests it was at Rieti.[160] There is not enough evidence to determine precisely where Hugolino was at the likely time of this interview, but the papal court was travelling to Rieti from the Lateran Palace in the spring of 1225, and reached Rieti in mid-June.[161] It is possible, even likely, that Hugolino was travelling with the court at that time, as is noted in passing in the *Vita prima*.[162] Having come to Rieti for the purpose of seeing an eye specialist, Francis did, in fact, see one. Indeed, he saw a doctor or doctors regularly, perhaps even daily, and submitted to receiving an invasive cauterization, in an effort to cure his eye disease, probably at the recommendation of the specialist. In many of the early sources, Francis appears reluctant to accept the treatment. The *Assisi Compilation* notes that Francis wanted to wait until Elias (who was presumably travelling to meet Francis) arrived before he was cauterized, but, since Elias was delayed, he went ahead with the treatment anyway, "chiefly on account of his obedience to the Bishop of Ostia and the minister general."[163] Interestingly, the *Remembrance* and the *Treatise on Miracles* further highlight Francis' reluctance to accept medical intervention, noting that "he was compelled (*coactus*) to undergo a cure for himself."[164] The anonymous author of the *Actus Beati Francisci in Valle Reatina* is even more direct, stating that Hugolino and Elias instructed (*preceperent* for *preceperunt*) Francis to accept the counsel given to him by his doctors and that he "ought to submit to a suitable remedy."[165] The AVR further notes that Francis sent the doctor away the first time he wanted to perform the cauterization, saying that he would wait for the arrival of Elias. But, once Elias was delayed, Francis was afraid ("timeo") to contradict the order ("preceptus") of the vicar and protector of the order. Thus, he called the doctor back to perform the cauterization.[166] Bonaventure, however, denies that Francis was ordered in any way to receive treatment, saying instead that Francis did so because he had been given advice (consilium) by doctors and had been vehemently urged (instanter sauderetur) by the brothers that he might open himself to be assisted through the remedy of cauterization.[167]

The cauterization procedure itself is described in detail in the *Assisi Compilation* (where it is authenticated by the "nos qui cum eo fuimus" phrase), the *Remembrance of the Desire of a Soul*, the *Treatise on Miracles*, the *Legenda maior*, and the *Actus Beati Francisci in Valle Reatina*. Unlike his companions,[168] Francis showed no fear as the *medicus* heated the cauterization iron and proceeded to burn the skin from Francis' ear to his eyebrow.[169] The treatment was harsh; it left scars[170] and, as the *Assisi Compilation* notes, it did not work,[171] nor did a second attempt at a surgical procedure, the piercing of Francis' ears, performed by another doctor.[172]

Angelo Sachetti Sassetti has suggested this expert who recommended and perhaps even performed the cauterization might have been a certain "Magister Nicolaus medicus" found in archival documents from Rieti between 1230 and 1233,[173] but as Schmucki points out, there is no evidence that he was a specialist who treated eye ailments. Further, Schmucki adds, he may not have been a trained physician at all, given that "operations at that time were performed by surgeons and charlatans."[174] While the history of the practice of medicine in the early thirteenth century in Italy has not been as well studied as that of the latter half of the thirteenth century, it is nonetheless clear that practitioners of surgery could be extremely well trained, with Parma and Bologna being centres for surgical training in the late twelfth and early thirteenth centuries.[175] It is unlikely that the *medicus* who was an expert in treating eye infections was a charlatan.

Medical specialists who worked primarily on the health of the eyes can also be found in the historical record in this period. There is evidence that eye specialists existed in Italy in the early part of the thirteenth century. Notarial records in Siena, for instance, capture the presence of an entire family of doctors who are listed as not just *medici* but as *medici oculorum*, operating in Siena from near the time of Francis' death.[176]

Circumstantial evidence suggests that the person Francis saw may have known the work of Beneventus Grassus or, perhaps, Beneventus' predecessors.[177] Beneventus was likely Italian and seems to have had a practice of treating eye disease. He is known now only through a treatise on diseases of the eye and in which, in the words of Laurence Eldredge, who has spent some time working on Beneventus' treatise in the last fifteen years, "[Beneventus] thinks highly of this cure [cautery]."[178] While he promotes different cures for different eye diseases, Beneventus appears to fall back on cautery as a treatment for many of them, though he often includes poultices and eye ointments as well. Beneventus' theory of cauterization, according to Eldredge, is that a burn near the infected or affected area would draw the infection (or ill humours) towards the burn, where they could be evacuated. The burn could then heal and the affected eye could be cured.[179] So sure was Beneventus of the benefits of cauterization for infected eyes that he claims to have written a treatise on the subject, though that treatise has not been identified.[180] The earliest extant manuscript of Beneventus' treatise on eye diseases is from the late thirteenth or early fourteenth century[181] and he is quoted by Jean Yperman in a text written circa 1328.[182] Beneventus' work is thus often dated to the late thirteenth century, though it has been dated as early as the eleventh century.[183] It is, of course, unlikely that Francis saw Beneventus himself, especially if the date of late thirteenth century is correct, but the use of cautery to treat ailments of the eye, which is clearly present in Beneventus' book, suggests that the idea that such an operation could provide relief for Francis was probably circulating in Italy near the time when Francis was treated in such a way.

That the expert Francis saw at Rieti was in fact an expert in diseases of the eye is actually supported in the early source *lives*. The *Assisi Compilation*, the *Remembrance*, the *Legenda major*, and the *Actus* recount a miracle that a woman had come from Machilone, a village some thirty kilometres from Rieti, to see the same doctor Francis was seeing.[184] The sources are all quite different in the details. In the *Assisi Compilation* Francis tells his guardian to give the woman a cloak he has been using so she can pay for her medical treatment, while in the *Remembrance* he must negotiate doing so with his guardian, who was reluctant to let Francis give up his cloak. The same event is described in the *Actus*, but in that narrative Francis admonishes his guardian for putting the needs of the order above the needs of the poor. Where the sources all agree, however, is that the poor woman had come to Rieti to see the doctor (the same doctor Francis was seeing) about her eye ailment. This does seem to support the idea that there was, at this time, an expert for eye diseases in Rieti. Whatever experts Francis saw in Rieti, and it seems he may have seen more than one,[185] their identity has not survived the movement of time. Their actions, however, were recorded in the early sources. The cauterization of Francis' face, so carefully described in the sources, makes sense in the context of a medieval theory that cauterization would draw the illness or ill humours out of the eye. Beneventus' treatise also suggests many cures that involve daily treatment. And indeed, most early *lives* of Francis report that he saw doctors regularly, perhaps even daily.[186] The doctor or doctors who saw Francis witnessed miracles – a good meal was provided at the moment a wealthy doctor agreed to stay for dinner,[187] a dangerous crack threatening to collapse a house was fixed by a lock of Francis' hair.[188] Yet, the miracle stories should not distract from the clear evidence that Francis was being treated by doctors regularly.

Sometime after he had his surgery, Francis went to the Bishop of Rieti's house to stay for several days. He also stayed at the church at San Fabiano and in the room of one Teobaldi Saraceno, but it is unclear if this was in the bishop's house, at San Fabiano or elsewhere in Rieti. The accounts of miraculous events suggest that, in all of the places he stayed, Francis continually suffered from his eye ailment as well as other illnesses. Thus, while his body was "afflicted with great infirmity and pain,"[189] Francis asked a brother who used to play the lute in the secular world before his conversion to acquire one to play a song of praise of the Lord for Francis. When the brother refused out of shame for taking part in so worldly a thing, Francis let the matter drop, but the next evening he heard lute music, which he considered to be from heaven.[190] At the bishop's house, again while "weak from the disease of his eyes,"[191] he cured a cleric named Gedeone.[192]

After his time in Rieti, Francis travelled to Siena for further treatment of his eyes.[193] It is difficult to ascertain when this occurred, but the *Vita prima* places Francis in Siena approximately six months before his death.[194] On the way there, Francis had his famous encounter with Lady Poverty, but, even more interesting, for our purposes, is with whom he was travelling when he saw that vision. The *Remembrance* reports that on that trip Francis had for a companion "a certain doctor who was bound to (*obligatus*) the order."[195] This phraseology is interesting, and it is impossible to know what precisely it means. Was the doctor a Franciscan novice or friar?[196] Was he bound by obedience to care for Francis on behalf of the order? Was he bound by a monetary agreement to care for Francis on his travels? Whatever the word does mean, it is unlikely to mean "very devoted," as it is translated in *Francis of Assisi: Early Documents*. That Francis travelled with a doctor seems to have been troubling for members of the later order, for while Bonaventure's *Legenda maior* tells the miracle of Francis' sighting of Lady Poverty on his trip to Siena, in that text the saint appears to be travelling to Siena alone. In fact, Bonaventure actually reports that Francis was travelling to that city for an unspecified "pressing cause,"[197] rather than noting that it was for treatment.

The reasons for Francis' transfer to Siena are are uncertain. Thompson argues that "the ministers decided that Francis should go to Siena, a larger city, to seek further medical attention";[198] this may be true, but there is nothing in the early *lives* to support this position. Yet Siena was a centre for early medicine, and, even more tellingly, seems to have had a family of eye doctors living and working there during Francis' lifetime.

While Siena never developed a fully realized faculty of medicine in the High Middle Ages, there were physicians and those who trained physicians operating there by the mid-1200s. Records in Siena suggest that the physician Petrus Hispanus[199] taught his trade in Siena circa 1240. Alcide Garosi has found records of a family of eye doctors working in Siena, alongside several other independent eye doctors, between approximately 1215 and 1280.[200] It is possible, and probably even likely, that Francis did travel to Siena to consult such a specialist. Certainly there were specialists in Siena to see. At the very least, this reality puts to rest the notion raised in Schmucki that ophthalmology as a special branch of medicine did not come into existence before the end of the thirteenth century.[201]

It is absolutely possible Francis saw an eye specialist in Rieti. It is also conceivable that those concerned with Francis' health, including the doctors who were caring for him, his guardian, the vicar general of the order, and the cardinal protector of the order, thought he might find a cure, probably from another such specialist, in Siena. The constant movement of Francis during this time and the continual search for a cure for his eye ailment indicate that those responsible for Francis' health, if not necessarily Francis himself, were desperate to find a cure for his eye disease and his encroaching blindness. There can be no other reason for this constant movement that is directed only by a search for a cure in the final years of the saint's life.

Francis was ill and probably unable to see very well in Siena when he arrived, but at the beginning of his stay he was not yet bedridden. He became so while in Siena. "[Francis] began to be gravely ill in all the rest of his body. With his stomach shattered from long-lasting illness, and his liver damaged, he vomited blood, and so it seemed that death approached."[202] The *Vita brevior* reports something similar, noting that "in the sixth month before the day of his death, when he was in Siena, [Francis'] failure of his stomach prevailed over the infirmity of his eye and he was habitually so painfully worn down in his whole body that he seemed to approach death."[203] The brothers travelling with him recognized how close Francis was to death and asked for a blessing. Francis granted this, asking that his brief words be recorded. He spoke for only a short time, citing his inability to speak due to weakness and the pain he was experiencing. Then he gave a short blessing and a series of instructions on how the brothers should live, which is sometimes referred to as a proto-testament.[204] So ill was Francis that the brothers with him sent for the vicar general, and Elias came to see him, thinking the saint was about to die.[205] Yet Thomas of Celano reports that Francis recovered enough to travel, this time to Le Celle, a hermitage near Cortona. Once there, however, Francis took a turn for the worse again, experiencing swelling in his stomach, legs, and feet. His stomach failed him more and more and "it was scarcely possible to receive any food."[206] Recognizing that this was, perhaps, his final illness, the order arranged for Francis to be carried back to Assisi.[207]

There is some minor confusion in the early sources about where precisely Francis travelled in the last few months of his life. Perhaps the two most reliable sources for Francis' movements, Thomas of Celano's *Vita prima* and the *Assisi Compilation*, do not agree. The *Vita prima* notes that Francis travelled from Siena to Le Celle de Cortona to Assisi directly[208] – and, indeed, this makes sense geographically – Le Celle is only a short way off a route that allowed travel between Siena and Assisi via Cortona.[209] The *Vita prima* then begins a discussion of Francis' descent into death, implying that the trip from Siena was Francis' last journey before death. However, in a text that contains an authenticating phrase, the *Assisi Compilation* notes that Francis travelled from Siena to Cortona to the Porziuncula, and then to Begnara to the north of Assisi, before returning to Assisi for a final time before his death.[210] Historians, often puzzling about what to do with this, suggest the saint had a bit of a recovery or needed to rest in a cooler place for a bit, and so travelled to Begnara, where he fell ill again and had to be returned home.[211] The *Assisi Compilation* also describes a miracle that happened near Begnara, in Nocera Umbria. The soldiers who were accompanying Francis back to Assisi were unable to buy anything they needed during their stop in the town. Having heard of their failure, Francis recommended they go back to the same houses, but to beg for alms rather than to offer to buy the needed goods. The knights did so and received what they needed.[212] The miracle is also recorded in the *Remembrance*, a testament to the story's provenance in the reminiscences of Francis' companions. Yet Thomas of Celano seems not to know quite where to place the miracle, owing to his different understanding of Francis' movements at the end of the saint's life. Thomas recounts the miracle, stating that it occurred at Nocera, when "blessed Francis was full of infirmities and already bending near to the end" [of his life, presumably].[213] That Francis did travel to Begnara near the end of his life is reiterated in AC 99, which records that, "when, in those days after he had returned from Begnara, blessed Francis lay very ill in the palace of the bishop of Assisi," he wanted to comfort his soul by listening to the brothers sing the *Praises of the Lord*.[214]

In spite of Thomas' confusion, we must accept that Francis either went or was taken to Begnara sometime after he returned to Assisi from Siena and Le Celle in the last months before his death. Indeed, that Francis was so close to death explains why soldiers from Assisi were enlisted to accompany him. Francis' holy body was already a valuable commodity for Assisi, and it needed protection. But the trip from Begnara to Assisi was to be his last. The soldiers took him to the bishop's palace in Assisi, as noted in AC 99. There he heard his brothers sing, though Elias believed it was not fitting for Francis to take such comfort and joy from the music.[215] He was also visited by a doctor, perhaps a family friend,[216] named Bon Giovanni, who confessed to Francis, when the saint asked for the truth, that the saint's dropsy was incurable and he would shortly die.[217] One last miracle was performed while Francis was at the bishop's palace. Francis was there, "during the time of his last illness,"[218] the *Remembrance* reports, and wished to have some parsley to settle his stomach. The saint had obviously been having quite a bit of parsley as the cook complained that he would be unable to find any as he had been picking it every day and would have an even worse time in the dark. Francis told him to pick the first herbs he came across, which, of course, were parsley.[219]

Shortly before his death Francis asked to be moved from the bishop's palace to the Porziuncula, wanting to end his life where his converted life had begun. He was so ill that he could not even ride a horse and had to be carried in a bed ("lecto"). On his trip he wanted to bless the city of Assisi, so he asked those carrying him to stop and turn the bed so that he would be facing the city. So ill was Francis that he was unable to stand even for a moment to finish his blessing. So blind was he that he could not tell which way the bed should be facing. Raising himself only a little in the bed,[220] the saint said his blessing and then was carried to the Porziuncula, where he would finish out his days.[221] He knew (and was told, again, this time by a brother) that he was dying. He was suffering from dropsy, swelling in his limbs and in his stomach, his body was desiccated ("desiccatus"), and he was suffering many other infirmities.[222] It had become impossible for him to see. Knowing the end was near, Francis asked for his close companions Brother Angelo and Brother Leo to come. Once there, they sang for him the *Canticle of the Sun* – to which Francis had recently added a final verse about death.[223]

Near the same time, the *Assisi Compilation* reports, he asked that Lady Jacoba, a long-time friend and supporter of the saint,[224] be informed that he was about to die. He asked that she send him a tunic the colour of ashes made by the Cistercian monks of France and a confection she made for him in the past called *mastacciolo*, which was made with almonds and honey. Miraculously the lady herself came to see Francis just as the letter was being sent. She visited for a time, and one day made the *mastacciolo*, though the saint could only manage eating a bit of it.[225] The meeting with Lady Jacoba is also recounted in the *Treatise on Miracles* by Thomas of Celano, though the *mastacciolo* is referred to only as a "certain dish she brought because the saint desired it."[226]

The *Assisi Compilation* notes that Francis remembered that brother Bernard of Quintaville, too, had always liked the *mastacciolo* Lady Jacoba had made, and so called him to his side. Francis wanted to bless him, and attempted to do so, yet the saint had become entirely blind and, as a result, inadvertently blessed another brother.[227] A similar episode is recorded in the *Vita brevior*, though many details are changed. In this legend, Francis raised his hand and asked over whom he held his right hand. When the answer was Brother Elias, Francis blessed him, calling him "son" and thanking him for taking Francis' burdens onto his own shoulders.[228] Near to the end, too, Francis called all the brothers with whom he was staying close to him and blessed them, sharing bread with them, in what the *Assisi Compilation* and the *Remembrance* clearly liken to the Last Supper.[229] A few days later, Francis passed away.

What does all this information tell us about Francis and illness? The picture emerges of a saint who was chronically ill from the time he was a prisoner of war in Perugia in his early twenties, though he also experienced periods of relative health in the earlier part of his converted life. Francis' vigorously ascetic life and his desire to spend much of his time preaching led him to exhaust himself, eventually forcing him to relax the rigour of his ascetic practices far more often than has been generally recognized. His always fragile health began to fail him even more when he returned from Egypt in late 1219, carrying an eye infection that would lead to his near total blindness. He was ill enough to require Elias to report his words at a general chapter in 1221, suggesting that, as was reported in the *Assisi Compilation*, it may have been his declining strength, his illnesses, and infirmities, as much (or more!) than his dislike of the direction in which the order was heading that caused him to abruptly step back from leading the order, circa 1220.

Francis' declining health becomes even more apparent in the early 1220s and clearly became a central concern in his life after his vision of the seraph in the fall of 1224. The two years of Francis' life between 1224 and his death in early October of 1226 were consumed with attempts to cure his various illnesses and care for his broken body. It is not an overstatement to say that Francis' handlers, the upper administration of the order, were desperately trying to find a cure for Francis' eye infection. All other illnesses or infirmities, including those supposed to be a result of receiving the *stigmata*, were not of nearly as much concern to the order as Francis' failing eyesight. Six months before the his death his health declined on other fronts, with his stomach, liver, and spleen failing and his body becoming swollen. Evading death's grasp once more with a slight recovery, Francis was nevertheless dead within the year, having lived a life in which he suffered from illness, as the *Assisi Compilation* consistently asserts, from the time of his conversion until his death.

A careful reading of early texts about Francis suggests that tensions existed in Francis himself, within his order, and within the church hierarchy around the saint's illnesses, even during his own lifetime. These tensions were centred on how Francis might effectively lead his order as an infirm man and the extent to which he should seek out secular medical care for his various illnesses and infirmities. The early hagiographical texts also suggest that tensions existed for authors as they grappled with making sense of the saint's suffering, of making his suffering a meaningful experience for the saint and a teachable example of faith and patience for the faithful.

Chapter Four

Disability and Tensions in Francis' Lived Experience

The previous chapters' focus on Francis' experiences of illness and infirmity sheds light on the many anxieties Francis' bodily health, or lack thereof, seem to have generated in his lived experience. The early *lives* of Francis suggest that gaps existed between Francis' desire to live a rigorously ascetic life and the requirement to address the needs of his delicate constitution. The interventions of Francis' guardians to ensure that he cared for his body demonstrate this. But it is also clear that sometimes it was not the needs of his weakened body, but his emotional well-being, that he addressed when he ate a particular food, most notably the marzipan that Lady Jacoba made for him at the end of his life. For it seems, if we read the sources closely, Francis had a bit of a sweet tooth and this weakness clashed with his goal of living an ascetic and disciplined life.

Other tensions were more serious. Francis' resignation, an event which appeared to shock his followers, indicates there was some turmoil within the order. Historians of Francis have noted these tensions before, generally arguing that Francis felt that the order had moved beyond his ability to control it. Perhaps this partially explains Francis' desire to step aside. Yet, as chapter 3 has demonstrated, there is enough evidence in the early *lives* and in Francis' own writings to suggest that Francis was ill at the time of his decision to step down and that his illness may have played more of a role in his withdrawal from leadership than has previously been recognized.

Francis quit his role as leader and turned to a life that appears to have been more and more secluded from his increasingly conventual, clerical order. However, when Francis' eye ailment became an impediment to his ascetic and spiritual goals, Elias of Cortona, who was then acting as vicar general of the order, and Hugolino dei Conti di Segni, the cardinal protector of the order, intervened and directed the saint to receive treatment. From that moment in 1224 until near the time of his death, Francis travelled from place to place, seeing doctors regularly, almost daily, in spite of the fact that his own stated philosophy was not to seek out medical treatment too readily, but to regard any ailment or infirmity as a means of God's correction and to accept it patiently. This approach saw its culmination in a shift of Francis' position on medicine and on the importance of obedience near the end of his life. Finally, there is a clear tension around Francis' failing eyes themselves, for the biblical association of blindness with sin seems likely to have been behind the desire to cure Francis' eye infection at all costs.

The Needs of the Delicate Body and the Requirements of Asceticism

From the time of his conversion to religious life, Francis was committed to a life of asceticism. Yet he was not always able to fulfil his commitment to so strenuous a life. "Francis was always sickly," states the *Assisi Compilation* baldly.[1] He was not able to tolerate going out and begging alms for food every day,[2] and in the beginning of his converted life, at least, he sought out elixirs and medical remedies to aid his ailing body.[3] More than that, Francis avoided foods that were contrary to his complexion, and, as the *Assisi Compilation* contends, illness sometimes required him to eat food that had been cooked in oil rather than other kinds of fat.[4] The *Vita prima* and the *Assisi Compilation* both recount another instance in which Francis ate a bit of chicken[5] or perhaps some other sort of delicacy when he was very sick.[6]

Francis clearly felt that such care of the body, when it was necessary, should also be confessed, for the early texts also report that Francis did penance, sometimes severe penance, for his perceived lapses in ascetic discipline. The *Assisi Compilation* reports that he regularly "confessed" the allowances made in his diet on account of his illness.[7] One of the most commonly reported stories, which likely occurred before 1221, discusses how Francis ate some delicacy, reported in the *Vita prima* as a piece or two of chicken, on account of his illness. After he had recovered, he did public penance by having a brother, identified as Peter Catani in the *Assisi Compilation*, tie a cord around his neck and drag him through the city, proclaiming him a glutton who grew fat by eating chicken.[8]

Francis and his early companions appeared to be aware of the saint's desire for asceticism and the compromises he was forced to make on account of his infirm body. The *Assisi Compilation* notes that Francis always wanted to follow the will of God, regardless of whether he was sick or healthy,[9] a seeming recognition on the part of both the saint and the author that such a goal was not always possible. And indeed, it was not. The previous chapter discusses several instances in which Francis relaxed his ascetic rigour. He rode on horseback when he was weak and ill, he accepted meat and even medicine when necessary, and even on occasion ate foods that were a delight to him – for instance crab cakes or the marzipan made by Lady Jacoba. Yet Francis' frustration with the need to relax his ascetic practices during times of illness is recorded only in the *Vita prima*, which notes that, when it was necessary on account of his illness to "temper his former rigour," he announced to the brothers that he and they ought to begin to serve the Lord. As Thomas' commentary suggests, Francis did not ever think that the asceticism he had practised in the past allowed him to be more temperate in the present. Instead he wanted to continually renew his rigorous practice.[10]

In a rather contradictory text, the *Assisi Compilation* also notes that Francis was "austere to his body," even though "from the time of his youth he was a frail and infirm man according to his nature and he could not live in this world except delicately."[11] The next paragraph provides more context for this comment, noting that in a sermon to the brothers, Francis worried that the allotment of meat he ate each week[12] was encouraging other brothers to be less austere in their diet and even in their possession of goods than they ought to be. Speaking to a group of friars, Francis noted, "Do the brothers not think that the *pitantia* is necessary for my body? But since it is right for me to be a model and example of all brothers, I wish to use and to be content with poor food and things and not delicacies."[13] Francis' meaning here is ambiguous, for while it is clear that he understands that his acceptance of foods for maintaining his health was necessary, such as meat, he also believes he may be encouraging other brothers to eat such fare when they had no need, and that he wishes *(velle)* to be content with only simple food. The verb *velle* is nebulous, as wishing and being willing are not actually doing. Indeed, it is possible to read Francis' words here as an attempt to excuse his continued acceptance of the *pitantia*.

It is also possible that the authors of the *Assisi Compilation* recognized this, for, in two later chapters, the idea that Francis needed to reject delicacies and even medicine as an example to the other friars is reiterated, this time with confirmation that the saint did indeed reject the necessities of his body. AC 79 notes that since Francis was "a model and example of all the brothers he did not wish to use *(uti nolebat)* the medicines and even foods necessary in his infirmity."[14] The text goes on to confirm that Francis was strict with his body, which was always sickly, even when he seemed healthy.[15] The idea that Francis was so infirm he often needed foods considered to be delicacies, though he most often rejected them, is reiterated a third time soon after, this time in a section which is attested to with the "nos qui fuimus cum ipso" authentication. AC 82 notes that although the *pitantia* was necessary for Francis' body on account of his infirmity,[16] Francis preferred to check the necessities of his body, as he needed to offer himself as an example to his brothers.[17] The text ends by noting, however, that even though Francis chose not to take the foods necessary for his body, he could have chosen to do so, as doing so was in obedience with God's directives and would not have negated his good example.[18]

These three discussions in the *Assisi Compilation* point to several probable realities about Francis' life. First, of course, they confirm that the saint was frail throughout his life, and often ill. Second, taken together they clearly demonstrate that at the time of composition there was likely a debate about the extent to which Francis had eaten meat and meat products on account of his illness. Indeed, it seems to have been well known that Francis occasionally needed to relax his ascetic practices to care for his body, something the *Assisi Compilation* addressed directly. Other early *lives* of Francis demonstrate that his contemporaries may have been aware of his need for delicacies and medicines. For instance, the *Legend of the Three Companions* recounts the story of how the priest at San Damiano recognized Francis' delicate constitution and that he was not up to the work of physically renovating a church so he sought out special foods and electuaries for Francis.[19] The *Remembrance* records that people used to pass on *electuaria* or medicaments to him, though Francis would not take them but passed them on to other ill individuals.[20] If these narratives can be trusted, Francis was so widely known to have a delicate constitution during his life that laypeople provided him with medicines and cures. Although the texts taken together suggest that for the most part Francis eschewed comforting foods and medicines, they also demonstrate that at times he did eat meat and further assert that it was not wrong or even setting a less than good example to do so.[21]

The repeated discussions of Francis eating special or refined food and delicacies and of taking medicines in the early *vitae* of Francis suggests that the propriety of Francis doing so may have been fiercely debated after the saint's death. Such discussions point to a larger societal debate ongoing in much of Europe at the time, the debate between the desire for ascetic life and the need to care for one's body. As a part of God's creation, the body could not be rejected, ignored, or neglected; its care was understood to be necessary and that need for care must be held in the proper tension with the desire for asceticism.

Medicine, Doctors, and Perfect Obedience

For a saint with whom the ideal of obedience is inextricably linked, Francis did not write a great deal on the subject. Wayne Hellmann counts the use of the term "obedience" 48 times in Francis' writings, most often concerning how living "in obedience" may be considered a "prized gospel value."[22] Hellmann makes this point while noting that Francis speaks about obedience often – obedience to the *Rule*, to the gospel life, to God – but he rarely speaks about the need for obedience to authority.[23] A closer examination of Francis' discussions of obedience suggests that this is not necessarily true. Especially towards the end of his life, Francis highlighted his desire to be perfectly obedient to the superiors of his order and his desire that other members of his order behave in the same way. This new emphasis on obedience to authority emerged only at the end of his life, and it reflected a fairly dramatic change from his earlier position.

The timing of Francis' changing position on obedience is significant. As late as 1223, Francis allowed for disobedience to one's superiors on the basis of conscience. By 1226, Francis left no room at all for disobedience to a superior. The timing of this change coincides precisely with Francis' period of intense illness, especially his failing eyesight and the treatments he received for it. Given that the earliest and most reliable sources for Francis' life suggest that he had to be ordered to accept treatment by his superiors, it seems possible, even likely, that this experience changed his perception of the importance of obedience to authority figures.

The *Regula non bullata*, *Regula bullata*, and the *Admonitions* suggest that Francis believed that obedience need not be perfect and absolute. There was space for disobedience of an authority figure if the requested act of obedience was at odds with one's own conscience or what one believed to be God's will. Perfect obedience was owed to God alone; human ministers and prelates could err and, as such, could be disobeyed. Thus, the *Regula non bullata* reflected Francis' will that "all of [his] other blessed brothers diligently obey [the ministers] in the things that deal with the health of the soul and in those things which are not contrary to our life."[24] However, Francis also noted that obedience should be to one's heart and conscience first and foremost, and to one's superior second. "But if any one of our ministers orders one of the brothers [to do] something contrary to our life or contrary to his soul, let him not be bound to obey him, since that in which a fault or a sin is committed is not obedience."[25] The *Regula bullata* repeats this idea, but puts the onus on the superiors not to ask anything of their charges that might be sinful or contrary to the life described in the *Rule*.[26] It also adds a reminder that those who have joined the Franciscan Order have "denied their own wills for the sake of God."[27] The change between the two rules is subtle but it does speak to changing realities in Francis' life. In the first place, the new statement concerning prelates not ordering things which are contrary to the Franciscan way of life probably reflects the saint's growing concern that the order had moved away from the ideals of apostolic poverty and mendicancy that he had initially espoused. But placing the onus on obeying the *Rule* to the prelates within the order also subtly shifts the responsibility for adherence away from individual friars and places it in the hands of the superiors of the order. Indeed, Francis reminds his followers that this must be so, as those who have joined the order have given up the right to express their own will. The *Regula bullata* still leaves room for disobedience to superiors in cases where a command contradicts God or the *Rule*, though, tellingly, not the custom of Franciscan life, as is found in the *Regula non bullata*.[28] This change seems to reflect a shift in Francis' position on the authority prelates had within the order and emphasized the need of individual friars to obey them even when their own conscience determined that the obedience might not perfectly reflect Franciscan ideals.

Francis' discussion of obedience in the *Admonitions* seems to provide evidence for the above interpretation of the *Regula bullata*. The date of the composition of the *Admonitions* is debated among scholars of Francis' work. In all likelihood, the individual texts were composed (or orated) at different times and gathered into a coherent collection sometime later, perhaps even after Francis' death.[29] Most commentators place the date of composition to the last years of Francis' life, between 1220 and 1226,[30] and possibly between 1223 and 1226.[31] It is uncertain whether the texts of the *Admonitions* were written by Francis or were reportations of speeches he gave, perhaps at the general chapters. Whichever is the case, most scholars agree that the words and ideas found in the *Admonitions* are Francis' own. There is enough similarity in ideas, sentence construction, and word choice between the *Admonitions* and other known works of Francis to support the idea that these texts reflect Francis' own phraseology.[32]

The *Admonitions* reflects a further emphasis on the importance of obedience to the prelate, and marks a middle ground between the discussion in the *Regula bullata* and the *Testament* with respect to obedience of authorities. Admonition III states:

> [t]hat man who renders himself wholly to obedience into the hands of his prelate relinquishes everything he possesses and loses his body. And

anything he does or says which he knows is not contrary to the will of his prelate, while what he does is good, this is true obedience. And if at some time, he who is subordinate sees better and more useful things for his soul than those things which the prelate advises to him, he ought to sacrifice to God with his will [his own wishes] but be eager to embrace those wishes of the prelate. For this is charitable obedience since it satisfies both God and neighbour. But if the prelate commands to his subordinate something contrary to his soul, although the subordinate ought not to obey him, nevertheless let him not abandon [his superior].[33]

Although in the *Admonitions*, Francis still leaves room for disobedience to a superior when one's soul might be compromised, the space is closing.

Robert Karras has found potential source texts for Francis' position on obedience in the *Admonitions* in both Gregory the Great's *Moralia in Iob* and in a pseudo-Bernardine text on obedience entitled *De statu virtutum*.[34] The idea that obedience sometimes requires that the good of the self or the self's soul be left aside is clearly present in both potential source texts, as Karras demonstrates, and the idea that a prelate who orders things contrary to the soul ought not to be abandoned is also present in the pseudo-Bernardine text.[35] Nonetheless, while it is possible that Francis had a familiarity with the *Moralia*, it is unlikely he had any knowledge of the much less well-known *De status virtutum*. And indeed, not long after the *Admonitions* were written, Francis would state that he desired an even deeper level of obedience for himself and for the members of his order – an absolute and unquestioning obedience to authority.

Dictated on his deathbed, the *Testament* records Francis' last discussion of his life and directions for his order. Concerning obedience, Francis wrote: "I firmly wish to obey the general minister of this fraternity and the other guardian whom it pleases him to give me. And I so wish to be a captive in his hands that I cannot go anywhere or do anything beyond obedience and his will, for he is my master."[36] Francis then adds that he expects that sort of obedience to Franciscan leaders from all members of his order. "And let all the other brothers hold such obedience to their guardians and make the office according to the *Rule*."[37] Unlike any of the early discussions concerning obedience, there is no space for disobedience or disregard for the directives of superiors. Obedience to authority, as discussed in the *Testament*, must be absolute.

Wayne Hellmann has argued that for Francis, obedience ultimately means obedience to living a gospel life, a life of apostolic poverty,[38] and notes that Francis rarely invoked an authority other than the gospels to whom his friars should be in obedience. This is true for some of Francis' discussions about obedience. Yet, as demonstrated above, Francis never suggests that authority figures need not be obeyed. In the *Admonitions*, and especially in the *Testament*, there is a request for obedience even against one's own conscience. Most dramatically, in the *Testament* Francis demanded absolute unquestioning obedience to superiors, both from himself and from other friars.

Circumstantial evidence of Francis' life suggests that his experience with his deteriorating health, and his superiors' insistence that his weakening eyesight be treated, may have impacted his views concerning the necessity of obedience. Recall that the earliest sources of Francis' life agree[39] that he had to be compelled to seek treatment by Elias of Cortona and/or Hugolino of Ostia. In the *Vita prima*, Thomas writes that Hugolino warned ("monere") Francis to take care of his eye infirmity. The *Assisi Compilation* puts this more strongly, stating that Hugolino ordered ("praecipere") Francis to let himself be cured. Focusing on Francis himself, rather than on who is giving the order, the *Remembrance of the Desire of a Soul* records that Francis was compelled ("coactare") to become open to the idea of being cured. These recollections all imply a degree of force or coercion on the part of those responsible for Francis' care. That Francis needed to be ordered can be explained by his early stance on medical intervention for himself and other member of the early Franciscan Order.

In all versions of the *Regula non bullata* that have been identified thus far, there has been a discussion of sick brothers which states, in part:

> I ask the infirm brother that he return thanks for everything to the Creator and whatever the Lord wishes for him; let him desire to be just that, whether healthy or infirm, since God preordains all things for the purpose of eternal life, teaching with the goads of lashes and infirmities and with the spirit of remorse, just as the Lord said "Those I love, I correct and chastise." But if anyone is agitated or angered either against God or against the brothers, or if they demand medicines very anxiously, desiring too much to be free of the flesh quickly about to die, a desire which is inimical to the soul, it occurs to him from evil, and it is a carnal desire. And he does not seem to be of the brothers since he delights more in his body than in his soul.[40]

Given the presence of this text in every extant version of the *Regula non bullata*, and the large amount of text given over to the topic relative to the short length of the RNB, this idea of the acceptance of infirmity must have been important to Francis. Yet, in the *Regula bullata*, written and accepted around 1223, the discussion of sick brothers changed dramatically. The discussion was much shortened, stating only, "And if anyone of [the brothers] falls into infirmity, all the brothers ought to serve him just as they would wish to be served."[41] This change could have come about as a result of several shifts within Francis' own thought and within the order itself. While the *Regula non bullata* was probably written by Francis himself, the early *lives* and chronicles testify that Francis was aided by other members of the order while composing the *Regula bullata*. To draft the final version of his new *Rule*, Francis retreated to Fonte Columbo, taking Brother Leo and Bonizzo of Bologne with him.[42] According to the *Assisi Compilation*, which is not necessarily to be trusted in this instance,[43] other brothers approached Elias and asked him to see Francis and ensure that the rule would not be so severe that they would not be able to observe it.[44] Perhaps more clear-cut is the presence of Hugolino of Ostia at Fonte Columbo during the composition of the rule. In his papal bull, *Quo elongati*, Hugolino (by then Gregory IX) wrote that he had stood by or assisted ("astare") Francis both during the composition of the second rule and when the *Rule* was confirmed by Pope Honorius III.[45] There is thus enough evidence to demonstrate that some prelates of the order, certainly Hugolino and possibly Elias as well, were present for at least part of the writing process. It seems possible, then, that the erasure of Francis' earlier statement on accepting one's illnesses as the will of God and not seeking out medical attention too readily reflects the position of Elias and Hugolino concerning Francis' failing health, and, more importantly, concerning the necessity for Francis to seek out and accept medical attention.

Thus, there is a decided chronological correlation between when Francis began to experience serious infirmities and was ordered to seek out treatment, and when he changed his positions on the desirability of friars seeking out medical attention and the necessity of obedience to authority figures within the order. Early sources suggested that obedience was generally understood to mean obedience to the Franciscan *Rule* and to living a life of poverty and humility. The *Testament*, however, implies a different kind of obedience – one with which Francis himself seemed uneasy throughout much of his life – obedience to those in positions of authority. It is highly likely that this newfound emphasis on hierarchical authority (with less or no room for following one's will or conscience) reflects the reality of Francis' own experience. Willing to suffer whatever illness he might experience as God's will for him, he avoided medical attention for his eye ailment until ordered to do so by his superiors in the Franciscan hierarchy. It is true that correlation does not always indicate causality, but here I think it is fair to say that Francis' being required to obey his superiors influenced both his discussion of when a friar should seek medical attention and his changing notions of what constituted ideal obedience.

The Problem with Blindness

It is clear from the above that Elias and Hugolino worked strenuously to ensure that Francis' eye impairment was treated. But we need to examine why these leaders were so adamant about seeking a cure for Francis' visual impairment. Traditionally in the Middle Ages, blindness was regarded as an impediment to ecclesiastical office. The root of this precept is found in Leviticus 21. This chapter of Leviticus is dedicated to the purity of priests; part of the chapter prohibits sacrifices being offered by anyone who is blind or has defects of the eye, is disabled, mutilated, or broken-limbed, or suffers from dwarfism, the itching disease, or hernias.[46] This notion was codified into canon law. The idea that members of the church hierarchy, especially those at the highest levels of authority, needed to be without impairment was of concern by the central Middle Ages, as the case of Pope Leo III (r. 795–816) demonstrates. For reasons that remain unclear, two papal officials attempted to blind Leo near the beginning of his tenure as pope.[47] The expectation of his attackers was that Leo's blindness would force him to retire his office as pope and remain confined to a monastery.[48] The attack was ultimately unsuccessful, but the mere possibility of a blind pope generated anxiety among the faithful. It is perhaps for this reason, Susan Wade suggests, that some Carolingian authors write that the pope's "eyes and tongues miraculously regenerated themselves." Such a miracle, she argues, "simultaneously vindicat[ed] the pope and dispell[ed] any notion of a lingering injury that might interfere with pontifical rule."[49] Other instances of individuals in roles of authority who stepped down when they became blind are found in various sources. For instance, as discussed in detail in the next section, Aymard of Cluny appointed a coadjutor to rule in his place as abbot because he believed his blindness prevented him from caring for the monastery as he saw fit. In the diocese of York, the records of Archbishop William Melton, who held the post from 1317 to 1340 demonstrate that he appointed coadjutors for blind priests on a somewhat regular basis.[50] Unfortunately, none of this provides evidence for how the blindness of the founding member of a new order would have been dealt with in the early thirteenth century and in a place much closer to Rome.

It is important to note, however, that such anxieties about priests and higher order ecclesiastics having impairments did not necessarily always apply to people in positions of leadership within the church. Wade presents the case of Abbot Erluin as a counterpoint to the story of Pope Leo. Erluin of Gembloux had been asked to reform the abbey of Lobbes in modern-day Belgium. Either angered by the reforms put in place, or by what they perceived to be inappropriate behaviour and the misuse of abbey revenues, three monks blinded Erluin and cut out his tongue.[51] However, Erluin's disfigurement did not result in his removal as abbot of Gembloux. He remained at Gembloux, in the position of abbot, until his death in 987, thirty years after the attack which made him blind and dumb.[52] Nor is there any mention in the chronicle of the abbey that Erluin governed his abbey with the help of a coadjutor.[53]

Tradition and canon law stipulated that blind men could not say mass. This proscription seems to have also had its roots in the Old Testament. Leviticus 21 notes that no man of the seed of Aaron with a blemish (*macula*) ought to offer bread to his God or approach to serve it.[54] The next sentence makes clear what precisely is meant by blemish, as several disabilities are listed.[55] The first mentioned in the long list is blindness. From this, then, came the directive that blind priests may not participate in the mass.[56] Aside from the clear biblical injunction, medieval authorities believed that the danger of spilling the precious wine, or dropping the host, was too great.[57] Recently, however, Irina Metzler has urged scholars not to overemphasize the proscriptions against the blind in medieval canon law. She suggests that, although those born blind were discouraged from entering the priesthood, priests who became blind after they had taken orders were not forced to leave it.[58] To prove this, she notes that some dispensations for disabilities (not only blindness) were given to priests, and demonstrates that the visibility of the disability appeared to impact ecclesiastical decisions concerning the suitability of an individual retaining their priestly duties.[59] Nonetheless, those who were completely blind, even if that injury occurred after taking holy orders, were generally expected to have a coadjutor to say mass in their place.[60]

Thus, medieval attitudes towards the blind were mixed. Moshe Barasche has argued that, in medieval Europe, the blind were often perceived as the least deserving of the disabled. In medieval literature, blindness often seems to reflect a flawed inner character.[61] Edward Wheatley has suggested that when the blind were managed and controlled within a society, for instance within a hospice, they could be tolerated, but when they were not so controlled, moving about unchecked within society, they were deemed dangerous.[62]

Francis may well have regarded his blindness as spiritually rewarding. Yet there is precious little evidence in Francis' own writings or in

the medieval society in which he lived that indicates this would be
so. As historians of medieval blindness have argued, society rarely
regarded blindness as a positive attribute, even among saints and mystics. Surely this must be the logical conclusion of Wheatley and Barasche's observationsthat blindness was linked to the Antichrist and the
refusal to recognize the "truth" of Jesus on the part of Jewish people
and in the consistent presence of cures for blindness found in medieval
miracle stories and hagiographies. In his earliest writings, Francis himself linked blindness with a refusal to accept the need for penance to be
with Christ. In both versions of the *Letters to the Faithful*, Francis argued
that those who lived according to the whims of the body were blind,
since they did not see the light of God.[63]

It is difficult to know whether the injunctions against blind individuals saying mass would have formally impacted Francis, though if he
was a deacon of the church, as Michael Cusato has argued,[64] it may well
have. Deacons had many roles in the Middle Ages, but one of the most
important was their care for the vessels and elements of the eucharist. Blindness also inhibited proper adoration of the eucharist during
mass. While the jury is still out on whether Francis was a deacon of the
church, he almost certainly had received formal permission to preach
from the papacy. But even this formal permission to preach may have
been jeopardized by Francis' encroaching blindness.

What is more clear is that, from early on, blindness and other infirmities were impediments to entering the Franciscan Order.[65] Examination
of a candidate's devotional worthiness was common even in Francis' own time, and, as Angela Montford notes, an amendment to the
order's statutes in 1239 suggests that a person who had an incapacity
of the body which was burdensome should not be admitted.[66] Further,
Franciscans who became ill during their novitiate ran the risk of being
sent home.[67] The Franciscan Order's early interventions to ensure that
members of its order could not be barred from the priesthood by canon
law and were generally healthy enough to take on the rigours of an
ascetic mendicant life do not prove that Francis himself would have
experienced difficulty in maintaining his position as the leader of the
order he founded as his sight became impaired and he became more
infirm. However, the statutes of 1239 were instituted not long after
Francis' death. Elias of Cortona oversaw the general chapter in Rome
in 1239, though he was deposed as the minister general of the order
there. Hugolino dei Conti di Segni, by then Pope Gregory IX, was also
still alive and in a position of authority. These are the same individuals
who so forcefully encouraged Francis to seek medical treatment, especially for his eye disease. Those individuals who were so concerned

with Francis' receiving medical care for his eyesight may very well have also been behind the drive to ensure all members of the order were as healthy as possible.

Disability and Leadership

It is well known that Francis resigned his leadership position in Franciscan Order sometime before 1221, turning that duty over, first, to Peter Catani and, upon Peter's death, to Elias of Cortona. It has long been argued that Francis' decision to resign was prompted both by his desire to lead a humble life and by his own recognition that he was not able to lead an order the size of the Franciscan Order, even as early as 1217.[68] This conjecture may in part be based on the fact that Bonaventure's official *lives* of Francis contain no reference to the saint's worsening impairments interfering with his ability or his legal right to lead his order. Though it is most often presented in Franciscan hagiography as Francis' personal decision to step down from his position of leadership, in fact, canon law of the early thirteenth century dictated that this was necessary, given the severity of his infirmities. While Francis and his early biographers believed that his illnesses and infirmities greatly aided his personal spiritual growth, they also obliquely attest that they undermined his ability to lead his order effectively.

The question of the suitability of infirm or ill prelates continuing in office was of some concern for canonists of the High Middle Ages. The subject is mentioned in Gratian's *Decretum*, completed circa 1145 and used as a textbook in the law school at Bologna almost since its completion.[69] Gratian queried whether canon law required that an ill or infirm[70] bishop should be replaced. Based upon a letter written by Pope Gregory I,[71] Gratian states that while a bishop can never be replaced while he is still alive, regardless of how sick or unable to perform his duties he might be, a steward can be appointed to perform his duties in his stead.[72] Gratian expands upon the necessity of such stewards in chapter three of the same question, suggesting that while sick or infirm clerics ought not to lose their benefices and thus their sources of income, a steward should be appointed to ensure that their duties to the community and the church are fulfilled.[73] Although the ecclesiastical law laid out in Gratian's work does not refer specifically to a situation such as Francis', one could expect that, rather than step down, an infirm cleric would have been asked to choose a suitable stand-in as a leader for the order.

Gratian's *Decretum* was never officially adopted by the church as a definitive statement of its laws; however, it did become a useful tool in the training of lawyers of canon law. Masters of law produced commentaries on the text as they lectured about it. One of the earliest of these commentaries was *Summa parisiensis*, written circa 1160 by an unknown Italian master teaching in or near Paris.[74] The *Summa parisiensis* largely echoes the position of Gratian on the issue of how ill clerics should be replaced by a steward and should not lose their income. However, he cites one exception to this rule: a bishop who is ill with leprosy should not retain his episcopacy. This, he explains, is a parallel application of canon law that prohibits those diagnosed with leprosy from living with their spouses.[75] In some communities, lepers were regarded by those around them as "dead to this world," a position with which the anonymous author of the *Summa parisiensis* would seem to agree.[76] In spite of his physicians' reluctance to provide a single cause, such as leprosy, for Francis' growing number of ailments, the symptoms the saint was experiencing, particularly after 1220, could have been enough of an issue for canonists of his own time.

While Gratian's *Decretum* was never officially adopted by the Catholic Church, Pope Gregory IX commissioned another collection of canons. These decretals, written by his chaplain and confessor Raymond of Peñafort, overshadowed Gratian's work and came to be promulgated as law by the church. They are important both for their content concerning ill clerics, which differs substantially from that of Gratian's work, and because of the close personal connection between Francis and Gregory, who, of course, began his life as Hugolino of Ostia and became cardinal protector of the Franciscan Order.

Given the close connection between Hugolino and Francis, and the interest the former took in both Francis' order and the saint's health, the differences on the subject of ill clerics between Gratian's *Decretum* and the concordance of canons commissioned by Gregory IX are intriguing. Like Gratian's work, Gregory's decretals insist that ailing clerics and bishops should keep their living, even if a steward must take over their duties. It was the church's duty to care for the sick.[77] However, the criteria given for when and why a person should be removed from his ecclesiastical duties are more clearly stated. Quoting another letter of Gregory the Great, the decretal states that churches ought not to be afraid of finding stewards to replace officials, since "if others were to be discouraged by the example of an individual's illness, it would perhaps not be possible to find [those] who are able to fight for the church."[78] Had this law been applied directly to Francis, the saint would have been forced to resign his position at the head of the order.

In the context of religious persons, neither Gratian's *Decretum* nor Raymond's *Decretals* promulgated by Gregory IX included a discussion of the replacement of sick abbots, nor does the *Rule of St. Benedict* or the *Rule of St. Augustine* speak of what is to be done should an abbot take ill. Further, monastic customaries do not generally discuss the actions that should be taken should an abbot fall so ill or disabled that he is unable to continue in his leadership role. Yet, there is evidence that a long tradition of using stewards or *coadiutores* in monastic and ecclesiastical settings existed in the Middle Ages. Thus, for instance, abbots of Cluny, would, at times, choose coadjutors who would aid them in the administration of the monastery and would, upon their death, become abbots. The clearest example of this occurred when Aymard, abbot of Cluny in the mid-tenth century, became blind and could no longer continue to perform his duties. Note that here, as possibly in Francis' own life, blindness was a detriment to service. Upon his request, a coadjutor, the future St. Mayeul of Cluny, was appointed. Mayeul became the abbot of Cluny in his own right after Aymard resigned his post.[79] Such a practice ensured an infirm abbot would not negatively impact the abbey and also alleviated the inevitable period of confusion that accompanies an abrupt change in leadership. James King's work on the memoranda rolls of Oliver Sutton, Bishop of Lincoln from 1280 to 1299, also suggests that in Lincoln, at least, the office of coadjutor was used regularly in cases where the primary holder of a benefice was incapacitated physically or mentally and could not perform his duties.[80]

In the Franciscan Order itself, the earliest extant legislation regarding the replacement of infirm individuals in leadership positions dates from a series of constitutional regulations promulgated at the general chapter of 1260. While the constitutions do not touch on the role of a steward for the minister general, they do instruct that a vicar may be appointed for a provincial general to administer the province when the provincial general travels to a general meeting, when he otherwise travels out of his province, or when he is infirm.[81] The vicar retains his authority even if the minister is dissolved of his leadership role, or if the minister dies, until he is replaced at the next provincial chapter.[82] *Custodes*, who oversaw all friaries in a given territory, could similarly appoint a vicar when they left their provinces. Though not explicitly stated, the proximity of the note on the provincial ministers and the *custodes*, along with the opening "Custodes similiter," suggests that, in the case of *custodes* as well, a vicar could be appointed should a *custos* become too ill to carry out his duties effectively.[83] Thus, from the time of Bonaventure's generalship, at the absolute latest, rules were in place within the Franciscan Order that specifically dealt with the replacement of ill individuals in positions of leadership. It is possible that these rules date from before 1260, possibly as early as 1239, given that the many *constitutiones* given in that year are not extant today. However, none of the handful of the constitutions that do survive refer to the possibility of a custodial vicar for any position or reason.[84]

In spite of the lack of written regulations providing for the use of stewards or vicars before 1260, there is evidence from an early chronicle of the order that such was the practice of the Franciscans from almost its earliest days. In Thomas of Eccleston's chronicle, composed (or perhaps collated) before 1258,[85] he records that Agnellus of Pisa, the first provincial minister of England, became ill with dysentery at Oxford, likely in 1236. Physicians treated him there, and the dysentery was cured; however, he then developed pain in his intestines and side. Believing himself about to die he received his last rites. With that done, Agnellus completed two final administrative tasks in the days before his death. He sent a representative to the minister general to ask for the appointment of his replacement, and he appointed a vicar who would act in his stead.[86] This story is interesting for several reasons. In the first place, it demonstrates that even before the Constitutions of Narbonne of 1260, it was common practice within the order to name a vicar if a prelate within the order was too ill to perform his duties. This may point to an earlier dating for that rule than 1260. Possibly it was included in the now fragmented collection of *constitutiones* of 1239, though, if Thomas can be trusted, Agnellus' decision to name a vicar predates even those regulations by three or more years. Certainly though, Thomas' story demonstrates that the canon law concerning the need to replace infirm prelates with stewards was taken seriously within the order.

The practice of appointing vicars for infirm abbots, the canon law collections of Gratian and Raymond of Peñafort, and the early use of stewards within the Franciscan Order itself provide a new framework for understanding Francis' often fraught position as spiritual leader and worldly chief administrator of his order. While Francis was not a bishop or a prelate of the church, or the abbot of a monastery, he was in a similar position of leadership with respect to his fledgling order. This was increasingly the case as the order grew rapidly and became more structured and regularized in the years after it was formally recognized in 1209/1210. To be sure, Francis chafed against his role as an authority figure, wanting in the first instance for his brothers to be guided by the gospel and the gospel alone, but other members of the order recognized the need to regularize expectations and community life. In the years after 1210, and especially after 1217, it was the second group who won out. Formal organization became inevitable and with formal organization came expectations around Francis' position as leader.

Francis was aided in the organization of his disparate order by Hugolino of Ostia, whom he met in Florence around 1217. Thompson argues that Hugolino advised Francis on a number of issues related to the administration of the order.[87] Perhaps as a direct result of Hugolino's intervention and advice, when Francis departed for Egypt in 1219, he left the day-to-day administration of the order in the hands of two vicars, Gregory of Narni and Matthew of Naples, instead of simply leaving as he had done on his aborted trip to France two years earlier.[88] In the time he was gone, Hugolino also incorporated many changes within the order. While not every change was to Francis' liking, from Hugolino's perspective, these changes were fundamental for the continued flourishing of the order. Thus, in the year of Francis' travels, Hugolino asked Pope Honorius to write letters ensuring that the friars would be welcomed wherever they preached.[89] Against Francis' wishes of absolute poverty, not just for the friars but also for the order itself, Hugolino also began the process of providing convents for the friars, a step that angered Francis upon his return.[90]

Thus, by 1217 at the latest, Francis had taken on a clear leadership role in his order, and had, probably with the help of Hugolino, created the beginnings of an administration. He had appointed vicars who would function as leaders in his absence and advocates who represented the interests of the order at the curia. He had also begun the process of formalizing the irregular meetings he called into formal yearly chapters;[91] the missions abroad, too, had become more professionalized.[92] In spite of his unwillingness to lead, Francis became the head of an order whose adherents numbered in the thousands.[93] Francis' leadership role, not wanted but taken on under duress, meant that his increasing infirmities in the years after his return to Italy in 1219 posed a serious problem for the order.

As chapters 2 and 3 have outlined in detail, Francis' health, always fragile, deteriorated rapidly after his return from Egypt. As early as 1221 and certainly by 1223, Francis was in no condition to lead his large and quickly growing order. Although Francis' decision to remove himself from the day-to-day administration of the Franciscan Order is most often described as voluntary, canonical legislation on the need to replace ill prelates and leaders, combined with the tension evident in the early hagiography between his stated withdrawal from leadership and his continued desire to shape the future of the order, suggests the possibility that Francis was encouraged to withdraw from an active role of leadership, perhaps against his own wishes.

In the hagiography and chronicles of the Franciscan Order extant today, Francis voluntarily and spontaneously says he will no longer lead the order at a chapter meeting.[94] He handed the onerous burden of leadership to Peter Catani, one of the earliest converts to Francis' new order.[95] The date of that meeting is debated, but certainly his withdrawal took place before 1221,[96] the year of Peter Catani's death. When Peter died, not long after his appointment, Francis did not take up the reins of leadership again. Instead, he appointed another to lead the order, Elias of Cortona.[97] The position of both Peter and Elias has been much debated within Franciscan scholarship; however, the fact that both were appointed by Francis rather than elected by the Franciscan brothers as later ministers general would be after Francis' death suggests they led the order at Francis' discretion.[98] Certainly the papacy regarded both men as vicars rather than as leaders of the order in their own right.[99] This lends credence to the possibility that Francis appointed individuals to lead the order in his stead because the curia expected him to do so in accordance with tradition and canon law, rather than purely as an act of humility.

The early narratives of Francis' life provide no direct evidence that Francis was forced to step down as the leader of his order as a result of the infirmities he was experiencing. However, it is clear in these texts that the prelates of the order were determined that Francis receive treatment for his illnesses, particularly his failing eyesight. Further, a careful consideration of what the sources do say about Francis' stepping away from a leadership position in the Franciscan Order does suggest that his illness may have been part of his rationale for doing so.

In the *Legend of the Three Companions*, a new story about Francis is told, one which was explicitly intended to explain the saint's reasons for his resignation from leadership within his order. Francis saw a vision of a black hen with a dove's feet with so many chicks she was unable to keep them under her wings. Francis interpreted this vision to mean that he would have so many followers that he would not "be able to protect them with his own strength."[100] The legend links this vision with Francis' decision to entrust the order to the church and to Hugolino, cardinal bishop of Ostia.[101]

While the *Legend of the Three Companions* suggests, albeit in the vaguest of terms, that Francis believed he would be incapable of providing guidance and protection for a large order, the *Assisi Compilation* contains many discussions of Francis' decision to step down, each emphasizing something different. AC 11 argues clearly that it was Francis' sense of humility, and only that, that persuaded him to remove himself from his leadership role. He promised always to obey the minister general, the provincial generals, and any guardian appointed to oversee him.[102] This rationale is repeated in AC 39, but that pericope also records Francis' prayer to the Lord on this occasion, which states, "O Lord, I commit this family, which you entrusted to me until now, [back] to you. And now, on account of my infirmities which you know, I am not able to have care of them [any longer], [and] I commit my family to the ministers."[103] This discussion is repeated exactly in Thomas of Celano's *Remembrance of the Desire of a Soul*.[104] Here, then, we have recorded the possibility that Francis stepped down from leading his order owing to his illnesses and infirmities. Francis again mentions his illness as a reason for his resignation in AC 106, but with an important caveat: he would have remained in a leadership position, even given his infirmities, had the brothers not strayed from the path he had set for his order. In the narrative, a young brother asks Francis why he tolerates brothers who do not follow the saint's example of living in poverty, humility, and simplicity. The saint's answer is that, in spite of his illness, which he had had since his conversion, he had taught them well by example and through his preaching. When he resigned, Francis said to his brothers that his increasingly severe infirmities meant that he would not be able to care for the brothers any longer as a minister, though he suggests to the friar that, had the brothers not already begun to fall away from his example and ideals, he would have felt well enough to lead the order in spite of his failing body.[105] Although not directly linked with this particular discussion, this section of the *Assisi Compilation* has an authenticating phrase, specifically noting, "But we who were with him when he wrote the *Rule* and nearly all of his other writing present testimony that he had made written many things in the *Rule* and in his other writings concerning which certain brothers, and chiefly the prelates, were opposed to him."[106]

The story itself and the authenticating phrase in AC 106 need further discussion. First, while the authenticating phrase is not in the narrative which describes Francis' resignation and the idea that he might not have resigned if members of the order had not gone astray, the authenticated text about the intention of the *Rule* is related to the account of the resignation. The authenticating phrase "nos qui cum ipso fuimus" refers specifically to the fact that Francis wrote things to which many members of the order were opposed. This is clearly linked to the story concerning Francis' resignation, which notes, as shown above, that Francis would have continued leading his order in spite of his infirmities had the brothers not strayed from what he believed to be the will of God and his vision for the order. It seems likely then that the narratives which the "nos qui cum ipso fuimus" authenticates may be extended to include the discussion of Francis' resignation. It is, perhaps, a reliable reminiscence. However, it also seems to be a politically motivated remembrance, specifically crafted to censure developments within the order in the 1240s, reminding the Franciscan leadership that, in the eyes of Francis' closest companions, the order was straying from what they believed to be Francis' message. We can see the roots of the coming Spiritual/Conventual divide in this and other authenticated passages in the *Assisi Compilation*. Nonetheless, this passage, which clearly does represent an early tradition about Francis, suggests that the saint did step down from his leadership position within the order and he did so, at least in part, because of his infirmities and illnesses.

A final discussion of Francis' resignation comes in AC 112. In this section, Francis notes that he resigned from "the office of the brothers," among other reasons, on account of his illnesses and for the greater utility of his soul and of all the brothers. Francis states, "I am not bound to the brothers except to show a good example." He reiterates that his infirmity excused him from leadership by saying that "even if infirmity had not excused me, the greater aid which I am able to devote to the brothers of the Religion, is that I am free daily for prayer to the Lord for the Religion that he govern, conserve, protect and defend it."[107]

Thus, perhaps the most reliable source for Francis' life suggests multiple times that Francis stepped back from leading his order owing to his increasing infirmity. For the most part, the resignation appears to be voluntary, but there are some hints that Francis may not always have been happy with his decision to step down. For instance, once when he was asked why he gave up his position as the leader of the order, Francis replied that he wished the brothers would follow in his footsteps more, as he believed that some prelates of the order were leading the friars astray. Later, during a bout of illness, the saint woke up and reportedly said, "who are those people who took my religion and my brothers from my hands? If I go to the general chapter, I will show them what I will."[108] This passage has most often been interpreted as showing the concern of some of the original companions of St. Francis that the order was already by the 1240s moving in a direction that was inimical to Francis' vision for his brothers, but should some version of the reported incident have actually occurred, it might also suggest that Francis, at times, felt that his order had been removed from his control, perhaps against his will.

In another chapter of the *Assisi Compilation*, just after Francis' resignation is discussed, there is an authenticated discussion of how Francis changed the *Rule* against his better judgment. Of the *Rule*, AC 106 notes that the saint wrote many things, to which certain brothers, "especially the prelates," were opposed, "[b]ut since he very much feared scandal, he condescended, although unwillingly, to the wills of the brothers." "Those who were with him" at the time stated that Francis "often said, 'Woe to those brothers who are against me on this, which is the will of God for the greater utility of the Religion, which I know, although I, reluctant, condescend to their will.'"[109] Again, politically, this passage is problematic, for it surely demonstrates the discomfort Francis' near companions felt with the direction the order had taken after the saint's death. Yet, if this passage is in any way reliable, and the authentication indicates it might be, Francis' withdrawal from leadership wass closely linked to his illnesses and infirmities, as well as to his dissatisfaction with the direction the order had taken. All of this admittedly circumstantial evidence suggests that on some level, at least, Francis felt pressured to retreat from leading his order, pressure likely exerted by the prelates that were the focus of his disdain in this passage.

That there were concerns around how and why Francis stepped down as the leader of his order is also made apparent by how the subsequent *lives* of Francis discuss his resignation. Most say nothing at all. Only the *Remembrance of the Desire of a Soul*, relying, as it does on a source shared with the *Assisi Compilation*, notes that Francis resigned owing to his humility and his infirmities.[110] Only one other text acknowledges the withdrawal at all, Bonaventure's *Legenda maior*. In this text, Bonaventure acknowledges the resignation, but says it was done out of humility, with no mention of illness at all.[111]

As many historians of Francis have noted, the tensions that play out in the earliest hagiographies of Francis, those written between 1228 and 1250, reflect tensions within the Franciscan membership about Francis' aspirations for the order and about what could be expected of the order as it grew in size and popularity. These conflicts ultimately resulted in a split between the Spirituals and Conventuals. However, with respect to illness and disability, the early hagiographies also reflect a different sort of tension, one which played out during Francis' life, between Francis' desire to still lead his order according to his vision and the illnesses and impairments that played a role in his decision to withdraw as leader. Francis' reasons for his resignation as the leader of the Order of Friars Minor ultimately remain unknown. While a surfeit of early hagiographies of St. Francis exists, there are very few records of early Franciscan chapters general or chapters provincial. No official record exists of the chapter at which Francis made his abrupt announcement of resignation. In fact, it is not known for certain in which year the saint resigned,[112] and indeed some early chronicles of Franciscan leadership (though, it should be noted, not the earliest chronicles) suggest that

Francis remained minister general until his death.[113] Moreover the earliest *lives* of Francis did not discuss the mechanics or ramifications of his decision to step down at all. Peter Catani and Elias of Cortona, the first individuals to take Francis' place at the head of the order, are referred to variously as vicars and ministers general in their own right.[114] Naturally these gaps and differences in the textual record have led to uncertainty about how and why Francis resigned his position. However, the role of Hugolino, later Pope Gregory IX, who promulgated Raymond of Peñafort's decretal collection, suggests a possible way to rationalize the evidence. Hugolino became the order's protector at Francis' request.[115] From that time, he began to exert greater and greater control over the order. It is not inconceivable that the same man, a canon lawyer himself, who, when he became pope, promulgated a collection of law that included new discussions of how ill clerics and prelates should appoint stewards in their place, encouraged Francis to do precisely this. While the evidence is circumstantial, as discussed above, Francis is reported to have cited his growing infirmities as one of the reasons for his resignation. Moreover, the role of Peter Catani and Elias of Cortona in the Order during Francis' lifetime seems less like that of a minister general and more like that of a steward. Neither was elected by the order, the common practice for choosing leaders within the order after Francis' death; rather, both were chosen by Francis himself,[116] and though Francis called both ministers general of the order, the papacy, in particular, referred to both as vicars or stewards.[117] This suggests that, although Francis may have regarded his removal from leadership as an act that was permanent, others within the ecclesiastical hierarchy and even within the order understood it to be an administrative necessity, one that created a situation of stewardship, which was, in fact, how Elias and, especially, Peter treated their positions.

The earliest *lives* of Francis and the earliest chronicles of the Franciscan Order point to tensions between Francis' desire for enduring harsh ascetic practices and the hard reality of Francis' delicate constitution, between the social and political ramifications of blindness and the visual impairment Francis experienced, and between Francis' desire to remain in control of his order after his resignation from leadership, likely due to illness, at least in part. In various cases it fell to Francis or to his minders (and often both) to navigate these tensions. Guardians to whom Francis had sworn obedience tried to limit Francis' ascetic practices and to temper his expectations to the needs of his body. Unsurprisingly, Francis sometimes chafed at these restrictions. While Francis himself seemed resigned to accept his encroaching blindness as the will of God and as a spiritual opportunity, the leadership of the order, aware of the negative social meanings often ascribed to blindness and the formal restrictions on blind priests and prelates that were sometimes applied, worked against Francis' own desire and insisted Francis be treated. Most poignantly, perhaps, leaders in the order and the church itself may have convinced an ill Francis to withdraw from the tasks of leadership, a move that, at times, the saint seems to have resisted and resented, as he watched the order become more rigorously institutionalized. Although such tensions in the texts likely reflect the beginnings of the coming conflict between the Spirituals and the Conventuals within the order, they are also evident around Francis' illnesses and his personal and institutional responses to those illnesses.

Chapter Five

The Hagiographers' Search for Meaning

If Francis' disabilities and how they might best be dealt with caused tension during his own lifetime, they were doubly problematic once the *poverello* had been declared a saint. For political reasons, Francis' canonization was fast-tracked through the official channels of the papacy. The saint had died in October of 1226 and by mid-July of 1228 he was canonized. Francis' canonization was hastened because Hugolino of Ostia, his long-time friend and protector of the order, became pope in March 1227. However, Hugolino, now Pope Gregory IX, also hoped to gather more support for himself in his entrenched dispute with the Holy Roman Emperor, Frederick II, by declaring the already popular holy man a saint. When Gregory was driven from Rome by Frederick, in 1227, he took refuge in Umbria. It is difficult not to read Francis' quick canonization as the return of a political favour, at least in part.[1]

Virtually no records of Francis' canonization procedure survive, beyond the bull *Mira circa nos* which promulgated Francis' elevation to sainthood at a time when the Holy See was trying to systematize canonization procedures; this suggests an unusual canonization process, but Francis' quick canonization was not the only outlier of the period. Anthony of Padua, another Franciscan, was canonized even faster than Francis had been, less than a year after his death in 1231. This rapid process, too, may have had its roots in political motives, but there is no doubt that the Franciscans, like the Dominicans, would become powerful tools in the papacy's fight against heresy. Promoting their sanctity was beneficial both because the holy men were clear symbols of orthodoxy and because declaring them saints bound the Franciscan Order to the political and religious exigencies of the papacy.[2] Miles Pattenden has argued that Clare of Assisi's quick canonization at the behest of the papacy after her death in 1253 was motivated by similar concerns as well as a desire on the part of the papacy to place the responsibility for the convents that had been united under her rule in 1218 squarely with the Franciscans.[3] Whatever the motivations behind the quick canonization of Franciscan leaders in the first half of the thirteenth century, Francis was declared a saint in 1228, and the process of presenting his virtues to the world through narratives of his life and miracles began in earnest.

There is no doubt that Francis' illnesses and infirmities, and how they might be best dealt with, had created some tension in the saint's own life, as discussed in chapter 4. After Francis had become a saint, his hagiographers were left with the task of normalizing his life and integrating it into the models of the thousands of saints who had come before him. Meaning was found in his suffering and his erratic or unusual behaviour, and behaviour that seemed at odds with what might be expected of a saint was elided or explained away. Francis' messy life was cleaned up for mass consumption. Scholars of Francis have the luxury of being able to see the process of this normalization and "hagiographication" in the several early *lives* of the saint still extant today. The reasons for the production of multiple early *lives* of Francis are a bit unclear and likely overlap – perhaps there were different perspectives on Francis' intentions and visions for the order, or people had different perceptions of the saint's actions and way of life. Certainly, a desire to collect as many different stories about Francis as possible, or a perception that previous *lives* were inadequate, also played a part. Whatever the case, by the time Bonaventure was tasked to write his official *life* of Francis in 1260, there were no fewer than ten *lives* and reminiscences of Francis circulating, and probably more. By examining the changes in discussions of the ailing Francis across these different early *lives*, it is possible to see the tensions early hagiographers felt in trying to reconcile Francis' lived reality with the expectations of those who read his *life* with preconceived notions of how a medieval saint was supposed to live and act.

Disappearing Blindness

Just as early sources suggest that the deterioration of Francis' eyesight was a source of tension in his life, so too do early hagiographies of the saint struggle to present Francis' blindness in a way that gives appropriate meaning to an impairment that could have had serious legal ramifications on the saint and been read as a negative sign of his moral fibre.[4] Certainly, as noted in chapter 4, Francis' blindness could have been an impediment to the his ability to preach publicly and to his right to lead his order. Canon law of the period stipulated restrictions on leaders of the church who were visually impaired. While Francis was not a prelate or a priest who said mass, his position as the leader of a popular religious order may have made his encroaching blindness equally problematic. All authors of formal *lives* of Francis struggled with how to present Francis' visual impairment, which was clearly remembered by those who had witnessed Francis' ministry and one which was readily apparent in the few autographs he had written.

Scott Wells' work on how blindness was represented in the various formal *lives* of Francis is instrumental in demonstrating how the saint's disability was managed by hagiographers from the earliest *vita*, written by Thomas of Celano, to the official *life* of Bonaventure promulgated within the order in 1266. Wells notes that Thomas linked Francis' failing eyesight with his imminent death, rather than acknowledging that it was something the saint suffered with for years.[5] The experience of the disease and the potential cures the saint sought out at the request of the leadership of the order are firmly placed in the last two years of Francis' life. Importantly, the discussion takes place after Francis' vision of the seraph and his reception of the *stigmata*, which clearly ties his blindness to the suffering he must endure on earth before he is united with Christ in heaven. Indeed, Thomas is explicit in this linkage, noting that it was "[i]n the course of this same time [as Francis experienced the *stigmata*], his body began to be bothered by various weaknesses even more severe than those to which he was previously accustomed."[6] Thomas more clearly links the eye disease to necessary temporal suffering by noting that "[Francis] incurred a grave illness of the eyes. In this way, God multiplied his mercy upon him."[7]

The *Assisi Compilation* is perhaps more reliable in its discussion of Francis' impending blindness because the remembrances were written by those close to Francis during his last years. It links the onset of Francis' eye disease to his return from Egypt and his subsequent withdrawal from the leadership of the order.[8] As Wells notes, the suffering that Francis experienced from his eye infirmity and his other illnesses after 1220 are read in the *Assisi Compilation* as experiences which enabled him to live a simple and humble life. They allowed him to resign and to ask for a guardian to obey, and gave him an opportunity, also, to obey the leadership of the order and to lead a simple life in the presence of his companions.[9] Interestingly, later *lives* written by Thomas of Celano, the *Vita brevior*, and the *Remembrance of the Desire of a Soul* also relate incidents of Francis' blindness as allowing him to practise humility. The *Remembrance*, for instance, includes the story from the *Assisi Compilation* which discusses Francis' obedience to his superiors in getting his eye treated by a surgeon. The story demonstrates both the saint's humility and his communion with nature. Indeed, most *lives* written after the *Assisi Compilation* include this compelling story.

Bonaventure's official *Legenda maior* also includes the episode, and although the discussion comes after a description of Francis' eye illness in Bonaventure's text, the cauterization procedure is never directly specified as one undertaken to cure Francis' eye infirmity, as it clearly is in the source text.[10] As Wells notes, Francis' visual impairment is mentioned only in chapter 5 of the *Legenda maior*, a chapter dedicated to his ascetic acts. In this chapter, Francis' "very grave eye disease" is said to have been the result of his continuous weeping; he persisted with his weeping even when a doctor advised him to stop lest he risk losing his sight.[11]

There are several important points of deviation in Bonaventure's discussion of Francis' blindness. Most important, in the *Legenda maior*, Francis' blindness is never actual, only potential.[12] This is a significant shift in the narrative of Francis' disability and reflects the discomfort Francis' official hagiographer had with reconciling Francis' visual impairment often linked with metaphorical blindness of those who did not accept Christ as their saviour, with the saint's holiness. So common was this idea that Francis himself made such a connection in both recensions of the *Letter to the Faithful*.[13] In Bonaventure's *life*, Francis was told by doctors that he should stop his ascetic weeping because he was endangering his eyesight. In complete opposition to the Francis in earlier *lives*, Bonaventure's Francis ignored the advice of his doctors, noting that he would rather give up his physical eyesight for the gift of spiritual light.

It is thus possible to trace a sort of genealogy of how Francis' failing eyesight was problematic during his life and, even more so, after his elevation to sainthood, as discussed by hagiographers. Thomas of Celano's earliest *vita* linked Francis' eye impairment to the suffering he experienced as an *alter Christus* after he had his vision of the seraph in 1224. His later texts and the *Assisi Compilation* present his eye impairment as an opportunity to practise humility, though they do acknowledge an earlier onset for his blindness. Bonaventure takes a different approach altogether, perhaps in recognition of how problematic a blind saint could be. He argued that it was Francis' own ascetic practices that endangered his eyesight and that, in spite of medical advice, his continued weeping, as a part of his penance to God, further endangered his sight. Yet Bonaventure never acknowledges that Francis lost his sight, an elegant solution of disappearing an impairment perceived as problematic and indicative of wilful ignorance in the Middle Ages.

Asceticism and Medicine

Scholars have written entire books on the relationship between medieval medicine and the medieval Christian devotion to suffering. As Judith Perkins has argued, since the origins of the Christian faith, Christian identity has been fundamentally linked with the suffering self.[14] In the early centuries of Christianity, martyrs suffered for their faith. As Christianity became a tolerated religion in the Roman Empire, and then the official religion of that state, suffering did not lose its importance. In the East, holy men demonstrated their religious devotion and their connection to the heavens by performing amazing feats of asceticism.[15] In both the Eastern and Western Roman Empires, monasticism, a way of living ascetically in a communal setting, became common. Christian men and women forwent food and sexual pleasure out of a desire to become like angels, and thus closer to God.[16] As even the earliest orthodox theologians had argued, a person's body and soul were inextricably bound in a person. Thus, mortification of the body was understood to benefit the soul. By the High Middle Ages, this idea had been adopted not just among the religious and extremely pious in society, but also within the general population. However, the late central and High Middle Ages also saw changing attitudes towards the body. Increased interest in how Christ experienced his human embodiment is apparent in texts emanating from cathedral schools and universities. Bodily experiences, such as illness, hunger, and even physical ecstasy, rather than the simple denial of bodily needs, became central to medieval spirituality in the West.

Illness, much more than impairment became the focal point of some medieval saints' *lives* in the High Middle Ages. It was not uncommon for hagiographies from that period to include a discussion of how illness led to contemplation and then a turn to a religious vocation.[17] Illness was not only regarded as a push from God to live a good life, but was seen as an opportunity to experience some of Christ's own earthly sufferings.[18] Yet, as Angela Montford notes, there was another way of approaching illnesses of the body in medieval Europe – the belief that one had a duty to keep one's body healthy to ensure it was as fit as possible for the Resurrection,[19] though this approach never seems to have been as popular as the first. Nonetheless, the presence of two very different positions on illness did lead to some difficulties in assessing whether or not a Christian should seek medical intervention for illnesses and impairments. On the one hand, God was the author of all things, including any infirmities experienced. Moreover, suffering was regarded as redemptive, so seeking out medical therapies to diminish suffering from infirmities could be regarded as counterproductive to salvation. On the other hand, from the second century forward, some Christian thinkers presented Christ as a healer, and thus medicine, like the ailments themselves, could be considered a gift from God.[20] Thus, from the patristic period to the High Middle Ages, ecclesiastical opinion was divided on the suitability of Christians consulting physicians. Vincent of Beauvais' massive encyclopedia, the *Speculum maius*, perfectly demonstrates this lack of consensus. His discussion entitled "How the Counsel of Doctors Is to Be Used," in the *Speculum naturale*, cites four authorities for consulting physicians, four against, and one opinion that is ambivalent.[21] In canon law, it was not until the Fourth Lateran Council of 1215 that the question of how a Christian should seek medical advice was addressed, and it comes in the form of an admonition to physicians, who were to ensure that a patient sought a "physician of the soul," that is, a priest, before applying a secular medical cure, as "corporeal infirmity is sometimes caused by sin."[22] It should be noted that this canon seems to expect that individuals will seek out medical attention when in need, though this is not particularly advocated. Rather, the goal of that canon is to ensure spiritual health is the first priority for both patient and physician.

As we have seen in the earliest *lives* of Francis, and then in the redactions of those *lives*, Francis embodies a tension between ascetic living and the need to care for the body as a part of God's creation – the tension between accepting inconveniences of the body as part of God's will and accepting medical intervention as a reflection of God's desire and ability to care. However, the early *lives* of Francis, especially the official *lives*, also suggest that members of the Franciscan Order were attempting to differentiate Francis' radical asceticism from the more reasoned asceticism they might expect from other members of the order. This was done in three different ways. First, discussions of Francis' own ascetic feats and their effects were somewhat minimized in later *lives*. Second, hagiographers included stories about how Francis recommended that his followers practise only moderate ascetic acts. Finally, by the time Thomas of Celano wrote *The Desire of the Remembrance of a Soul* circa 1244, he had found the space to include a long exchange between Francis and his brothers that suggested that Francis, along with other members of the order, relax their expectations around ascetic devotion, particularly in the later years of life. All of these strategies indicate that Francis' hagiographers were aware that Francis' own brand of asceticism was to be admired, but not imitated.

Francis' own relationship with ascetic practice changed over time. The earliest writings of Francis suggest that he saw the body as the locus of sin and believed that bodies needed to be controlled and chastised. This idea can be found in the shortest recension of the *Letter to the Faithful*[23] and in the *Regula non bullata*.[24] "The Spirit of the Lord," suggests an early version of the *Rule*, "wants the flesh to be mortified and despised, considered of little worth, rejected, and insulted."[25] There are hints in the earliest *lives* that Francis practised often extreme acts of mortification, at least until his body could no longer tolerate them. For instance, he fasted to the point of physical exhaustion. Early on in his ministry, the *Remembrance* tells us, Francis was debilitated by fasting, so much so that he could not complete his hike to Bevagna.[26] The *Assisi Compilation* reports that even as he encouraged moderation in terms of ascetic acts and fasting for his friars, he himself was always austere.[27] Yet, by 1221, Francis had relaxed the fervour of his ascetic acts out of deference to the needs of his body. This reality was sometimes enforced by his guardian or other members of the Franciscan hierarchy, but Francis also appears to have accepted the need to relax his ascetic rigour as he grew older as a result of a conversation with another brother.

In a narrative recounted in *The Remembrance*, which has no known earlier source, Francis is distressed by the needs of his body. It had become necessary to use soothing medicinal treatments, though he did not want to acknowledge the ailments of his body. Francis feared that he was indulging his body too much, eager as he was for poultices and compresses. The brother to whom Francis relayed his fears reminds him that, for many years, Francis' body obeyed his will to practise asceticism absolutely and without fail. Now, as his body was failing, the brother suggests, Francis owed it to his faithful limbs to care for them.[28] Celano's text here is working in complicated ways, for it is certainly encouraging the brothers to accept their bodies' increased demands for care as they aged, as well as demonstrating the need to accept some medical interventions. Angela Montford has noted that in mendicant texts, at least, it appears that submission on the part of ill friars to the authority of physicians was actively supported in the thirteenth century.[29] Most of the evidence she presents to support her observation comes from sources connected to the Dominican Order. However, Celano's *Remembrance* is doing similar work for the Franciscan Order by asserting that care for one's health was important, and that the authority of the physician, along with the needs of the body, should be respected. For this reason, we might suspect that this narrative in the *Remembrance* is structured to be a teachable moment for the friars of the mid-thirteenth century.

Like many religious in the thirteenth century, Francis was ambivalent about the role of medicine in the life of a person dedicated to God. His early work suggests an outright hatred of the corporeal body. "Let us chastise our body, crucifying it with its vices, desires and sins,"[30] says what is likely an intermediate version of the *Rule*, written between 1221 and 1223,[31] now preserved in a manuscript held at Worchester Cathedral. The punishment of the body, for Francis, extended to acceptance of illness. The *Regula non bullata* stipulates that a sick brother should "desire to be whatever God wishes him to be, whether that is healthy or sick." Nor should the sick brother seek out medical treatment too precipitously, for that desire is born of the flesh ("carnalis est") and shows the individual loves his body more than his soul. All early versions of the *Rule* repeat this stipulation that brothers not see doctors too freely.[32] It was clearly considered to be an important directive. Interestingly, however, this injunctive is left out of the *Regula bullata* altogether. It only required that sick brothers be cared for by their companions.[33] Yet in the *Remembrance*, Celano tried to negotiate this stipulation, reminding Francis (and, by extension, others in the order) that at, times, medical intervention was necessary.

Other *lives* do not necessarily record Francis' changing ascetic practices, so much as they downplay or minimize the consequences of Francis' ascetic acts. Early on in the *Vita prima*, Thomas writes that, shortly after his conversion, Francis' friends found him "consumed by exhaustion of the body," which they believed to be the consequence of bodily purging and madness.[34] According to Thomas, Francis' (former) friends also mocked him and threw stones. The entire story, including the references to Francis' weakened body, is told again in *Legend of the Three Companions*, almost word for word. A reference to his friends throwing rocks is also found in the newly discovered *Vita brevior* and in Bonaventure's *Legenda maior*. The *Vita brevior* notes again that Francis' friends believed his behaviour had changed radically and that the citizens of Assisi attacked Francis, believing him to be out of his mind.[35] The *Legenda maior*, however, massages the narrative found in the *Vita prima* and the *Legend of the Three Companions* a bit to suggest that Francis' friends believed that he had taken leave of his senses due to his "filthy face and altered mind."[36] It is only in earlier *lives* of Francis, then, that there is a suggestion that the townspeople who had known the young, decadent Francis believed his new way of life to be the product of a weakened body and mind. Certainly, part of the reason Bonaventure modified the story of people's reaction to Francis' conversion is that by the 1260s Francis had been a saint for thirty years and widely recognized as such. It was perhaps not fathomable (and certainly not to be highlighted) that some citizens of Assisi, and even friends of the Bernardone family, might not have immediately recognized Francis' behaviour for the pious and divinely inspired acts later hagiographers would ascribed them to be. However, another likely reason for Bonaventure's change was to highlight to followers of the saint the importance of moderation in ascetic practice, an idea that became increasingly imperative in the thirteenth century.[37] The stark reality of Francis' own life and suffering presented a counternarrative to this new initiative, one that had to be managed by authors of the saint's *lives*.

The attempt to encourage moderation in ascetic practices begins early in the hagiographies of Francis, certainly earlier than in Bonaventure's *Legenda maior*. One of the most obvious invocations to moderation is found in the *Assisi Compilation*, where it is given in the words of Francis himself. That such a plea for moderation comes in a text often considered to be the most closely aligned with proto-Spiritual Franciscan sensibilities is perhaps surprising; however, as David Burr suggests, the emphasis in the *Assisi Compilation* is on Francis' devotion to apostolic poverty, rather than asceticism.[38] For the authors of that text, elderly by the time it was completed, Francis' rejection of money or property for the order was a far more important theme to highlight than fasting and other kinds of bodily mortification – though Francis' own suffering was by no means ignored. In a pericope in the *Assisi Compilation*, authenticated by the witnessing phrase "nos vero qui cum ipso fuimus," the ascetic rigour of the first friars is described – how they mortified themselves not just by abstaining from food and drink, but also in keeping vigils, by remaining out in the cold, and with manual labour. They wore things similar to chain mail or hair shirts next to their skin. However, according to the text, some of the friars became ill in just a short time, and recognizing this, Francis prohibited the wearing of anything next to the skin unless it was the friar's habit. The prohibition was announced at a chapter meeting.[39] Early Franciscan records are sparse, and there is no other evidence of such a prohibition made at a chapter meeting. Without answering the question of whether Francis himself did, in fact, prohibit the use of hair shirts and other such tools of asceticism, it is clear that the authors of the *Assisi Compilation* believed it necessary to attribute such a restriction to the founder and to give it legal force by suggesting the prohibition was made at a chapter meeting.

Most *lives* of Francis strongly suggested that even Francis himself advocated moderation in ascetic practices by members of the order and, at the end of his life, even for himself. This message reflects what appears to have been, if not official policy, at least a general feeling on the part of the order that friars ought to avoid excessive practices of mortification. The moderation of asceticism outlined in the early *lives* of Francis also parallels a movement in the Dominican Order to ensure their novices did not commit self-harm due to ascetic practices.[40] Minimizing discussions of Francis' ascetic acts, along with a great deal of the discussion of his illness, also allowed for another new trend found the later *lives*: the removal of most discussions of medical care received by Francis.

Disappearing Doctors

Just as Francis' blindness disappeared by the time Bonaventure wrote the *Legenda maior*, so too did many of the doctors that Francis encountered in earlier *lives*. Indeed, one would be hard-pressed to recognize in Bonaventure's discussion of Francis that the saint spent the last years of his life in the care of doctors. To be sure, Bonaventure does retain the discussion of the surgical intervention to cure his ailing eyes, a story which almost certainly makes its first appearance in the source material for the *Assisi Compilation*, but which is told in all later *lives* of St. Francis. In all of these *lives* Francis is ordered to seek out the treatment, either by Brother Elias, as in the accounts in the *Assisi Compilation* and the *Actus beati Francisci in Valle Reatini* or by unnamed brothers or individuals in the other accounts. In all cases, the treatment is given by an individual described as a *medicus* (AC, LM) or a *chirurgicus* (VS, TM), and in the case of the narrative in the *Actus Beati Francisci in Valle Reatini* the specialist is described as a "doctor who was an expert in the art of surgery and chiefly surgery of the eyes before all other things."[41] In this one instance, Francis' visit to the doctor seems to have been made acceptable in later *lives* as it was an opportunity for teaching about God's role in nature and about faith itself. The story is told in its fullest detail in the *Assisi Compilation*. In it, Francis welcomes the fire that makes the cauterizing iron hot, as its author is, of course, God. And indeed, Francis' understanding, and his lack of fear about the procedure, are proven correct when he feels no pain at all. The readers of the *life* are meant to understand that Francis' perception of nature is the correct one, and that God's authorship in nature allows for his intervention on behalf of the faithful. The story and its attendant message are repeated in the later *lives*, including Bonaventure's *Legenda maior*.

In spite of the presence of many doctors in the source texts for the *Legenda maior*, only one other doctor is found in Bonaventure's hagiography of Francis. A doctor who visited Francis regularly to treat him was repaid by Francis, not with money, but with a hair from the saint that fixed a dangerous crack in the wall of the doctor's house.[42] In this episode too, Francis' medical care is not the point of the narrative. Rather the story highlights the miracle Francis' hair performed.

Discussions of Francis' care at the hands of medical professionals are far more often found in *lives* of Francis written before Bonaventure's *Legenda maior*, especially in the *Assisi Compilation* and the *Remembrance of the Desire of a Soul*. That Francis was in the care of physicians at the end of his life is apparent even in the *Vita prima*. Thomas notes that the physicians (*medici*) who treated Francis "were amazed and the brothers marvelled at how the spirit was able to live in flesh so dead, the flesh having been so consumed that only his skin clung to his bones."[43] Francis was also warned twice, by multiple doctors, of his coming death, according to the *Assisi Compilation*, implying that at the end of his life, he was in the care of not one doctor, but probably many.[44]

As chapter 3 has demonstrated, Francis saw many doctors before the end of his life and seems to have been in the near constant care of physicians from shortly after his vision at La Verna. The *Vita prima*, the *Assisi Compilation*, the *Remembrance of the Desire of a Soul*, the *Treatise on Miracles*, and the *Actus beati Francisci in Valle Reatini* all record how the saint went to Fonte Columbo, near Rieti, expressly for the purpose of seeing an eye specialist.[45] Several of the texts record that Francis saw multiple doctors there; indeed it was the need to cure his eye disease that drove him to Rieti and then to Siena.

Yet, while the presence of doctors is recorded regularly in early *lives* of Francis, their presence is deliberately minimized in Bonaventure's *Legenda maior*. To be sure, Bonaventure does not deny that Francis saw doctors. However, when a doctor's professional status was not directly relevant to the point of the story he retold, it appears that Bonaventure deliberately removed the physicians from the story. There are two important examples of this in the *Legenda maior*. The first occurs during a discussion of Francis' now famous vision of Lady Poverty, first described in Thomas of Celano's *Remembrance of a Soul*. In that account Francis was travelling from Rieti to Siena, for the purpose of visiting a physician to cure his eyes. Remember that, according to the *Remembrance*, Francis was travelling to Siena with a doctor as a companion, one who was bound to the order.[46] When Bonaventure retells this story, however, Francis appears to be travelling alone. Bonaventure writes that the vision occurred when Francis, "driven there for cause, was conveying himself to Siena."[47] There is no mention of a companion. Bonaventure's diversion from his source text seems to be a deliberate attempt to obfuscate both the reason for Francis' travel and that Francis was travelling with, and was, perhaps, even in the care of, a doctor. Nor is this the only time Bonaventure disappears doctors from earlier sources.

Remember, too, the story of the doctor who cared for Francis' pheasant for a time, told in the *Remembrance of the Desire of a Soul* and the

Treatise on Miracles. When Bonaventure describes this miracle, he records it more or less as told in Thomas of Celano's texts; however, in the *Legenda maior* the doctor who takes the pheasant in the earlier narratives is described simply as a "man who was accustomed to visit out of devotion to the servant of God."[48] The Latin of Thomas and the Latin of Bonaventure are sufficiently different that it is possible that Bonaventure used a different, unknown, source for this story, but if, as is generally believed, Thomas' *Remembrance* and *Treatise on Miracles* are the sources, Bonaventure's removal of the doctor from the story was calculated and deliberate. Indeed, both stories suggest that Bonaventure was uncomfortable with the reality, presented in earlier sources, that Francis spent much of the last years of his life in the care of one or more doctors.

This discomfort with Francis' medical care on the part of Bonaventure was the product of many different concerns. In the first place, it was reasonably well known in the early decades of the order that Francis himself had been reluctant to accept medical care and that he had required his earliest followers to follow suit, although this proscription was eventually relaxed in the *Regula bullata*.[49] Yet, a dedication to representing the authentic Francis was probably not Bonaventure's primary motivation in excising references to doctors from Francis' *life*. A far more likely reason is the thirteenth-century Franciscan leadership's position on the presence of doctors and sick individuals within the order.

Angela Montfort has persuasively argued that Franciscans, in particular, were reluctant to allow sick or disabled individuals into their order. She cites three different examples from the 1230s and 1240s to support this assertion, including that of a man refused entry into the order for scrofula and that of two other men who hid their injuries, presuming they would be denied entry into the order.[50] These actions suggest that the order tried to ensure that ill or disabled individuals wishing to join the order were denied entry. This is borne out by some of the early rules that governed the Franciscan Order. Indeed, even before 1260, the constitutional mandate of the Franciscan Order insisted that every novice be asked about his health and that he be turned away "if he had any infirmity or corrupt quality of his body on account of which he would be later be a burden on others; if he had any mutilated member or were an invalid in any way."[51] This institutional interest in the health of a potential novice is unique to the Franciscan Order and probably reflects an appreciation of the time and energy commitment required to care for the sick – as perhaps borne out by the circumstances of the order's own founder.

That this concern is readily seen in Franciscan constitutions, chronicles, and hagiographies, while it is largely absent from Dominicans texts of the same period, is significant. From the earliest decades of the order, Franciscans were clearly aware of the difficulties that might result in accepting ill and infirm individuals. Before 1254 they had a mechanism to replace any *discretus* who could not fulfil the office of visiting the friaries in his province, especially because of reasons of illness or death.[52] The constitutions of 1260 contained the above stipulation and also put clear procedures in place to ensure that if a provincial minister was freed of his duties, or became ill or perhaps died, he would be replaced in the interim and then permanently at the next provincial chapter.[53]

Was this wary acceptance of the need to deal with ill administrators borne of the Franciscan experience with Francis? The emphasis on health screening for novices and the protocols for dealing with sick friars found in the Franciscan constitutions, chronicles, and hagiographies, and the nearly complete absence of such attention in the contemporary Dominican sources, suggest a possible relationship. The Franciscan Order's experience of Francis' chronic illnesses seems to have determined future policy in the order.

The Changing Role of Guardians

The structure of early Franciscan government, especially within Francis' own lifetime, is the subject of intense debate.[54] While various positions or offices of the Franciscan Order were named in Francis' writing, rarely did the saint define these in any way; that was left to other, later, writers and commentators. By the time commentaries on the *Rule* were being written by the four masters[55] and Hugh of Digne[56] in the middle of the thirteenth century, the title of *guardian* had come to mean, essentially, the head of a group of Franciscans, the superior of a Franciscan house. This is the way it is used in Thomas of Eccleston's mid-thirteenth-century chronicle; in it he names the first guardians in the various foundations the Franciscans established in England.[57] Yet the origin of the term makes its original meaning much less clear.

Francis uses the term *guardian* in only three of his writings, all of which probably date to 1223 or after. It is surprising that a term which came to mean the leader of a community of friars was not used in any version of the Franciscan *Rule*. Rather, the term is found in two letters of Francis' and in the *Testament*.

The first use, chronologically, appears to be in a letter Francis wrote to a minister.[58] Like so much about early Franciscan sources, the manuscript tradition of the *Letter to a Certain Minister* is not as clear as might be hoped. It is usually dated to around 1223, based on the fact that some of its phraseology is similar to that found in the *Regula bullata*, which was promulgated at the end of 1223.[59] Carlo Paolazzi has argued that the letter should be seen as a bridge between the *Regula non bullata* and the *Regula bullata* and thus should be dated slightly earlier, to between 1221 and 1223.[60] The letter itself is an exhortation to a minister who is feeling beleaguered in his position and who has perhaps even been physically assaulted by those in his care. It contains two references to guardians. After urging the minister in question to accept whatever behaviours the brothers might heap upon him with acceptance, mercy, and forgiveness, Francis instructs him to "announce this to the guardians, when you are able to do so, that you are resolved within yourself to act in such a manner."[61] The second passage reads, "If anyone of the brothers, with the enemy urging him on, has sinned mortally, let him be held through obedience to return to his guardian … Similarly let [all the friars] be bound through obedience to send him [the sinner] to the *custodes* with a companion."[62] This would suggest that the role of guardians and the roles of the *custodes* were similar and that both terms referred to administrators within the order.

Yet the role of guardians was not clearly established, for Francis' *Regula bullata*, written at nearly the same time as the *Letter to a Certain Minister*, does not mention the role of guardians at all. Instead, the *Rule* notes, "If any of the brothers, with the enemy instigating, have sinned mortally, for those sins, let it be arranged among the brothers concerning them, that [the sinful brothers] be restored to the provincial ministers alone."[63] The guardians, whatever role they might have played, are simply not mentioned.

Francis also used the term *guardianus* in a letter which probably dates to around the same time as the *Letter to a Certain Minister*. The *Letter to the Entire Order* has variously been dated between late 1221 and 1224, but most scholars place it circa 1223 or later.[64] In this letter, too, Francis uses the term to describe the administrators of his order. The letter has several injunctions about how members of his order ought to act. To emphasize that he was speaking to the entire order, present and future, members and superiors, Francis wrote near the end that he was addressing the minister general (probably Elias of Cortona at the time), and the ministers general who came after him, along with the "other *custodes* and *guardiani*" of the Friars Minor who existed or would exist in the future.[65] In this letter, too, the term *guardianus* is best understood as some kind of administrator within the order.

Francis noted the presence of the guardians once more, in his *Testament*, written at the end of his life, in 1226. Here he uses the term quite differently. Francis writes, "And I firmly wish to obey the minister general of this fraternity and to obey the other guardian whom it pleases him to give to me. And I so wish to be a captive in his hands so that I am not able to go or do anything beyond obedience and his will, since he is my Lord ... And let all other brothers be so bound to obey their guardians and make the office according to the *Rule*."[66] Having noted the obligation of brothers to obey their guardians, however, Francis goes on to say that if someone is found not reciting the office, or not orthodox in his belief, then all the brothers should be "bound through obedience to present him to the *custodes* nearest the place where they found him."[67] Francis thus appears to understand "guardian" to mean the keeper or leader of a small group of friars, perhaps itinerant friars. Although the *Rule* does not specify this, the early hagiographies make clear that, at least in the case of Francis himself, a guardian could be assigned to a single individual.

Francis appeared to have understood that his requested guardian would guide him in all things and that Francis would owe him absolute obedience. By subsuming his own will to the will of the guardian, the usual narrative goes, Francis was a living *exemplum* of spiritual humility. Yet Francis' choice of the word "guardian," in Latin *guardianus*, is unusual in and of itself. The term seems to have been used only sparingly before its adoption into the Franciscan administrative language in the thirteenth century. Its primary meaning until that point was a person who provides protection, such as a warden.[68] Francis could have as easily chosen another word adopted into the administrative language of the Franciscan Order: *custos*. This term generally means keeper, and, with different modifiers, it could apply to the custodians of a town or a prison guard. In English law, the term *custos* was often applied to a person who was charged with the care of another person deemed mentally incapable by the courts.[69] This was not, however, Francis' context – he chose to put an overseer in his place, and the language of the hagiographies, regardless of the role of the guardian in Francis' *life*, was one of obedience and service. Indeed, both words implied two distinct semantic senses in medieval Latin, the first care for others and the second protection and service. Perhaps Francis wanted to instil these values in the members of his order by eschewing the traditional hierarchical language of leadership.[70] Yet the role of guardians and *custos* in the early years of the Franciscan Order, and especially in Italy, is not well understood.

While the term *custodes* was used regularly in Francis' early writing, the term *guardianus* came later, as demonstrated above. Chronologically, if the hagiographies can be trusted, the first introduction of the term into Franciscan history occurred after Francis withdrew from the leadership of the order and after he had received a guardian to whom he swore obedience.[71] Francis then began to use the term in his writing to refer to some kind of superior within the order. Perhaps his request for a guardian was the origin of the term within Franciscan government. Indeed, it is possible that at the very chapter in which Francis resigned his leadership of the order and received a guardian, the decision to send friars to Germany was also made, which could account for the seemingly early use of the term *guardian* among Franciscans in that province.[72] Cajetan Esser has argued that in Germany and England the term *guardianus* was used to mean the leader of a community of friars from the time Franciscan communities were founded in these provinces in the 1220s.[73]

While hagiographers suggest that Francis' original request for a guardian was grounded in the saint's determination to be humble, it is important to remember that other sources report that Francis withdrew from leadership because he was ill. For this reason, we might also consider that Francis' guardian had another purpose, one linked to the saint's declining health. As early sources of Francis' life demonstrate, Francis' guardian protected the saint's physical well-being as well as his spiritual health.

There is no doubt that at times Francis' guardian acted as a sort of protector, defending Francis' physical well-being from the saint's inclination to destroy his already infirm body with severe ascetic practices. There is more evidence of this kind of role for the guardian than any other in the early *vitae* of the saint. In these early texts, Francis' guardian is not mentioned often, and, interestingly, never by name, but when his guardian is mentioned, it is most often in the context of ensuring Francis' health. Francis' guardian acts in Francis' physical self-interest even when his decisions do not accord with the saint's. For example, the *Assisi Compilation* includes a story of how Francis' pants caught fire when he was sitting too close to the hearth. Francis did not permit the fire to be extinguished by anyone until his guardian was called in and began to put out the flames "against Francis' wishes."[74] More often, the guardian ensured that Francis cared for his ailing body. Twice in the *Assisi Compilation* Francis was asked by his guardian and Elias of Cortona not to give away his tunic, for doing so would endanger the saint's already fragile health.[75] The story included in AC 91 is particularly telling; in it Francis secretly gives a beggar a portion of his tunic, for fear his guardian will forbid him to do so. And in this, Francis is proven correct, for the guardian, "as if he sensed what Francis wished to do," found him and forbade him to share his tunic because the weather was very cold and Francis was sick. Francis appears almost petulant when he retorts, "if you do not want me to give my tunic to the man, it is only right the you make some piece [of cloth] as a gift to the poor brother."[76] This report makes clear the caregiver role of Francis' guardian and also, more interestingly, Francis' seeming inability to obey his guardian in all things, as he had promised to do. Yet another instance where such irritation on the part of Francis with his guardian becomes clear is recorded in both the *Assisi Compilation* and the *Remembrance*. Because Francis suffered from an ailing stomach and spleen, his guardian required him to sew fox fur on his tunic.[77] The *Remembrance* also records that the guardian insisted that Francis keep his tunic on at the end of his life, rather than face death naked. He did so by telling Francis that he owned the tunic Francis was wearing; thereby the saint could not give it away as he did not have the authority to do so. This story, again, was couched in the need to preserve Francis' health as much as possible even on the eve of his death.[78]

In spite of his stated desire to obey his guardian in all things to make himself humble, Francis seems to have had some difficulty with his promise of absolute obedience to his guardian, especially with respect to injunctions around health. Thus, when asked to seek treatment for his eyes, early *vitae* record that Francis had to be ordered to do so, not only by his fellow friars and his guardian, but also by his vicar, Elias of Cortona, and even the cardinal protector of the order, Hugolino. The story in AC 91 recounted above, in which Francis tries to give away pieces of his tunic against the wishes of his guardian, also demonstrates that Francis was not as careful with his health as others wished him to be. Francis' stated desire to obey his guardian thus seems not to have extended to matters of his own health. It is clear that, at times, Francis' wishes conflicted with those to whom he submitted to obey. Yet ultimate authority rested with Francis' guardian, not with Francis himself, as the few stories about Francis' interactions with his guardians suggest. Far from having authority over the whole order, Francis did not even have bodily autonomy in the period after his withdrawal from leadership.

In conclusion, then, it seems possible that Francis' request for a guardian at the moment of his withdrawal from leadership is the origin of the use of the term *guardianus* within the Franciscan Order. This hypothesis neatly explains why the term is not used in Francis' writing until 1223, why it is not used in either of the two *Rules*, and why it *is* used in the *Testament*. By the time the *Testament* was written, in 1226, the term was being expanded to apply not only to Francis' own companion but to other members of the order, primarily those leading groups of itinerant Franciscans, and perhaps especially in the provinces of Germany and England. Further, it seems likely that one of the roles that Francis' guardian played was to protect the saint's fragile physical health, even when Francis himself did not wish it to be protected. In an act of extreme humility (though the *vitae* are fairly clear in demonstrating that this humility was not *always* voluntary), Francis' very bodily autonomy was given over to his guardian.

Disappearing Humanity, New Sanctity

It has long been understood that saints seem to become less differentiated and more stereotypically holy the further removed their hagiographies are from their subjects. Indeed, the revisions of saint's *lives* often have more to do with responding to current political and social realities than with returning to explore the realities of a saint's experience. By the thirteenth century, the methods for canonization were being formalized and had become quite rigorous. These formal processes included a papal investigation into the actions and miracles of a would-be saint. Many witnesses were called to attest to the holiness of the individual. Three uncontested miracles were required for consideration. The holy behaviour expected of saints was becoming limited by the thirteenth century as well. Increasingly, there were expected patterns of holy behaviour saints needed to exhibit. Erratic behaviour that did not conform to expectations was minimized in hagiographical texts.[79]

Unsurprisingly, Francis' *lives* follow this general trend, although the trend is complicated by the more casual and personal reminiscences found in the *Assisi Compilation*. Later, however, Francis seems to shed his personality, and even his humanity, in the narratives of his life that continued to be written throughout the thirteenth century. The saint also becomes emotionally and physically stronger, and less in need of medical care and physical, and even emotional, comfort. One of the most obvious ways this is demonstrated in the early *lives* of Francis is in how Francis interacts with music.

It is clear from many of the earliest discussions of Francis' life that the saint loved music.[80] Of course he composed the *Canticle of Brother Sun*, which is his best known work, though he composed other pieces as well. Even hearing music inspired Francis and raised his spirits. Unsurprisingly, most of the evidence for Francis' enjoyment of music comes from the *Assisi Compilation*.[81] Those reminiscences, when they are included at all in the later *lives*, especially Bonaventure's *Legenda maior*, are changed in ways that diminish Francis' enjoyment of an earthly pleasure.

If one of the narratives in the *Assisi Compilation* can be trusted, Francis' love of music was considered problematic by leaders of his order even in his own lifetime. AC 99 tells of how, near the end of his life, Francis used to comfort himself by singing the *Praises of the Lord*, a song of his own composition. Brother Elias, though, appears to have suggested that some people might find it unseemly for Francis to find joy in music so near the end of his life. The text records Elias' words to Francis:

> Most dear brother, I am greatly consoled and edified from every joy which you show for yourself and your companions in such affliction and infirmity. However, granted that the people of this city venerate you for a saint in life and in death, nevertheless since they firmly believe that you are near death on account of your great and incurable infirmity, hearing *Laudes* of this sort being sung, they can think or say among themselves: "How can he who is near death show such joy at this time? For he ought to be thinking about his death."[82]

Although not authenticated by the usual testamentary phrase, this story has a ring of authenticity. Elias was concerned to preserve Francis' saintly image – an image that did not include a sick and dying Francis who was joyfully singing.

It is likely that even during Francis' life the leadership of the order was attempting to shape Francis into a model of perfect sanctity. This is certainly the case in the formal *lives* written after the saint was canonized. AC 66 reports that when Francis was staying in Rieti seeking treatment for his eyes, he requested that a brother trained to play the lute find an instrument and play him a song that praised the Lord. Francis said that he would appreciate this music, "especially since [his] body was afflicted with great infirmity and pain." With the music he would "reduce the pain of his body to consolation and the joy of the spirit." Unfortunately for Francis, the brother he asked to play was reluctant to do so, since the people of Rieti knew him and he feared they would think he was being tempted by the lute and the lifestyle it represented. Francis let the idea go, but the next night, he heard lute music, more beautiful than he had ever heard before. Francis considered the presence of the lute the work of God rather than man, and gave thanks to God accordingly.[83] The Latin is interesting here, for it does not deny that there was a person playing the lute; rather, Francis believed that God had encouraged the lute player to play in Francis' hearing.[84]

The story is repeated in Thomas of Celano's *Remembrance*, but with a significant change – Francis' words in this *life* imply that he thought the lute was not played by human hands. Francis said: "The Lord, who is a source of comfort to the afflicted, has never left me without consolation. For look! I, who was not able to hear the lutes of men, was able to hear a sweeter lute."[85] This reconfiguration of the *Assisi Compilation* narrative would seem to imply that Francis' enjoyment of human music was potentially problematic. Far less of a concern was Francis' enjoyment of heavenly music.

The story is reworked again in Bonaventure's *Legenda maior*, with more changes. To be sure, in this narrative, too, Francis' body is described as oppressed, having been attacked by his many infirmities, "yet [the saint] desire[d] music not solely as a consolation for his current predicament, but to "excite the agreeable qualities of his spirit."[86] Consolation, it seems, was not reason enough for the music. Nor could the music be of earthly origin, for Bonaventure states explicitly that "it was not fitting to [Francis'] honour that he be open to this [music] occurring through human work; the care of angels was present for the purpose of pleasing the holy man."[87] Bonaventure further implies that Francis believed the music was heavenly – that he had perhaps been transported to the heavenly realm for a time.[88] But even this was not enough to emphasize the importance of Francis accepting heavenly consolation rather than human. Bonaventure alone finishes the story of the heavenly lute music with a discussion of how Francis' companions would often see the Lord visit Francis to provide him with "abundant and excessive consolation."[89] Bonaventure's phrasing here is interesting, as the word *excessivus*, rarely used in the Middle Ages and with no known classical uses, means only immoderate and/or excessive.[90] Bonaventure's use here might imply that the saint did not require the consolation he received from God, but that God, loving Francis as one of his saints already, consoled him anyway.

That Francis ought to have willingly accepted his infirmities and his suffering without seeking comforts from the secular world around him is perhaps best expressed in the *Remembrance of the Desire of a Soul*. The text implicitly acknowledges that Francis' pain was recompense for sin.[91] Having burned "anything combustible within himself," Thomas notes, "[Francis], thoroughly cleansed [by the suffering his infirmities had caused], would suddenly fly up to heaven."[92] Then Thomas inserts a rare authorial note in the text, saying that he believed that the saint bore his sufferings knowing that in such suffering there was great reward.[93] In both of these statements, the *Remembrance* reflects one of the central themes in saints' *lives* since the time of the martyrs – a trope that Judith Perkins notes is embedded in Christian thought and ways of being – that Christians suffer and then they ascribe a higher meaning to their suffering.[94] Nearly forty years ago Peter Brown noted that feats of heroic athleticism were performed to prove a saint's devotion to God in the early Christian East.[95] The work of Caroline Walker Bynum[96] and Amy Hollywood,[97] to name only two scholars, demonstrated that saints and mystics of the High Middle Ages used suffering as a means of achieving nearness to Christ, whether by imitating his experiences of pain or suffering or using suffering to create a kind of sublime *aporia* that allowed for a mystical connection with the divine. By the time that the *lives* of Francis were written, saints suffered and welcomed that suffering. Human consolation was unnecessary – divine consolation was all that was required.

And yet the very *life* that notes the importance of Francis' suffering is also one of the few formal texts that acknowledges the reality of the emotional and mental impact Francis' infirmities took, for in that same chapter in which Thomas of Celano notes the reasons why Francis bore his sufferings, he also tells of how on a certain night, Francis, "exhausted more than usual on account of his serious illnesses and diverse troubles, began to feel pity for himself in the inner recesses of his heart."[98] While self-pity was surely a common reaction in an individual suffering greatly from various infirmities, this moment is the only time such a human response to Francis' own plight is even acknowledged in the *Remembrance*. In other texts, however, there are subtle signs that, at times, Francis craved and received comfort when he experienced the pains of his infirmities during his more active ministry and towards the end of his life. For instance, AC 71 records how once, while Francis was ill at the bishop's palace in Assisi, his brothers were trying to encourage him to eat. He could not, but said that if he might have some *squalo* fish, he might be able to eat that. Miraculously, someone arrived with the fish and some crab cakes, both of which Francis was able to eat. The point of the story in the *Assisi Compilation* is to demonstrate that the appearance of a man with these treats was miraculous because they were not in season, but the narrative also demonstrates Francis' desire for what today we might call comfort food. That both the fish and the crab cakes were comfort foods for Francis is elaborated on in the *Actus beati Francisci in valle Reatini*, when, in a lovely turn of phrase, the narrator reports that "[Francis'] sense (*sensualitas*) of taste desired nothing except *squalo*" – for it was only this fish, and crab cakes, that the saint "freely ate."[99]

At the end of his life, too, Francis found comfort not just in the Lord, but in human companionship and, again, in special food. Certainly having his closest companions nearby gave him comfort. But, according to the *Assisi Compilation*, Francis also asked that Jacoba de Setti be informed of his impending death. He further specified that she should send a grey tunic to him, along with the delicacy she often made for him when he visited her in Rome.[100] As noted in chapter 3, the ingredients named suggest the comestible was something like marzipan, a sweet confection and something Francis enjoyed.

In the Middle Ages, as today, marzipan consists primarily of almonds and sugar. Although the narrative does not allude to it at all, the humoral properties of both almonds and sugar would have been understood to be beneficial to Francis during his last days. Sugar was considered to be moderately hot,[101] but almonds were extremely so.[102] The medicinal qualities of the marzipan would have been understood to be able to momentarily invigorate Francis on his deathbed, providing a small amount of heat to his increasingly cold body. Yet the narrative clearly implies that, for Francis, the importance was not the medicinal properties of marzipan, it was the comfort of tasting a treat he enjoyed one last time. The *Assisi Compilation* notes that one day after her arrival, Lady Jacoba "prepared that edible for the holy father, [part of which] he desired to eat,"[103] though he could only eat a little owing to the weakness of his body.

Francis' need for human comforts seems to have been troubling for his later hagiographers. In later *lives* of Francis, and certainly in the official *life* written by Bonaventure, many of the human comforts Francis craved while ill and during his last days have been taken out of the narrative. Gone are the comforting and desired foods of *squalo*, crab cakes, and marzipan. Lady Jacoba and her marzipan disappear entirely.[104] Francis does not, as in earlier texts, feel saddened, because, of course, as a saint, he could not do other than look forward to his union with God. Even in the very text that noted that he was in danger of self-pity, the *Remembrance of the Desire of a Soul*, Francis is not allowed to actually dwell in his self-pity, for, Thomas writes, Francis "preserved [himself from this feeling] with an unmovable shield of patience by praying to Christ."[105] Bonaventure's narrative disappears that part of Francis' human experience entirely.

As those with living memories of Francis died, and as the hagiographies of the saint were more removed from the saint and his companions, examples of Francis' humanity, especially in the face his suffering, configured as redemptive, vanished from the narratives. Francis had become a saint. A close examination of the early *lives* of Francis makes absolutely clear the process in which hagiographers engaged to ensure the image of Francis they presented was wholly in line with the expectations of saintly behaviour. In the case of Francis, this activity was less about shoring up support for canonization as most of the *lives* were written after Francis had been declared a saint. Instead these redactions were related to reconciling a man who experienced significant infirmities and suffered greatly with them to the image of a saint who patiently accepted his suffering and saw living with his infirmities as being obedient to God's will. Many worldly interventions to care for Francis' infirm body were written out entirely, as was the case in Bonaventure's *Legenda maior*, with its description of Francis' blindness and much of the medical care he received. When such episodes remained, they were crafted into teachable moments, as the narrative of the cauterization Francis received eventually was.

Of course, this textual "clean-up" happens in many, if not most, saints' *lives* as they are rewritten over time. Francis' *vitae* are unusual, however, in how quickly the pattern of eliding certain behaviours and events developed. That much of this revision occurs around Francis' illnesses and infirmities, and in particular, around the secular interventions to provide care and comfort for the saint, suggests an uneasiness on the part of hagiographers about those secular interventions and how they might be interpreted by those interested in the saint and his cult.

Chapter Six

On Disability, Power, and Gender:
A Speculative Conclusion

If Francis' hagiographers were uncomfortable with the saint's infirmities and the medical care the he received, they also struggled to map the events of his life as a founder onto the narratives of other saints who remained as leaders of the orders they founded until their death, even if they were pressured or had a desire to resign. Medieval hagiography includes several examples: St. Benedict, Robert of Moselme, and Bruno of Cologne, to name only three. St. Dominic, to whom Francis was (and still is) often compared, worked tirelessly as the leader of his order until his death in 1221. Indeed, the first *lives* of Dominic emphasized his role as a founder, more than any other aspect of his life.[1] That Francis had voluntarily retreated from his position as the head of the order he founded needed to be explained. This is most clearly seen in the *Assisi Compilation*, in which Francis' resignation was discussed on three separate occasions; in each, different reasons were given for his withdrawal.

As we have seen, one of the ways hagiographers explained Francis' unusual withdrawal was to argue that he stepped down out of a sense of humility. Francis rejected the power and authority that came with his position as a founder. The first of the three discussions of Francis' resignation in the *Assisi Compilation*, along with Bonaventure's *Legenda maior*, emphasize this reasoning, having Francis say, "I would obey a novice for one hour if he were given to me as my guardian just as though he were the oldest, and as diligently as I would obey the oldest and most distinguished brother."[2] This desire for humility also explained the presence of Francis' guardian, whom the saint pledged to obey in all things. Yet, as will become clear in this chapter, a desire for humility is clearly only a part of the explanation for Francis' resignation. In fact, Francis' actions after his resignation suggest that he was not always comfortable with his choice to leave the leadership of the order behind. More pragmatic, and more likely than a consequence of his desire for humility, is that Francis recognized that the social barriers he would encounter as a result of his infirmities would not easily allow him to continue to lead. By stepping down, Francis forwent a more direct, masculine mode of authority. He himself recognized this and used different strategies to challenge those in formal positions of authority and to assert his own power after his decision to withdraw. Chiefly, Francis turned to acts of disobedience, to a letter-writing campaign, and to demonstrating his own authority through his nearness to God as a means of fostering his own power in the face of traditional forms within the church hierarchy.

Francis' early hagiographers, faced with the stark reality that, despite his spiritual charisma, Francis was unwilling, and perhaps even unable, to retain the traditional forms of power that came with founding a popular religious order, employed different strategies to demonstrate how the saint retained authority in spite of his loss of position. Of course, as this book has demonstrated, many early *vitae* simply downplayed the impact that Francis' illnesses and infirmities had in his life and leadership. When that proved impossible, they presented alternative reasons for Francis' choice to withdraw. They also were at pains to demonstrate that Francis retained some forms of authority after his resignation. Evidence of acts of disobedience practised by the saint were elided. Instead his hagiographers endowed Francis with a higher authority than that of those who governed the order and the church, an authority predicated on his suffering and demonstrated by God in the saint's reception of the *stigmata*.

Resistance and Power in Francis' Lived Experience

As earlier chapters in this book have demonstrated, Francis' access to traditional modes of power were diminished as his body became more infirm. While this culminated in his withdrawal as the leader of his order, there were other ways in which the saint felt his own lack of authority. For instance, in the later years of his life, Francis preached less. Although the Fourth Lateran Council forbade preaching by laypeople who did not have the express permission of the church, Francis was able to continue preaching, possibly because he had received the required permissions or because, as Michael Cusato has argued, Francis was made a deacon of the church.[3] As we have seen, in the last years of his life, Francis spent more time in contemplation and far less time preaching publicly, likely owing to his increasingly infirm body, and the time he spent in treatment. As result of this, the saint's public voice, his dramatic presentations of how a Christian life should be lived, weakened, as did his public authority. That public authority was also weakened by Francis' inability to attend chapter meetings after 1224.[4] Chapter meetings were where the order's business was conducted and, had Francis attended, his position would have been presented and respected, if not followed.

That members of the Franciscan Order and the church perceived that Francis lacked formal authority in the later years of his life is clear from discussions of the composition and adoption of the *Regula bullata*, which was likely composed after he stepped down from leading the order. Francis' first draft of a new rule was "lost" after he handed it over the order's *de facto* head, Elias of Cortona.[5] The loss has been much debated, and scholars such as Moorman have argued that the *Rule* was deliberately lost because it was considered too harsh.[6] The premise for this speculation, however, arises from a problematic report in the *Assisi Compilation*, which describes various ministers and prelates who visited Francis, along with a reluctant Elias of Cortona, to convince him to moderate the *Rule* he had been tasked to write. If the *Assisi Compilation* is accurate – and this is a very big if in this instance, the proto-Spiritual bias of the authors being very apparent in this section – it had already become evident by 1223 that Francis' authority as a founder has been eroded, not just by his resignation but by his perceived inability to write a workable rule.

After his first draft was lost, Francis wrote another rule, and appears to have consulted Hugolino about it shortly afterward. After Francis died, Hugolino, by then Pope Gregory IX, wrote in his papal bull *Quo elongati*, which explained how the *Regula bullata* should be observed, that he had "assisted [Francis] as he composed the *Rule* and obtained its confirmation from the Apostolic See," and was thus in a good position to interpret its true meaning.[7] Yet Gregory's intervention in the meaning of the *Rule* was not always perceived as helpful. The Franciscan theologian and future archbishop of Canterbury John Pecham recorded that detractors argued that friars lived under the *Rule* of Gregory, rather than the *Rule* of Francis,[8] perhaps a sign of future tensions within the order. The tensions around Francis' composition of the *Regula bullata* demonstrate how quickly after his resignation the saint lost formal authority over the order he had founded.

Yet, Francis' separation from modes of authority runs deeper than his inability to preach or his stepping away from positions of power and governance within the order. At times, Francis was unable even to exhibit autonomy over his own body. In many cases it was the leaders of the order or Francis' guardian who had ultimate authority over Francis' care for his body. When Francis' eye impairment became severe, he was ordered by Hugolino and Elias to receive treatment for it. Francis no longer had autonomy of choice in his self-care. Even more telling in this regard is the way that Francis' guardian acted to ensure the saint cared for his body. As chapter 5 has demonstrated, Francis' guardian acted in Francis' physical self-interest even when his decisions did not accord with the saint's, as for instance, in the famous story where Francis would not extinguish his pants which were on fire until his guardian told him to do so.[9] Besides this dramatic example, there is more evidence of Francis' lack of bodily autonomy, especially as it relates to his guardian. The *Assisi Compilation* in particular notes several instances in which Francis' guardian insisted that Francis care for his body over and above Francis' own wishes. It is clear, then, that at times, Francis' wishes conflicted with those to whom he submitted to obey. Yet, ultimate authority rested with Francis' guardian, not with Francis himself, as the few stories about Francis' interactions with his guardians suggest. By the end of his life, Francis had virtually no authority over the order and, in the last two years, he was, at times at least, denied autonomy even over his own body.

Yet the early writings of the saint and *lives* of Francis, and especially the *Assisi Compilation*, suggest that Francis resisted his diminished authority over his body and his order. With respect to his inability to remain in control of his own health-care decisions, Francis sometimes practised a strategy of resistance, a resistance that appears surprising given the narratives of humility and obedience that built up around the saint after his death. But the evidence in the *Assisi Compilation* is clear, sometimes Francis just disobeyed his guardian. For instance, AC 91 records how Francis secretly gave a beggar a piece of his tunic because he knew his guardian would not allow it. Even though Francis was found out, it is clear his intention was to subvert his guardian's orders. Similarly, in a story told in the *Assisi Compilation*,[10] Francis obeyed his guardian's request that he sew some fox fur into his tunic to protect his body. Francis did so only grudgingly, keeping the fur lining only for a short time. If this story can be trusted, Francis did his best to circumvent his obedience to his guardian especially, it seems, as it related to matters of his personal health.

The story above is repeated in Thomas of Celano's *Remembrance of the Desire of a Soul*, but with one significant difference – Francis obeys his guardian. Although Francis insisted that he wear fur on the outside of his tunic as well as the inside so people would know he did so, he wore the fox-lined tunic without later discarding it as noted in the *Assisi Compilation*.[11] Francis' disobedience disappeared.

At other times, Francis obeyed the directives given to him about the care of his body, but texts indicate that he did not wish to do so. The clearest example of this is the episode in which Francis is ordered to receive a cauterization for his eye impairment. He was ordered to do so by the cardinal protector of the order, Hugolino dei Conti di Segni, and by the vicar of the order, Elias of Cortona. Francis then travelled to meet the surgeon, but elected to wait until Elias arrived before he began the procedure. When it became clear that Elias could not come to meet Francis, Francis agreed to go ahead with the treatment, though the *Assisi Compilation* notes that receiving this treatment was against his own wishes. Hesitating, but resigned, Francis finally "proposed that he be obedient to [Hugolino and Elias], although it was burdensome enough to him to have cares of this sort [taken] for him. And for that reason, he wished his minister to compel this."[12] Only one other early *life* of Francis discusses his reluctance to obey his superiors to receive treatment: the *Actus beati Francisci in Valle Reatini*. In this work, Francis is recorded as saying, "But since I do not wish to hold the cure of the body in the same way as the cure for the soul, I ask that you do not conduct [the surgery] unless first Brother Elias, vicar of the order, hold that the cure be done."[13] Again, once Francis understood that Elias would not be able to join him, he agreed to move forward with the operation, lest he seem to be "contradicting the directive of the protector and vicar of the order."[14] In all other works, the possibility of Francis' hesitating to obey or not wishing to obey was simply left aside. He proceeded with the surgery after he was ordered to do so.

It is clear, then, that at times Francis' wishes conflicted with those to whom he submitted to obey. While, most often, ultimate authority over the care he received rested with his guardian and the leadership of the order, Francis sometimes hesitated to obey or outright disobeyed the directives he received. This suggests that the narrative of holy humility that was carefully constructed by many of his earlier hagiographers was not necessarily always present in his lived experience. And as Dalarun has noted, that carefully constructed narrative of humility has been picked up by many modern biographers of Francis, some of whom also fall into repeating hagiographic tropes.[15]

If Francis lacked bodily autonomy towards the end of his life, his formal authority within his order and the church hierarchy at large was also compromised. His public voice was being silenced by his inability to preach (or perhaps societal expectations that he ought not to preach) and his inability to lead his order as he wished following his formal resignation. Although Francis contributed to the order's governance for a time after his resignation, as demonstrated in his role in composing the *Regula bullata*, that episode also clearly demonstrates his diminished authority. To deal with this reality, Francis employed many strategies. The first, and arguably his most effective, was to engage in a letter-writing campaign. Until his resignation, Francis wrote only infrequently. But after he withdrew from leadership, he began to write extensively, to individuals in the order, the order at large, and even those outside of his religious community. Many of the letters are directive in their nature.

Within those letters that can with some surety be dated until after 1221 or so, the tone shifts significantly. Of course, Francis wrote much about the idea of servitude and styled himself as a servant of people and of God in many of his writings. In later writings, however, his use of the language of service shifts in such a way as to highlight his nearness to Christ. He uses that nearness to bolster his spiritual authority in the face of potentially resistant secular authorities. For example, in a letter dedicated to the whole order, almost certainly written after 1223,[16] Francis notes (in a more florid way than usual) that he sends greetings in the Lord. Referencing the Acts of the Apostles, Francis asks his brothers to attend him carefully and "obey the voice of the Son of God."[17] Of course the brothers should obey God's commands, but it is clear in the letter that Christ's commands and Francis' own are conflated. While Francis begins by asking the brothers to show due reverence to the eucharist, he quickly homes in on his own position on the role of priests within the order. He exhorts them to be content with celebrating mass only once a day, contrary to the norm at the time when priests in religious orders would sometimes say multiple masses for the dead each day. In houses with more than one priest, Francis wrote, mass still should only be said once a day. These are Francis' commands, not God's, of course.

Later in the letter he exhorts his vicar, Brother Elias, to ensure that his *Rule* is observed "inviolably (*inviolabiliter*)" by the Friars Minor. Again, although Francis perceived the order to be doing God's work, the expectation that friars should follow the *Rule* exactly, a preoccupation of Francis' towards the end of his life, is a collapse of God's commands into Francis' own. That this was an intentional strategy in the letter is made especially clear near the end, when Francis states explicitly, "I, brother Francis, a useless man and an unworthy creature of the Lord God, speak through (*per*) the Lord Jesus Christ to Brother H, the minister of the whole religion and to all general ministers who will be after him and the other custodians and guardians who are and will be."[18] By speaking through Christ, Francis merged his will and Christ's own in the letter.

A second example of Francis' use of his nearness to God to establish his own authority can be found in the *Testament*, in a passage in which Francis notes that his way of living a religious life, outlined in the *Regula non bullata* and modified in the *Regula bullata*, was, in fact, revealed to him by God. It is clear that by the time of the *Testament* Francis was worried that the way of living he had envisioned for the order was under threat. The *Testament* can be read as a last attempt to wrest the order back into an approximation of the vision Francis had for it. The authority by which he did so, given that he no longer had any official standing in the order, was that God himself had given him the *Rule*, an idea largely absent in both the earlier *Rule* and the text of the *Regula bullata* that have come down to us. Francis reiterated at the end of the Testament that the Lord dictated the *Rule* directly to him, saying "[b]ut as the Lord has given me the *Rule* to speak and to write simply and purely, just as [he did] these words, understand them simply and purely, without gloss."[19] Francis argued for the authority of his *Rule* and his *Testament* by explaining that the content of the *Regula bullata* did not originate with him, but was revealed to him directly by God. Of course, this imbued Francis' wishes and words with authority beyond his own.

But the *Testament* goes further than simply asserting that the *Rule* came from God; rather, it insists that Francis' way of life was shown to him by God himself. Francis wrote, "and after the Lord gave the brothers to me, no person showed me what I ought to do, but the Almighty (*Altissimus*) himself revealed to me that I ought to live according to the pattern of the Holy Gospel, and I had written [a rule to this effect] simply and with few words and the Lord Pope confirmed it for me."[20] With this statement Francis inserted himself at the centre of his order, even at the end of his life and after removing himself from formal authority within it. The Lord revealed to Francis and Francis alone a gospel-inspired life, the rules of which Francis and Francis alone caused to be written down. When Honorius approved the *Rule*, he did it "for Francis." In this way, Francis makes plain that the way of life for the Friars Minor comes directly from God, who imbued Francis with his vision for the order. By appealing to God for his authority, Francis insulated himself from criticisms that he no longer held a formal position of authority and demonstrated that his authority came from a higher power than the church *magisterium* or the commands of the order's current leadership.

While his letters and other works do not directly testify to his feelings of powerlessness, his energetic letter-writing campaign, begun towards the end of his life, along with his increasing insistence on the divinely revealed nature of his instructions for the order, suggests that Francis was trying to combat an order moving in directions with which Francis was uncomfortable and his impotence in stopping that undesired move. Faced with the reality that he no longer had access to traditional modes of power in the leadership of his order, he invoked a new source of authority, his holiness and his mystical nearness to Christ. In Francis' own writings, this nearness to God was not predicated on his disabilities, illness, or suffering. Instead Francis suggested it was God's divine revelations to him that were the source of his authority for directing his order outside formal mechanisms of power. However, as Francis' early hagiographers began to struggle with how to reconcile Francis' position as the founder of an order who still wished to exert his authority even after he had withdrawn from leadership, they increasingly turned to narratives of holy suffering to explain the saint's access to alternative modes of authority.

Reshaping Francis' Authority: The Work
of Early Hagiographers

While Francis could actively work to combat his loss of formal authority, hagiographers had a different task. In normalizing the story of the Francis, his hagiographers had to ensure that his authority was maintained throughout his life. In particular, even if Francis had not maintained his authority over his order after his withdrawal from leadership, the future saint's personal autonomy and ability to pursue his own religious goals had to be maintained. Yet constructing such a narrative was difficult because it was well known that Francis had been in ill health in the last years of his life, and accounts of his care by physicians (and perhaps guardians), and his frustration with the leadership of the order, were well attested. To manage the image of the saint, early hagiographers turned to different strategies that downplayed his lack of personal autonomy and authority. First, they provided alternative explanations for his lack of formal authority and bodily autonomy, especially referencing the his desire to be humble and obedient. In service to this narrative, hagiographers sometimes elided instances of outright disobedience found in source texts. Second, the authors of Francis' formal *lives* sometimes downplayed the impact that Francis' illnesses and infirmities had on his wordly authority. When that proved difficult the authors employed a third, related, strategy: they demonstrated the ways in which Francis' spiritual authority was more important than his secular power.

To deal with earlier stories, especially those from the presumed source for the *Assisi Companion* that demonstrated Francis' lack of authority, hagiographers sought to provide explanations for his behaviour that described his actions without reference to loss of autonomy or power. Perhaps the most obvious example of this is that, at times, Francis' reason for resigning from the leadership of his order or obeying his guardian was linked to his desire for humility, his desire *for* a lack of power. Francis' resignation was very much on the minds of his companions as they were recounting their remembrances, as recorded in the *Assisi Compilation*, for the story is mentioned in three separate narratives, with many possible motivations for the withdrawal given,[21] including Francis' infirmities and his desire for humility. In the *Remembrance of the Desire of a Soul*, in words that echo (or perhaps inspired) those found in the *Assisi Compilation*, Thomas of Celano relates that Francis himself believed he had become too infirm to continue to lead his order.[22] Yet, by the time Bonaventure rewrote the story of Francis' resignation, all references to Francis' being too ill to lead had been removed. Instead the focus is only on Francis' desire to be humble and to practise obedience, a link that Thomas' works did not make.[23] Bonaventure wrote that Francis "wished not to be above, but rather under, he wished not so much to order as to be subservient. For this reason, withdrawing from the office of [minister] general, he sought a guardian under whose will on all things he wished to cast himself."[24] There is no mention here of Francis' infirmities forcing a resignation; rather, Francis' withdrawal is described as a personal choice, freely given, out of a sense of humility; a narrative which allowed the saint the fiction that any infirmities he may have experienced [and society's response to them] had nothing to do with his withdrawal from leadership. Francis' access to formal mechanisms of authority would have remained intact, in Bonaventure's conception of the resignation, had Francis not freely chosen to deny himself that authority.

Another example of hagiographic choice that limits discussion of Francis' lack of formal authority pertains to a vision Francis had. The story is told only twice in the early *lives*: in the *Legend of the Three Companions* and again in the *Remembrance of the Desire of a Soul*. In it the saint saw a black hen who had so many chicks it could not protect them all with her wings.[25] Francis' interpretation of the vision, given in both texts, is that he is the hen, and the chicks his many followers in the Franciscan way of life, so many that he became "unable to protect with [his] own power." Recognizing this, Francis then suggested he would need to commend his followers to the church itself, who would be able to "protect and govern" the order.[26] In the *Legend of the Three Companions*, this vision is linked to choosing Cardinal Hugolino as the protector of the order. The story is told only once more, in the *Remembrance*. It is told in much the same fashion, Francis having the vision and then interpreting it himself, saying that it means that "Francis' power would not suffice to defend the brothers from the disorder of men and the contradiction of tongues."[27] Although the *Remembrance* puts the interpretation of the vision in Francis' own voice, the use of the third person suggests the interpretation probably came from a third party and perhaps a different source than was used in the slightly earlier *Legend of the Three Companions*. Yet the vision and its meaning are found nowhere else in the early *lives*. Even the *Fioretti*, perhaps based on early sources, does not contain this vision, a suggestion that later sources were unsure what to do with a story that suggests Francis' *virtus* could not protect and guide the members of his order.

The word choice in both versions of Francis' analysis of the vision is vague. *Virtus* can mean strength but it can also mean power – physical and political.[28] In the Roman period, the word, as its linguistic root suggests, was inherently linked with representations of manliness. By the Middle Ages, it had picked up other meanings, such as virtue and miracle.[29] It was a complex and ambiguous term. Yet, however we understand the specific term *virtus*, it does seem clear that Francis acknowledged the reality of his lack of power (personal, political, or otherwise) in the episode. In later hagiographies, those less dependent on reminiscences of the saint and more focused on creating a coherent narrative of the founder of the Franciscan Order, this episode, minor and problematic, was left aside.

Just as narratives of Francis' life that suggest his access to authority was diminished by his infirmities and not by personal choice were altered or outright ignored by later writers, early accounts of Francis' disobedience were also elided, especially in later, more formal, *lives*. Evidence of disobedience, of course, suggests a Francis who was unhappy with his chosen position of humility – a Francis who was resisting his lack of autonomy and authority. Thus, for instance, while the *Remembrance of the Desire of a Soul* recounts the story from the *Assisi Compilation*, discussed above, about how Francis resisted his guardian's advice about lining his tunic with fox fur, all the *Remembrance* says about the incident is that Francis and the guardian finally agreed that he would wear the fur as long as his tunic also had fur on the outside, so everyone would know he was wearing it.[30] The little addition from the *Assisi Compilation*, that Francis did not wear the fox fur for long, is left out entirely. Francis' obedience is absolute in the more formal life, though the story also suggests Francis' retained some authority to negotiate his behaviour with his guardians.

Another story in the *Assisi Compilation*, also recounted above, about how Francis tried to secretly give a beggar a part of tunic against the wishes of his guardian, is left out entirely of the later *Remembrance*, nor is it found in any later *life*, though much of the surrounding material from the *Assisi Compilation* is added. Of course, the story had to be left aside, for it suggests that Francis chafed at his guardian's orders, and rather than having the authority to negotiate or advocate to change his guardian's mind, he felt he had to disobey in secret. This is hardly the behaviour one would expect from the founder of an order, and it is at odds with the image of a humble and obedient Francis that began to be crafted by even the earliest of his hagiographies. The inconvenient remembrances of Francis' companions were thus left aside in the later *Remembrance* and *Legenda maior*.

Another way that later *lives* and especially the official *life* of Francis written by Bonaventure circa 1260 demonstrated that Francis retained authority unless he voluntarily relinquished it was to downplay the role that guardians and doctors played in the saint's life and especially in maintaining his health. Chapter 5 has already demonstrated that Bonaventure's *Legenda maior*, in particular, did not acknowledge the reality of Francis' blindness, and several doctors were elided from narratives of Francis' life. In Bonaventure's *life*, too, the guardians who cared for Francis' health are largely absent. Although the episode in which Francis asks for a guardian to obey at the time of his resignation is repeated, the only time his guardian makes an appearance after that is on the saint's deathbed, when he lends Francis a tunic to wear so that he can pass away owning nothing.[31] All instances of guardians caring for Francis' well-being found in earlier texts, especially the *Assisi Compilation*, are simply not included in Bonaventure's *Legenda*. Such disappearances can only be explained as an attempt to limit discussions of the saint's vulnerabilities and the consequent lack of personal autonomy and formal authority he experienced.

A last strategy employed by Francis' hagiographers was to show that Francis' spiritual authority, based on his nearness to God through his imitative suffering and reception of the *stigmata*, was far more important than his secular role as a founder of an order. A cursory comparison of the early *lives* of St. Francis and St. Dominic, another founder of an early thirteenth-century religious order, makes this abundantly clear. Dominic's early *lives* were recorded in the *Libellus de principiis Ordinis Praedicatorum* by Jordan of Saxony,[32] Peter Ferrand's *Legenda sancta Dominici*,[33] and the *legendae* of Constantine of Orvieto[34] and Humbert of Romans.[35] All of these texts portray Dominic absolutely as the founder of his order – even Dominic's dedication to apostolic poverty was presented in these early *lives* as a function of his desire to convert heretics. In contrast, Francis' hagiographers, even the earliest ones, tend to present Francis as a person drawn to a spiritual life, who imitated Christ's suffering so thoroughly he received the wounds of Christ. The disparities between Dominic, the founder, and Francis, the mystic marked with God's favour by the wounds of Christ, as presented in the early hagiographies would eventually cause concern in the Dominican Order. Only with Catherine of Siena in the fourteenth-century would the Dominicans be able to celebrate their own saint with (secret) *stigmata*. Yet, the Dominicans were not the only order with concerns. On the Franciscan side, the very different visions many later Franciscan leaders and Francis himself had for the order caused fissures in the order that rippled through the later Middle Ages.[36] While Francis' role as a founder was perhaps not deliberately positioned as incidental to his life, this was the effect of the hagiographic emphasis on Francis' personal style of devotion and on his personal relationship with God. It also likely reflects Francis' own positioning of the place from which his authority came in the latter part of his life.

After Francis withdrew as the head of the Franciscan Order, he found his access to authority, both personal and institutional, curtailed. To deal with this reality, he adopted a number of strategies to bolster his position. To maintain some control over the direction of the order, he engaged in a persistent letter-writing campaign, and in these letters and in other texts he demonstrated that his vision for the Franciscan Order had come directly from God himself. Francis sometimes used simple disobedience as a strategy of resistance and a way to maintain some level of personal autonomy. This practice was especially apparent in his dealings with those responsible for his personal care, especially his guardians.

Early hagiographers of Francis were faced with explaining Francis' discomfort with his loss of authority. Instances of disobedience, infrequently found in hagiographies to begin with, disappeared entirely in the later official *life* by Bonaventure. Bonaventure also diminished discussions of Francis' illnesses and the medical care he received, especially as reasons for the saint's withdrawal as leader of the Franciscan Order. Franciscan hagiographers emphasized aspects of Francis' personal spirituality and devotional practices at the expense of discussions of the saint as a founder. Francis' imitation of Christ was celebrated by his official biographers, but generally not in a way that suggests the saint could derive institutional authority from such acts of devotion. Even God's approval of Francis, written on his body in the form of the *stigmata*, did not suggest that the saint could or should derive any formal authority within the order because of this approval.

Francis in the Feminine Mode?

Since Caroline Walker Bynum published *Holy Feast and Holy Fast* in 1987,[37] historians have generally recognized that holy women who were denied access to traditionally masculine forms of authority in the Middle Ages sought to establish alternative modes of authority for themselves. By linking their bodily experiences to those of Christ, Catherine of Siena, Catherine of Genoa, and many other devout women participated in a dialogue that emphasized Christ's embodied humanity. Like women, Christ both fed and was food to the Christian faithful. Like women, Christ suffered and bled. Women's experience was Christlike, and in that similarity, a deep authority for religious women, one that transcended and surpassed the entrenched male authority of the traditional church hierarchy, was established.[38]

This claim to authority may have had its origins in a move towards a more experiential, more femininized Christianity in the High Middle Ages. Francis was an inheritor of the eleventh- and twelfth-century tradition that regarded women as capable of intense spirituality.[39] Robert of Arbrissel, for instance, created a space for pious women who wanted to withdraw from the world alongside their male counterparts and even allowed women to lead his entire community of male and female religious. Bernard of Clairvaux's famous sermons on the *Song of Songs* positioned the soul as feminine,[40] or perhaps *virago*.[41] He, like other Cistercians, often described the characteristics of successful religious leadership as being those of a loving mother,[42] a metaphor Francis used in his own writings.[43] Such actions and discussions destabilized the expectations of spiritual behaviour in a time when the majority of canonized individuals were clerical men,[44] and perhaps opened a space for a different, more affective, kind of piety that has come to be coded as feminine. Historians do not hesitate to argue that Francis of Assisi participated in this general trend towards the feminization of religion that occurred during the High Middle Ages. Jacques Dalarun suggests that Francis was best understood as a "bridge between a masculinized religion and a new religion, feminized as the languishing body of Christ is feminized."[45] Though Bynum herself takes pains to demonstrate that Francis' piety was different from the sort exhibited by female mystics in the High Middle Ages, she understands Francis to have engaged in this kind of devotion that was far more common amongst women than men. Indeed, Bynum regularly lists Francis alongside several women when discussing feminine piety, though she argues that food and fasting were not as central to Francis' spirituality as to that of contemporary female religious. Poverty, rather than food, was the primary metaphor of Francis' life, Bynum notes,[46] even as he exhibited other characteristics of a more feminine piety.

For Bynum and Dalarun especially, Francis' experiential, embodied spirituality was an extension of the eleventh-century Cistercian practices that positioned the soul as the bride to Christ's bridegroom, and the caring prelate as a nurturing mother figure, regardless of gender. Yet a parallel explanation exists, one linked to Francis' illnesses and disabilities and the feminized perceptions of his body which resulted from them. Even as a man whose spiritual focus initially revolved around the notion of apostolic poverty, Francis displayed a more feminine somatic piety, particularly at the end of his life. *Pace* Bynum, Francis' experiential spirituality, linked though it was to an expression of apostolic poverty, *did* revolve around eucharistic piety, suffering, and extreme fasting, although this link was weakened in Bonaventure's official *life*. As in many female saints' *lives* of the later Middle Ages, the Francis of the oldest hagiographies displayed a mystical piety that emphasized a direct relationship with God, without priestly meditation. That Francis exhibited patterns of piety that would come to be more associated with female saints (or could be written as doing so) can be attributed to the social feminization the saint experienced himself, likely as a result of his illnesses and infirmities. Francis' leaky, imperfect, impaired body rendered him ineligible to act in the typically masculine arena of clerical power. Instead, by highlighting his nearness and accessibility to God through physical suffering and devotion, his hagiographers attempted to assert that he had a higher authority, one that eclipsed the authority granted through traditional channels. Francis' nearness to God ensured that he retained a spiritual authority that allowed him some access to the halls of religious power which would otherwise have been closed to him both as a non-prelate and as a disabled person.

That Francis' infirmities and disabilities allowed his body to be read as humorally feminine needs some discussion. Of course, Francis was anatomically and physiologically male, but as Christ's pierced and tortured body was in some ways read as feminized, so was Francis'. In the modern world, there is little doubt that the presence of an impairment, especially a readily apparent impairment, and perceptions about am impaired persons' gender performance intersect. This appears to be particularly true for infirm men, especially those who have experienced a sudden impairment, such as the loss of a limb or paralysis.[47] In their foundational study on the subject, Thomas Gerschick and Adam Miller suggest that disabled men react to the ideals of what they termed "hegemonic masculinity" in different ways. Some accept the necessity of exhibiting these characteristics.[48] Others modifiy or "reformulat" these ideals to suit their own experiences.[49] Still others "reject" hegemonic masculinity entirely. Instead those men subscribe to alternative forms of masculinity,[50] which can could challenge hegemonic masculinity, or create yet another "other" against which hegemonic, heterosexual masculinity is constantly defined. Since the publication of Gerschick and Miller's study, many other scholars from various disciplines have noted that disabled men often feel the need to meet the characteristics of hegemonic masculinity, characteristics such as virility and strength, and when they cannot, they feel, in some way, "othered" and, at times, emasculated.[51] In the words of Tom Shakespeare, "white heterosexual men construct themselves in opposition to women, nature, black people, gay men." Thus "masculine ideology rests on a negation of vulnerability, weakness and, ultimately, even the body itself." Shakespeare then suggests that a disabled body is one of the things against which heterosexual men define themselves.[52] In keeping with the two (dominant)-sex model of gender that posits a relatively stark separation of gender identities, neither Gerschick and Miller nor Shakespeare argue explicitly that disabled male bodies can be read as feminized; rather they are other or subaltern.

Other scholars clearly link perceptions of the disabled other and perceptions of the feminine. For Rosemarie Garland-Thomson, the same characterizations that mark woman as "other" are those that mark a person as disabled.[53] This link, she argues, is embedded within Aristotle's formulation of woman as malformed man, inextricably linking disability and the feminine.[54] Both disabled bodies and feminine bodies, for Garland-Thomson are read as inferior to what she terms "normate" bodies, and their access to agency is thus affected. However, Garland-Thomson's work also highlights the complexity of reading disabled bodies in any culture, for disabled bodies can be read in multiple ways simultaneously, sometimes engendering them with power by their very difference, as she demonstrates in the case for Toni Morrison's character Eva Peace.[55] Francis' stigmatized and broken body was also read in different ways – as the body of a living martyr devoted to God and as the body of a broken man unable to summon the stamina to continue to lead his order.

Other scholars have used Garland-Thomson's ideas and categories to examine linkages between how disabled bodies are represented and and how they are perceived in different societies. Thus, Catherine Kudlick has argued that Jean-Denise Jameu, a blind cloth merchant who lived in Paris in the eighteenth century, was treated in ways a woman might have been treated, both by his wife and by the courts.[56] Tory Pearman has argued that medieval English literature represents women's bodies as inherently disabled, but that a disabled body also could allow for spiritual growth, as it did in the case of Margery Kempe.[57] None of these authors, however, explicitly suggest a disabled male body was in any way read as physically feminized, even as they were read in such a way socially and politically.

In the premodern West, where the dominance of Aristotle in the universities was not seriously challenged until the late sixteenth century and where differences in gender seemed less rigidly defined as separate and untouchable (though anatomical sex remained so), the link between disability and femininity seems even more clear. To be sure, Irina Metzler has recently argued that, in the medieval world as in the modern, disabled people were seen as "asexual" and "defined by their impairment and not by their male and female traits,"[58] but this position seems a bit rigid and, in light of the Aristotelian conceptions of gender, unlikely to be absolutely true in the Middle Ages. As Metzler herself has argued, in the context of the medieval world, being productive was regarded as critical, certainly for survival but also to demonstrate that a person was toiling, as God had decreed, as a necessary punishment after the fall.[59] To be productive was to be active, a characteristic Aristotle had attributed to males rather than females.[60] Passivity of any sort, sexual or otherwise, was perceived as a feminine trait.[61] Thus, some impaired individuals who were unable to be productive members of society, who had perhaps been reduced to begging outside their parish church, were regarded as socially and economically (and perhaps physiologically) passive, a characteristic more often linked with women than men. Not only were Aristotle's theories of sex and gender, highlighted (but not systematized) in his biological works as well as his *Ethics* and *Politics*, tremendously influential in medieval universities in the High Middle Ages, his linking of femininity and passivity seems to have reached far beyond the classroom.

Medieval medical theory fit well with Aristotle's position on sex and gender. This is perhaps not surprising given that the building blocks of medieval humoral theory predate Aristotle and that, indeed, Aristotle incorporated them into his works.[62] The second-century physician Galen, whose articulation of humoral theory in *De temperamentis* became the backbone of medieval humoral theory, referenced Aristotle regularly. Humoral theory, as Galen and his followers defined it, can also support the link between passivity and illness and/or impairment. Basic humoral theory in the Middle Ages held that every individual was made up of a complexion of the (usually) four natural humours: blood, phlegm, black bile or *melancholia*, and yellow bile. Complexions were further differentiated by non-natural elements, such as climate, age, exercise, and diet.[63] Normal, healthy complexions could be dominated by an individual humour; hence individuals could be characterized as phlegmatic, melancholic, sanguine, or choleric, descriptions which still resonate today. In general, heat was regarded as the most necessary element of life and vitality, and men were believed to have more innate heat in comparison to women. The widespread acceptance of humoral theory and Aristotle's ideas on gender in the High Middle Ages created a context in which the feminine gender and disability could be aligned. The medieval emphasis on the complementarity of masculinity, heat, and activity, juxtaposed with femininity, coolness, and passivity, allowed medieval society to read disabled bodies as embodying more feminine characteristics than able bodies.

In humoral theory, men, especially young men or those in the prime of their life, tend to be dominated by yellow bile or blood, humours that allowed men to be active and passionate. In contrast, women were thought to be dominated by the wetter and cooler humours of phlegm and black bile.[64] One's age intersected with the expectations of humoral balance based on gender; younger individuals, regardless of sex, were expected to have more blood or choler, while more mature people would be dominated more by melancholy, or, in the last stages of life, by phlegm.[65] Aging was thought to be caused by a gradual drying out of the body, with an infusion of *melancholia* and/or phlegm at the end of life.[66] In spite of this, women, who were generally considered cooler and moister than men, were thought to age more rapidly than men.[67] While this notion may be linked to a general perception that a woman's youth was dependent upon her reproductive capabilities,[68] in terms of humoral theory, it was explained by women's tendency towards the cooler complexions that became dominant in maturity and old age. In any case, in terms of humoral theory, as men aged, their complexion became coloured with more black bile and phlegm, humours more commonly associated with women. Like women, they became more passive than men in the prime of their life. As Gail Kern Paster has noted, in the premodern world, the single most important characteristic that differentiated men and women in terms of humoral theory was heat.[69] As heat waned in an aging male body, that body became feminized, in humoral if not anatomical terms.

Within humoral theory, illness and disability were most generally caused by an imbalance in the humoral complexion of an individual. Such an imbalance could be an overabundance or deficiency of a particular humour. Yet, certain humoral complexions were thought to be more prone to illness, especially the phlegmatic and the melancholic.[70]

Unsurprisingly, given the higher prevalence of disability and illness in older people both today and in the Middle Ages, these were the humours believed to dominate in maturity and old age, which, as noted above, were also the humours most closely associated with women. Thus, as Tory Pearman has noted, women were always in some way regarded as disabled (men) in medieval society.[71] Medieval humoral theory, then, created a nexus which linked disability, old age, and femininity.

Yet even disabilities that occurred as the result of accidents or war wounds, rather than age, had a feminizing effect. Literary theorists such as Kathleen Kelly have suggested that in Arthurian romance, at least, men managed potential identification and empathy with their combatants in tournaments or the battlefield by understanding a body wounded by swords as feminine rather than masculine. A pierced bleeding body was understood by others in the narrative to be, in the moment of wounding, at least, feminine and passive, and fundamentally unlike the active male bodies of the unwounded knights.[72] This position has been challenged by Kenneth Hodges, who argues that knights in romances who overcame their wounds could assert their masculinity even more strongly.[73] However, both Kelly and Hodges were examining knights in literature whose wounds healed and allowed them to fight again. If the wounds did not heal, the knight perished. There was no place in Arthurian romance, it appears, for a permanently disabled knight who could no longer fight. Even the Fisher King was eventually healed though note that while he was wounded his role was largely passive, save for fishing. Even to fish, he first had to be carried down from his bed to the boat and set out on the sea.[74]

In the real medieval world, outside of literature, permanently disabled veterans of war were surely a reality. Indeed, archaeological evidence suggests that many, perhaps most, of the wounds sustained in battle were healed, meaning that a majority of individuals survived battlefield wounds.[75] However, there has been precious little written about the life experiences of these survivors.[76] Unsurprisingly, those few injured warriors who are found in historical records remained active in military life.[77] More such warriors are found in the archaeological record.[78] But those whose injuries were so severe that their previous way of living was not a possibility for them seem to virtually disappear from the historical record. Both Carole Rawcliffe and Irina Metzler suggest that most soldiers who became too injured to fight were often reduced to begging.[79] Interestingly, Metzler notes that a knight who returned home seriously injured was described (in a letter asking those who read it to support the wounded knight) as *impotens*,[80] a word that by the Middle Ages had come to mean disabled, but retained its earlier meaning of powerless and connotations of sexual dysfunction.[81] While the word choice appears to make its meaning ambiguous, in fact such a description perfectly captures the fundamentally medieval link between ability, productivity, and masculinity.

Practising Piety in the Feminine Mode

In the Middle Ages there were exceptions to the general rules about gender established above. Issues of disability and gender did not always play out in the same way in discussions of Jesus and even of the saints. Caroline Walker Bynum has famously noted that medieval textual and visual representations of Christ focus on his materiality, in some ways feminizing him.[82] Leah deVun has argued that late medieval texts sometimes regarded Jesus as a hermaphrodite, able to embody "a unity of contrary parts – the human and the divine, the male and female" – much in the way that alchemists believed the philosopher's stone embodied a perfect unity of contraries.[83] While this reading of a holy body balancing both masculine and feminine characteristics is less likely in the case of male saints, especially founder-saints,[84] it still must be kept in mind as we explore Francis' particular traits. As noted at the beginning of this chapter, Francis' piety embodies many typically feminine features. In medieval texts, female saints, by their very nature, were regarded as more embodied than men. Francis, too, in many ways, lived an experienced, embodied, spiritual life. This is, indeed, a hallmark of his spirituality.[85] Modern readers sometimes need to be reminded of Francis' embodied spirituality, in spite of the suffering, eucharistic piety, and forms of abstinence and fasting described in early *lives* of the saint, because he was anatomically male. The shadow of Aristotle is long. But an infirm, chronically ill Francis is an embodied Francis and a feminized Francis.

Holy Feast and Holy Fast outlines several markers of feminine piety. These include an embodied spirituality which featured focus on control of food, borne of women's associations with food preparation and as nursing mothers; a strong devotion to the eucharist, again borne of the eucharist's association with food; and ascetic acts to discipline the body and suffering on account of illness and impairment rather than athletic ascetic feats. The early *lives* of Francis suggest he embodied all of these markers of a more "feminine" medieval spirituality.

That Francis' religious life centred around the idea of apostolic poverty cannot be doubted. But food, both its renunciation and its necessity in times of ill health, are a consistent theme in most early *lives* of Francis written before Bonaventure's official *life*. No fewer than ten episodes of Francis' illness are linked in some way to food. For instance, early *lives*, such as the *Vita prima* and the *Legend of the Three Companions*, suggest that, just after his conversion, Francis' former friends thought he was mad, as his body had become so emaciated.[86] On another occasion, Francis was unable to complete his journey to Bevegna because he was so weak from fasting.[87] The *Assisi Compilation* reiterates Francis' refusal of food and medicine even when he was ill.[88] Later *lives*, like Bonaventure's *Legenda maior* and the *Actus beati Francisci in Valle Reatina*, note that Francis hardly ever ate cooked food when he was healthy.[89] Of course this implies that he did eat cooked food when he was ill, although the later *lives* do not note such instances. The earlier *lives* do, however, record several situations in which Francis was forced to adjust his ascetic food habits owing to his weakened state: when the priest at San Damiano recognized Francis' delicate constitution and brought him special food,[90] when his companions begged him to eat while he was sick in the bishop's palace at Assisi,[91] when he ate chicken while ill and then later confessed it dramatically,[92] and when he ate food cooked in lard rather than oil.[93]

Desires for various foods also featured in Francis' last days as he struggled with illness and infirmity. The *Remembrance of the Desire of a Soul* recounts how, during his final illness, Francis wanted to eat some parsley. The cook at the Porziuncula replied that he had been picking parsley constantly and did not think he could find any at night. By some miracle, though, he found some parsley, which Francis then ate.[94] This reference to Francis eating parsley at the end of his life is interesting for several reasons. Its mention in the *Remembrance* could be a trope; parsley had long been linked with death in the Mediterranean world. Further, it was a known to aid in passing urine; Galen, for instance, had recommended it for dropsy, the swelling of the limbs from which Francis was said to have suffered at the end of his life. Finally, humorally, it was considered warm and dry, and was thus recommended to older people and to those with cooler and moister temperaments.[95] A second request on Francis' behalf for special food was not linked to medicinal care, but simply reflected a desire to taste a favoured treat once more, a morsel of which he enjoyed on his deathbed.[96]

Several episodes in the earliest and most reliable *lives* of Francis suggest that food and its renunciation were of rather central importance to Francis' pious practices. Other practices were equally important of course, especially the renunciation of wealth and the living of a mendicant life, but this ought not to obscure the fact that food and fasting, and especially Francis' worry over food, are present in nearly all early *lives* of the saint. It is a reasonably central part of Francis' own devotional piety.

Interestingly, while early *lives* of Francis do not generally emphasize the importance the saint placed on seeing and receiving the body and blood of Christ, his own surviving writings do.[97] The eucharist was an important component of Francis' own understanding of his religious devotion, especially towards the end of his life. This is most clearly seen in comparing the two recensions of Francis' *Letter to the Faithful*. In the shorter version of the *Letter*, Francis hardly mentions the eucharist, noting only that failure to receive it is among the many sins of those who are not living in penance.[98] Yet, in the longer (and perhaps later) redaction, the eucharist was a central concern. In this letter Francis spends some time discussing the importance of Christ's sacrifice and linking it to the reception of the eucharist.[99] Francis then outlines the necessity of the receiving of communion for salvation. "Accordingly, we must confess all our sins to a priest. And we should receive the body and blood of our Lord, Jesus Christ, from him, since those who do not eat his flesh or drink his blood are not able to enter the Kingdom of God."[100] Francis continues to emphasize the importance of the eucharist to salvation and to the importance of the priests who administer communion. Because this position became the cornerstone of some of his later writing, it is worth translating in full.

> Also, we ought to visit churches frequently and to venerate and revere clerics, not so much because they are sinners but on account of their office and administration of the most holy body and blood of Christ, which they sacrifice on the altar and receive and administer to others. And we should all firmly understand that since no one is able to be saved except through the holy words and blood of our Lord, Jesus Christ, whom clerics proclaim, announce, and minister. And they alone ought to minister and not others.[101]

The importance of the eucharist and of the priests who administer it is repeated in almost the same language in other later texts written by Francis. In his *First Letter to the Custodians*, Francis wrote that the custodians should ask their clergy to revere "the most Holy Body and Blood of our Lord Jesus Christ and his holy names and the written words that sanctify His Body."[102] The letter again emphasized the importance of doing penance and receiving the eucharist for personal salvation. So important did Francis believe this message to be that he wrote a second letter to the custodians shortly afterward, in which he asked that bishops and other members of the clergy be given the first letter, which reflected upon, in the words of Francis, "the most holy Body and Blood of our Lord." Nearer the date of his death, Francis reiterated the importance of celebrating the eucharist with a pure heart during mass,[103] and included a discussion of the true body of Christ being in the eucharist in the first of his *Admonitions*.[104] In it, Francis explicitly linked salvation with recognizing Christ's body in the eucharist. Indeed, this point is hammered home several times in the text. Just as Christ had been flesh and blood, seen by the apostles, so too was the eucharist flesh and blood. The last paragraph is yet another recapitulation, but lovely in its parallelisms:

> And just as those who only saw [Christ's] flesh through the sense of [their own human] flesh, but contemplating him with spiritual eyes believed that he was God, so we, seeing the bread and wine with corporeal eyes, should see and believe firmly that they are the most sacred body and living and true blood. And in such a way, the Lord is always with his faithful, just as he said, "Lo, I am with you until the end of the age."[105]

It is possible, and most likely correct, to read Francis' emphasis on the importance of penance and the eucharist as part of the church's program of reform and as a way to emphasize the importance of the sacrament in the wake of its rejection by heretical groups. Indeed, several of the texts above note that denial of the necessity of the eucharist, or the reality of transubstantiation, will result in condemnation.[106]

In his final work, the *Testament*, as in his longer *Letter to the Faithful*, Francis again emphasizes the importance of priests in the transmission of the sacrament, and that it is their office and position, rather than their personal rectitude, which should inspire trust and veneration. In the *Testament*, Francis writes of priests that "he [did] not want to consider any sin in them because [he] discern[ed] the son of God in them and they [were] his Lords."[107] He goes on to once more emphasize the corporeality of the eucharist and reiterate the importance of the priestly role in the sacrament. "And on account of this," Francis notes, "I act [as though priests were his Lords] since I see nothing corporeally of the highest son of God himself in this world except his most holy body and his most holy blood, which [priests] receive and which they alone minister to others."[108] The echoes of similar phrasing in his letters, in the *Admonitions* and in the *Testament*, suggest that centrality of the eucharist, and the important place priests had in administering it was a central message of Francis' teachings. Certainly, both were included, in part, to combat heretical beliefs, but such theological and political awareness on Francis' part does not negate the centrality of the eucharist in Francis' writings. To be sure, he did not, like later medieval mystics such as Catherine of Siena, subsist wholly on the eucharist or have visions of the bleeding host. Francis' emphasis was different and clearly more tied to doctrinal concerns. And, of course, there were other important aspects of Francis' devotion, especially his apostolic poverty. However, discussions of the importance of the eucharist for salvation figures in 11 of 28, or 39 per cent, of Francis' known works. When songs, prayers, and offices are removed, one can find the discussion in 10 of 16 works, or 62.5 per cent, of the letters, rules, and other exhortatory writings of the saint. Clearly, reception of the eucharist was of crucial importance to Francis, not as a meal[109] but as a symbol of faith and salvation.

That Francis, whose love of Christ was literally written on his body in the shape of Christ's wounds, practised a somatic piety cannot be doubted. Yet Francis' relationship with his body was not one of easy acceptance. His early writings speak of a mind and soul which hated the vices and sins of the body, and name the flesh as an enemy of salvation – a flesh that must be chastised and disciplined into submission.[110] Thus, he practised rigorous asceticism and, in his earliest works, encouraged others to do the same. "Let us chastise our body by crucifying it with its vices, sins, and desires," Francis wrote in an early edition of his *Regula non bullata*.[111] Although other versions of the RNB do not include this phrasing, they do suggest one ought to hate one's body as a site of potential sin.[112]

Looking to the earliest *lives* of Francis, it is clear that he practised a severe asceticism, at least when his health permitted and perhaps even when it did not. The *Assisi Compilation*, in particular, notes several times that Francis practised rigorous asceticism and refused to look to his body's needs in terms of comfort, food, or medicines.[113] So severe was Francis' earliest asceticism that the *Legend of the Three Companions* notes that on account of it, "at the very day of his death, [Francis] confessed that he had sinned greatly against his brother body."[114] This was, unsurprisingly, a problematic statement in a hagiographic text, but it does illustrate a constant theme found in Francis' own writings, that the body, as the locus of sin, was to be hated and controlled. The *Assisi Compilation* responds directly to the above passage in the *Legend of the Three Companions*, reassuring its readers that Francis did not sin in his treatment of his body. The passage, which ostensibly reports Francis' own words, notes that one should ensure that the needs of "Brother Body" are met so that one can continue to function.

If, however, on account of lack or poverty, Brother Body is not able to have its necessities in sickness or in health, after he had honestly and with humility sought his necessities from his brother or his prelate, and they were not given to him, he should patiently sustain this for his love of the

Lord and it will be charged to him by the Lord for his witness for Christ (*martyrio*). And since he did what is his [to do], namely that he sought out his necessity, he is excused from sin, even if his body is thus more ailed.[115]

This passage is interesting, not least because it is clearly an answer to the idea found in the LTC that Francis sinned against his body by practising severe acts of asceticism. The passage is also exhortatory, encouraging followers of Francis to at least try to ensure that their bodily needs were met. In this it agrees with another, authenticated, passage of the *Assisi Compilation* that suggests Francis encouraged moderation in his followers but was severely ascetic himself.[116] It also, however, demonstrates that Francis' asceticism was known to have caused him to experience more severe illnesses.

While Francis' ascetic practices are discussed in early *lives* of the saint, a far more common theme is his acceptance of illness as a way of devoting himself to God. Francis' first rule encouraged sick brothers to thank God for their illnesses and to remember that God corrects with ailments of the body. For this reason, Francis argued, one should not seek out medical attention too quickly.[117] Francis himself practised this approach, as he had to be strongly encouraged – indeed, one might say forced – to seek medical treatment for his ailing eyes.

Francis' patient suffering of disease allowed him to be linked to the suffering Christ by his hagiographers. This is a common trope of all early *lives*, even Bonaventure's *Legenda maior*. Thomas of Celano's *Vita prima* has Francis comparing the suffering he is experiencing to martyrdom and finding suffering his illness more difficult.[118] The *Remembrance of the Desire of a Soul* goes further, recording a vision seen by members of the Franciscan Order the night the saint died. In the vision the brothers saw both Francis and Christ as one person.[119] Francis' image was superimposed over Christ's. Indeed, with the exception of the *Assisi Compilation*, which focuses much more closely on Francis as a holy man, most early *lives* of Francis deliberately demonstrate Francis' affinity to Christ, not only in terms of the miracles he performed, but also in terms of his suffering, especially in the years after he was reported to have received the *stigmata*.[120]

In the early part of his converted life, Francis also ministered to the sick. One of Francis' earliest acts as a man newly devoted to God was to live among and minister to the lepers of his community. Francis himself notes that he did so because he had found the sight of lepers "bitter," and that after he had lived with them, "what had seemed bitter was changed into sweetness of the mind and body for me."[121] The *Vita prima* describes Francis' time with the lepers, noting especially the care that Francis visited upon the lepers' bodies. [Francis] served all of them most diligently on account of [his love for] God, and wiped away "all rottenness, sores, and puss from them."[122] In the *Assisi Compilation* Francis scolds a fellow brother for taking lepers with many sores to church, since "men are accustomed to abhor lepers who have many wounds."[123] Francis immediately recognized the error in his statement and confessed his sins to Peter Catani, whom the text states was minister general at the time.[124] Francis declared that, as penance, he would eat from the same dish as the leper. The *Assisi Compilation* spends some time describing the event itself, noting that the leper with whom Francis shared his dish "was wholly wounded and ulcerated, and his fingers, especially, with which he ate, were drawn in and bloody so that when [the leper] cast his fingers into the bowl, blood flowed into it."[125] In spite of Bynum's characterization of this episode as "eating with a leper,"[126] it is far closer in its description to some of the acts of later female saints, such as Angela of Foligno and Catherine of Siena, who licked pus from the wounds of the sick for whom they cared.[127] Although the discussion of Francis' interaction with people with leprosy is less graphic in the *Remembrance of the Desire of a Soul*, it does describe how Francis regularly gave alms and kissed them on the hands and mouth.[128]

Demonstrating Power in the Feminine Mode

The examples above suggest that Francis' brand of spirituality had a great deal in common with modes of piety more often associated with women than men in the High and Late Middle Ages. While Francis' devotion to the eucharist was perhaps driven by a desire to correct heretics, hagiographic descriptions of Francis' approach to food, his passive acceptance of illness, and care of people with leprosy all reflect acts and practices that came to be more commonly associated with female mystics than male saints. Yet Francis himself appears not to have used his highly embodied spirituality as a source for any authority he might project. That was left to his hagiographers, though the authority he gained in such texts was always personal, not institutional.

Initially, of course, Francis had formal authority within his order. He wrote the *Rule*, chose who was accepted into the brotherhood, and generally determined the spiritual and secular directions of the order. If Michael Cusato is correct, Francis' functional authority as the leader of the order was strengthened when he was formally accepted into the lower secular orders as a deacon.[129] Even without that formal rank, in the early years of his the Franciscan foundation, Francis frequently interacted with bishops and cardinals and had regular access to the members of the *magisterium*. As the male founder of a papally approved order, as a deacon, and one associated with access to prelates, Francis had access to traditional modes of power within the medieval Catholic Church. That changed, however, when Francis withdrew from the leadership of his order.

After Francis refused to continue his leadership role, the saint was slowly excluded from the normative routes to power he had previously accessed. He was forced to find other ways to influence members of his order. Michael Cusato suggests that he began to emphasize his moral authority within the order. While he had remained in a leadership role, Francis had exerted both functional and moral authority, but upon his resignation, he was left only with moral authority.[130] Testimonies, especially in the *Assisi Compilation* and the *Remembrance*, suggest that, at times, Francis regretted giving up his functional authority.[131] While this may reflect the frustration of the authors about the direction the order had taken by the 1240s, it also may indicate a genuine desire on the part of Francis to take back functional authority within the order. Certainly it indicates regret on the part of Francis' companions that the founder of their order had given up his formal, functional authority.

Francis himself appears not to have used his embodied spirituality, nor his affinity to Christ through his suffering, as a source for his moral authority. Rather, he used the example of his life and his mystical knowledge of God's will as such a source. Francis' frustration that he was no longer able to direct the order unilaterally can be seen in his writings to the order, which increased dramatically in number after 1220. These letters became more strident as he saw fissures developing between his vision for the order and how the already large and rapidly growing order was being governed, actual governance of an order that included thousands of people.[132] His early biographers, however, saw another way of demonstrating the saint's religious authority – illustrating the saint's likeness to Christ and writing God's approval of Francis' life and deeds directly on his body.

The process of linking Francis to Christ began with Elias of Cortona's testimony of the *stigmata*, written as a letter to the order upon Francis' death. Elias wrote:

> Not long before [Francis'] death, our father and brother appeared crucified. He carried on his body five wounds which were truly the *stigmata* of Christ. For his hands and feet had the puncturing of nails, pierced through from each side, holding onto scars, and showing the black of nails. And his side appeared to be lanced and often leaked out blood.[133]

While Elias' testimony was initially contested by some, confirmation that Francis bore the wounds of Christ given to him by a seraph at La

Verna in 1224 is present in Francis' first official *life* and every other *life* written thereafter. In 1237, an initial doubter of the *stigmata*, Hugolino of Ostia, then Pope Gregory IX, mentioned them in three different proclamations, though his reversal likely had more to do with political considerations than a true belief in the saint's wounds of Christ.[134] According to the early *lives*, Francis' way of life, his modes of expressing his devotion to God, had received approval from the highest of authorities, one that no secular authority, even the pope himself, could deny. God's approval of Francis was literally written on his body in his wounds which mimicked Christ's own. In this way, the early biographers could suggest Francis' lack of what Cusato calls functional authority was ultimately unimportant. He had approval from a higher authority. Yet, this authority derived from God's approval was always formulated as a personal rather than institutional authority. Never do early authors of Francis' formal *lives* suggest that Francis' vision for his order must be correct because he had received the *stigmata*.

It should come as no surprise, then, that Francis' *lives* bear similarities to those of later women saints composed in the High Middle Ages. Like Francis, their bodies were regarded as inherently problematic, cooler and wetter than the ideal, leaky, uncontrollable, and inherently disabled. Like the Francis in the hagiographies, women sought direct contact with God himself, and received his direct approval through mystical revelations. In the High Middle Ages, women, far more than men, carried the *stigmata*.[135] Like these women, Francis channelled his apparent nearness to God into personal authority. Indeed, as Grace Jantzen has argued, devotional practices such as caring for the seriously ill and outcast of society as Christ had done, suffering in an imitation of Christ's experience on the cross, and extreme fasting and eucharistic devotion allowed women to access non-traditional channels of authority.[136] One need only look to the example of Catherine of Siena, who at times was capable of directing even the pope, to see the veracity of this claim.

That Francis, who suffered like Christ and who received God's clear approval through the reception of the *stigmata* on his infirm body and, in doing so, *was* able to effect some change, fits into this feminine mode of establishing authority seems clear. That this affinity to the feminine is based in medieval Umbrian and Tuscan perceptions of similarities between women and a sick and impaired Francis can only be made visible if we understand how Francis' infirm body would be regarded in the Middle Ages – as unproductive, passive, and feminized. Reading Francis' own writings and his early *lives* through the lens of disability theory makes this affinity that much clearer.

Postscript: On the Importance of Disability as a Category of Analysis

Like all books written about the saint, this one does not present the historical truth about Francis. Instead, it offers a particular reading of Francis, highlighting aspects of his life as recorded in early Franciscan sources that have traditionally been marginalized. It is not a corrective. It is one of many perspectives that allow a glimpse of what the life of the historical Francis might have been like: a man who struggled to humble himself for God, a man who struggled to balance the needs of his growing order with his desire for his followers to lead a life of absolute apostolic poverty, and, yes, a man who struggled with impairments and infirmities, and their implications, all of his life.

Reading Francis' life through the lens of disability significantly alters the way many events in his life can be interpreted. It recentres the saint's illnesses in his life and insists that they and the social responses to them be read as a part of the saint's lived experience. It challenges the traditional narrative of Francis' humility and authority found in both medieval hagiographies and modern biographies of the saint. Further, it forces us to see that the very infirmities that enabled Francis' hagiographers to link the saint's suffering to Christ's own, and from which Francis appeared to have derived some personal power and authority, also resulted in his being barred access to the traditional masculine modes of authority, both in the leadership of the order and in the hierarchy of the Catholic Church. The lens of disability also makes the role of the guardian more explicable and makes visible the desperation with which Franciscan leadership sought to cure Francis' encroaching blindness. It demonstrates the care with which allusions to Francis' illnesses and infirmities were glossed or elided in later versions of the saint's life, especially Bonaventure's *Legenda maior*. Above all, it highlights the need for scholars to acknowledge that Francis was ill for most of his converted life, impaired and in the constant care of doctors for his last two years, and to recognize that these realities had an impact on the saint's lived experience beyond his spirituality.

That this work has provided some radically different conclusions about events in Francis' life is, in itself, support for arguments made by Catherine Kudlick, Kim Nielson, Lennard Davis, and others that disability must be added to the historian's usual categories of social analysis of race, class, and gender.[1] Paying attention to disability, rather than marginalizing it from methodological considerations or historical analyses, adds richness and nuance to our understanding of the past, not just about medicine and illness but about all aspects of past cultures. Surely it is time for disability analysis to become an integral part of the historian's tool box.

Recentring Illness: A Revised Chronology of Francis' Life

Date	Event
Date	**Event**
ca. 1204	Francis is captured as a prisoner of war by Perugian forces.
ca. 1205	Francis' release as a prisoner of war is negotiated, likely because he is ill.
1205–1208	Francis converts to religious life.
ca. 1208	Francis' body is weakened by his ascetic activities. The priest at San Damiano offers him medicines and foods to strengthen his weakened body. Francis' friends and family believe his ascetic activities have impaired him physiologically and psychologically.
ca. 1209	Francis travels to Rome to have his *Rule* approved.
ca. 1210	Francis spends time working with lepers in a hospital near Assisi.
1213–1214	Francis is stricken with an illness in Spain while travelling to Morocco.
1214	Francis is stricken with a second illness while on his way home from Spain.
Before 1218	Francis is sick at the bishop's palace in Assisi (while he is still receiving brothers into the order himself).
1219	Francis travels to Egypt and contracts an eye ailment.
ca. 1220	Francis returns from Egypt; he is so weak he needs to ride a donkey while travelling through Italy.
ca. 1220	Francis does penance for eating chicken while ill.
ca. 1221	Hugolino dei Conti di Segni, bishop of Ostia, becomes protector of the Franciscan Order.
ca. 1221	Francis resigns from leading the Franciscan Order, at least in part on account of his illnesses and infirmities. At the same time he receives a guardian, whom he swears to obey in all things.

1221–1224	Francis spends time in contemplation and preaching, but often travels with the aid of a mule or donkey owing to mobility issues.
1224	Francis has his vision of the seraph at La Verna. His hagiographers will suggest he received the *stigmata* of Christ at this time.
1224	Francis relaxes the "rigour of his life" owing to his illnesses and infirmities.
1225	Francis seeks treatment for his eye impairment in Assisi, having been ordered to do so by Elias of Cortona and Cardinal Hugolino.
1226	Francis seeks treatment for his eye impairment at Rieti.
1226	Francis travels to Siena in the company (care?) of a physician.
1226	Francis receives specialized eye care from an eye doctor in Siena.
1226	Francis falls seriously ill, experiencing ailments of the stomach, liver, and spleen.
1226	Francis is carried back from Siena to Cortona, as he is too frail to walk.
1226	Francis is moved to the bishop's palace in Assisi.
1226	Francis asks to be moved to the Porziuncula in preparation for his death. He asks for Lady Jacoba de Settesoli of Rome to be informed of his death; she visits him.
1226	Francis dies at the age of approximately 46.

Notes

Introduction

1 As much as possible, this book uses terminology found in early
   hagiographies of St. Francis. The most commonly used term to describe
   Francis' experiences of chronic illness and physiological distress is *infirmitas*,
   which I have most often translated as its cognate "infirmity," and on occasion,
   when the circumstances of the discussion suggest it, illness or impairment.
   I avoid using the term disability to describe Francis' experiences since I find
   the distinction made by proponents of the social model of disability helpful.
   On the multiplicity of ways *infirmitas* was understood in the Middle Ages, see
   Jenni Kuuliala, Katariina Mustakallio, and Christian Krötzl, "Introduction:
   Infirmitas in Antiquity and the Middle Ages," in *Infirmity in Antiquity and the
   Middle Ages*, ed. Jenni Kuuliala, Katariina Mustakallio, and Christian Krötzl,
   1–11 (Abingdon: Routledge, 2016), 5–6.
2 On this phenomenon, see Bill Hughes, "Medicine and the Aesthetic
   Invalidation of Disabled People," *Disability and Society* 15:4 (2000), 555–68, 558.
3 While Davis seems to have meant that one's own disabilities dare not be
   spoken of in professional circles, his discussion of the poor attendance
   at conference talks on the topic of disability suggests that, until recently,
   disability itself was not discussed as a category of analysis by the majority
   of scholars. Lennard J. Davis, *Enforcing Normalcy: Disability, Deafness and
   the Body* (London and New York: Verso, 1995), xi.
4 Davis, *Enforcing Normalcy*, 1–49, 157.
5 The number of works dedicated to the importance of religious suffering
   in the Middle Ages is enormous. The most significant include Caroline
   Walker Bynum, *Holy Feast and Holy Fast: The Religious Significance of Food
   to Medieval Women* (Berkeley: University of California Press, 1987); Amy
   Hollywood, *The Soul as Virgin Wife: Mechtild of Magdeburg, Marguerite Porete
   and Meister Eckhart* (South Bend, IN: University of Notre Dame Press,
   1995); Ellen Ross, "'She Wept and Cried Right Loud for Sorrow and for

Pain': Suffering, the Spiritual Journey, and Women's Experience in Late
Medieval Mysticism," in *Maps of Flesh and Light: The Religious Experience
of Medieval Women Mystics*, ed. Ulrike Wiethaus, 45–59 (Syracuse, NY:
Syracuse University Press, 1993); Jo Ann McNamara, "The Need to Give:
Suffering and Female Sanctity in the Middle Ages," in *Images of Sainthood
in Medieval Europe*, ed. Renate Blumenfeld-Kosinski and Timea Szell,
199–221 (Ithaca, NY: Cornell University Press, 1991).

6 Irina Metzler, *A Social History of Disability in the Middle Ages: Cultural
Considerations of Physical Impairment* (Abingdon and New York: Routledge,
2013), 43–5.

7 As Lawrence Cunningham notes, this combination of active with
contemplative was especially common in the first generations of
Franciscans. See Lawrence Cunningham, *Francis of Assisi: Performing the
Gospel Life* (Grand Rapids, MI: William B. Eerdmans Publishing, 2004), 71–3.

8 André Vauchez, *François d'Assise: Entre histoire et mémoire* (Paris: Fayard, 2009).

9 André Vauchez, *Francis of Assisi: The Life and Afterlife of a Medieval Saint*,
trans. Michael Cusato (New Haven, CT: Yale University Press, 2012).

10 Augustine Thompson, *Francis of Assisi: A New Biography* (Ithaca, NY:
Cornell University Press, 2012).

11 For a discussion of the likely date, see Rosalind Brooke, *Early Franciscan
Government: Elias to Bonaventure* (Cambridge: Cambridge University Press,
1959), 76–7; and John Moorman, *A History of the Franciscan Order* (Oxford:
Clarendon Press, 1968), 51.

12 Vauchez, *Francis of Assisi*, 95.

13 Vauchez, *Francis of Assisi*, 95.

14 Vauchez, *Francis of Assisi*, 99.

15 Vauchez, *Francis of Assisi*, 125.

16 See Vauchez, *Francis of Assisi*, 131.

17 See Vauchez, *Francis of Assisi*, 140, 141.

18 In fact, Thompson says that Francis "resigned" as the leader of the
Franciscan Order at that time – a problematic statement as Francis had
no designated title within the Franciscan movement at the time. See Jean-
François Godet-Calogeras, "Francis of Assisi's Resignation: An Historical
and Philological Probe," in *Charisma und religiöse: Gemeinschaften im
Mittelalter*, ed. G. Andenna, M. Breitenstein, and G. Melville (Münster:
Verlag Münster, 2005), 281–300.

19 Thomson, *Francis of Assisi*, 78–9.

20 Jordan of Giano, *Chronica* in *Analecta Franciscana* (Quaracchi: Collegium S.
Bonaventurae, 1885), I.1–19, 7; English translation available in *Thirteenth
Century Chronicles*, trans. P. Hermann (Chicago: Franciscan Herald Press,
1984), 17–77, 33.

21 Thompson, *Francis of Assisi*, 89.

22 Thompson, *Francis of Assisi*, 113.
23 Thompson, *Francis of Assisi*, 191.
24 Thompson, *Francis of Assisi*, 127.
25 Thompson, *Francis of Assisi*, 113.
26 Thompson, *Francis of Assisi*, 127.
27 Thompson, *Francis of Assisi*, 118.
28 Michael Cusato, "Francis and the Franciscan Movement, 1181/82–1226," *The Cambridge Companion to Francis of Assisi*, ed. Michael J.P. Robson, 17–33 (Cambridge: Cambridge University Press, 2012), 29.
29 Cusato, "Francis and the Franciscan Movement," 31.
30 Cusato, "Francis and the Franciscan Movement," 31.
31 Cusato, "Francis and the Franciscan Movement," 31.
32 Thomas of Celano would have had access to Elias' letter to the entire order and, of course, oral testimony from those who knew the saint.
33 Michael Blastic, "Francis and His Hagiographic Tradition," in Robson, *The Cambridge Companion*, 71.
34 Steven J. McMichael, "Francis and the Encounter with the Sultan (1219)," in Robson, *The Cambridge Companion*, 127–42, 131.
35 Henri-Jacques Stiker, *A History of Disability*, trans. William Sayers (Ann Arbor, MI: University of Michigan Press, 2002), 83.
36 Angela Montford, *Health, Sickness, Medicine and the Friars in the Thirteenth and Fourteenth Centuries* (Aldershot: Ashgate, 2004), 5–7, 235.
37 This is true of both of Metzer's books on the topic of physical disability. See Irina Metzler, *Disability in Medieval Europe: Thinking about Physical Impairment during the High Middle Ages, 1100–1400* (Abingdon and New York: Routledge, 2006), 137–8; and Metzler, *A Social History of Disability in the Middle Ages*. In the latter text, Francis is discussed as a handy and well-known example of someone who adopted a life of voluntary poverty.
38 For a recent historiography of disability studies in the medieval world, see Rick Godden and Jonathan Hsy, "Encountering Disability in the Middle Ages," *New Medieval Literatures* 15 (2015), 314–39.
39 Julie Singer, "Disability and the Social Body," *Postmedieval: A Journal of Medieval Cultural Studies* 3:2 (2012), 135–41, 136.
40 Marno Retief and Rantoa Letšosa, "Models of Disability: A Brief Overview," *HTS Teologiese Studies/Theological Studies* 74:1 (2018), 1–8.
41 Singer, "Disability and the Social Body," 136.
42 Edward Wheatley, *Stumbling Blocks before the Blind: Medieval Constructions of a Disability* (Ann Arbor, MI: University of Michigan Press, 2010), 204–5.
43 Wheatley, *Stumbling Blocks*, 11.
44 On the complexity of medieval people's perceptions of links between sin and illness, see Metzler, *Disability in Medieval Europe*, 46–8.

45	Lateran IV, Canon 22. "Cum infirmitas corporalis non numquam ex peccato proveniat, dicente Domino, languido quem sanaverat: Vade et amplius noli peccare, ne deterius aliquid tibi contingat, decreto praesenti statuimus et districte praecipimus medicis corporum, ut cum eos ad infirmos vocari contigerit, ipsos ante omnia moneant et inducant, quod medicos advocent animarum, ut postquam infirmis fuerit de spirituali salute provisum, ad corporalis medicinae salubrium procedatur, cum causa cessante cesset effectus."

	The rest of the canon proceeds as follows: "Hoc quidem inter alia huic causam dedit edicto, quod quidam in aegritudinis lecto iacentes, cum eis a medicis suadetur, ut de animarum salute disponant, in desperationis articulum incidunt, unde facilius mortis periculum incurrunt. Si quis autem medicorum huius nostrae constitutionis postquam per praelatos locorum fuerit publicata, transgressor extiterit, tamdiu ab ingressu ecclesiae arceatur, donec pro transgressione huiusmodi satisfecerit competenter. Ceterum cum anima sit multo pretiosior corpore, subinterminatione anathematis prohibemus, ne quis medicorum pro corporali salute aliquid aegroto suadeat, quod in periculum animae conuertatur." See *Decrees of the Ecumenical Councils: Nicaea to Lateran V*, ed. N. Tanner. 2 vols. (Washington, DC: Georgetown University Press, 1990), 245–6. The English translation of this canon can be found in H.J. Schroeder, *Disciplinary Decrees of the General Councils: Text, Translation and Commentary* (St. Louis: B. Herder, 1937), 236–96. Now in public domain and available at http://www.fordham.edu/halsall/basis/lateran4.html. Accessed 15 July 2009. Although I have often included readily available English translations for many texts used herein, translations are my own unless otherwise stated.
46	Metzler, *Disability in Medieval Europe*, 9.
47	Metzler, *Disability in Medieval* Europe, 4–5. See also Singer, "Disability and the Social Body," 135.
48	On this, see Singer, "Disability and the Social Body," 136.
49	Julie Singer, "Towards a Transhuman Model of Medieval Disability," *Postmedieval: A Journal of Medieval Cultural Studies* 1:1–2 (2010), 173–9, 175–6.
50	Rosemarie Garland-Thomson, "Integrating Disability, Transforming Feminist Theory," in *Gendering Disability*, ed. Bonnie G. Smith and Beth Hutchison (New Brunswick, NJ: Rutgers University Press, 2004), 73–103, 77.
51	Little work has as yet been done in this field in the area of medieval studies. The only book-length study is Tory Vandeventer Pearman's *Woman and Disability in Medieval Literature* (New York: Palgrave MacMillan, 2010), which suggests that the female body was conflated with the disabled body in the High Middle Ages.
52	See, for instance, Garland-Thomson, "Integrating Disability," 78; Pearman, *Women and Disability*, 5; and Kristen Lindgren, "Bodies in Trouble: Identity, Embodiment and Disability," in *Gendering Disability*, ed. Bonnie G. Smith

and Beth Hutchison, 145–65. (New Brunswick, NJ: Rutgers University Press, 2004), 147.

53 This general understanding can be seen in much of Aristotle's corpus, but is perhaps most clearly laid out in his *On the Generation of Animals*, esp. I.2: I.20–1; II.1; II.3; IV.1–2. Aristotle, *On the Generation of Animals*, trans. Arthur Platt. eBooks@Adelaide available at http://ebooks.adelaide.edu.au/a/aristotle/generation/. University of Adelaide Library. Last updated 23 March 2013. Retrieved 17 September 2013. For a discussion of Aristotle's humoral hierarchy and its impact on his discussions of sex, see Joan Cadden, *Meanings of Sex Differences in the Middle Ages: Medicine, Science and Culture* (Cambridge: Cambridge University Press, 1993), 22–4.

54 Aristotle, *On the Generation of Animals*, II.3.

55 On this topic, see Cadden, *Meanings of Sex Differences*, 33.

56 Daniel J. Wilson, "Fighting Polio Like a Man: Intersections of Masculinity, Disability and Gender," in Smith and Hutchison, *Gendering Disability*, 121.

57 Catherine J. Kudlick, "'Disability' and 'Divorce': A Blind Parisian Cloth Merchant Contemplates His Options in 1756," in Smith and Hutchison, *Gendering Disability*, 134–4. (New Brunswick, NJ: Rutgers University Press, 2004).

58 Thomas J. Gerschick and Adam Stephen Miller, "Gender Identities at the Crossroads of Masculinity and Physical Disability," in *Toward a New Psychology of Gender*, ed. Mary M. Gergen and Sara N. Davis, 455–5 (Abingdon and New York: Routledge, 1997), 455.

59 Quotations are from *The Riverside Chaucer*, ed. Larry D. Benson. 3rd ed. (Boston: Houghton Mifflin, 1987), I(A), p. 35, ll. 675–91.

60 There is a long bibliography that examines the sex, gender, and sexuality of Chaucer's Pardoner. For overviews, see Robert S. Sturges, *Chaucer's Pardoner and Gender Theory: Bodies of Discourse* (New York: Palgrave, 2000), 35–59; and Vern L. Bullough with Gwen Whitehead Brewer, "Medieval Masculinities and Modern Interpretations: The Problem of the Pardoner," in *Conflicted Identities and Multiple Masculinities*, ed. J. Murray (New York, Taylor and Francis, 1999), 93–110.

61 Elspeth Whitney, "What's Wrong with the Pardoner: Complexion Theory, the Phlegmatic Man, and Effeminacy," *Chaucer Review* 45:4 (2011), 357–89.

62 Whitney, "What's Wrong with the Pardoner," 360.

63 See, for instance, Ruth Mazo Karras, *Sexuality in Medieval Europe: Doing unto Others*. 3rd ed. (Abingdon and New York: Routledge, 2017), 6. Joan Cadden, *Nothing in Nature Is Shameful: Sodomy and Science in Late Medieval Europe* (Philadelphia: University of Pennsylvania Press, 2013).

64 On the Pardoner as effeminate (and even gendered as female), see Henry Ansgar Kelly, "The Pardoner's Voice, Disjunctive Narrative, and Modes

of Effemination," in *Speaking Images: Essays in Honor of V.A. Kolve*, ed. R. Yeager and C. Morse (Asheville, NC: Pegasus Press, 2001), 411–44.

65 Francis of Assisi, *Epistola toti ordini missa*, 39, in FAS, 210–20, 218.

66 For a discussion of Francis' autographs, see Atillio Bartoli Langeli, *Gli Autografi di Frate Francesco e di Fratre Leone* (Turnhout: Brepols, 2000), 13–75; Jean-Baptiste Auberger, "A Short Note on the Autographs of Francis of Assisi," trans. E. Hagman, *Greyfriars Review* 17:1 (2004), 1–4.

67 For the most recent discussion of these sources, see Carlo Paolazzi, *Francisci Assisiensis: Scripta* (Grottaferrata: Collegi S. Bonaventurae, 2009).

68 Engelbert Grau, "Thomas of Celano: Life and Work,",trans. X.J. Seubert, *Greyfriars Review* 8:2 (1994), 177–200, 180.

69 Grau, "Thomas of Celano," 181.

70 This *vita* was reconstructed and posited by Jacques Dalarun in 2007 and was fortuitously confirmed in 2015, when a manuscript being auctioned was found to include a new life which paralleled much of what Dalarun had reconstructed. Moreover, since it had a dedication to Brother Elias, named as minister general of the Friars Minor, it can be dated with near certainty to between 1232 and 1239 – the dates of Elias' generalship. See Jacques Dalarun, "Thome Celanensis *Vita beati patris nostri Francisci (Vita Brevior)*: Presentation et edition critique," *Analecta Bollandiana* 133:1 (2015), 23–86, especially 23–33; and Jacques Dalarun, *The Rediscovered Life of Francis of Assisi*, trans. T. Johnson (St. Bonaventure, NY: Franciscan Institute Publications, 2016).

71 Dalarun, "Thome Celanensis," 33.

72 Théophile Desbonnets, *From Intuition to Institution: The Franciscans*, trans. Jerry DuCharme and Paul Duggan (Chicago: Franciscan Herald Press, 1988), 155–7.

73 "'Qui sunt isti,' ait, 'qui religionem meam et fratrum de meis manibus rapuerunt? Si ad generale capitulum venero, tunc eis ostendam qualem habeam voluntatem.'" VS 2.141.188. FA:ED 2.367, FF 607. This incident is lifted directly from the more informal *Assisi Compilation*, AC 44, FA:ED 2.145, FF 1517.

74 Rosalind Brooke, "Introduction," in *Scripta Leonis*, 55 ff. John Moorman, *The Sources for the Life of St. Francis of Assisi* (Manchester: Manchester University Press, 1970), 97–109.

75 David Burr, *The Spiritual Franciscans: From Protest to Prosecution in the Century after Francis* (University Park, PA: University of Pennsylvania Press, 2001), loc. 298 ff, Kindle.

76 See Brooke, "Introduction," 3–78.

77 See infra, 23–4.

78 Jordan of Giano, *Chronica* in *Analecta Franciscana*, I.1–19. English translation available in *Thirteenth Century Chronicles*, 17–77. On Jordan of Giano as a reliable narrator, see A.G. Little, "Chronicles of the Mendicant Friars," in A.G.

Little, *Franciscan Papers, Lists and Documents*, 25–41 (Manchester: Manchester University Press, 1943), 28–9; and Brooke, *Early Franciscan Government*, 20–7.

79 On Thomas of Celano's life, see Grau, "Thomas of Celano," 180–1.

80 Dalarun makes this point, while noting that Thomas of Celano's description of Francis' *stigmata* as protuberances of flesh that looked like nails never changed in any of the works known to have been written by him, even as that description differed from Elias of Cortona's presentation of the *stigmata* as wounds. Jacques Dalarun, *The Misadventure of Francis of Assisi*, trans. E. Hagman (St. Bonaventure: Franciscan Institute Publications, 2002), 130.

81 Desbonnets, *From Intuition to Institution*, 165. These are labelled N, M, Z, and X on his diagram.

82 Dalarun, *The Misadventure*, 63.

83 Raoul Manselli, *"Nos qui cum eo fuimus": Contributo alla questione francescana* (Rome: Istituto storico dei Cappuccini, 1980). English translation in Raoul Manselli, *"Nos qui cum eo fuimus": A Contribution to the Franciscan Question*, trans. Edward Hagman, ed. Regis J. Armstrong and Ingrid Peterson, supplement, *Greyfriars Review* 14 (2000) 1–196.

84 The seminal work of New Testament form criticism is Rudolf Bultmann's *History of the Synoptic Tradition*, published in German in 1921. A recent English translation is Rudolf Bultmann, *History of the Synoptic Tradition*, trans. J. Marsh (Peabody, MA: Hendrickson Publishing, 1994).

85 Manselli, *"Nos qui cum eo fuimus,"* 23.

86 The *Speculum lemmens* is a fourteenth century text (MS Isidoriano 1/73), which contains many of the same narratives as are found in the better known (and better organized) *Speculum perfectionis*, first studied by Little. Unlike the *Speculum perfectionis*, however, the stories contained within it are ordered in no obvious way. MS Little is the shorthand name for Bodleian Lat. th. d. 23, which is a collection of Franciscan documents that dates from circa 1400 (Bodleian online manuscript catalogue, http://www .bodley.ox.ac.uk/dept/scwmss/wmss/online/medieval/lat/latin-th .html, accessed 27 November 2013) or the first half of the fifteenth century (Manselli, *"Nos qui cum eo fuimus,"* 28). It contains, among other texts, papal bulls relating to the order, commentaries on the *Rule*, and various stories about Francis. Manselli, *"Nos qui cum eo fuimus,"* 27.

87 Manselli, *"Nos qui cum eo fuimus,"* 30.

88 On Leo's *rotuli* and their loss and recovery see Duncan Nimmo, *Reform and Division in the Franciscan Order: 1226–1538* (Rome: Capuchin Historical Institute, 1987), 81–8.

89 Manselli, *"Nos qui cum eo fuimus,"* 31.

90 Manselli, *"Nos qui cum eo fuimus,"* 38. Rosalind Brooke makes a similar point in her introduction to *Scripta Leonis*, 10.

91 On this see Christopher Brooke's review of Augustine Thompson's
     Francis of Assisi: A New Biography in the *Journal of Theological Studies* 64:1
     (April 2013), 300–3, 303.
92 Manselli, *"Nos qui cum eo fuimus,"* 110.
93 On the judicious editing and "sugar coating" of Bonaventure's sources
     for the *Legenda Maiora*, see Dalarun, *The Misadventure*, 243–58.
94 Rosalind Brooke, *The Image of St. Francis: Responses to Sainthood in the
     Thirteenth Century* (Cambridge: Cambridge University Press, 2006), 115–16.
95 Rosalind Brooke's detailed argument for the unity of the stories preserved
     in the *Assisi Compilation* can be found in Brooke, "Introduction," 43–66.
96 Thompson, *Francis of Assisi*, 162–3.
97 Thompson, *Francis of Assisi*, 165–6.
98 Manselli, *"Nos qui cum eo fuimus,"* 26–7.
99 Manselli, *"Nos qui cum eo fuimus,"* 26–7. Even Brooke agrees with this
     assessment, see Brooke, "Introduction," 22.
100 On this see the introduction to the English translation of the *Anonymous of
     Perugia* in FA:ED II, 31–2, and Lorenzo di Fonza, *"L'Anonimo Perugino* Tra
     Le Fonti Francescane del Secolo XIII: Rapporti Letterari e Testo Critico in
     Miscellaneo Franciscana," 72 (1972), 117–483, 396–8.
101 See Dalarun, *The Misadventure*, 177.
102 See Desbonnets, *From Intuition to Institution*, 161–2.
103 Desbonnets, *From Intuition to Institution*, 161–2; Maurice Causse, "Des
     sources Primatives de *La Legende des Trois Compagnons," Collectanea
     Franciscana* 68/3–4 (1998) 465–91, 473–7, and the introduction to *The
     Legend of the Three Companions* in FA:ED II, 61–5, 63.
104 Jacques Dalarun, *Vers une résolution de la question franiscaine: La Légende
     ombrienne de Thomas of Celano* (Paris: Fayard, 2007), 184–6. See also the
     chapter on dating the *Umbrian Choir Legend*, 113–42.
105 Attilio Cadderi and P. Carlo, "Introduzione," in Anonymous of Rieti,
     Actus beati Francisci in valle Reatina, ed. A. Cadderi and P. Carlo. 5–128
     (Porziuncola: Edizioni Porziuncola, 1999), 62–3.
106 Cadderi, "Introduzione," 53–7.
107 Cadderi, "Introduzione," 58. On Bernard of Besse's *Praises*, see David
     Amico, "Bernard of Besse: *Praises of the Blessed Francis (Liber de laudibus
     beati Francisci), Franciscan Studies*, 48 (1998), 213–68.
108 Cadderi, "Introduzione," 53
109 Cadderi, "Introduzione," 53.
110 "Angelus Reatinus, qui de rebus a Francisco gestis inter suae patriae
     terminos [scribit]." Luke Wadding, *Annales minorum*, 1209, XXII, p. 65.
111 Cadderi, "Introduzione," 59.
112 Cadderi, "Introduzione," 57.

1. Francis Overdiagnosed and Undiagnosed

1 On this hagiographic trope in various eras, see Andrew Crislip, *Thorns of the Flesh, Illness and Sanctity in Late Ancient Christianity* (Philadelphia: University of Pennsylvania Press, 2006), and Massimo Leone, *Conversion and Identity* (Abingdon and New York: Routledge, 2003), 38–9.

2 Sabatier's biography of Francis was published in 1893 and translated into many different languages, including English, in the years after that. The text has been continually reissued since then.

3 A useful summary of medical studies of Francis until the mid-1970s can be found in Octavian Schmucki, "The Illnesses of Francis during the Last Years of His Life," trans. Edward Hagman, *Greyfriars Review* 13:1 (1999), 21–59, 21–3.

4 Albert Bournet, *S. François d'Assise: Étude Sociale et Médicale* (Lyon: A. Storch, 1893).

5 For a good exploration of how Charcot, Freud, and others believed hysteria and mysticism intersected, see Cristina Mazzoni, *Saint Hysteria: Neurosis, Mysticism and Gender in European Culture* (Ithaca, NY: Cornell University Press, 1996), 17–49.

6 Bournet, *François d'Assise*, 117.

7 Bournet, *François d'Assise*, 127.

8 Two studies, both published in 1885, noted outbreaks of jaundice (a symptom of hepatitis) in dock workers in Germany and among those housed in a mental institution in Merzig after the communities had received inoculations for small pox, suggesting the disease was bloodborne and could be shared through needles. On this see Adrian Rueben, "Landmarks in Hepatology," *Hepatology* 36:3 (2002), 770–3, 771.

9 Sigmund Freud and Josef Breuer, *Studies on Hysteria*, trans. James Strachey, standard edition, vol. 2 (London: Basic Books, 1955), 244.

10 Bournet, *François d'Assise*, 104–7.

11 Nitza Yarom, *Body, Blood and Sexuality: A Psychoanalytic Study of St. Francis' Stigmata and Their Historical Context* (New York: Peter Lang, 1992).

12 Lisa Cataldo, "Religious Experience and the Transformation of Narcissism: Kohutian Theory and the Life of St. Francis of Assisi," *Journal of Religion and Health* 46 (2007), 527–40.

13 Lorenzo Gualino, *L'uomo d'Assisi* (Turin: Fratri Bocca, 1927).

14 Jean-Martin Charcot, *La foi qui guerit* (Paris: Bureaux du Progrès Medical, 1897), 10.

15 Gaulino, *L'uomo d'Assisi*, 59–63.

16 Gualino, *L'uomo d'Assisi*, 66.

17 Gualino, 41. See also his discussion of the impossibility that Francis suffered from hallucinogenic depression on pages 42–8.

18 Roberto Zavalloni, *La personalità di Francesco d'Assisi:Sstudio psicologico* (Padua: Edizioni Messaggero, 1991).

19 Lino Temperini, *Francesco di Assisi: Cronistoria psicologia initerario spirituale* (Rivoli: Neos Edizioni, 2012).

20 Temperini, *Francesco di Assisi*, 158.

21 Temperini, *Francesco di Assisi*, 162.

22 Théodore Cotelle, *Saint François d'Assise: Étude medicale* (Paris: Libr. Ch. Poussielgue, 1895).

23 Cotelle, *Saint François d'Assise*, 3–5

24 Cotelle does not suggest this categorically. See Cotelle, *Saint François d'Assise*, 74.

25 Cotelle, *Saint François d'Assise*, 75.

26 Cotelle, *Saint François d'Assise*, 76.

27 Cotelle, *Saint François d'Assise*, 179.

28 Cotelle, *Saint François d'Assise*, 182.

29 Cotelle, *Saint François d'Assise*, 183.

30 Cotelle, *Saint François d'Assise*, 182.

31 Cotelle, *Saint François d'Assise*, 125.

32 Cotelle, *Saint François d'Assise*, 129.

33 Cotelle, *Saint François d'Assise*, 129–32.

34 Cotelle, *Saint François d'Assise*, 136.

35 Cotelle, *Saint François d'Assise*, 156.

36 Orestes Parisotti, *Quo morbo oculi sensum amisit Francescus ab Assiso* (Rome: Tipografia pontificia, 1918).

37 Parisotti, *Quo morbo oculi*, 13–14.

38 Parisotti, *Quo morbo oculi*, 25–6.

39 Josef Stebel, "Kulturhistorisches aus der Geschichte der Opthalmologie und Medizen. Diagnose des Augenleidens des hl. Franziskus von Assisi. Ein Beitrag zu Behandlung der Augenleiden im Hochmittelalter. Die Todesursache A. Dürers," in *Klinische Monatsblätter für Augenheilkunde* 99 (1937), 252–60.

40 See Rosario Zeppa, "San Francesco's Blindness," *Journal of Paleopathology* 3:3 (1991), 133–5.

41 E.F. Hartung, "St. Francis and Medieval Medicine," *Annals of Medical History* 7 (1935), 85–91.

42 Hartung, "St. Francis and Medieval Medicine," 86.

43 Shannen K. Allen and Richard D. Semba, "The Trachoma 'Menace' in the United States" in *History of Opthamology* 47:5 (September/October 2002), 500–9, 501–2. However, it is not at all clear that Egypt was the source of the trachoma outbreak.

44 Katherine Schlosser, "History of Trachoma," special edition, *Trachoma Matters: Newsletter of the International Trachoma Initiative*, http://trachoma .org/other-resources.

45 Hartung, "St. Francis and Medieval Medicine," 86.

46 Hartung, "St. Francis and Medieval Medicine," 90.

47 Santo Cianciarelli, *Francesco di Pietro Bernardone: Malato et santo* (Florence: Nardini, 1972).

48 Cianciarelli, *Francesco di Pietro Bernardone*, 20.

49 Ciancarelli, *Francesco di Pietro Bernardone*, 24.

50 Ciancarelli, *Francesco di Pietro Bernardone*, 52.

51 Ciancarelli, *Francesco di Pietro Bernardone*, 82.

52 Ciancarelli, *Francesco di Pietro Bernardone*, 86.

53 Ciancarelli, *Francesco di Pietro Bernardone*, 87.

54 Ciancarelli, *Francesco di Pietro Bernardone*, 85.

55 Ciancarelli, *Francesco di Pietro Bernardone*, 123–4.

56 Ciancarelli, *Francesco di Pietro Bernardone*, 119.

57 Ciancarelli, *Francesco di Pietro Bernardone*, 132–4.

58 Ciancarelli, *Francesco di Pietro Bernardone*, 126, 128, 132. Indeed, Ciancarelli suggests a stomach ulcer is responsible for Francis' illness in the liver, spleen, and stomach, as recounted in Thomas of Celano's *Vita prima*.

59 Ciancarelli, *Francesco di Pietro Bernardone*, 77–8.

60 Ciancarelli, *Francesco di Pietro Bernardone*, 77.

61 Ciancarelli, *Francesco di Pietro Bernardone*, 80–1.

62 Keith Haines, "The Death of Francis of Assisi," *Franziskanische Studien* 58 (1976), 27–46, 39.

63 Haines, "The Death of Francis of Assisi," 42–3. On common symptoms, see Centers for Disease Control and Prevention, "Signs and Symptoms of Brucellosis," http://www.cdc.gov/brucellosis/symptoms/index.html. Retrieved 13 November 2013.

64 Haines, "The Death of Francis of Assisi," 41–5.

65 Haines, "The Death of Francis of Assisi," 45–6.

66 For a quick discussion of symptoms of lepromatous form of leprosy see http://www.cdc.gov/leprosy/symptoms/index.html. Accessed 8 November 2013.

67 This appears to be the general consensus as to why Elias hastened the burial of Francis (see Brooke, *The Image of Saint Francis*, 467–8), though other reasons have been proposed. André Vauchez has suggested that Elias hid Francis' body to prevent the development of a popular and highly policitized cult centred on his tomb. See Vauchez, *Saint Francis of Assisi*, 154. Richard Trexler has claimed, controversially, that Elias moved Francis' body quickly and in secret as a means of hiding the fact that Francis did not have the stigmata, or if he did, that they disappeared soon after his death. See Richard Trexler, "The Stigmatized Body of Francis of Assisi Conceived, Processed, Disappeared," *Frömmigkeit im Mittelalter*, ed. Klaus Schreiner (Munich: Fink, 2002), 463–97.

68 See Brooke, *The Image of St. Francis*, 469.

69 Brooke, *The Image of St. Francis*, 469.

70 Brooke, *The Image of St. Francis*, 457–561.

71 Brooke, *The Image of St. Francis*, 461.

72 Joanne Schatzlein and Daniel Sulmasy, "The Diagnosis of St. Francis: Evidence for Leprosy," *Franciscan Studies* 47:25 (1987), 181–217, 203.

73 Schatzlein and Sulmasy, "Diagnosis," 202.

74 Schatzlein and Sulmasy, "Diagnosis," 204.

75 Schatzlein and Sulmasy, "Diagnosis," 204.

76 Schatzlein and Sulmasy, "Diagnosis," 205. This assumption is not necessarily correct because we know that something happened that caused Elias to translate and bury Francis' body three days before a planned ceremony. That Elias was concerned that pieces of Francis' body may have been taken as relics is not out of the question. Indeed, the iron bars surrounding Francis' sarcophagus were likely put in place soon after his death, when he lay at San Giorgio, to prevent pilgrims from taking the contents of the sarcophagus, including pieces of Francis' body. On this topic see Brooke, *The Image of St. Francis*, 464–5.

77 Schatzlein and Sulmasy, "Diagnosis," 210. They also carefully describe why other suggested diagnoses for Francis are unlikely. See pages 207–10.

78 There are several scholars who have argued this point. See, for instance, Ian Hacking, *Mad Travelers: Reflections on the Reality of Transient Mental Illness* (Cambridge: Harvard University Press, 2002); Ian Hacking, *Rewriting the Soul: Multiple Personalities and the Sciences of Memory* (Princeton, NJ: Princeton University Press 1995); Roger Smith, "The History of Psychological Categories," *Studies in History and Philosophy of Biological and Biomedical Sciences* 36:1 (March 2005), 55–94; Kurt Danziger, *Naming the Mind: How Psychology Found Its Language* (Thousand Oaks, CA: Sage, 1997); and Graham Richards, *Putting Psychology in Its Place: An Introduction from a Critical Historical Perspective* (Abingdon and New York: Routledge, 1996).

79 Mark Spigelman and Eshitu Lemma, "The Use of the Polymerase Chain Reaction (PCR) to Detect *Mycobacterium tuberculosis* in Ancient Skeletons," *International Journal of Osteoarchaeology* 3:2 (1993), 137–43.

80 Evilena Anastasiou and Piers D. Mitchell, "Palaeopathology and Genes: Investigating the Genetics of Infectious Diseases in Excavated Human Skeletal Remains and Mummies from Past Populations," *Gene* 528 (2013), 33–40, 33.

81 Anastasiuo and Mitchell, "Palaeopathology and Genes," 33.

82 This is not actually the case for Francis of Assisi, of course, as his body was recovered in the nineteenth century. However, modern tests to confirm diagnoses are unlikely to be undertaken.

83 See Chiara Frugoni, *Francis of Assisi: A Life*, trans. John Bowden (London: SCM Press, 1998), 141; and Daniel Spoto, *Reluctant Saint: The Life of Francis of Assisi* (New York: Penguin, 2002), 188.

2. Recentring Illness and Infirmity in Francis' Lived Experience

1 Of the early hagiographies, *The Legend of the Three Companions* gives the
   most detail about Francis' early *life*. See LTC 1, 2–3, FF 1376–7; FA:ED 2.68–9.
2 For a useful summary, see Michael Cusato, "The Letters to the Faithful," in
   The Writings of Francis of Assisi: Letters and Prayers, Studies in Early Franciscan
   Sources, (St. Bonaventure: Franciscan Institute Publications, 2001), loc.
   2567–4580, Kindle. Even the use of this title is hotly debated. On this, see
   Margaret Carney, "The 'Letter' of Fourteen Names: Reading the
   'Exhortation,'" in *Francis of Assisi: History, Hagiography and Hermeneutics
   in the Early Documents*, ed. J.M. Hammond, 90–104 (New York: New City
   Press, 2004).
3 Enrico Menestò, "A Re-reading of Francis of Assisi's *Letter to the Faithful*,"
   Greyfriars Review 14:2 (2000), 97–110, 101.
4 Cusato, "The Letters to the Faithful," loc. 2591.
5 This has been suggested by many twentieth-century scholars of the
   letter. See, for instance, Menestò, "A Re-reading," 97–110; Théophile
   Desbonnets,"La lettre à tous les fidèles de François d'Assise," in *I frati
   Minori e il Terzo Ordine: Problemi e discussioni storiografiche*, ed. Stanislao da
   Campagnola (Todi: Accademia Tudertina, 1985), 53–76; Cusato, "The Letter
   to the Faithful," loc. 2613.
6 On this see Walter Goetz, *Die Quellen zur Geschichte des heiligen Franziskus
   von Assis*. (Gotha: F.A. Perthes, 1904), 24–5.
7 As Cusato notes, Esser and Lehmann have argued that the short version
   is the original, while David Flood and Cusato himself suggest the longer
   version is the first. See Cusato, *"Letter to the Faithful*," loc. 2700–957; and
   Manestò, "A Re-reading," for overviews of the different positions.
8 "quod, cum personaliter propter infirmitatem et debilitatem mei corporis
   non possim singulos visitare." FAS 186, FA:ED 1.45.
9 "Et quamvis sim simplex et infirmus, tamen semper volo habere clericum,
   qui michi faciat officium sicut in regula continetur." *Testamentum* 29;
   FAS 400, FA:ED 1.126.
10 Jean-Baptiste Auberger, "A Short Note on the Autographs of Francis of
   Assisi," trans. E. Hagman, *Greyfriars Review* 17:1 (2004), 1–4.
11 Jean-François Godet-Calogeras, "The Autographs of Brother Francis,"
   in *The Writings of Francis of Assisi: Letters and Prayers* (St. Bonaventure:
   Franciscan Institute Publications, 2011), loc. 917, Kindle.
12 There has been much debate about the hand in which Francis wrote and
   how he was trained to write in it. Jean-François Godet-Calogeras, "The
   Autographs," loc. 914, suggests the letters are Carolingian minuscule, but
   an Umbrian book hand is suggested by Pratesi. A. Pratesi, "L'autografo
   di San Francesco nel Duomo di Spoleto," in *San Francesco e i Franciscani a
   Spoleto* (Spoleto: Accademia Spoletina, 1984), 17–26, 20.

13 Langeli suggests the writing is "tormented and irregular"; it is certainly
so when compared with the usual production of medieval scribes. Attilio
Bartoli Langeli, *Gli autografi di Frate Francesco e di Frate Leone*, Corpus
Christianorum Augographa Medii Aevi V (Turnhout, Brepols 2000), 22.

14 See Langeli's extensive notes on his transcription of the *The Praises*.
Langeli, *Gli autografi*, 36–8.

15 Godet-Calogeras, "The Autographs," loc. 1215.

16 See Langeli's transcription of Brother Leo's rubric, in Langeli, *Gli autografi*,
31–2. The cohesiveness of the narrative of Francis' vision and the subsequent
reception of the stigmata imply that Leo wrote this rubric much later than
1224, perhaps as late as 1270, just before his death.

17 Langeli, *Gli autografi*, 22.

18 Auberger, "A Short Note," 2.

19 For a summary of the debate about the date of the letter, see Godet-
Calogeras, "The Autographs," loc. 1350–76.

20 The inclusion of this "not" in the letter has been open to debate, but most
scholars of Francis' autographs now seem to have sided with the position
of Bartoli Langeli, who argues that this was the best reading of the text.
See Langeli, *Gli autografi*, 48. On this controversy, see also Felice Accrocca,
"The 'Unlettered One' and His Witness: Footnotes to a Recent Volume on
the Autographs of Brother Francis and Brother Leo," trans. E. Hagman,
Greyfriars Review 16:3 (2002), 265–82, 268–9.

21 Francis of Assisi, *Letter to Brother Leo*, ed. Attilio Bartoli Langeli, in A.B.
Langeli, *Gli autografi di Frate Francesco e di Frate Leone* (Turnhout: Brepols,
2000), 49–51.

22 Langeli, *Gli autografi*, 45–6.

23 LM 4.9, FA:ED 2.556, FF 810; and LM *Miracula* 10.6, FA:ED 2.681, FF 960.
See also Langeli, *Gli autografi*, 45.

24 Godet-Calogeras, "The Autographs," loc. 1463.

25 "faticoso et spezzato." Langeli, *Gli autografi*, 22.

26 On Francis' lack of learning and his autographs, see, for instance, Bartoli,
who argues that Francis' state of education placed him between "illiteracy"
and "full and complete literacy." Langeli, *Gli autografi*, 28.

27 On poor transcriptions see Carlo Paolazzi, "Francis and His Use of Scribes:
A Puzzle to Be Solved," trans. E. Hagman, *Greyfriars Review* 18:3 (2004),
481–97.

28 Francis himself attests that he is "ignorant and unlearned (*ignorans sum et
idiota*)" during a confession about how he had broken the *Rule* in his *Letter
to the Order*, though, as Octavian Schmucki has demonstrated, this was
probably hyperbole for emphasis since Francis was able to read French,
Italian, and simple Latin, though he could not easily write in Latin. He
may have been more at ease in Italian, but no samples of Francis' writing

in Italian survive. Octavian Schmucki, "St. Francis' Level of Education," trans. P. Bennett, *Greyfriars Review* 10:2 (1996) 153–70.

29 Auberger, "A Short Note," 3.

30 There has been some discussion on the part of Langeli and Godet-Calogeras that this blessing is a sort of magic square which can be read to mean the same thing regardless of which corner of the square a person begins to read. See Langeli, *Gli autografi*, 40, and Godet-Calogeras, "The Autographs," loc. 1277. While I am not convinced that this placement of words was meant to be a magic square – most medieval magic squares contained palindromes and not simply text that could be read in any direction – there is no doubt that those four words do appear to be carefully placed on the blessing *Chartula*.

31 Thus, based on the palaeographical evidence in the two texts, I agree with the majority of scholars who have studied it and date it after the *Chartula*, likely in 1225.

32 Pratesi noted that the writing in the letter demonstrated the saint's advanced stage of illness, using what he saw as a significant difficulty on the part of the scribe to write in an ordered fashion to date the letter in Francis' life. See A. Pratesi, "L'autografo," 17–26, 23. See also Cajetan Esser, "Über die Chonologie der Schriften des hl. Franziskus," *Archivum Franciscanum Historicum* 65 (1972), 20–65, 48–9. Esser backs away from a discussion of Francis' illnesses impacting his ability to write.

33 See Langeli's line-by-line analysis of all three autographs in Langeli, 31–56.

34 Langeli, *Gli autografi*, 37.

35 Langeli, *Gli autografi*, 37.

36 Langeli, *Gli autografi*, 38; Godet-Calogeras, "The Autographs," loc. 914.

37 Langeli, *Gli autografi*, 38–9.

38 See the discussions of these in Langeli, *Gli autografi*, 46–56; and Godet-Calogeras, "The Autographs," loc. 1486–501.

39 "la giudicavo della mano di Francesco, basandomi sul brutto disegno dell *t*, indegne di Leone." Langeli, *Gli autografi*, 50.

40 See Langeli, *Gli autografi*, 47; and Godet-Calogeras, "The Autographs," loc. 1486.

41 Langeli, *Gli autografi*, 49; Godet-Calogeras, "The Autographs," loc. 1486.

42 Langeli, *Gli autografi*, 47–8; Godet-Calogeras, loc. 1485.

43 Francis of Assisi, *Testamentum*, 2.15, FAS 396, FA:ED 1.125.

44 Paolazzi, "Francis and His Use of Scribes," 324.

45 VP 1.10.23; FF 298; FA:ED 202.

46 Robert Black, *Humanism and Education in Medieval and Renaissance Italy: Tradition and Innovation in Latin Schools from the Twelfth to the Fifteenth Century* (Cambridge: Cambridge University Press, 2001), 29–30.

47 Schmucki, "St. Francis' Level of Education," 153–70, 156.
48 See Godet-Calogeras, "The Autographs," loc. 914.
49 Much has been written about the blessing on the *Chartula*. For recent
   work that summarizes much of the literature, see Godet-Calogeras, "The
   Autographs," loc. 1199–296.
50 Godet-Calogeras, "The Autographs," loc. 1492.
51 On the various interpretations of the meaning of this image, see Duane
   Lapsanski, "The Autographs on the *Chartula* of St. Francis of Assisi,"
   Archivum Franciscanum Historicum 67 (1974), 36–37; Chiara Frugoni,
   *Francesco e l'invenzione delle stimmate: Una storia per parole e immagini
   fino a Bonaventura e Giotto* (Turin: Einaudi, 1993), 72; Damian Vorreaux,
   The Tau: A Franciscan Symbol: History, Chronology, Iconography, trans.
   M. Archer and P. Lachance (Chicago: Franciscan Herald Press, 1977),
   70–1; Francis De Beer, *François, que disait-on de toi* (Paris: Éditions
   Franciscaines, 1977), 108.
52 Frugoni, *Francesco e l'invenzione dell stimmata*, 76.
53 Thomas Madden, *Enrico Dandolo and the Rise of Venice* (Baltimore: Johns
   Hopkins University Press, 2003), 64–8.
54 Madden, *Enrico Dandolo*, 85–96.
55 The entire dedication reads as follows: "Beatus Franciscus acquisivit
   hoc breviarium sociis suis fratri Angelo et fratri leoni. eo quod tempore
   sanitatis sue voluit dicere semper officium sicut in regula continetur et
   tempore infirmitatis sue, cum non poterat dicere volebat audire. et hoc
   continuavit dum vixit. Fecit etiam scribi hoc evangelistare. ut eo die, quo
   non posset audire missam occasione infirmitatis vel alio aliquo manifesto
   impedime[n]to: faciebat sibi legi evangelium, quod eo die dicebatur in
   ecclesia in missa. Et hoc continuavit usque ad obitum suum. Dicebat
   enim. 'Cum non audio missam, adoro corpus christi oculis mentis in
   oratione quemadmodum adoro cum video illud in missa.' Audito vel lecto
   evangelio beatus Franciscus ex maxima reverentia Domini obsculabatur
   semper evangelium. Quapropter frater Angelus et frater leo supplicant
   sicut possunt domine Benedicte, abbatisse pauper[u]m dominarum
   Monasterii Sancte Clare et omnibus abbatissis eiusdem monasterii que
   post ipsam venture erunt. Ut in memoria et devocione sancti patris
   librum istum in quo multotiens legit dictus pater semper conservent
   in monasterio Sancte Clare." Brother Leo, *Dedication in the Breviary of
   St. Francis*, ed. Attilio Bartoli Langeli, in *Gli Autografi di Frate Francesco e di
   Frate Leone*, ed. A.B. Langeli (Turnhout: Brepols, 2000), 83.
56 Brother Leo, *Dedication*, 83.
57 Brother Leo, *Dedication*, 83.
58 Brother Leo, *Dedication*, 83.

3. Testimonies of Illness in the Early *Lives* of St. Francis

1 As the chapter title suggests, *Et licet infirmus fuisset semper*, AC 117, FF 1681, FA:ED 2.225.

2 See for instance, chapter 83 of the *Assisi Compilation*. FF 1597–8, FA:ED 2.185.

3 There is some debate about the veracity of this encyclical, at least as it has come down to us today. While evidence from the *Chronicle* of Jordan of Giano shows that Brother Elias wrote an encyclical to the Franciscan Order that announced Francis' death and proclaimed the presence of the *stigmata* on his body, the encyclical preserved today contains evidence it was written after Thomas of Celano's *Vita prima* was composed, and perhaps as late as 1260, and thus long after the moment of Francis' death. On this see the introduction to the letter found in FA:ED 2.485–488 ; Felice Accrocca, "Is the Encyclical Letter of Brother Elias on the *Transits* of Saint Francis Apocryphal?," trans. Robert Stewart, *Greyfriars Review* 13 (1999), 19–63.

4 Chiara Frugoni, *Francis of Assisi: A Life*, trans. J. Bowden (New York: Continuum, 1998), 142.

5 Carolyn Muessig, "Signs of Salvation: The Evolution of Stigmatic Spirituality before Francis of Assisi," *Church History* 82:1 (March 2013), 40–68, 43–4.

6 Muessig, "Signs of Salvation," 47.

7 Muessig, "Signs of Salvation," 49–50.

8 Muessig, "Signs of Salvation," 52–6.

9 Fortini, *New Life*, 155.

10 See, for instance, Thompson, *Francis of Assisi*, 10, and Vauchez, *Francis of Assisi*, 12.

11 LTC 2.4, FF 1378, FA:ED 2.69–70.

12 "post paucos vero annos." LTC 2.5, FF 1378, FA:ED 2.70.

13 "et [Franciscus] convinculatus cum caeteris squalores carceris patitur." VS, 1.1.4, FF 447, FA:ED 2.243.

14 Vauchez, *Francis of Assisi*, 12.

15 "Sicque diu infirmitate attritus." Thomas of Celano, VP 1.2.3, FF 280, FA:ED 1.184.

16 Thompson, *Francis of Assisi*, 10.

17 Arnaldo Fortini, *Francis of Assisi: A Translation of the "Nova Vita" di San Francesco*, trans. Helen Moak (New York: Crossroads, 1981), 165. The Italian is even more evocative: "L'ombra della notte li avvolgeva poco a poco." Arnaldo Fortini, *Nova vita di San Francesco*, 4 vol. (Assisi: Edizioni Porziuncula, 1959), 1.210.

18 Fortini's dating on the peace between Assisi and Perugia differs from that of other scholars. See Paul V. Riley Jr., "Francis' Assisi: Its Political and Social History, 1175–1225," *Franciscan Studies* 34 (1974), 393–424, 413.

19 LTC 2.4, FF 1378, FA:ED 2.70.

20 "Post paucos vero annos, quidam nobilis de civitate Assisii militaribus
    armis se praeparat ut ad pecuniae vel honoris lucra augenda in Apuliam
    vadat. Quo audito, Franciscus ad eundum cum illo aspirat, et ut a quodam
    comite Gentili nomine miles fiat." LTC 2.5, FF 1378, FA:ED 2.70.

21 Arnaldo Fortini, *Francis of Assisi*, 169 and 169 n.c. Fortini, *Nova Vita*, 1.217.
    See also Fortini's discussion of his reasoning in *Nova Vita*, 2.178–9, and a
    transcription the document, *Assisi, Archive of the Cathedral*, fasc. II, n114,
    which recounts a payment in exchange for freeing a captive, one Bernardo,
    son of Figura, in 1164, described in *Nova Vita*, 3.537.

22 "[Franciscus] vincula ridet et spernit." VS 1.1.4, FF 447. FA:ED 2.242.

23 I am especially sceptical of the reliability of this account given that Francis
    claims that he is exulting "because he will be adored by the whole world."
    "Adhuc sanctus adorabor per saeculum totum." VS 1.14, FF 447, FA:ED 2.243.

24 Guy Geltner, "Medieval Prisons: Between Myth and Reality, Hell and
    Purgatory," *History Compass* 4:2 (March 2006), 261–74, 264.

25 Geltner, "Medieval Prisons," 264.

26 On the lack of sick wards in medieval Italian prisons see Guy Geltner, *The
    Medieval Prison: A Social History* (Princeton, NJ: Princeton University Press,
    2008), 66.

27 "Cumque iam paululum respirasset et baculo sustentatus, causa
    recuperandae sanitatis coepisset huc atque illuc per domicilium ambulare."
    VP 1.2.3, FF 280, FA:ED 1.185.

28 "Sicque diu infirmitate attritus, ut meretur pervicacia hominum quae vix
    nisi suppliciis emendatur, coepit intra se alia solito cogitare." VP 1.2.3,
    FF 279, FA:ED 1.184–5.

29 These include the LTC 2, FF 427, FA:ED 319; LM 1.2, FF 782, FA:ED 2.540.
    A discussion of illness in the LTC seems related in terms of time, for
    Francis is described as getting ill on his way to Apulia, yet this is the only
    text in which he is described as becoming ill while travelling. LTC 2.6,
    FF 1379, FA:ED 2.71.

30 The *Assisi Compilation* is quick to report that, in spite of Francis' infirmities,
    he did without the necessities his sickness required as an example to
    the other brothers. "Et licet infirmus fuisset semper beatus Franciscus,
    quoniam in seculo fuit fragilis et debilis homo secundum naturam
    et cotidie usque ad diem mortis sue, eo quod esset infirmior, tamen
    considerabat ut fratribus exhiberet bonum exemplum et ut occasionem
    murmurandi semper de se tolleret eis, videlicet ut non possent fratres
    dicere. Ipse habet necessitates suas, et nos non habemus." AC 117, FF 1682,
    FA:ED 2.225.

31 "Quia in sanitate eius et infirmitate, usque ad diem mortis, tot voluit pati
    necessitates, quod quicumque fratrum scirent sicut nos, qui per aliquod
    tempus usque ad diem mortis eius cum ipso fuimus, quod, si vellent

reducere ad memoriam, non possent se a lacrimis continere (Since in his health and in his illness, up to the day of his death he wished to suffer such needs, such that any of the brothers who knew him as we who were with him for some time up to the day of his death [knew him], if they wished to recall it to memory, they would not be able to contain themselves from tears)." AC 117, FF 1682–3, FA:ED 2.225–6.

32 See Manselli, *"Nos qui cum eo fuimus,"* 108.

33 AC 117, FF 1682, FA:ED 225.

34 LTC 5.14, FF 1388, FA:ED 2.75; AC 120, FF 1690, FA:ED 2.229.

35 AC 79, FF 1589, FA:ED 2.181.

36 AC 117, FF 1681–2, FA:ED 225–6.

37 Two examples of this phraseology can be found within passages with the authenticating phrase in the *Assisi Compilation*, AC 89, FF 1612, FA:ED 2.193; AC 117, FF 1681–2, FA:ED 225–6.

38 "Propterea sicut multotiens dicebat fratribus quia oportebat, ipsum esse formam et exemplum omnium fratrum, ideo non tantum medcinis, sed etiam cibis necessariis in infirmitatibus suis uti nolebant. Et propterea quia hec predicta considerabat, non tantum quando videbatur esse sanus, licet semper esset debilis et infirmus, sed etiam in suis infirmitatibus, suo corpore erat austerus." AC 79, FF 1590, FA:ED 2.181.

39 "Quo viso, cuncti qui noverant eum, comparantes ultima, primis, coeperunt illi miserabiliter exprobrare et insanum ac dementem acclamantes, lutum platearum et lapides in ipsum proiciunt. Cernebant eum a pristinis moribus alteratum et carnis maceratione valde confectum, et ideo totum quod agebat exinanitioni et dementiae imputabant." VP 1.5.11, FF 288, FA:ED 1.191.

40 "Quem videntes illi qui prius noverant eum sibi miserabiliter exprobrabant insanumque ac dementem clamantes, lutum platearum et lapides proiciebant in eum. Cernentes enim eum sic a pristinis moribus alteratum et carnis maceratione confectum, totum quod agebat exinanitioni et dementiae imputabant." LTC 6.17, FF 1391, FA:ED 2.78.

41 "Quem cum cives cernerent facie squalidum et mente mutatum, ac per hoc alienatum putarent a sensu, luto platearum et lapidibus impetebant et tamquam insano et dementi clamosis vocibus insultabant." LM 2.2, FF 789, FA:ED 2.537.

42 "Cum cepisset beatus Franciscus habere fratres, tantum letabatur de conversione illorum, et quod Dominus sibi dedit societatem bonam, in tantum diligebat eos et venerabatur quod non dicebat eis ut irent pro helemosina et maxime quia videbatur ei quod verecundarentur ire; sed parcens illorum verecundie, ipse cotidie solus ibat pro helemosina. Ex hoc nimis fatigabatur corpus suum, maxime cum fuisset homo delicatus in seculo et debilis secundum naturam, et propter nimiam abstinentiam et afflictionem quam sustinuerat et ab illo die quo exivit de seculo esset

debilior. Unde considerans quod tantum laborem non poterat tolerare, et quia ad hoc vocati erant…. Et exinde unusquisque libentius petebat licentiam eundi pro helemosina." AC 51, FF 1527–8, FA:ED 2.150–1.

43 "ipse enim, qui tam delicatus fuerat in domo paterna, propriis humeris lapides ferebat in Dei servitio multipliciter se affligens. Sacerdos autem praedictus, considerans eius laborem quod scilicet tam ferventer ultra vires divino se obsequio manciparet, licet esset pauperculus, procurabat pro eo fieri aliquod speciale ad victum, sciebat autem ipsum delicate vixisse in saeculo. Quippe, ut ipse vir Dei postea confessus est, frequenter electuariis et confectionibus utebatur et a cibis contrariis abstinebat." My translation differs substantially from that found in *Francis of Assisi: Early Documents*. LTC 7.21, FF 1395–6, FA:ED 2.81.

44 On the history of the term *electuaria* see L. Plouvier, "Le 'Lectuaire': Une confiture du bas Moyen Âge," in *Du Manuscrit à la Table*, ed. C. Lambert., 243–56 (Montreal: Les Presses de l'Université de Montréal, 1992); L. Plouvier, "L'electuaire, un medicament plusieurs fois millenaire," in *Bulletin-Cercle Benelux d'histoire de la pharmacie* 86 (1994), 7–21. See also Mary Carruthers, "Sweetness," *Speculum* 81:4 (October 2006) 999–1013, 1010.

45 Plouvier, "Le 'Lectuaire,'" 244.

46 Both definitions can be found in J.F. Niermeyer, *Mediae Latinitatis Lexicon Minus: Abbreviationes et index fontium* (Leiden: Brill, 1997), 242.

47 See Plouvier, "Le Lectuaire," 254.

48 "Ex quo communi omnium Domino coepit servire, communia facere semper amavit, singularitatem in omnibus fugiens, quae omnium vitiorum labe sordescit. Nam cum in opere illius desudaret ecclesiae, de qua mandatum a Christo susceperat, de delicato nimium rusticanus et patiens laboris effectus, sacerdos ad quem ecclesia pertinebat, cernens illum assidua fatigatione attritum, pietate permotus, aliquid singularis victus, licet non sapidi quia pauper, coepit ei quotidie ministrare. Qui sacerdotis discretionem commendans et pietatem amplectens. 'Non invenies sacerdotem istum ubique', ad semetipsum ait, 'qui semper tibi talia subministret. Non est haec vita hominis paupertatem profitentis; non expedit tibi assuescere talibus; paulatim ad contempta redibis, iterum ad delicata perefflues. Surge iam, impiger, et ostiatim pulmenta commixta mendica!'" VS 1.9.14, FF 456–7, FA:ED 2.253.

49 "Quadam autem vice, solus ibat prope ecclesiam Sanctae Mariae de Portiuncula, plangendo et eiulando alta voce. Quem audiens, quidam vir spiritualis putavit ipsum pati infirmitatem aliquam vel dolorem, et pietate motus circa eum, interrogavit illum cur fleret. At ille dixit: 'Plango passionem Domini mei, pro quo non deberem verecundari alta voce ire plorando per totum mundum. Ille vero coepit cum, ipso similiter plangere alta voce.'" LTC 5.14, FF 1388, FA:ED 2.76. "Unde,

quodam tempore, paucis annis post conversionem suam cum ambularet
quadam die solus per viam non multum longe ab ecclesia Sancte Marie de
Portiuncula, ibat alta voce plangendo et eiulandoa. Cumque sic ambularet,
quidam spiritualis homo, quem novimus et ab eo istud intelleximus, qui
multam misericordiam et consolationem fecerat sibi antequam haberet
fratrem aliquem et postea similiter, obviavit illi, et motus pietate circa
ipsum interrogavit eum dicens, 'Quid habes, frater?' Putabat enim quod
haberet dolorem alicuius infirmitatis. At ille, 'Ita deberem ire plangendo et
eiulando sine verecundia per totum mundum passionem Domini me!'"
AC 78, FF 1588–9, FA:ED 2.180–1.

50 "cum iam ivisset usque in Hispaniam, in faciem ei restitit, et ne ultra
procederet, aegritudine intentata, eum a coepto itinere revocavit."
VP 1.20.56, FF 332, FA:ED 1.230.

51 "Sed cum iam usque in Hispaniam perrexisset, divina dispositione,
quae ipsium reservabat ad alia, gravissima ei supervenit infirmitas, qua
praepeditus, quod cupiebat adimplere nequivit." LM 9.6, FF 859,
FA:ED 2.661.

52 "De Hispania regrediens sanctus Franciscus, cum non potuisset iuxta
votum Marrochium proficisci, aegritudinem incurrit gravissimam. Nam
egestate cum languore afflictus et hospitio hospitis rusticitate pulsus, per
triduum loquelam amisit. Viribus tandem utcumque resumptis, per viam
gradiens fratri Bernardo dixit se, si haberet, de una avicula comesturum."
TdeM 5.34, FF 671, FA:ED 2.416.

53 "Et ecce, per campum quidam eques accurrit, avem portans peroptimam; qui
beato Francisco dixit, 'Serve Dei, suscipe diligener quod tibi elementia divina
transmittit!' Suscepit cum gaudio munus, et Chrstum sui habere curam
itelligens, ipsum per omnia benedixit." TdeM 5.34, FF 671, FA:ED 2.416.

54 "Contigit semel cum sanctus Franciscus Mevanium pergeret, prae
debilitate ieiunii ad castrum pervenire non posse. Socius vero, misso
nuncio ad quamdam spiritualem dominam, panem et vinum pro sancto
humiliter petiit. Illa, ut audivit, cum filia virgine Deo devota, cucurrit
ad sanctum, portans quae necessaria erant. Refectus autem sanctus et
aliquantulum confortatus, verbo Dei matrem et filiam versa vice refecit."
VS 2.80.114, FF 548, FA:ED 2.323.

55 "In tempore quo nullus recipiebatur in vita fratrum sine licentia beati
Francisci, venit cum aliis, qui volebant intrare Religionem, filius cuiusdam
nobilis secundum seculum de Luca ad beatum Franciscum qui erat tunc
infirmus et manebat in palatio episocopi Assisii." AC 70, FF 1574–5,
FA:ED 2.173.

56 Chapter 11. See Jordan of Giano, *Chronica*, 11.4, and the translation of
Jordan of Giano, *Chronicle*, 11.26.

57 VS 2.11.40, FF 481, FA:ED 2.273.

58 See, for example, discussion of this event in Fortini, *Francis of Assisi*, 598.
Seton also places this event in the last few weeks, even days, though he
notes that "the phrase is difficult to understand as the time up to October
[when the saint died] would not be called winter. Possibly the incident
occurred during some earlier period of illness." William Seton, "The Last
Two Years of the Life of St. Francis," in *St Francis of Assisi: 1226–1936:
Essays in Commemoration*, ed. W. Seton (London: University of London,
1926), 219–41, 232n4.

59 "Quodam tempore, cum maneret in eodem palatio valde infirmus, fratres
rogabant ipsum et confortabant ut comederet. Ipse autem respondit eis,
'Fratres mei, non habeo voluntatem comedendi, sed si haberem de pisce
qui dicitur squalus, forsitan comederem.' Et hiis dictis, 'ecce quidam
apportabat canistrum, in quo erant tres magni squali bene parati et cuppi
de gammaris, de quibus libenter comedebat sanctus pater, quos miserat ad
ipsum frater Girardus, minister Reate.'" AC 71, FF 1576, FA:ED 2.173–4.

60 "Et admiranti sunt valde fratres considerantes sanctitatem eius et
laudaverunt Dominum qui servo suo satisfecit, de quibus impossibile erat
eis tunc satisfacere illi, maxime quia hiems erat et in illa terra de talibus
habere non poterant." AC 71, FF 1576, FA:ED 2.174.

61 "Sed sensualitas gustus nichil appetiti nisi squalum. Hunc enim et
coppum gammarorum pater libenter comedebat. Est enim squalus
quidem piscis fluminalis et albus. Coppus est enim quidem pastillus
ex pulpa et suco gamararorm [sic] et nucibus et spetiebus compositus."
AVR 3.36–8, 182.

62 Melitta Weiss Adamson, *Food in Medieval Times* (Westport, CT: Greenwood
Publishing, 2004), 25.

63 Ken Albana, "Fish in Renaissance Dietary Theory," in *Fish: Food from the
Waters*, ed. Harlan Walker, 9–19 (Oxford: Oxford Symposium, 1998), 15.

64 "Et gustans de predictis in paucis diebus fuit divina virtute sanitati
pristine restitutus." AVR 3.44, 184.

65 Francis' companion Angelus was certainly from Rieti. On this see
Attilio Cadderi, *Fra Angela da Rieti Compagno di San Francesco*
(Assisi: Frascati, 1996).

66 Cadderi and Carlo, "Introduzione," 5–128, 59–60.

67 "mastilla gammarorum," AC 68, FF 1571, FA:ED 2.171; "pastillis
gammarorum," VS 2.15.44, FF 485, FA:ED 2.276; "pastillis gammarorum,"
TdeM 5.36, FF 672, FA:ED 2.416; "coppi grammatorum," AVR 3.58, 188.

68 "Ecce, videte glutonem, qui impinguatus est carnibus gallinarum."
VP 1.19.52, FF 328, FA:ED 1.228.

69 David Grumett and Rachel Muers, *Theology on the Menu: Asceticism, Meat
and the Christian Diet* (Abingdon and New York: Routledge, 2010), 161n68.
Francis' relatively novel approach to food and fasting is discussed on
pages 41–2.

70 "licet parum comederet quoniam propter multas et varias et longas infirmitates comedere not poterat." AC 80, FF 1590, FA:ED 181.

71 "Et ceperunt fere omnes plangere ex pietate et compassione ipsius, maxime quia tunc erat magnum frigus et tempus hiemale et nondum erat a febre quartana liberatus." AC 80, FF 1589–92, FA:ED 181–2.

72 AC 80, FF 1591, FA:ED 182.

73 Brooke, *Early Franciscan Government*, 77.

74 Chapter 11. Jordan of Giano, *Chronica*, in 11.4, and Jordan of Giano, *Chronicle*, 11.26.

75 See VP 2.4.97–8. FF 374–6, FA:ED 1.266–7.

76 Hugh Taylor, *Trachoma: A Blinding Scourge from the Bronze Age to the Twenty-first Century* (East Melbourne: Centre for Eye Research Australia, 2008).

77 "Cum beatus Franciscus per longum tempus habuisset, et habuit usque ad diem mortis sue, infirmitates epatis, splenis et stomachi, et a tempore quo fuit in ultramarinis partibus ad predicandum Soldano Babilonie et Egypti habuisset infirmitatem maximam oculorum propter multum laborem ex fatigatione itineris, qui in eundo et redeundo sustinuit magnum calorem." AC 77, FF 1587–8, FA:ED 2.177.

78 "Eo tempore cum reverteretur sanctus de ultra mare." VS 2.5.31, FF 472, FA:ED 2.266. "Eo quoque tempore, quo revertebatur de ultra mare." LM 11.8, FF 876, FA:ED 617.

79 "Beatus Franciscus, quia debilis homo erat and infirmus equitabat in asino." AC 72, FF 1576, FA:ED 2.174.

80 Chapter 15. Jordan of Giano, *Chronica*, 15.5. Jordan of Giano, *Chronicle*, 15.30.

81 Although I will use the term "resignation" to refer to this event in Francis' life, Jean-François Godet-Calogeras has suggested that we cannot necessarily speak of Francis resigning as minister general, since he never took on that role within the order. See Jean-François Godet-Calogeras, "Francis of Assisi's Resignation," 281–300.

82 See, for instance, Moorman, *A History of the Franciscan Order*, 51; Fortini's *Francis of Assisi* suggests that Francis was ill and wished to remove himself from the contradiction of exercising authority as the leader of his order and wanting a life of absolute humility. See also Michael Cusato, in *"La Renonciation au pouvoir chez les freres Mineurs au 13e siècle*, PhD thesis, Université de Paris IV, Sorbonne, January 1991; Cusato argues that Francis was tempted by the power of leadership and so resigned. André Vauchez argues that, although Francis justified his resignation by saying he was ill, the real reason was "probably his desire to avoid putting himself into conflict with the papacy"; Vauchez, *Francis of Assisi*, 95.

83 "Idcirco generali cedens officio, guardianum petiit, cuius voluntati per
    omnia subiaceret." LM 6.4, FF 826, FA:ED 2.571.

84 "Ad servandam humilitatis sancte virtutem, paucis annis elapsis, post
    suam conversionem, in quodam capitulo, coram omnibus fratribus
    de Religione, prelationis officium resignavit dicens, 'Amodo sum
    mortuus vobis. Sed ecce,' inquit, 'frater Petrus Cathanii, cui ego et vos
    omnes obediamus.' Et inclinans se protinus coram ipso, obedientiam et
    reverentiam promisit eidem." AC 39, FF 1513, FA:ED 2.142.

85 It is included in AC 106, FF 1649, FA:ED 2.211, and AC 112, FF 1669,
    FA:ED 2.219. The phrase is also found in the Lemmens *Speculum*, LS 41,
    FF 1819–20 and in Sabatier *Speculum*, SS 81, FF 1983.

86 AC 106. Manselli does not discuss the first part of AC 106 as being clearly
    linked to the authenticating phrase – though he does not actively discount
    it either. See Manselli, *"Nos qui cum eo fuimus,"* 132–41. Brooke, however,
    suggests that we need not necessarily dismiss as unauthenticated those
    narratives closest to the phrase in favour of presuming only the closest
    story in the text is meant to be verified by the phrase. See Brooke, *The
    Image of St. Francis*, 115–16.

87 The text is unclear here. It reads, "Iterum dum maneret beatus Franciscus
    in eodem palatio"; however, there is no palace mentioned in the text
    near this episode. As Brooke argues, this presents clear evidence that
    the *Assisi Compilation* was copied from either loose sheets of parchment,
    perhaps copied out of order or a source that had done so. See Brooke,
    "Introduction," 48.

88 "Quoniam licet tempore quo renuntiavi et dimisi officium fratrum, coram
    fratribus me excusarem in capitulo generali, quod propter infirmitatem
    meam de ipsis curam et sollicitudinem habere non possem." AC 106,
    FF 1650, FA:ED 2.211.

89 "si secundum voluntatem meam fratres ambularent et ambulassent,
    propter ipsorum consolationem nollem, quod alium ministrum haberent
    preter me, usque in diem mortis mee." AC 106, FF 1650, FA:ED 2.211

90 "Unde sepe dicebat beatus Franciscus fratribus in capitulis et etiam in
    collatione verborum suorum. "Ego iuravi et statui fratrum Regulam
    observare et fratres omnes similiter ad hoc se obligaverunt; quapropter,
    ex quo dimisi officium fratrum, de cetero, propter infirmitates meas et pro
    maiori utilitate anime mee et omnium fratrum, non teneor fratribus nisi
    exhibere bonum exemplum. Nam illud a Domino reperi et scio in veritate
    quoniam, etiam si infirmitas non me excusaret, maius adiutorium quod
    fratrum Religioni impendere possim, est ut cotidie vacem orationi pro ea
    ad Dominum, ut ipsam gubernet, conservet, protegat et defendat." AC 112,
    FF 1668–9, FA:ED 2.219–220.

91 *Testamentum*, 3.27–8; FAS 400, FA:ED 1.126.

92　On the meaning of *guardianus* within the order, see *Francis of Assisi: Early Documents*, 98, note a, and Robson, *Cambridge Companion*, xi.

93　"5 guardianus," by P. Carpentier, 1766, in du Cange et al., *Glossarium mediae et infimae latinitatis*, t. 4, col. 125a, http://ducange.enc .sorbonne.fr/GUARDIANUS5. Accessed 23 July 2016.

94　That Francis wants a guardian to obey is clearly outlined in the *Testament*. Francis wrote "And I so wish to be a captive in [my guardian's] hands that I cannot go anywhere or do anything beyond obedience and his will, for he is my master." "Et ita volo esse captus in manibus suis, ut non possim ire vel facere ultra obedientiam et voluntatem suam, quia dominus meus est." Francis of Assisi, *Testamentum*, 3.28, FAS 400, FA:ED 1.126.

95　AC 87, FF 1609–10, FA:ED 2.191–2.

96　Guardians and their role in Francis' life and in the hagiographies will be discussed in greater detail in chapters 4 and 5.

97　"Fratres autem … in campo spatioso et circumsepto [sic] sub umbraculis habitabant, comedebant et dormiebant." Jordan of Giano, *Chronica*, 6; Jordan of Giano, *Chronicle*, 31.

98　"Dum beatus Franciscus esset in capitulo generali apud sanctam Mariam de Portiuncula, quod dictum est capitulum sestoriorum." AC 18, FF 1498, FA:ED 132.

99　Thompson, *Francis of Assisi*, 246–7.

100　On early fractures within the order, see Burr, *The Spiritual Franciscans*, loc. 301 and ff, Kindle.

101　"In fine autem huius capituli, videlicet quando iam capitulum erat terminandum, venit in memoriam beato Franciscus, quod Ordinis aedificatio in Theutoniam non venisset. Et quia Franciscus tunc debilis erat, quidquid ex parte sui capitulo dicendum erat, frater Helias loquebatur. Et beatus Franciscus, sedens ad pedes Helias fratris, traxit eum per tunicam. Qui inclunatus est ad ipsum, quid vellet aucultavit et se erigens ait, 'Fratres, ita dicit Frater' – significans beatum Franciscum, qui quasi per excellentiam a fratribus frater dicebatur. Est quaedam regio Theutonia, in qua sunt homines christiani et scitis." Jordan of Giano, *Chronica*, 7; Jordan of Giano, *Chronicle*, 33.

102　"'Fratres, ita dicit Frater' – significans beatum Franciscum." Jordan of Giano, *Chronica*, 6.

103　Thompson, *Francis of Assisi*, 89.

104　Fortini, *New Life*, 476; Fortini *Nova vita*, 1.2.159.

105　Fortini, *New Life*, 476; Fortini *Nova vita*, 1.2.159.

106　Jordan of Giano, *Chronicle*, 31–2n33

107　"Ad cuius mandatum episcopus quidam missam celebravit, et beatus Franciscus creditur tunc evangelium legissem et frater aiius epistolam." Jordan of Giano, *Chronica*, 6; Jordan of Giano, *Chronicle*, 31.

108 "In hoc capitulo beatus Franciscus, assumpto themate: *Benedictus Dominus Deus meus, qui docet manus meus ad praelium,* fratribus praedicavit." Jordan of Giano, *Chronica*, 6, Jordan of Giano, *Chronicle*, 33.

109 "[Dominus Ostiensis], qui est dominus, protector et corrector totius fraternitatis." *Testamentum*, 3.33, FAS 402, FA:ED 1.127.

110 Brooke, *Early Franciscan Government*, 65.

111 VP 1.27.73, FF 349, FA:ED 1.245; LTC 16.64, FF 1437–8, FA:ED 2.105–6. Thomas of Celano's *Remembrance of the Desire of a Soul* also places the meeting in Rome. VS 1.17.25, FF 467–8, FA:ED 2.261–2.

112 For a quick reference see the useful chart in Jane E. Sayers, *Papal Government in England during the Pontificate of Honorius III (1216–1227)* (Cambridge: Cambridge University Press, 1984), 86–8. The chart is based on the registers of Honorius' letters found in Potthast.

113 On this topic and the various ways in which early Franciscan sources discuss Hugolino's role within the early order, see Edith Pásztor, "St. Francis, Cardinal Hugolino and 'The Franciscan Question,'" trans. P Colbourne, *Greyfriars Review* 1:1 (Fall 1987), 1–29.

114 "Viderat enim beatus Franciscus quamdam visionem quae ipsum poterat induxisse ad petendum cardinalem et ad recommendandum ordinem romanae ecclesiae." LTC 16.63, FF 14367, FA:ED 2.105.

115 "Viderat namque gallinam quamdam paruam et nigram, habentem crura pennata cum pedibus in modum columbae domesticae, quae tot pullos habebat quod non poterat eos sub alis propriis congregare, sed ibant in circuitu gallinae exterius remanentes. Evigilans autem a somno coepit cogitare de huiusmodi visione, statimque per Spiritum sanctum cognouit se per illam gallinam figuraliter designari et ait 'Ego sum illa gallina, statura pusillus nigerque natura, qui debeo esse simplex ut columba et affectibus pennatis virtutum volare ad caelum. Mihi autem Dominus per misericordiam suam dedit et dabit filios multos quos protegere mea virtute non potero, unde oportet ut eos sanctae Ecclesiae recommendem quae sub umbra alarum suarum eos protegat et gubernet.'" LTC 16.63, FF 1437, FA:ED 2.105.

116 This entire episode can be found in LTC 16.64–6, FF 1437–9, FA:ED 2.105–6. While much of the information in this chapter is based in AP 45, the LTC is the first to explicitly link the request of Hugolino with Francis' vision of the black hen.

117 VS 16–17, 23–5, FF 465–7, FA:ED 2.260–2.

118 FF 1615, FA:ED 2.194.

119 "propter guardiandum suum ut non prohiberet illi." AC 91, FF 1616, FA:ED 2.195.

120 "maxime quia tunc erat magnum frigus et ipse infirmus et frigidus erat valde." AC 91, FF 1616, FA:ED 2.195.

121 AC 77, FF 1587, FA:ED 1.119.

122 AC 119, FF 1688, FA:ED 2.228.

123 See Thomas Spalatensis, *Historia Pontificum Salonitanorum et Spolatinorum*, MGH Scriptores 29 (Hanover: Impensis Bibliopolii Hahniani, 1892), 568–98, 580.

124 On other contemporary chronicles that record the earthquake on Christmas Day 1222, see Pierre Alexandre, *Les séismes en Europe occidentale de 394 à 1259: Nouveau catalogue critique* (Brussels: Observatoire Royale de Belgique, 1990), 174–80.

125 Francis' *Rule* was approved in *Solet annuere*, dated 29 November 1223. See *Bullarium Franciscanum*, ed. G. Sbaralea (Assisi: Edizione Porziuncula, 1759–), 1:15–19.

126 See Fortini, *Life of Francis of Assisi*, 664n10.

127 It is important to note that although tradition stipulates that Francis wrote the *Rule* at Fonte Columbo, no sources state his location explicitly. See AC 17, FF 1496–7, FA:ED 131, which state that Francis was on a certain mountain ("Cum beatus Franciscus in quodam monte"), and LM 4.11, FF 813, FA:ED 559, which state that Francis was led up a certain mountain ("in montem quemdam") by the Holy Spirit.

128 Thomas notes that the Christmas at Greccio occurs some three years before Francis' death, so time and place are both clarified in this narrative. VP 1.30.84–87, FF 360–4, FA:ED 1.254–7.

129 This is also recorded in Thomas of Celano's *Vita prima*. Thomas notes that Francis' time at La Verna occurred two years prior to his death. VP 2.3.94, FF 370–1, FA:ED 263.

130 Vauchez, Francis of Assisi, 131.

131 Paul Sabatier, *Life of Francis of Assisi*, trans. L.S. Houghton (New York: Charles Scribner's Sons, 1919), 300. Following Sabatier, many easily accessible chronologies of Francis' life include such a preaching tour just after the saint received the stigmata.

132 Walter Seton, "The Last Two Years of the Life of St. Francis," in *St. Francis of Assisi: Essays in Commemoration, 1226–1926*, ed. W. Seton (London: University of London, 1926), 219–41, 224.

133 Fortini suggests that, although Francis occasionally travelled during the period from late 1224 to early spring 1225, he was quite infirm and exhausted. Preaching, certainly, is not discussed. See Fortini, *New Life*, 558–60.

134 Thompson does not even mention the possibility of a preaching tour, arguing that Francis was so infirm when he descended from La Verna that he needed "what amounted to nursing care," Thompson, *Francis of Assisi*, 119. To bolster his position, Thompson cites Octavian Schmucki, *The Stigmata of St. Francis of Assisi: A Critical Investigation in Light of Thirteenth Century Sources*, trans. C.F. Connors (St. Bonaventure: Franciscan Institute

Publications, 1991), 230, as saying that the most likely reason for the
descent from La Verna was medical (Thompson, 267), but *pace* Thompson,
Schmucki does not. Schmucki actually notes that "there was nothing
impeding the saint, *before the fresh outbreak of his infirmity,* from traveling
for the last time around the villages of the Umbrian region riding on an
ass" (230n31, emphasis mine).

135 "Tantum quoque animarum, diligebat salutem, et proximorum sitiebat
lucra, ut cum per se ambulare non posset, asello vectus circuiret terras."
VP 2.4.98, FF 375, FA:ED 266–7.

136 Emphasis added. "Sed quoniam secundum iura naturae, humanaeque
conditionis modum necesse est quod de die in diem homo exterior
corrumpatur, licet is qui intus est renovetur, illud pretiosissimum
vasculum in quo caelestis thesaurus erat absconditus, coepit undique
conquassari et virium omnium pati defectum. Verum quia cum
consummatus fuerit homo tunc incipiet, et cum finierit tunc operabitur, in
carne infirma spiritus promptior efficiebatur. Tantum quoque animarum
diligebat salutem et proximorum sitiebat lucra, ut cum per se ambulare
non posset, asello vectus circuiret terras.

Frequenter eum monebant fratres, illi omni precum instantia
suggerentes, ut infirmum corpus et valde debilitatum medicorum
auxilio utcumque recreare deberet. Ipse autem, illo suo nobili spiritu
in caelum directo, qui solvi solummodo cupiebat et cum Christo esse,
hoc facere penitus recusabat. Verum quia nondum impleverat ea quae
passionum Christi deerant in carne sua, licet stigmata eius in corpore suo
portaret, infirmitatem oculorum incurrit gravissimam, quemadmodum
multiplicavit in eo misericordiam suam Deus. Cumque de die in diem
infirmitas illa succresceret et ex incuria videretur quotidie augmentari,
frater Helias tandem, quem loco matris elegerat sibi et aliorum fratrum
fecerat patrem, compulit eum ut medicinam non abhorreret, sed eam
reciperet in nomine Filii Dei, per quem creata erat, sicut scriptum est:
Altissimus de terra creavit medicinam, et vir prudens non abhorrebit
eam. Sanctus pater vero tunc benigne acquievit et humiliter obtemperavit
sermonibus se monentis." VP 2.4.98, FF 375–6, FA:ED 255–67.

137 Luigi Pellegrini has noted that even the *Vita prima*, which states within
itself that it will present the events of Francis' life in chronological order,
cannot always be trusted to accurately date events. See Luigi Pellerini,
"Considerazioni e proposte metodologiche per una analisi delle fonti
Francescane," *Laurentianum* 18 (1977), 292–313, 300–1.

138 "Per eiusdem igitur temporis curricula coepit corpus suum variis urgeri
languoribus et vehementioribus quam prius solitum esset. Frequentes
namque patiebatur infirmitates, utpote qui perfecte castigaverat corpus
suum, et illud in servitutem redegerat ex multis iam praecedentibus
annis." VP 2.4.97, FF 374, FA:ED 1.266.

139 On a donkey: VP 2.4.98, FF 375, FA:ED 1.267. On a horse: VP 1.23.63.
FF 340, FA:ED 1.238.

140 On a donkey: AC 72, FF 1576, FA:ED 2.174; and AC 91, FF 1616,
FA:ED 2.195. On a horse: AC 91, FF 1817; AC 119, FF 1688, FA:ED 2.228;
AC 120, FF 1689, FA:ED 2.229.

141 VS 2.17.46, FF 488, FA:ED 2.278. The VS also records that Francis was so
exhausted when he returned from Egypt that he rode a donkey then too.
VS 2.5.31, FF 472, FA:ED 2.266.

142 The incident of Francis riding on a donkey in the TdM might date before
1224, as he was travelling to visit a hermitage. See TdeM 3.15, FF 658–9,
FA:ED 2.409. On horseback: TdM 12.108, FF 714, FA:ED 2.444

143 Bonaventure, too, includes examples, taken from earlier sources, of Francis
riding donkeys that appear to have occurred before 1224. See LM 7.12,
FF 842, FA:ED 2.584; LM 11.8, FF 876, FA:ED 2.617; and LM 13.7, FF 895–6,
FA:ED 2.635. On horse: LM 12.11, FF 889, FA:ED 2.628.

144 "Quanta nempe in sola Francia Franciscus mirabilia patrat, ubi ad
deosculandum et adorandum capitale, quo sanctus Franciscus in
infirmitate fuerat usus, Francorum rex et regina et universi magnates
accurrunt." VP 3.120, FF 401, FA:ED 1.290.

145 Benedict uses the term in chapter 55 of the *Rule* to mean something like
pillow.

146 Discussion of this relic is found only in the VP. No other early sources
record its existence. The earliest inventories of Sainte-Chapelle, where a
relic intended for the king and queen of France would likely have been
placed, record only a tunic of St. Francis, not a pillow or headband. See
A. Vidier, "Le Trésor de la Sainte-Chapelle," *Mémoires del a Société de
l'histoire de Paris et de l'Ile-de-France* 34 (1907), 199–234. The inventories
of 1341 and pieces from the 1349 inventory not included in the 1341
inventory can be found on pages 209–29 and 231–4 respectively. Francis'
tunic is noted as item 51 on page 214. While this might cast some doubt
on the historicity of the relic, the narrative does provide support for
Francis' continued suffering of his eye disease.

147 "Itaque cum oporteret ipsum etiam nolentem proprii corporis
incommoda, quae vires eius excesserant, blandimentis remediabilibus
delinire." VS 2.160, 210, FF 626, FA:ED 2.382.

148 "Similiter duobus annis ante obitum suum, cum iam esset valde
infirmus et specialiter de infirmitate oculorum, et moraretur in quadam
cellula facta de storiis apud Sanctum Damianum." AC 83, FF 1596,
FA:ED 2.184.

149 Thompson, *Francis of Assisi*, 119, 267.

150 Fortini, *New Life*, 565; Carlo Paolazzi, *Il Cantico di frate Sole* (Genoa:
Marietti, 1992), 37; Vauchez, *Francis of Assisi*, 131; Thompson, *Francis of
Assisi*, 122, Paolazzi, "Introduzione a *Cantico di Fratre Sole*," in FAS 118–20,

118. Brian Mooney's work on the *Canticle* agrees, although he collapses what appear to be separate incidents about Francis composing praises into the single act of writing the *Canticle of the Sun*. See Brian Mooney, *Francis of Assisi and His "Canticle of Brother Sun" Reassessed* (New York: Palgrave-Macmillan, 2013), 34–7.

151 The AC clearly suggests that the *Canticle of Exhortation* was written in the same place as the *Praises of the Lord* (probably the *Canticle of the Sun*), and most historians of Francis echo this without question. See Paolazzi, "Introduzione a *Audite Poverelle*," in FAS 124.

152 See AC 83, FF 1598–9, FA:ED 2.186 for the *Canticle of the Sun*, and AC 85, FF 1603–4, FA:ED 2.188–9 for the *Canticle of Exhortation*.

153 Thompson, for instance, notes only that the two had a falling out, "probably over court jurisdiction." Thompson, *Francis of Assisi*, 124.

154 See Fortini, *New Life*, 569–580

155 See AC 84, FF 1600–1603, FA:ED 2.187–8.

156 "Cumque iaceret ibi beatus Franciscus usque ad quinquaginta dies et plus, non potuit lumen diei videre de die nec de nocte lumen ignis, sed semper in domo et in cellula illa manebat in obscuro; insuper et magnos dolore in oculis die noctuque habebat, ita quod de nocte quiescere et dormire fere non poterat; quod erat valde erat contrarium et magnum gravamen infirmitate oculorum et aliis eius infirmitatibus." AC 83, FA:ED 1.185, FF 1596–7.

157 This event is recorded in VP 2.4.98, which links Elias' visit and command to Francis' worsening condition. It is also found in AC 83.

158 "Factum est autem, cum plures accederent suis eum medicaminibus adiuvare, non invento remedio, accessit ad civitatem Reatinam, in qua illius infirmitatis curandae morari vir peritissimus dicebatur." VP 2.5.99, FF 376, FA:ED 1.267. The *Assisi Compilation* confirms that the purpose of Francis' trip to Rieti was to see an expert in eye disease. See AC 86, FF 1604–5, FA:ED 2.189. According to the *Assisi Compilation*, the expert knew how to cure the Francis' infirmity of the eye: "cum quodam medico Reate qui noverat oculorum infirmitati medicinari." See also AVR 3.45, 184, and 7.7, 220.

159 "habens in capite quoddam magnum caputium sicut fratres fecerant sibi,et pannum de lana et lino consutum cum caputio ante oculos." AC 86, FF 1604–5, FA:ED 2.189.

160 Compare VP 2.5.101, FF 379–80, FA:ED 2.271, and AC 86, FF 1604–5, FA:ED 2.184.

161 See the chart in Sayers, *Papal Government in England*, 86–8.

162 VP 2.5.99, FF 376–7, FA:ED 1.267.

163 "maxime propter obedientiam domini episcopi Hostiensis et generalis ministri,." AC 86, FF 1605, FA:ED 2.189.

164 "Tempore infirmitatis oculorum, coacto ut mederi sibi pateretur."
      VS 2.125.166, FF 592, FA:ED 2.354. The TdeM repeats the same
      phraseology. See TdeM 3.14, FF 655, FA:ED 2.408.

165 "Videns autem dominus hostiensis ordinis procurator [sic] et frater
      heylas vicarius ordinis eius infirmitatem sibi et aliis in multis nocivam.
      preceperent [sic] per obedientiam sibi ut concilum acciperet a medicis
      qualiter sibi subveniret [sic – for *subvenire*] deberet de remedio oportuno
      [sic]." AVR 7.4, 218–20.

166 AVR 7.9–23, 220–4.

167 "Cum autem semel daretur consilium a medicis, et instanter suaderetur
      a fratribus, ut pateretur sibi per remedium subveniri cocturae." LM. 5.9,
      FF 820, FA:ED 2.566.

168 The moral of the story, in all the texts, is to demonstrate Francis' love of
      all parts of nature, even those parts which are dangerous, like fire.

169 The wound is described in AC 86, FF 1607, FA:ED 2.190; VS 2.125.166,
      FF 593, FA:ED 2.355; TdeM 3.14, FF 658, FA:ED 2.409; LM 5.9, FF 820,
      FA:ED 2.566; AVR 7.20, 224.

170 See VS 2.162.215, FF 631, FA:ED 2.385, in which Francis wears a cap made
      of sackcloth to cover his scars.

171 AC 86, FF 1608, FA:ED 2.191.

172 AC 86, FF 1608, FA:ED 2.191.

173 Angelo Sachetti Sassetti, *Analecta Franciscana Reatina* (Reiti: Soc. Tip.
      "Giornale di Basilicata," 1926), 40–4.

174 Schmucki, "Francis' Illnesses during the Last Years of His Life," 37–8

175 See Nancy Siraisi, *Medieval and Early Renaissance Medicine: An Introduction
      to Knowledge and Practice* (Chicago: University of Chicago Press, 1990), 163–4.

176 Alcide Garosi, *Siena nella storia della medicina, 1240–1555* (Florence:
      Olschki, 1978), 366.

177 Not much is known about Benvenutus Grassus with the exception that
      he wrote a treatise on diseases of the eye, which had moderate success in
      the fourteenth and fifteenth century and was printed in several editions
      in the fifteenth and sixteenth centuries. It was also translated into French,
      Provençal, and English. See David C Lindberg, *A Catalogue of Medieval and
      Renaissance Optical Manuscripts* (Toronto: PIMS, 1975), #190, 102–5. The
      few people who have worked on Beneventus Grassus tend to date him
      to the mid to late thirteenth century, based on the age of the manuscript
      survivals and internal evidence provided by the text. However, without
      explanation or evidence, the *Dictionnaire biographique des médecins en
      France au Moyen Âge* argues that he should be dated to the second half
      of the twelfth century rather than the thirteenth century, as is commonly
      done. See Ernest Wickersheimer, *Dictionnaire biographique des médecins en
      France au moyen âge* (Paris: Droz, 1936), 85–6.

178 Laurence M. Eldredge, "A Thirteenth-Century Ophthalmologist,
      Benvenutus Grassus: His Treatise and Its Survival," *Journal of the Royal
      Society of Medicine* 91:1 (1998), 47–52, 49.
179 Eldredge, "A Thirteenth-Century Ophthamologist," 49.
180 Eldredge, "A Thirteenth-Century Ophthamologist," 49.
181 Laurence M. Eldredge, "The Latin Manuscripts of Beneventus Grassus'
      Treatise on Diseases and Injuries to the Eye," in *Beneventus Grassus: On the
      well-proven Art of the Eye: Pratica oculorum et De probatissima arte oculorum:
      Synoptic Edition and Philological Studies*, ed. A. Miranda-García and S.G.
      Fernández-Corugedo (Bern: Peter Lang, 2011), 19–33, 24. The manuscript
      is Erfurt, Universitäts Bibliothek, MS Dep. Erf. CA. 4° 193.
182 Laurence Eldredge, "The Textual Tradition of Beneventus' Grassus' *De
      arte probatissima oculorum*," *Studi Medieval* 34 (1993), 95–138, 95–6.
183 For a summary of likely dates, see Eldredge, "The Textual Tradition," 96.
      Indeed, the likely *terminus a quo* for the text is the eleventh century, when
      the translation of Hunayn ibn Ishaq's work on ophthalmology, referenced
      in Beneventus Grassus' treatise, had been translated into Latin under the
      name Johannitius. Eldredge uses this information to suggest a *terminus a
      quo* of the ninth century, but it seems unlikely Grassus would have been
      educated enough to read Arabic. See Eldredge, "The Textual Tradition," 95.
184 See AC 89, FF 1611–12, FA:ED 2.192–3, VS 2.59.92, FF 528–9, FA:ED 2.306–7;
      AVR 9.4–29, 242–8.
185 Only one source suggests that the surgeon who performed the
      cauterization and the doctor who looked after him regularly were
      one and the same. The AVR 3.456, 184, states "Cuum [sic] enim
      beatus franciscus ex continuo fletu infirmitatem oculorum incurrisset
      gravissimam venit Reate ubi erat in arte cirugica [sic] et maxime oculoum
      medicus expertissimus. Et cum maneret in heremitorio fontis columarum
      [sic] prope reate predictus medicus pro cura oculorum Santum visitabat
      assidue et devote."
186 "quotidie." See VS 2.15.44, FF 485, FA:ED 2.276; TdM 5.36, FF 672,
      FA:ED 2.416. The AVR notes that the doctor visited "assidue et devote."
      AVR 3.46, 184.
187 This miracle is recounted in AC 68, FF 1571, FA:ED 2.171; VS 2.15.44,
      FF 485, FA:ED 2.276; TdeM 5.36, FF 671, FA:ED 2.416, and in
      AVR 3.58, 188.
188 LM 7.11, FF 841–2, FA:ED 2.583–4; AVR 9.30–5, 248–50.
189 "maxime quia corpus affligitur magna infirmitate et dolore." FF 1566,
      AC 66, FA:ED 2.169.
190 See AC 66, FF 1566–7, FA:ED 2.168–9; VS 2.89.126, FF 559–60, FA:ED 2.330.
      Radically altered, the miracle is also found in the *Legenda major*. See
      LM 5.11, FF 822, FA:ED 2.567.

191 "Hiisdem temporibus cum beatus Franciscus esset infirmus infirmitate
    oculorum et per aliquot dies maneret in palatio episcopi Reate." AC 95,
    FF 1621, FA:ED 2.197

192 The first part of this story is found in AC 95, FF 1621–3, FA:ED 2.197–8.
    The cure was conditional though, and when Gedeone returned to his old
    and suspect ways of life, God intervened to take his life by collapsing a
    house on top of him. The *Assisi Compilation* does not contain the end of
    the story (in which Gedeone is killed) but it can be found in VS 2.12.41,
    FF 482–3, FA:ED 2.274. The miracle (and that Francis was ill at Rieti at
    the time) can be found in the LM 11.5, FF 873–4, FA:ED 2.615–16, and
    AVR 8.1, 234.

193 VS 2.60.93, FF 529–30, FA:ED 2.307–8.

194 VP 2.7.105, FF 383, FA:ED 1.274.

195 "comitem itineris habens medicum quemdam Ordini obligatum."
    VS 2.60.93, FF 530, FA:ED 2.307.

196 Darrel Admundsen has shown that the often-presumed prohibitions
    of clerics, monks, and later friars being doctors in generally inaccurate.
    See Darrel Admundsen, "Medieval Canon Law on Medical and Surgical
    Practice by the Clergy," *Bulletin of the History of Medicine* 52:1 (1977),
    22–43, 26. See also Angela Montford, "Brothers Who Have Studied
    Medicine: Dominican Friars in Thirteenth-Century Paris," *Social History
    of Medicine* 24:3 (2011), 535–3, 536.

197 "causa exigente." See LM 7.6, FF 837, FA:ED 2.580.

198 Thompson, *Francis of Assisi*, 129.

199 There were, apparently, as many as three different Peter Hispani active
    in Italy during the thirteenth century. On this see Iona McCleery,
    "Opportunities for Teaching and Studying Medicine in Medieval
    Portugal before the Foundation of the University of Lisbon (1290),"
    Dynamis 20 (2000), 305–29, 308–9; and Renzo Console and Christopher
    Duffin, "Peter Hispanus (ca 1215–1277) and the 'Treasury of the Poor,'"
    Pharmaceutical Historian: British Society for the History of Pharmacy 42:4
    (Autumn 2012), 82–8, 82. The articles which provide evidence for three
    individual people operating as Peter Hispanus are José Francisco
    Meirinhos, "Petrus Hispanus Portugalensis: Elementos para uma
    differenção de autores," *Revista Española de Filosofia Medieval* 3 (1006),
    51–76; and Angel D'Ors, "Petrus Hispanus, O.P.," *Auctor Summularum,
    Vivarium* 35 (1997), 21–91.

200 Garosi, *Siena nella storia della medicina*, 367.

201 Schmucki, "Francis' Illnesses during the Last Years of His Life," 37.

202 "In mense autem sexto ante obitus sui diem, cum esset apud Senas pro
    infirmitate oculorum curanda, coepit in toto reliquo corpore graviter
    infirmari, et fracto stomacho infirmitate diuturna et vitio hepatis,

sanguinem multum evomuit, ita quod visus est morti appropinquare."
VP 2.7.105, FF 383, FA:ED 1.274.

203 "In mense autem sexto ante obitus sui diem, cum esset apud Senas,
stomacho defectus infirmitati prevaluit oculorum et, gravius solito corpore
toto attritus morti visus est propinquare." VB 63.

204 AC 59, FF 1550–2, FA:ED 2.161–2.

205 VP 2.7.105, FF 383, FA:ED 2.274, and VB 63, FA:ED 2.474.

206 "intumuit venter eius, turguere crura, tumueruntque pedes et stomachi
magis ac magis defectum incurrit, ut cibum aliquem recipere vix valeret."
VP 2.7.105, FF 383, FA:ED 1.274. See also VB 63, which notes only that
"Ubi morbo gravius invalescente, fecit se Asisium deportari."

207 VP 2.7.105, FF 383, FA:ED 2.174.

208 VP 2.7.105, FF 383, FA:ED 2.174.

209 Fortini, *Nova Vita*, 2.463.

210 AC 96, FF 1623, FA:ED 2.198.

211 See Fortini, *New Life*, 589. Vauchez and Thompson do not posit a cure;
rather they explain the move as a way for Francis to get relief from the
heat in Assisi. See Vauchez, *Francis of Assisi*, 139, and Thompson, *Francis
of Assisi*, 131. There is no evidence to support this supposition in the
source documents. In placing this event in Francis' life near the end,
after his failed trip to Siena to cure his eye ailment, the historians follow
Wadding, *Annales minorum*, II.129, so the traditional dating is a long
storied one.

212 AC 96, FF 1623–4, FA:ED 2.198–9.

213 "Contigit beatum Franciscum infirmitatibus plenum et iam fere ad
extrema vergentem, in loco Nuceriae requiri a populo Assisii." VS 2.47.77,
FF 515, FA:ED 2.297–8.

214 "Cum in palatio episcopatus Assisii beatus Franciscus iaceret valde
infirmus illis diebus quando reversus est de loco Bagnarie." AC 99, FF 1633,
FA:ED 2.202.

215 AC 99, FF 1633–4, FA:ED 2.202–3.

216 On the possible connection between Bon Giovanni and Francis' family,
see Fortini, *New Life*, 599–601. Fortini suggests that the notation in the
Assisi Compilation that Bongiovanni was from Arezzo is a scribal error and
that it should have read Assisi. Fortini has, in fact, found a doctor and
notary named Bongiovanni in the records of Assisi.

217 AC 100, FF 1635–6, FA:ED, 2.203–4.

218 "In ultimo suae infirmitatis tempore." VS 2.22.51, FF 492, FA:ED 2.281.

219 VS 2.22.51, FF 492, FA:ED 2.281.

220 "erigens se parum in lecto." AC 5, FF 1475, FA:ED 2.120.

221 AC 5, FF 1474–6, FA:ED 2.120.

222 AC 90 notes that this was his condition "a few days before his death";
"Nam paucis diebus ante obitum suum, quia erat hydropicus et quasi

totus desiccatus et per alias plures infirmitates quas habebat." AC 90, FF 1615, FA:ED 2.194.

223 AC 7, FF 1476–8, FA:ED 2.120–1.

224 Jacoba dei Settesoli appears to have been a privileged noblewoman of Rome who knew and supported Francis from the earliest years of his movement. Not a great deal has been written about her (and not much is known). Perhaps the best source of information about her is Carol Reilley Urner, *The Search for Brother Iacopa: A Study on Jacopa Deo Settesoli, Friend of Francis of Assisi and His Movement*, unpublished MA thesis, Manila University, 1980. See also Jacques Dalarun, *Francis of Assisi and the Feminine*, trans. P. Pierce and M. Sutphin (St. Bonaventure, NY: Franciscan Institute Press, 2006), *passim*. Dalarun notes that Jacoba can be understood as the Mary Magdalene to Francis' Christ. Perhaps casting her in this role allowed the friars to make sense of her closeness to Francis. Finally, Francesco Di Ciaccia suggests that Jacoba's part in the Franciscan story was suppressed in Bonaventure's life because he could not make sense of her role in the saint's trajectory, though Di Ciaccia himself notes that she was necessary to the Franciscan story. See Francesco Di Ciaccia, "S. Chiara 'Domina' e Jacopa dei Dettesoli 'Fratello' di S. Francesco d'Assisi," *Studi Franciscani* 79:3 (1982), 327–241, 336 and 340.

225 "'mittat etiam de illa comestione, quam, pluries fecit michi, cum fui apud Urbem.' Illam autem comestionem vocant Romani 'mortariolum,' que fit de amigdalis et zucaro vel melle et aliis rebus." AC 8, FF 1478–81, FA:ED 1.121–3.

226 "ferculum quoddam quod sanctus appetierat detulit." TdeM, 6.38, FF 674, FA:ED 2.418.

227 AC 12, FF 1488, FA:ED 2.126.

228 "Cumque a sinistris ipsius resideret frater Helyas, circumsedentibus reliquis filiis, cancellatis manibus dexteram posuit super caput eius. Sed exteriorum oculorum lumine pene privatus et usu: 'Super quem' inquit, 'teneo dexteram meam?' 'Super fratrem Helyam,' inquiunt. 'Et ego sic volo,' ait. 'Tibi,' inquit, 'fili, in omnibus et per omnia benedico, qui, humeris propriis honera mea suscipiens, fratrum necessitates viriliter supportasti. Et sicut in manibus tuis eos augmentavit et conservavit Altissimus, ita et in te omnibus benedico.'" VB 63.

229 AC 22, FF 1501–3, FA:ED 2.135; VS 2.162–3, 2.216–17, FF 631–3, FA:ED 2.386–8.

4. Disability and Tensions in Francis' Lived Experience

1 "Et licet infirmus fuisset semper beatus Franciscus." AC 117, FF 1682, FA:ED 2.225.

2 AC 51, FF 1527–8, FA:ED 2.150–1.

3 LTC 7.21, FF 1394–5, FA:ED, 2.81.

4 AC 81, FF 1592–3, FA:ED 2.181–2.

5 VP 1.19.52, FF 327, FA:ED 1.228.

6 AC 80, FF 1590, FA:ED 2.181.

7 See this particular discussion in AC 79–80, FF 1589–92, FA:ED 2.182–3.

8 This episode is recounted in many early *lives:* VP 1:19.52, FF 327–8, FA:ED 1.228; AC 80, FA:ED 2.181–2, FF 1590–2; LM 6.2, FF 824–5, FA:ED 2.570.

9 AC 6, FF 1475, FA:ED 2.120.

10 "Cumque infirmitatis suae occasione rigorem pristinum necessario temperaret, dicebat, 'Incipiamus, fratres, servire Domino Deo, quia hucusque vix vel parum in nullo profecimus.' Non arbitratur se adhuc comprehendisse et infatigabilis durans in sanctae novitatis proposito, semper inchoare sperabat." VP 2.6.103, FF 381–2, FA:ED 1.273.

11 "ipse tamen suo corpori, etiam antequam haberet fratres, a principio sue conversionis et toto tempore vite sua fuit austerus, cum a tempore sue iuventutis esset homo fragilis et debilis secundum naturam, et in seculo non posset vivere nisi delicate." AC 50, FF 1525, FA:ED 2.150.

12 Although *pitantia* can mean food in a general sense, the context here seems to imply the more specific meaning mentioned in du Cange et al, "Pictantia," t. 6, col. 313b, http://ducange.enc.sorbonne.fr/PICTANTIA. Accessed 14 January 2015.

13 "Unde quodam tempore considerans quod fratres iam excederent modum pauperitatis et honestatis in cibus et rebus, in quadam sua predicatione quam fecerat, quibusdam fratribus in persona omnium fratrum dixit. 'Non putant fratres quod corpori meo necessaria esset pitantia? Sed quia oportet me esse formam et exemplum omnium fratrum, volo uti et esse contentus pauperculis cibus et rebus, et non delicatis.'" AC 50, FF 1525–6, FA:ED 2.150.

14 "ipsum esse formam et exemplum omnium fratrum." AC 79, FF 1590.

15 "ideo non tantum medicinis, sed etiam cibis necessariis in infirmitatibus suis uti nolebat. Et propterea quia hec predicta considerabat, non tantum quando videbatur esse sanus, licet semper esset debilis et infirmus, sed etiam in suis infirmitatibus, suo corpore erat austerus." AC 79, FF 1590, FA:ED 2.181.

16 "Et licet suo corpori propter eius infirmitatem [esset] necessaia pitantia." AC 82, FF 1594, FA:ED 2.184. Note that this is the precise language used in AC 50.

17 AC 82, FF 1594, FA:ED 184.

18 "Et licet suo corpori propter eius infirmitatem [esset] necessaia pitantia, tamen inde considereabat fratribus et aliis de sua bonum exemplum semper exhibere, ut tolleret eis ocassionem murmurandi et mali exempli, quod malebat patienter et libenter sustinere corporis necessitates et sustinuit saepe usque ad diem mortis sue, quam sibi satisfarcere, licet

secundum Deum et bonum exemplum illud facere potuisset." AC 82, FF 1594, FA:ED 2.184.

19 LTC 7.22, FF 1395–6, FA:ED 1.81

20 VS 2.133.175, FF 598–9, FA:ED 2.359.

21 On the flexibility of Francis' eating habits, see David Grumett, "Vegetarian or Franciscan: Flexible Dietary Choices Past and Present," *Journal of the Study of Religion, Nature and Culture* 1:4 (2007), 450–67.

22 Wayne Hellmann, "Authority According to St. Francis: Power or Powerlessness," in *Theology and Authority* (Peabody, MA: Hendrickson Publishers, 1987), 24–31, 24.

23 Hellmann, "Authority According to St. Francis," 24.

24 "Et omnes alii fratres mei benedicti diligenter obediant eis in hiis quae spectant ad salutem anime et non sunt contraria vite nostre." RNB, 4, FAS 248, FA:ED 1.66 That *eis* refers to ministers is clear from the preceding context, a discussion of ministers' need to visit their charges frequently.

25 "Si quis autem ministrorum alicui fratrum aliquid contra vitam nostram praeciperet vel contra animam suam, non teneatur ei obedire; quia illa obedientia non est, in qua delictum vel peccatum committitur." RNB 5, FAS 248, FA:ED 1.67.

26 On the differences between the *Regula non bullata* and the *Regula bullata* on the importance of obedience see Jens Röhrkasten, "Authority and Obedience in the Early Franciscan Order," *Episcopacy, Authority and Gender: Aspects of Religious Leadership in Europe, 1100–2000*, ed. Jan Wim Buisman, Marjet Derks, and Peter Raedts (Leiden: Brill, 2015), 98–115, 98–103.

27 "Fratres qui sunt ministri et servi aliorum fratrum, visitent et moneant fratres suos et humiliter et caritative corrigant eos, non praecipientes eis aliquid, quod sit contra animam suam et regulam nostram. Fratres vero, qui sunt subditi, recordentur, quod propter Deum abnegaverunt proprias voluntates. Unde firmiter precipio eis, ut obediant suis ministris in omnibus quae promiserunt Domino observare et non sunt contraria anime et Regule nostre (Brothers who are ministers and servants of other friars ought to visit and advise those brothers and humbly and charitably correct them, not ordering them to do anything which is against the soul and our *Rule*. But the brothers who are subordinate ought to remember that they have denied their own wills on account of God. Whence I firmly order them that they obey their ministers in all things which they promised to observe for the Lord and those things which are not contrary to the soul and our *Rule*)." RB 10, FAS 334, FA:ED 1.105.

28 RNB 5.

29 This cannot have occurred long after Francis' death, however, as a recently discovered manuscript now in the hands of a private owner can apparently be reliably dated to before Francis' canonization in 1228. See Michael Robson and Patrick Zutshi, "An Early Manuscript of the

Admonitions of St. Francis of Assisi," *The Journal of Ecclesiastical History* 62:2 (April 2011), 216–54.

30 Robson and Zutshi, "An Early Manuscript of the *Admonitions*," 225.

31 Robert Karras, *The Admonitions of St. Francis: Sources and Meanings* (St. Bonaventure, NY: St. Bonaventure University Press, 1999), 3.

32 G. Pozzi, "Lo stile di San Francesco," *Italia medievale e umanistica* 41 (2000), 7–72, 71.

33 "Ille homo relinquit omnia que possidet et perdit corpus suum qui se ipsum totum prebet ad obedientiam in manibus sui prelati, et quicquid facit aut dicit, quod ipse sciat quod non sit contra voluntatem sui prelati, dum bonum sit quod facit, vera obedientia est. Et si aliquando subditus videat meliora et utiliora anime sue quam ea que prelatus sibi precipiat sua voluntate Deo sacrificet, que autem sunt prelati studeat adimplere. Hec est caritativa obedientia quia Deo et proximo satisfecit. Si vero prelatus precipiat aliquid subdito contra animam suam, licet ei non obediat, tamen ipsum non dimittat." Transcription from Robson and Zutshi, "An Early Manuscript of the *Admonitions*," 244.

34 Karras, *Admonitions*, 60–1.

35 See Pseudo-Bernard, *De statu virtutum*, PL 184, columns 805–6.

36 "Et firmiter volo obedire ministro generali huius fraternitatis et alio gardiano quem sibi placuerit michi dare, et ita volo esse captus in manibus suis ut non possim ire vel facere ultra obedientiam et voluntam suam quia dominus meus est." *Testamentum*, 27–8; FAS, 400; FA:ED 1.126.

37 "Et omnes alii fratres teneantur ita obedire guardianis suis." *Testamentum*, 30, FAS 400; FA:ED 1.126.

38 Hellmann, "Authority According to St. Francis," 24–31.

39 See VP 2.5.101, AC 83, and VS 2.125.166.

40 "Et rogo fratrem infirmum ut referat de omnibus gratias Creatori, et qualem vult eum Deus, talem se esse desideret, sive sanum sive infirmum, quia omnes quos Deus ad vitam preordinauit eternam, flagellorum atque infirmitatum stimulis et compunctionis spirito erudit sicut dicit Dominus. Ego quos amo arguo et castigo. Si autem quis turbabitur vel irascetur sive contra Deum, sive contra fratres, vel si forte sollicite postulauerit medicinas, nimis desiderans liberare carnem cito morituram, que est anime inimica, a malo sibi evenit et carnalis est, et non uidetur esse de fratribus, quia plus diligit corpus quam animam." RNB 10, FAS 258–60. FA:ED 1.71–2.

41 "Et si quis eorum in infirmitatem ceciderit, alii fratres debent ei servire, sicut vellent sibi serviri." RB, FAS 330, FA:ED 1.103.

42 The earliest tradition that records this is AC 17, FA:ED 2.131, FF 1496.

43 Thompson notes, correctly I think, that the narrative in the *Assisi Compilation* more likely reflects tensions within the order in the 1240s and 1250s than those in the early 1220s. Nonetheless Thompson

allows for the possibility, even probability, that Elias did visit Francis during the composition of the *Regula bullata*. See Thompson, *Francis of Assisi*, 253.

44 Thompson, *Francis of Assisi*, 253.

45 "Et cum ex longa familiaritate, quam idem Confessor nobiscum habuit, plenius noverimus intentionem ipsius et in condendo predictam Regulam et obtinendo confirmationem ipsius per sedem apostolicam sibi astiterimus, dum adhuc essemus in minori officio constituti (And since from the long familiarity, which that same confessor [Francis] had with us, we would have known his intention more fully, and since we aided him in the composing of the aforesaid *Rule* and in obtaining its confirmation from the apostolic seat while we were placed in a lesser office)." Transcription found in Herbert Grundman, "Die Bulle '*Quo elongati*' Papst Gregor IX," *Archivum Franciscanum Historicum* 54 (1961): 20–5.

46 Leviticus 21:17–21.

47 See T.S. Brown, "Urban Violence in Early Medieval Italy: The Cases of Rome and Ravenna," in *Violence and Society in the Early Medieval West*, ed. Guy Halsall (Woodbrige: Boydell, 1998), 77–89, 81; and Susan Wade, "Abbot Erluin's Blindness: The Monastic Implications of Violent Loss of Sight," in *Negotiating Community and Difference in Medieval Europe: Gender, Power, Patronage and the Authority of Religion in Latin Christendom*, ed. Katherine Allen Smith and Scott Wells (Leiden: Brill 2009), 207–22, 219–20.

48 T.S. Brown, "Urban Violence, 81.

49 Wade, "Abbot Erluin's Blindness," 219–20.

50 See the discussion, original documents, and transcriptions in "Medieval Clergy and Disability"archive, University of York, Borthwick Institute for Archives. www.york.ac.uk/borthwick/holdings/guides/research-guides/disability/medieval-clergy-and-disability/. Accessed 19 February 2015.

51 Wade, "Abbot Erluin's Blindness," 207, 211–12.

52 Wade, "Abbot Erluin's Blindness," 220.

53 See Sigbert of Gembloux, *Gesta abbatum Gemblacensium*, ed. G. Pertz, MGH SS 8, 523–42, especially 532–4.

54 Leviticus 21:17–18: "loquere ad Aaron homo de semine tuo per familias qui habuerit maculam non offeret panes Deo suo nec accedet ad ministerium eius."

55 Leviticus 21:18–21: "Si caecus fuerit si claudus si vel parvo vel grandi et torto naso si fracto pede si manu si gibbus si lippus si albuginem habens in oculo si iugem scabiem si inpetiginem in corpore vel hirniosus omnis qui habuerit maculam de semine Aaron sacerdotis non accedet offerre hostias Domino nec panes Deo suo."

56 Irina Metzler suggest that the influence of Leviticus 21 can be overstated, noting that dispensations for some disabilities were given in the thirteenth century. Unfortunately, it is unclear the extent to which such dispensations were given, or for which disabilities they were most likely to be granted.

See Irina Metzler, "Medieval Blindness and the Law," *Scribd*, https://www
.scribd.com/document/157675720/Irina-Metzler-EN-Medieval-blindness-
and-the-law-visual-impairment-in-canon-law-and-civil-jurisprudence-
and-as-judicial-consequence, 1–2. Last updated 2 August 2013. Ninon
Dubourg's recent doctoral work on dispensations and the use of coadjutors
to replace ill clerics suggests that both increased throughout the high and
late Middle Ages. Her research and primary sources are outlined on her
website at ninondubourg.com.

57 Joy Hawkins, "Blindness and Sanctity in Later Medieval History," *Studies in Church History* 47 (2011), 148–58, 150.

58 See Metzler, "Medieval Blindness and the Law," 3

59 Metzler, "Medieval Blindness and the Law," 2–3.

60 More research needs to be done on the role of coadjutors for the blind, but Metzler cites two early fourteenth century cases. Metzler, "Medieval Blindness and the Law," 3.

61 Moshe Barash, *Blindness: The History of a Mental Image in Western Thought* (Abingdon and New York: Routledge, 2001), 108.

62 Edward Wheatley, "Blind Jews and Blind Christians: Metaphors of Marginalization in Medieval Europe," *Exemplaria* 14:2 (2002), 351–79, 367.

63 "ceci sunt, quia verum lumen non vident, Dominum nostrum Jesum Christum." *Epistola ad fideles I*, II.7 FAS 176. A few lines later Francis exhorts the blind, "Videte, ceci, decepti ab inimias vestris, a carne, mundo et diabolo": *Epistola ad fideles I*, II.11, FAS 176. The same phrases are also found in the *Epistola ad fideles II*, 66, 196, and 69, 196.

64 Michael Cusato, "Francis of Assisi, Deacon?" in *Defenders and Critics of the Franciscan Life*, ed. M. Cusato and G. Geltner (Leiden: Brill, 2009). To the evidence marshalled by Cusato, I would add Francis' own voice. In both recensions of Francis' *Epistola ad clericos*, he begins the letter by saying, "Attendamus, omnes clerici." This phraseology would seem to imply that Francis is claiming clerical status for himself. FAS 140 and 142.

65 Angela Montford, "Occupational Health in the Mendicant Orders," in *The Use and Abuse of Time in Christian History*, ed. R. N. Swanson, Studies in Church History 37 (Cambridge: Cambridge University Press, 2002), 95–106, 103.

66 Montford, "Occupational Health," 103.

67 Monftord, "Occupational Health," 103.

68 On this reasoning, see for instance, Moorman, *A History of the Franciscan Order*, 50–52, and Brooke, *Early Franciscan Government*, 76–83. Jacques Dalarun has recently lamented the tendency of many scholars to unquestioningly believe the truthfulness of Francis' humility described in early Franciscan sources. See Jacques Dalarun, *Francis of Assisi and Power* (St. Bonaventure, NY: Franciscan Institute, 2007), 194.

69 On the history of Gratian and his *Decretum* see James Brundage, "The
Teaching and Study of Canon Law in the Law Schools," in *The History
of Medieval Canon Law in the Classical Period,* ed. Wilfried Hartmann and
Kenneth Pennington (Washington: Catholic University of America Press,
2008), 98–120; Peter Landau, "Gratian and the Decretum Gratiani," in
*The History of Medieval Canon Law in the Classical Period: From Gratian
to the Decretals of Pope Gregory IX*, ed. Wilfried Hartmann and Kenneth
Pennington (Washington, DC: Catholic University of America Press, 2008),
22–54; and Anders Winroth, *The Making of Gratian's Decretum* (Cambridge:
University of Cambridge Press, 2000), 5–8.

70 As Irina Metzler has argued, the Latin words *infirmus, aeger,* and *egrotus*
were used almost interchangeably to mean either a sick or impaired
individual. See Metzler, *Disability in Medieval Europe*, 4–5.

71 Letter 11.29. See the *Patrologia Latina*, ed. J.P. Migne (Paris: Garnier fratres,
1866–1882), 77:1141–2. An English translation can be found in Gregory the
Great, *The Letters of Gregory the Great*, trans. John R.C. Martyn (Toronto,
PIMS, 2004), 774–5.

72 "Et quod nusquam canones precipiunt, ut pro egritudine episcopi
episcopus succedat, et ideo iniustum est, ut, si molestia corporis irruit,
honore suo privetur egrotus. Sed suggerendum est, ut si quid, in regime,
egrotat, dispensator illi talis requiratur, qui possit eius curam omnem
agere et locum illius in regimine ecclesiae (ipso non deposito) conservare,
ut neque Deus omnipotens offendatur, neque civitas neglecta esse
inveniatur." Gratian, *Decretum*, ed. A.L. Richter (Graz: Verlagsanstalt,
1959), 2.7.1.1, col. 566.

73 This is the particular topic of 2.7.1.3, col. 567; the chapter begins with the
rubric "infirmitatis causa loco suo quis priuare non debet."

74 For an overview of what is known about the author of the *Summa
parisiensis*, see Terence McLaughlin's introduction to the critical edition.
Terence P. McLaughlin, "Introduction," in *The "Summa parisiensis" on the
"Decretum gratiani"* (Toronto, PIMS, 1952), xvii–xx and xxxi–xxxiii.

75 "Sed solum si fuerit leprosus, tunc non debet retinere cathedram, sicut in
corpore canonun est, ubi similiter inuenitur quod propter lepram aliquis
separatur a cohabitatione uxoris." McLaughlin, ed., *Summa parisiensis*,
VII.2, 134.

76 The extent to which communities considered the lepers in their midst
officially dead and had rituals to affirm that status has been debated.
Carole Rawcliffe has argued that there is no evidence that leper masses
or other rituals that allowed lepers to become "dead to the world" ever
existed in England. She further argues that such rituals, if they did exist,
need not mean that the leper was marginalized or persecuted, a conclusion
this commentary on Gratian's *Decretum* would seem to refute. On the

historiography of the leper mass, see Carole Rawcliffe, *Leprosy in Medieval England* (Woodbridge: Boydell, 2006), 21–8.

77 "fraternitas tua divini contemplatione iudicii praebeat aegrotanti.".Raymond of Peñafort, *Decretalium gregorii*, in *Decretalium collectiones*, ed. A.L. Richter (Graz: Akademische Druck-u. Verlagsanstalt, 1959), cc. 1–928, 3.6.1, c. 481.

78 "quia, si alii eius essent exemplo deterriti, forte non posset qui militaret ecclesiae inveniri." Raymond of Peñafort, *Decretalium gregorii*, 3.6.1, c. 481. The decretal is repeated nearly word for word from the register of Gregory's letters. "quia diversis in Ecclesia militantibus, varia, sicut nosti, saepe contingit infirmitas. Et si hoc fuerunt exemplo deterriti, nullus de caetero qui Ecclesiae militet poterit inveniri." See the *Patrologia Latina*, 77:544–5. No recent translation of this letter into English exists.

79 See the *Vita sancti Maoili*, 2.1, in the *Patrologia Latina*, 137:733. I am grateful to Dr. Isabelle Cochelin for providing me with the above information.

80 King sees a parallel between guardians for individuals determined to be of unsound mind who are appointed by the king and coadjutors appointed for the same reason by prelates of the English church. James R. King, "The Mysterious Case of the 'Mad' Rector of Bletchingdon: The Treatment of Mentally Ill Clergy in Late Thirteenth-Century England," in *Madness in Medieval Law and Custom*, ed. W. Turner (Leiden and Boston: Brill, 2010), 57–80. I am grateful to Dr. Turner for drawing this article to my attention.

81 "Minister autem provincialis, quando vadit ad capitulum generale vel alias extra suam provinciam, vel sic infirmatur quod non possit provinciali capitulo interesse, instituat vicarium de consilio decretorum." *Constitutiones generalis narbonensis (1260)*, in *Constitutiones generalis ordinis fratrum minorum* in n.s. 1, ed. C. Cenci and R.G. Maillaux (Grottoferrata: Editiones Collegii S. Bonaventurae, 2007), 69–104, 11.7, 99.

82 "Vicarius vero, sic institutus a ministro, si minister in generali capitulo absolutus fuerit vel ipsum interim mori contingerit, remaneat vicarious auctoritate generalis ministri usquequo provinciale capitulum congregetur." *Constitutiones generalis narbonensis (1260)*, 11.8, 99.

83 "Custodes similiter, cum ad generale vadit capitulum, instituat vicarium in custodia, de aliquorum suae custodiae consilio discretorum." *Consitutiones generalis narbonensis (1260)*, 11.9, 99.

84 On the relatively few constitutions found from the meeting of 1239, see "Statua generalia ordinis edita in capitulis generalibus celebratis Narbonae an 1260, Assisii an. 1279 atque Parisiis an. 1292," ed. M. Bihl, in *Achivum franciscanum historicum* 36 (1941), 13–94, 284–358, and 338–9; Brooke, *Early Franciscan Government*, 210. For the most recent edition of the Constitutions of 1239, see *Fragmenta Priscarum Constitutionum Praenarbonensium (1239)*, in *Constitutiones generalis ordinis fratrum minorum*, ed. C. Cenci and

R.G. Mailleux (Grottaferrata: Editiones Collegii S. Bonaventurae, 2007), 5–12; *Constitutionum praenarbonensium particulae (1239–1254)*, in *Constitutiones generalis ordinis fratrum minorum*, ed. C. Cenci and R.G. Mailleux (Grottaferrata: Editiones Collegii S. Bonaventurae, 2007), 17–36; and *Vetigia constitutionum praenarbonensium (1239–1257)*, in *Constitutiones generalis ordinis fratrum minorum*, ed. C. Cenci and R.G. Mailleux (Grottaferrata: Editiones Collegii S. Bonaventurae, 2007), 43–63.

85 On the date of Eccleston's chronicle, *De adventu fratrum minorum in Angliam*, see Bert Roest, *Reading the Book of History: Intellectual Contexts and Educational Functions of Franciscan Hagiography, 1226–ca 1350* (PhD diss., Groningen University, 1996), 40, and Brooke, *Early Franciscan Government*, 27. On the way in which the narrative was collected see, most recently, Annette Kehnel, "The Narrative Tradition of the Medieval Franciscan Friars on the British Isles: Introduction to the Sources," *Franciscan Studies* 63 (2005), 477.

86 Thomas of Eccleston, *De adventu fratrum minorum in Angliam*, in *Analecta Franciscana I*, ed. Patres Collegii S. Bonaventurae (Quarrachi: Typographia Collegii S. Bonaventurae, 1885), 217–56, 246. See the English translation in *Thirteenth Century Chronicles*, trans. P. Hermann (Chicago: Franciscan Herald Press, 1961), 93–191,163–4.

87 Thompson, *Francis of Assisi*, 60.

88 Chapter 11. Jordan of Giano, *Chronica*, 4; Jordan of Giano, *Chronicle*, 26.

89 Honorius III, *Cum delicti*, *Bullarium Franciscanum*, 1.2. An English translation can be found in FA:ED 1.558. See also Moorman, *History of the Franciscan Order*, 50.

90 See also Brooke, *Early Franciscan Government*, 64, and Moorman, *History of the Franciscan Order*, 51.

91 On this, see Thompson, *Francis of Assisi*, 50.

92 Michael Robson, *The Franciscans in the Middle Ages* (Woodbridge: Boydell Press, 2006), 25.

93 Jordan of Giano states that 3000 Franciscans attended the Pentecost chapter of 1221, a number Thompson argues in high but not impossible. Chapter 16, Jordan of Giano, *Chronica*, 6; Jordan of Giano, *Chronicle*, 30–1; Thompson, *Francis of Assisi*, 88.

94 Until quite recently, this has been called Francis' "resignation" as minister general, but as Jean-François Godet-Calogeras has argued, Francis could not resign from the position of minister general of the order because he never possessed such a title. The use of the term minister general began after Francis' death. See Godet-Calogeras, "Francis of Assisi's Resignation," 281–300.

95 According to VS 2.111. On Francis' withdrawal in favour of Peter Catani, see Brooke, *Early Franciscan Government*, 76; Moorman, *History of the Franciscan Order*, 51; and Thompson, *Francis of Assisi*, 80.

96 Rosalind Brooke suggests an early date of 1219, while most other
     biographers follow Moorman in placing the chapter in 1220. See Brooke,
     Early Franciscan Government, 77–81; Moorman, *History of the Franciscan
     Order*, 50–1, Thompson, *Francis of Assisi*, 80.
97 See Jordan of Giano, chapter 16, which refers to Elias as the vicar
     (*vicarius*) of Francis. See also Brooke, *Early Franciscan Government*, 83;
     Moorman, *History of the Franciscan Order*, 51; and Thompson, *Francis of
     Assisi*, 88.
98 Brooke, *Early Franciscan Government*, 113.
99 On this see Brooke, *Early Franciscan Government*, 111.
100 "Viderat namque gallinam quamdam paruam et nigram, habentem crura
     pennata cum pedibus in modum columbae domesticae, quae tot pullos
     habebat quod non poterat eos sub alis propriis congregare, sed ibant in
     circuitu gallinae exterius remanentes. Evigilans autem a somno coepit
     cogitare de huiusmodi visione, statimque per Spiritum sanctum cognouit
     se per illam gallinam figuraliter designari et ait 'Ego sum illa gallina,
     statura pusillus nigerque natura, qui debeo esse simplex ut columba et
     affectibus pennatis virtutum volare ad caelum. Mihi autem Dominus per
     misericordiam suam dedit et dabit filios multos quos protegere mea
     virtute non potero, unde oportet ut eos sanctae Ecclesiae recommendem
     quae sub umbra alarum suarum eos protegat et gubernet.'" LTC 16.63,
     FF 1437.
101 LTC 16.63, FF 1437–8, FA:ED 2.105.
102 AC 11, FF 1484–5, FA:ED 2.125.
103 "Domine recommendo tibi familiam, quam michi hactenus commisisti.
     Et nunc, propter infirmitates quas tu nosti, dulcissime Domine, curam
     eius habere non valens, ipsam recommendo ministris." AC 39, FF 1513,
     FA:ED 2.142.
104 AC 39, FF 1513, FA:ED 2.142; VS 2.104.143, FF 571–2, FA:ED 2.340.
105 "Quoniam licet tempore quo renuntiaui et dimisi officium fratrum, coram
     fratribus me excusarem in capitulo generali, quod propter infirmitatem
     meam de ipsis curam et sollicitudinem habere non possem, tamen modo,
     si secundum voluntatem meam fratres ambularent et ambulassent,
     propter ipsorum consolationem nollem, quod alium ministrum haberent
     preter me, usque in diem mortis mee." AC 106, FF 1650, FA:ED 2.211.
106 "Nos vero qui cum ipso fuimus, quando scripsit Regulam et fere omnia
     alia sua scripta, testimonium perhibemus, quod plura fecit scribi in
     Regula et aliis suis scriptis, de quibus quidam fratres fuerunt sibi
     contrarii, et maxime prelati." AC 106, FF 1653, FA:ED 2.212.
107 "quapropter, ex quo dimisi officium fratrum, de cetero, propter
     infirmitates meas et pro maiori utilitate anime mee et omnium fratrum,
     non teneor fratribus nisi exhibere bonum exemplum. Nam illud a
     Domino reperi et scio in veritate quoniam, etiam si infirmitas non me

excusaret, maius adiutorium quod fratrum Religioni impendere possim, est ut cotidie vacem orationi pro ea ad Dominum, ut ipsam gubernet, conservet, protegat et defendat." AC 112, FF 1670, FA:ED 2.219–20.

108 "Et paulo post cum infirmitate nimia grauaretur, in vehementia spiritus in lectulo se direxit. 'Qui sunt isti, ait, qui Religionem meam et fratrum de meis manibus rapuerunt? Si ad generale capitulum venero, eis ostendam qualem habeam voluntatem.'"AC 44, FF 1518. This anecdote likely dates from circa 1247, as it appears to be drawn from the *Remembrance of the Desire of a Soul* of Thomas of Celano. See VS 2.141.188, FF 608, FA:ED 2.366.

109 "Nos vero qui cum ipso fuimus, quando scripsit Regulam et fere omnia alia sua scripta, testimonium perhibemus, quod plura fecit scribi in Regula et aliis suis scriptis, de quibus quidam fratres fuerunt sibi contrarii, et maxime prelati. Unde accidit quod in hiis, in quibus fratres fuerunt contrarii beato Francisco in vita sua, nunc post mortem essent valde utilia toti Religioni. Sed quia ipse plurimum timebat scandalum, condescendebat, licet involuntarius, voluntatibus fratrum. Sed sepe dicebat hunc sermonem: 'Ve illis fratribus qui sunt michi contrarii de hoc, quod cognosco, quod voluntas Dei est pro maiori utilitate Religionis, licet invitus condescendam voluntati eorum.'" AC 106, FF 1653, FAED: 2.212.

110 "Et nunc propter infirmitates quas tu nosti, dulcissime Domine, curam eius habere non valens, ipsam recommendo ministris." VS 2.104.143, FF 572, FA:ED 2.140.

111 "Ut autem pluribus modis negotiatior hic evangelicus lucraretur ac totum praesens tempus conflaret in meritum, non tam praeesse voluit quam subesse, nec tam praecipere quam parere. Idcirco generali cedens officio, guardianum petiit, cuius voluntati per omnia subiaceret." LM 6.4, FF 826, FA:ED 2.571.

112 Moorman, *History of the Franciscan Order*, 51, suggests 1220, while Rosalind Brooke, *Early Franciscan Government*, 78–83, suggests as early as 1217.

113 See *A List of the General Ministers Dating from the 1260s*, FA:ED 3.824. This list, which survives in a single manuscript, may be of non-Franciscan origin, which may account for the confusion. The first unquestionably Franciscan source about the early minister generals of the order dates from just after the turn of the fourteenth century, and does suggest, though does not explicitly state, that Elias of Cortona had taken over the role of minister general during Francis' lifetime. Peregrine of Bolonga, *An Abbreviated Chronicle of the Succession of General Ministers*, FA:ED 3.827–8. It is significant that neither text mentions Peter Catani. On this subject also see Brooke, *Early Franciscan Government*, 110

114 Brooke, *Early Franciscan Government*, 106–15; Dalarun, *Power*, 190.

115 Moorman, *History of the Franciscan Order*, 46, Brooke, *Early Franciscan Government*, 64.

116 Brooke, *Early Franciscan Government*, 113; Dalarun, *Power*, 88.
117 Brooke, *Early Franciscan Government*, 111.

5. The Hagiographers' Search for Meaning

1 On this, see Michael Goodich, "The Politics of Canonization in the Thirteenth Century: Lay and Mendicant Saints," *Church History* 44:3 (September 1975), 294–307, 306, and especially Donald Prudlio, *Certain Sainthood: Canonization and the Origins of Papal Infallibility in the Medieval Church* (Ithaca, NY: Cornell University Press, 2016), 79.

2 Prudlio, *Certain Sainthood*, 83–4.

3 Ultimately this manoeuvre did not work. Miles Pattenden, "The Canonization of Clare of Assisi and Early Franciscan History," *The Journal of Ecclessiastical History*, 59:2 (April 2008), 208–26.

4 As noted in chapter 4, scholars such as Moshe Barasch and Edward Wheatley have suggested that the physical disability of blindness was at times seen as evidence of a person's sinful nature or refusal to recognize the reality of Christ as redeemer. See Moshe Barash, *Blindness: The History of a Mental Image in Western Thought* (Abingdon and New York: Routledge, 2001), esp. 113–14, and Edward Wheatley, "Blind Jews and Blind Christians: Metaphorics of Marginalization in Medieval Europe," *Exemplaria* 14:2 (2002), 351–79.

5 Scott Wells, "The Exemplary Blindness of Francis of Assisi," in *Disability in the Middle Ages: Rehabilitations, Reconsiderations, Reverberations*, ed. J. Eyler. (Farnham: Ashgate, 2010), 67–80, 70–1.

6 "Per eiusdem igitur temporis curricula coepit corpus suum variis urgeri languoribus et vehementioribus quam prius solitum esset." VP 2.4.97, FF 374, FA:ED 1.266.

7 "[Franciscus] infirmitaten oculorum incurrit gravissimam, quemadmodum multiplicavit in eo misericordiam suam Deus." VP 2.4.98, FF 376, FA:ED 1.267.

8 See Wells, "Exemplary Blindness," 72–6. See also AC 77, FF 1587–8, FA:ED 2.180.

9 Wells, "Exemplary Blindness," 74.

10 Compare the *Assisi Compilation*, which explicitly states that Francis travelled to Fonte Columbo for the express purpose of consulting with a doctor from Rieti and then describes the cauterization extending from Francis' jaw to the eyebrow of the weaker of his two eyes, with Bonaventure's text, which notes that Francis was once advised by doctors to undergo cauterization. It notes that the cauterization extended from Francis' ear to his eyebrow, with no reference to his eye at all. See AC 86, FF 1604–9, FA:ED 189–90, and LM 5.9, FF 820–1, FA:ED 2.566.

11 "Licet enim adeptus iam esset cordis et corporis puritatem mirabilem, non cessabat tamen lacrimarum imbribus iugiter oculos expiare mentales, corporeorum luminum non ponderando iacturam. Cum enim ex continuo fletu infirmitatem oculorum incurrisset gravissimam, suadente sibi medico, quod abstineret a lacrimis, si corporei visus caecitatem vellet effugere, vir sanctus respondit, 'Non est, frater medice, ob amorem luminis, quod habemus commune cum muscis, visitatio lucis aeternae repellenda vel modicum, quia non spiritus propter carnem, sed caro propter spiritum beneficium lucis accepit'. Malebat siquidem corporalis visus lumen amittere quam lacrimas, quibus oculus mundatur interior, ut Deum videre valeat, repressa devotione spiritus impedire." LM 5.8, FF 820, FA:ED 2.565–6.

12 Wells, "Exemplary Blindness," 78.

13 *Epistola ad fideles*, 2.7 and 2.11. FAS 176.

14 Judith Perkins, *The Suffering Self*.

15 Peter Brown, "Rise and Function of the Holy Man in Late Antique Society," *The Journal of Roman Studies*, 61 (1971), 80–101.

16 See Peter Brown, *The Body and Society: Men, Women and Sexual Renunciation in Early Christianity* (New York: Columbia University Press, 1988), and Theresa Shaw, *The Burden of the Flesh: Fasting and Sexuality in Early Christianity* (Minneapolis: Fortress Press 1998).

17 Francis himself exemplifies this pattern. On the pattern itself, see Bynum, *Holy Feast and Holy Fast*, loc. 1619 of 6615, Kindle.

18 Bynum, *Holy Feast and Holy Fast*, loc. 1619, Kindle.

19 On this see Montford, *Health, Sickness, Medicine and the Friars*, 34.

20 On the complexities of the position of medicine within medieval Christian faith see, for instance, Joseph Ziegler, *Medicine and Religion c. 1300: The Case of Arnau da Vilanova* (Oxford: Oxford Historical Monographs, 1998), 215–22, and Metzler, *Disability in Medieval Europe*, 38–47.

21 Vincent of Beauvais, *Speculum naturale* (B. Belleri, 1624, repr., Graz: Akademischen Druck-u. Verlagsanstalt, 1967), xxxi, 99. See also Ziegler, *Medicine and Religion*, 223.

22 Lateran IV, Canon 22. "Cum infirmitas corporalis non numquam ex peccato proveniat, dicente Domino languido quem sanaverat. Vade et amplius noli peccare, ne deterius aliquid tibi contingat, decreto praesentistatvimus et districte praecipimus medicis corporum, ut cum eos ad infirmos vocari contigerit, ipsos ante omnia moneant et inducant, quod medicos advocent animarum, ut postquam infirmis fuerit de spirituali salute provisum, ad corporalis medicinae salubrium procedatur, cum causa cessante cesset effectus. Hoc quidem inter alia huic causam dedit edicto, quod quidam in aegritudinis lecto iacentes, cum eis a medicis suadetur, ut de animarum salute disponant, in desperationis articulum incidunt, unde facilius mortis

periculum incurrunt. Si quis autem medicorum huius nostrae constitutionis postquam per praelatos locorum fuerit publicata, transgressor extiterit, tamdiu ab ingressu ecclesiae arceatur, donec pro transgressione huiusmodi satisfecerit competenter. Ceterum cum anima sit multo pretiosior corpore, sub interminatione anathematis prohibemus, ne quis medicorum pro corporali salute aliquid aegroto suadeat, quod in periculum animae conuertatur." See *Decrees of the Ecumenical Councils: Nicaea to Lateran V*, ed. N. Tanner, 2 vols. (Washington, DC: Georgetown University Press, 1990), 245–6. The English translation of this canon can be found in H.J. Schroeder, *Disciplinary Decrees of the General Councils: Text, Translation and Commentary* (St. Louis: B. Herder, 1937), 236–96. Now in public domain and available at http://www.fordham.edu/halsall/basis/lateran4.html. Accessed 15 July 2009. See also Metzler, *Disability in Medieval Europe*, 46–7.

23 FAS 174, FA:ED 1.45.

24 RNB 22, FAS 276, FA:ED 1.79. See also the Worchester Fragment of the *Rule*, FAS 300, FA:ED 1.87.

25 Found in the Worcester Cathedral fragment of the *Rule*, FAS 298, FA:ED 1.90.

26 "Contigit semel cum sanctus Franciscus Mevanium pergeret, prae debilitate ieiunii ad castrum pervenire non posse." VS 2.80.114, FF 548, FA:ED 2.323. The source of this story is unknown.

27 See AC 50.

28 "Itaque cum oporteret ipsum etiam nolentem proprii corporis incommoda, quae vires eius excesserant, blandimentis remediabilibus delinire, quemdam fratrem, quem sciebat consilium sibi daturum expediens, benigne die quadam alloquitur, "Quid tibi videtur, fili carissime, quod conscientia mea de cura corporis frequenter submurmurat? Timet ne infirmanti nimis indulgeam, et exquisitis ei studeam fomentis succurrere. Non quod ipsum iam aliquid delectet accipere infirmitate longa confectum, a quo totius saporis recessit impulsus." See VS 2.160.210–11, FF 626–8, FA:ED 2.382–3.

29 Montford, *Health, Sickness, Medicine and the Friars*, 39–40.

30 "Et castigemus corpus nostrum crucifigentes illud cum vices et concupiscentiis et peccatis." Francis of Assisi, *Fragmeta Codicis Wigorniensis*, FAS 294–304, 301. This version of the *Rule* is significantly harsher in tone towards bodies than the RNB (see chapter 22 for a comparison) or the RB, where no such discussion exists.

31 On the likely dating see Carlo Paolazzi's introduction to the *Rule* fragments in FAS 291.

32 The injunction is included in Hugh of Digne's *Exposition of the "Rule" of the Friars Minor* and in the fragmented parts of the RNB included in Thomas of Celano's *Remembrance of the Desire of a Soul*. See *Fragmenta inserta in Hugo de Digne: Expositio super Regulam fratrum minorum*, ed. David Flood (Grottaferrata: Editiones Collegii S. Bonaventurae, 1979), included in

FAS 304–14, 310; and *Fragmenta in Thomas de Celano, Vita secunda sancto Francisci Conservata*, in FAS 314–16, 316.

33 RB in FAS 390.

34 "Cernebant eum a pristinis moribus alteratum et carnis maceratione valde confectum, et ideo totum quod agebat exinanitioni et dementiae imputabant." VP 1.5.11, FF 288, FA:ED 191.

35 "Cives et qui eum noverant universi, eum insanum ac dementem acclamantes, lutum platearum in ipsum et lapides proiecerunt." VB, Lectio 5:6, 38.

36 "Quem cum cives cernerent facie squalidum et mente mutatum, ac per hoc alienatum putarent a sensu." LM 2.2, FF 789, FA:ED 2.537.

37 On the increasing importance of moderating asceticism in the Dominican and Franciscan Orders see Montford, *Health, Sickness, Medicine*, 37.

38 On the *Assisi Compilation*'s political alignment within the early order and the text's emphasis on apostolic poverty, see Burr, *The Spiritual Franciscans*, 18–19.

39 See AC 50, FF 1525, FA:ED 2.150.

40 On this see Angela Montford, *Health, Sickness, Medicine*, 37.

41 "misit ad dictam civitatem pro medico qui in arte cirugica et maxime oculorum pre aliis erat expertus." AVR 218–24.

42 LM 7.11, FF 841–42, FA:ED 2.583–4.

43 See VP 2.7.107.

44 See AC 7, in which a brother says to Francis, "Pater, scias in veritate quod, nisi de celo Dominus suam medicinam mitteret corpori tuo, tua infirmitas est incurabilis, et parum vivere debes, sicut et medici iam dixerunt." FF 1477, FA:ED 2.121. The *Assisi Compilation* also includes another incident in which a doctor, perhaps a family friend of Francis', reports that he will soon die, a reality Francis welcomes. See AC 100, "Alia vice in illis diebus quidam medicus, nomine Bonus Iohannes, de civitate Aretii, qui notus et familiaris erat beato Francisco, in eodem palatio visitavit eum. Quem beatus Franciscus interrogavit de sua infirmitate dicens, 'Quid tibi videtur, frater Janni, de hac mea infirmitate hydropisi?' Dixit ergo ad eum medicus manifeste: 'Pater, secundum physicam nostram infirmitas tua est incurabilis et aut in fine mensis septembris aut quarto nonas Octobris morieris.'" FF 1635, FA:ED 2.203–4.

45 VP 2.5.99, AC 68, VS 2.15.44, TM 6.36, AVR 186–8.

46 "Cum pauper Christi Franciscus de Reate Senas properaret pro remedio oculorum, transitum faciebat per planum prope roccam Campilii, comitem itineris habens medicum quemdam Ordini obligatum." VS 2.60.93, FF 529–30, FA:ED 307.

47 "Accidit post haec quiddam mirabile viro sancto, dum se ad civitatem Senensem, causa exigente, transferret." LM 7.6, FF 837, FA:ED 2.580.

48 "Deinde cuidam collatus viro, qui ex devotione servum Dei visitare solebat,
    velut sibi molestum foret a pii patris absentari conspectu, escam recusavit
    omnino." LM 8.10, FF 852, FA:ED 2.594.
49 See *Regula non bullata* 10, FAS 259–60. FA:ED 1.71–2.
50 Montford, *Health, Sickness, Medicine*, 30–1.
51 "si infirmitatem aliquem habeat vel pravam corporis qualitatem, propter
    quam foret postea aliis onerosus; si membrum aliquod mutilatum habeat
    vel inefficax quoquomodo." *Contitutionum praenarbonensium particulae*,
    in *Constitutiones Generales Oridinis Fratrum Minorum*, ed. C. Cenci and
    R.G. Mailleux, *Analecta Franciscana XIII*, n.s. 1.15-15-36 (Quaracchi:
    Collegium S. Bonaventurae, 2007), no. 31, p. 23. The translation is my own.
    Angela Montford translates this phrase somewhat differently, "if they have
    any illness or any particular bodily quality which might later become a
    burden to others, or if they have a mutilation or any other incapacity."
    See Angela Montford, *Health, Sickness, Medicine*, 31–2.
52 "Cui detur sociis unus discretus, qui succedat ei in visitationsi officio
    tempore infirmitatis vel mortis. Cum quo etiam habere possit collationem
    et consilium in dubiis, non expressis personis de quibus, agitur, si fieri
    potest." *Contitutionum praenarbonensium particulae*, no. 8, p. 18.
53 "Minister autem provincialis, quando vadi ad capitulum generale vel alias
    extra suam provinciam, vel sic infirmatur quod non possit provinciali
    capitulo interesse, instituat vicarium de consilio descretorum."
        "Vicarius vero, sic institutus a ministro, si minister in generali
    capitulo absolutus fuerit vel ipsum interim mori contigerit, remaneat
    vicarius auctoritate generalis ministri usquequo provinciale capitulum
    congregatur."*Contitutionum generalis narbonensis, anni 1260*, Rubric XI,
    nos. 7 and 8, p. 99.
54 To name only a few monographs on early Franciscan government, see
    Brooke, *Early Franciscan Government*; Cajetan Esser, *Origins of the Franciscan
    Order*, trans. A. Daly and I. Lynch (Chicago: Franciscan Herald Press, 1970);
    Desbonnets, *From Intuition to Institution: The Franciscans*; and Moorman,
    A History of the Franciscan Order.
55 "Guardiani vero intelliguntur sicut ministri et custodes, qui sic solebant
    primitus nominari ("But guardians are known as ministers and custodians,
    which they were accustomed to being named originally)." *Expositio quatuor
    Magistrorum Super Regulam Fratrum Minorum*, ed. L. Oliger (Rome: Edizioni
    di Storia e Letteratura, 1950), 146. The text dates to the early 1240s. The four
    masters are traditionally given as Gaufridus of Brie, Alexander of Hales,
    John of Rupella, and Robert of Bascia.
56 "Unde hoc loco minister generalis custos vocatur et inferius ministrorum
    provinciae cutodiae nuncupantur. Sic nomen ministri ad generalem et
    provincialem et secundum antiquam ut dicitur nominationem etiam ad
    localem ministrum extenditur. Antiquitus enim ut praetactum est qui

singulis praeerant locis ministri dicebantur, licet etiam ad pleniorem forte distinctionem officii dicti sunt guardiani. (Thus, in that place, the minister general is called *custos* and the lower provincial ministers were called custodians. Thus the name of minister was extended to the general and to the provincial and according to old nomenclature, it is said to be extended even to the local minister. For formerly, as has been touched upon before, those who were responsible for single areas were called ministers, although they were also called guardians to more fully satisfy the distinction of offices.)" *Hugh of Digne's Rule Commentary*, ed. David Flood (Grottaferrata: Collegium S. Bonaventurae, 1979), 174. Hugh's commentary dates to around 1252. See David Flood, "Introduction," in *Hugh of Digne's Rule Commentary*, 13–87, 54.

57　Thomas of Eccleston, *De adventu fratrum minorum in Angliam*, 220–1; Hermann, English translation in *XIIIth Century Chronicles*, 93–191, 101–2.

58　See Paolazzi, FAS 160.

59　See Paolazzi, FAS 160.

60　Carlo Paolazzi, "Le Epistole Maggiori di Frate Francesco," *Archivum Fratrum Historicum* 101 (2008), 3–154, 43–6. It is possible, but generally deemed unlikely, that the language of guardians was added later in the manuscript tradition. Nonetheless, our earliest manuscript of the letter dates from the fourteenth century. See Michael Blastic, "Letter to the Clergy," in *The Writings of Francis of Assisi: Letters and Prayers*, ed. M. Blastic, J. Hammond, and J A.W. Hellmann (St. Bonaventure, NY, Franciscan Institute Publications, 2011), loc. 2049–164, 2049–76, Kindle.

61　"Et istud denunties guardianis, quando poteris, quod per te ita firmus es facere." *Epistola ad quendam ministrum*, FAS 164–6, 164, FA:ED 1.97–8.

62　"Si quis fratrum instigante inimico mortaliter peccaverit, per obdientiam teneatur recurrere ad guardianum suum … Similiter per obedientiam teneantur eum mittere custodi suo cum socio." Francis of Assisi, *Epistola ad quendam ministrum*, FAS 164–6, FA:ED 97–8, 1.98.

63　"Si qui fratrum, instigante inimico, mortaliter peccaverint, pro illis peccatis de quibus ordinatum fuerit inter fratres ut recuratur ad solos ministros provinciales." RB, FAS 322–339, 330. FA:ED 1.99–106, 1.103.

64　Michael Blastic, "Letter to the Entire Order," *The Writings of Francis of Assisi: Letters and Prayers*, loc. 2332–59.

65　"[D]ico per Dominum Jesum Christum fratri. H. ministro totius religionis nostrae et omnibus generalibus ministris, qui post eum erunt, et ceteris custodibus et guardianis fratrum, qui sunt et erunt, ut hoc scriptum apud se habeant, operentur et studiose reponant." *Epistola toti ordini missa*. FAS 210–20, 220.

66　"Et fimiter volo obedire ministro generali huius fraternitatis et alio guardiano quem sibi placuerit michi dare, et ita volo esse captus in manibus suis, ut non possim ire vel facere ultra obedientiam et voluntatem suam, quia dominus meus est … Et omnes alii fratres teneantur ita obedire guardianis suis et facere offitium secondum Regulam." Francis of Assisi, *Testamentum*, FAS 394–405, 400. FA:ED 1.124–7, 1.126.

67 *Testamentum*, FAS 400. FA:ED 1.126.

68 "5 guardianus" by P. Carpentier, 1766, in du Cange, et al., *Glossarium mediae et infimae latinitatis*, t. 4, col. 125a, http://ducange.enc.sorbonne.fr/GUARDIANUS5.

69 See Wendy Turner, "Mental Health and Homicide in Medieval English Texts," in *The Medieval Brain*, ed. Deborah Thorpe. Open Library of the Humanities, 12 September 2018. DOI doi.org://10.16995/olh.295.

70 Cusato, "Guardians and the Use of Power," 262–3.

71 AC 11, LTC 57, LM 6.4.

72 The dating of the various general chapters discussed in the early Franciscan sources has been subject to an exhaustive amount of debate. A summary of some of the debates can be found in Thompson, *Francis of Assisi*, 238–8 *passim*.

73 Esser, *Origins of the Franciscan Order*, 173.

74 "Nam quadam vice cum sederet iuxta ignem, ipso nesciente, ignis invasit pannos eius de lino iuxta crus. Cumque sentiret calorem ignis et socius eius videret quod ignis combureret pannos eius, cucurrit volens extinguere ipsum. Qui dixit ei, 'Carissime frater, noli male facere fratri igni'. Et ita non permisit ei, ut ullo modo ipsum extingueret. Ille vero statim ivit ad fratrem, qui erat eius guardianus, et duxit illum ad eum et sic, illo nolente, cepit extinguere ipsum." AC 86, FF 1608, FA:ED 2.191.

75 In AC 89 and 91.

76 "Ut autem non reverteretur vacuus pauper, ivit occulte beatus Franciscus, propter guardianum suum ut non prohiberet illi, et tulit cultrum, et sedens in loco secreto cepit tollere quandam petiam tunice sue, que erat interius suta cum tunica, volens illi pauperi dare secrete. Sed statim ut guardianus eius sensit quod volebat agere, ivit ad ipsum et prohibuit ut non daret, maxime quia tunc erat magnum frigus et ipse infirmus et frigidus erat valde. Dixit autem ad eum beatus Franciscus: 'Si vis ut non dem illi, oportet penitus quod aliquam petiam facias dari fratri pauperi.'" AC 91, FF 1616, FA:ED 2.195–6.

77 Found in AC 81 and VS 2.83.130.

78 VS 2.162.215.

79 See André Vauchez, *Sainthood in the Later Middle Ages*, trans. J. Birrell (Cambridge: Cambridge University Press, 2005).

80 See Thompson, *Francis of Assisi*, 42.

81 See AC 7, 66, 83, 99.

82 "Beatus Franciscus licet esset infirmus valde, ad consolandum tamen spiritum suum, ne deficeret aliquando ex magnis et diversis suis infirmitatibus, sepe de die suos socios Laudes Domini cantare

faciebat, quas ipsemet longo tempore ante in sua infirmitate fecerat;
similiter etiam de nocte, maxime ad hedificationem illorum custodum,
qui de nocte extra palatium propter ipsum vigilabant. Cumque
consideraret frater Helias, quod beatus Franciscus ita se confortaret
et gauderet in Domino in tanta infirmitate positus, quadam die dixit
ad ipsum: 'Carissime frater, de omni letitia quam pro te et sociis tuis
in tanta afflictione et infirmitate ostendis, sum plurimum consolatus
et hedificatus; sed licet in vita et in morte homines istius civitatis te
venerentur pro sancto, tamen quia credunt firmiter propter tuam
magnam et incurabilem infirmitatem te in proximo moriturum, audientes
huiusmodi Laudes cantari, possent cogitare aut dicere intra se: Quomodo
tantam letitiam hie ostendit qui est prope mortem? Deberet enim de
morte cogitare.'" AC 99, FF 1633–4, FA:ED 2.202–3.

83 "Quodam tempore cum esset apud Reate beatus Franciscus et maneret
in camera Tebaldi Sarraceni per aliquot dies pro infirmitate oculorum,
quadam die dixit uni de sociis suis, qui noverat in seculo cytharizare.
"Frater, filii huius seculi a divina non intelligunt; quoniam instrumenta
scilicet cytharas, psalteria decem cordarum et alia instrumenta, quibus
sancti homines in antiquo tempore ad laudem Dei et consolationem
animarum utebantur, ipsi ea ad vanitatem et peccatum contra voluntatem
Domini utuntur. Vellem igitur ut secreto ab aliquo honesto homine
cytharam acquireres, cum qua faceres michi versum honestum et
diceremus de verbis et laudibus Domini cum ipsa, maxime quia corpus
affligitur magna infirmitate et dolore. Unde vellem sub ista occasione
ipsum dolorem corporis reducere ad letitiam spiritus et consolationem.

Nam beatus Franciscus in sua infirmitate fecerat quasdam Laudes
Domini, quas suos socios ad laudem Domini et pro consolatione anime sue
ac etiam ad hedificationem proximi aliquando dicere faciebat.

Respondit frater et dixit ei, 'Pater, verecundor eam acquirere, maxime
cum sciant homines istius civitatis me in seculo nosse cytharizare; timeo
ne suspicentur me esse temptatum de cytharizando.' Dixit ad eum beatus
Franciscus, 'Ergo, frater, dimittamus.'

Nocte vero sequenti, fere in media nocte, vigilabat beatus
Franciscus et ecce circa domum ubi iacebat, audivit cytharam
pulchriorem versum facientem et magis delectabilem quam umquam
audiverat in vita sua. Et cytharizans ibat tantum longe quantum posset
audiri et postea revertebatur semper cytharizando. Et sic per magnam
horam hoc fecit.

Unde considerans beatus Franciscus quod opus Dei esset et non
hominis, maximo repletus est gaudio et cum exultatione cordis toto affectu
laudavit Dominum, qui tali ac tanta consolatione ipsum dignatus est
consolari." AC 66, FF 1566–7, FA:ED 2.168–9.

84 Francis' companions, however, are under the impression that the music was of a non-human origin since there was a curfew in the city, and the lute was heard after curfew. See AC 66, FF 1567, FA:ED 2.169.

85 "Dominus qui consolatur afflictos, numquam me sine consolatione dimisit. Ecce enim, qui citharas hominum audire non potui, citharam suaviorem audivi." VS 2.89.126, FF 560, FA:ED 2.330.

86 "Cum enim tempore quodam, ex multarum infirmitatum concursu aggravato corpore, ad iucunditatem spiritus excitandam." LM 5.11, FF 822, FA:ED 2.567.

87 "... nec id honestatis decentia per ministerium fieri pateretur humanum, affuit Angelorum obsequium ad viri sancti placitum adimplendum." LM 5.11, FF 822, FA:ED 3.567.

88 "Non videbatur aliquis, sed transitum et reditum citharoedi ipsa hinc inde auditus volubilitas innuebat. Spiritu in Deum directo a tanta fuit in illo dulcisono carmine suavitate perfruitus, ut aliud se putaret saeculum commutasse." LM 5.11, FF 822, FA:ED 2.567.

89 "Hoc et fratres sibi familiares non latuit qui per certa frequenter conspiciebant indicia, eum tam excessivis et crebris consolationibus Domino visitari, ut nec ipsas omnino occultare valeret." LM 5.11, FF 822, FA:ED 2.568.

90 "Excessivus," in du Cange et al., *Glossarium mediae et infimae latinitatis*, t. 3: 344b, http://ducange.enc.sorbonne.fr/EXCESSIVUS.

91 "Nec, nulla causa, fuit perfecta in valle lacrimarum a purgatio, quo sic de quadrante novissimo redderet rationem, si quid inhaesisset cremabile, ut tandem purgatissimus raptim ad superos evolaret. Potissimam vero tormentorum suorum existimo rationem, quia, ut ipse asserebat de aliis, in sustinendis illis retributio multa." VS 2.161.212, FF 628, FA:ED 2.384.

92 "si quid inhaesisset cremabile, ut tandem purgatissimus raptim ad superos evolaret." VS 2.161.212, FF 628, FA:ED 2.384.

93 "Potissimam vero tormentorum suorum existimo rationem, quia, ut ipse asserebat de aliis, in sustinendis illis retributio multa."

94 On suffering as a Christian *mentalité* see Perkins, *The Suffering Self*.

95 Peter Brown, "The Rise and Function of the Holy Man in Late Antiquity."

96 Bynum, *Holy Feast and Holy Fast*.

97 Hollywood, *The Soul as Virgin Wife*. See also her *Sensible Ecstasy*.

98 "Nam nocte quadam, cum propter infirmitatum suarum graves et diversas molestias plus solito lassaretur, coepit de intimo cordis compati sibi ipsi." VS 2.161.213, FF 628–9, FA:ED 2.384.

99 "Sed sensualitas gustus nichil appetit nisi squalum. Hunc enim et coppum gammarorum pater libenter comedebat." AVR 3.36–7, 182.

100 AC 8, FF 1478–9, FA:ED 2.121.

101 See Tim Richardson, *Sweets: A History of Candy* (New York: Bloomsbury, 2002), 202.

102 J. Salas-Salvadó, P. Casas-Agustench, and A. Salas-Huetos, "Cultural and Historical Aspects of Mediterranean Nuts with Emphasis on Their Attributed Healthy and Nutritional Properties," Supplement 1, *NMCD: Nutrition, Metabolism and Cardiovascular Diseases* 21 (2011), S1–S6, S2.

103 "Paravit illa domina quadam die illam comestionem sancto patri, de qua desideravit comedere; sed parum comedit ex ea, quoniam quotidie eius corpus ex infirmitate maxima deficiebat et morti appropinquabat." AC 8, FF 1481, FA:ED 2.123.

104 On this see Francesco Di Ciaccia, who suggests that Jacoba's part in the Franciscan story was suppressed in Bonaventure's life because he could not make sense of her role in the saint's trajectory – though Di Ciaccia himself notes that she was necessary to the Franciscan story. Di Ciaccia, "S. Chiara 'Domina' e Jacopa dei Dettesoli, 'Fratello' di S. Francesco D'Assisi," 327–41, 336 and 340.

105 "Sed ne spiritus ille promptus carni carnaliter consentiret in aliquo vel ad horam, patientiae scutum, orando ad Christum, servat immobile." VS 2.161.213, FF 629, FA:ED 2.384.

6. On Disability, Power, and Gender

1 On this see David Haseldine, "Early Dominican Hagiography," *New Blackfriars* 75 (1994), 400–14.

2 "[Francisus] [d]ixit aliquando sociis "quod ita diligenter novitio unius horae obedirem, si mihi guardianus daretur, sicut antiquissimo et discretissimo fratri." LM 6.4, FF 826, FA:ED 2.571. The *Assisi Compilation*'s version is much the same: "Immo quadam vice dixit sociis, ' quod ita diligenter obedirem novitio, qui intraret hodie Religionem, si esset meus guardianus, sicut illi, qui esset primus et antiquus in vita et in Religione fratrum.'" AC 11, FF 1486, FA:ED 2.125.

3 Cusato, "Francis of Assisi: Deacon?"

4 Francis' inability to attend chapter meetings is recorded in AC 44. There are no records for the chapter of 1223, but given that the future *Regula bullata* had just been drafted and was slated for discussion, it is likely Francis was present at that chapter.

5 AC 17, LM 4.11

6 Moorman, *A History of the Franciscan Order*, 56.

7 "Licet in condendo predictam Regulam et obtinendo confirmationem ipsius per sedem Apostolicam sibi astiterimus, dum adhuc essemus in minori officio constituto." *Quo elongati*, in Herbert Grundmann, "Die Bulle 'Quo elongati' Papst Gregor IX," *Archivum franciscum historcum* 54 (1961), 20–5, 21.

8 "Et hec omnia de pecunia et rebus dicit Gregorius nonus in exposition super regulam quam ipse condiderat, propter quod, quidam detractores dicere presumpserunt fratres minores non vivere secundum regulam Francisci, sed secundum regulam beati Gregorii. Quod est calumpniam imponere apostolici sanctitati. Ipse et enim se divit regula dubia ex intentione beati Francisci, quam noverat, declarare." John of Pecham, *Tractatis contra Kilwardly*, ed. F. Tocco. British Society for Franscan Studies I (Aberdeen: Typis Academicis, 1910), 140.

9 AC 86.

10 "Unde quodam tempore in hieme propter infirmitatem splenis et stomachi frigiditatem, unus de sociis qui erat eius guardianus acquisivit unum corium vulpis, et rogavit ipsum ut permitteret ipsum consui subtus cum tunica iuxta splenem et stomachum, maxime quia tunc erat magnum frigus, et ipse ex quo Christo servire incepit omni tempore usque ad diem mortis sue noluit portare nec habere nisi tunicam unam repetiatam, cum volebat illam repetiare. Cui respondit beatus Franciscus, 'Si vis ut habeam intus ad tunicam pellem illam, facias michi poni quandam petiole illius pellis de foris et consui ad tunicam, in testimonium hominibus quod ego habeo pellem interius.' Et ita fecit fieri; sed non multum portavit, licet sibi necessaria esset propter suas infirmitates." AC 81, FF 1593–4, FA:ED 2.183.

11 "Tempore hiemali cum nonnisi unica tunica sanctum eius corpusculum tegeretur, peciis admodum vilibus resarcita, guardianus suus, qui et socius eius erat, unum corium vulpinum acquirens et ad ipsum perferens dixit, 'Pater, infirmitatem pateris splenis et stomachi; precor caritatem tuam in Domino, ut subtus tunicam patiaris istud consui corium. Quod si totum non placet, saltem supra stomachum fieri sine.' Cui beatus Franciscus, 'Si vis ut sub tunica patiar istud, fac mihi eiusdem mensurae petiam exterius applicari, quae consuta de foris, indicet hominibus pellem intus absconditam.' Audit frater, nec approbat, instat, nec impetrat aliud. Acquiescente tandem guardiano, pecia supra peciam suitur, ne alius foris quam intus Franciscus esse monstretur." VS 2.93.130, FF 562–3, FA:ED 2.332.

12 "Cumque expectaret ipsum et non veniret, quia propter multa impedimenta que habuit venire non potuit, et ipse dubitabat incipere curam; sed necessitate coactus, maxime propter obedientiam domini episcopi Hostiensis et generalis ministri, proposuit eis obedire, licet satis grave illi esset de se habere huiusmodi sollicitudines. Et propterea volebat ut minister eius illud ageret." AC 86, FF 1604, FA:ED 2.191.

13 "Sed quia de anima et corpore simul curam habere non valeo rogo ut hoc non fiat nisi prius veniat frater helyas vicarius ordinis qui de fiendis curam habebit." AVR 7.4, 220.

14 "et timens protectis et vicario (*sic* vicarii) precepto non contradicere." AVR 7.4, 220.

15 Dalarun, *Francis of Assisi and Power*, 187.

16 As with nearly every letter written by Francis, the dates are uncertain. Paolozzi dates the letter to about 1224. On the debate as a whole, see Blastic, "Letter to the Entire Order," in *The Writings of Francis of Assisi*, loc. 2348.

17 "Audite, Domini, filii et fratres mei, et auribus percepite verba mea. Inclinate aurem cordis vestri et obedite voci Filii Dei." *Epistola toti ordinis missa*, FAS, 210, FA:ED 1.116.

18 "Ego frater Franciscus, homo inutilis et indigna creatura Domini Dei, dico per Dominum Jesum Christum fratri Helie ministro totius religionis nostre et omnibus generalibus ministris, qui poste eum erunt, et ceteris custodibus et gardianis fratrum, qui sunt et erunt." *Epistola toti ordinis missa*, FAS 220. The entirety of the letter can be found in FAS 210–20, FA:ED 1.116–21.

19 "sed sicut dedit michi Dominus simpliciter et pure dicere et scribere Regulam et ista verba, ita simpliciter et pure sine glossa intelligatis." *Testamentum IV*, FAS 402, FA:ED 1.127.

20 "Et postquam Dominus dedit michi de fratribus, nemo ostendebat michi quid deberem facere, sed ipse Altissimus revelavit michi quod deberem vivere secudum formam sancti Evangelii, et ego paucis verbis et simplicter feci scribi, et dominus Papa comfirmavit michi. *Testamentum II*, FAS 396, FA:ED 1.125.

21 See discussion above, 63–5.

22 "Ad servandam humilitatis sancte virtutem, paucis annis elapsis, post suam conversionem, in quodam capitulo, coram omnibus fratribus de Religione, prelationis officium resignavit dicens, 'Amodo sum mortuus vobis. Sed ecce, inquit, frater Petrus Cathanii, cui ego et vos omnes obediamus.' Et inclinans se protinus coram ipso, obedientiam et reverentiam promisit eidem.

Flebant igitur fratres, et altos extorquebat gemitus dolor, cum videbant se tanto patre quodammodo orphanos fieri. Surgens beatus Franciscus, iunctis manibus et oculis in celum erectis, dixit 'Domine, recommendo tibi familiam, quam michi hactenus commisisti. Et nunc, propter infirmitates quas tu nosti, dulcissime Domine, curam eius habere a non valens, ipsam recommendo ministris.'" AC 39, FF 1513, FA:ED 2.142. This is repeated verbatim at VS 2.104.143, FF 571–2, FA:ED 2.340.

23 Röhrkasten, "Authority and Obedience," 109.

24 "[Franciscus] non tam praeesse voluit quam subesse, nec tam praecipere
   quam parere. Idcirco generali cedens officio, guardianum petiit, cuius
   voluntati per omnia subiaceret." LM 6.4, FF 826, FA:ED 2.571.
25 "Viderat namque gallinam quamdam parvam et nigram, habentem crura
   pennata cum pedibus in modum columbae domesticae, quae tot pullos
   habebat quod non poterat eos sub alis propriis congregare, sed ibant in
   circuitu gallinae exterius remanentes." LTC 16.63, FF 1437, FA:ED 2.105.
26 "Ego sum illa gallina, statura pusillus nigerque natura, qui debeo esse
   simplex ut columba et affectibus pennatis virtutum volare ad caelum. Mihi
   autem Dominus per misericordiam suam dedit et dabit filios multos quos
   protegere mea virtute non potero, unde oportet ut eos sanctae Ecclesiae
   recommendem quae sub umbra alarum suarum eos protegat et gubernet."
   LTC 16.63, FF 1437, FA:ED 2.105.
27 "Pulli sunt fratres numero multiplicati et gratia, quos a conturbatione
   hominum et a contradictione linguarum defendere Francisci virtus non
   sufficit." VS 1.16.24, FF 466, FA:ED 2.260.
28 On the varied meanings of *virtus* in the Roman world, see Myles
   McDonnell, *Roman Manliness: Virtus and the Roman Republic* (Cambridge:
   Cambridge University Press, 2006).
29 On these meanings, see Virtus 1–3, du Cange et al., *Glossarium mediae et
   infimae latinitatis*, t. 8, col. 352c–353a, http://ducange.enc.sorbonne.fr/
   VIRTUS. Accessed 19 September 2018.
30 VS 2.93.130, FF 561–2, FA:ED 2.332.
31 LM 14.4.
32 Jordan of Saxony, *Libellus de principiis Ordinis Praedicatorum*, in *Santi Patris
   Nostri Dominici*, ed. D. H-C. Scheeben, MOPH 16 (Rome: Institutum
   Historicum Fratrum Praedicatorum, 1935), 25–88.
33 Peter Ferrand, *Legenda sancti Dominici*, MOPH 16, 209–60.
34 Constantine of Orvieto, *Legenda sancti Dominici*, MOPH 16, 286–352.
35 Humbert of Romans, *Legenda sancta Dominici*, MOPH 16, 355–43.
36 There is much written on the conflict between the Spirituals and
   Conventuals in the Franciscan Order. For an overview see Burr, *The Spiritual
   Franciscans*.
37 Bynum, *Holy Feast and Holy Fast*.
38 The interplay between these two types of authority has been explored
   by John Coakley. See John Coakley, "Gender and the Authority of the
   Friars: The Significance of Holy Women for 13th Century Franciscan and
   Dominican Women," *Church History* 60:4 (December 1991), 445–60, esp.
   449–50 and 458–9; and John Coakley, *Women, Men and Spiritual Power:
   Female Saints and Their Male Collaborators* (New York: Columbia University
   Press, 2006), esp. 337–63. See also Grace Jantzen, *Power, Gender and
   Mysticism* (Cambridge: Cambridge University Press, 1995), 158–9.

39 However, Jacques Dalarun has argued that Francis' devotion to women's spirituality has perhaps been overstated by scholars. He points out that Francis does not mention Clare at all in his writings, and that his interest in the community of Clares at San Damiano was, at best, a far secondary concern to his medicancy. See Jacques Dalarun, *Francis of Assisi and the Feminine*, ed. Jean-François Godet-Calogeras (St. Bonaventure, NY: St. Bonaventure University Press, 2006). 49–53, 71–73.

40 David Damrosch, "*Non alia sed aliter:* The Hermeneutics of Gender in Bernard of Clairvaux," in *Images of Sainthood in Medieval Europe*, ed. Renate Blumenfeld-Kosinski and Timea Szell, (Ithaca, NY: Cornell University Press, 1991), 181–95.

41 Shawn M. Krahmer, "The Virile Bride of Bernard of Clairvaux," *Church History* 69:2 (2000), 304–27.

42 Caroline Walker Bynum, *Jesus as Mother: Studies in the Spirituality of the High Middle Ages* (Berkeley: University of California Press, 1984), 117–19.

43 See, for instance, both iterations of the *Epistola ad fideles*.

44 See Donald Weinstein and Rudolph M. Bell, *Saints and Society* (Chicago, University of Chicago Press, 1982), 202–4.

45 Dalarun, *Francis and the Feminine*, 279.

46 Bynum, *Holy Feast and Holy Fast*, loc. 1261–5, Kindle.

47 The experience of masculinity on the part of men who have been disabled from birth or early childhood has not yet been much explored. On this topic see Russell Shuttleworth, Nikki Wedgewood, and Nathan Wilson, "The Dilemma of Disabled Masculinity," *Men and Masculinities* 15:2 (2012), 174–94, 183 ff.

48 Gerschick and Miller, "Gender Identities at the Crossroads," 455–75, 461.

49 Gerschick and Miller, "Gender Identities at the Crossroads," 458.

50 Gerschick and Miller, "Gender Identities at the Crossroads," 468.

51 See, for instance, Judith Lorber and Lisa Jean Moore, *Gender and the Social Construction of Illness* (Walnut Creek, CA: Alta Mira Press, 2002), 55 and 66, and Daniel Wilson, "Fighting Polio Like a a Man," in *Gendering Disability*, ed. Bonnie Smith and Beth Hutchison (New Brunswick, NJ: Routledge, 2004), 119–33, 121.

52 This concept is discussed briefly in Tom Shakespeare, "The Sexual Politics of Disabled Masculinity," *Sexuality and Disability* 17:1 (1999), 53–64, 58–9.

53 See for instance, Rosemarie Garland-Thomson, "Integrating Disability, Transforming Feminist Theory," *NWSA Journal* 14:3 (Fall 2002), 1–32, 7, and Rosemarie Garland- Thomson, *Extraordinary Bodies: Figuring Physical Disability in American Culture and Literature* (New York: Columbia University Press, 1997), 19.

54 Garland-Thomson, "Integrating Disability," 6, and Garland-Thomson, *Extraordinary Bodies*, 27.

55 Eva Peace is a character in Tony Morrison's novel *Sula*. On Eva Peace as a disabled character who at times must be read as an agent and a powerful one, see Garland-Thomson, *Extraordinary Bodies*, 116–17.

56 Kudlick, "'Disability' and 'Divorce,'" 134–44.

57 Pearman, *Woman and Disability in Medieval Literature*.

58 Metzler, *Social History of Disability in the Middle Ages*, 204.

59 Genesis 3:17–18. See also Metzler, *Social History of Disability in the Middle Ages*, 43–4.

60 Aristotle, *On the Generation of Animals*, 1:21.

61 See Cadden, *Nothing in Nature Is Shameful*, 189 ff (especially linking sexual passivity and femininity). Prudence Allen, *The Concept of Woman: The Aristotelian Revolution, 750 BC–AD 1250* (Grand Rapids, MI: Eerdmans Publishing, 1985), esp. 118–21. On the dominant Aristotelianism of the Middle Ages as discussed by Albert the Great and Thomas Aquinas, see 362–407. For a summary, see 411.

62 On this see Noga Arikha, *Passions and Tempers* (New York: Ecco, 2007), 72.

63 For a succinct introduction to the basics of humoral theory see Arikha, *Passions and Tempers*, 20–2.

64 On this see Gail Kern Paster, "The Unbearable Coldness of Female Being: Women's Imperfection and the Humoral Economy," *English Literary Renaissance* 28:3, 416–40 (1998), 422. Paster argues that while these two humours are more commonly associated with women, it is really only phlegm that utterly encompasses the premodern "normative" description of women as "cold and clammy."

65 On this see Arikha, *Passions and Tempers*, 41.

66 On this see Carolina Warren, "Aging and Identity in Premodern Times," *Research on Aging* 20:1 (1998) 11–35, 17.

67 Warren, "Aging and Identity," 27.

68 Warren, "Aging and Identity," 27.

69 Paster, "The Unbearable Coldness," 428. See also Gail Kern Paster, *Humoring the Body: Emotions and the Shakespearean Stage* (Chicago: University of Chicago Press, 2004), 88.

70 Arikha, *Passions and Tempers*, 41.

71 Pearman, *Women and Disability in Medieval Literature*, 7–11.

72 See Kathleen Coyne Kelly, "Malory's Body Chivalric," *Arthuriana* 6:4 (Winter 1996), 52–71, 64.

73 Kenneth Hodges, "Wounded Masculinity: Injury and Gender in Sir Thomas Malory's *Le Morte Darthur*," *Studies in Philology* 106:1 (Winter 2009), 14–31, 19.

74 Chrétien de Troyes, *Perceval* in *Arthurian Romances*, trans. William Kibler. (London: Penguin, 1991), 381–494, 424.

75 Exhumed medieval skeletons often show healed wounds. Piers Mitchell, *Medicine in the Crusades: Warfare, Wounds and the Medieval Surgeon* (Cambridge: Cambridge University Press, 2004), 110–11.

76 See Irina Metzler's discussion of the paucity of medieval sources in
    Metzler, *A Social History of Disability*, 36–7.

77 Metzler, *A Social History of Disability*, 37–8.

78 See Metzler's summary in Metzler, *A Social History of Disability*, 39.

79 Carole Rawcliffe, *Medicine and Society in Later Medieval England*
    (Stroud: Sutton Publishing, 1995), 3, and Metzler, *A Social History of
    Disability*, 40–1.

80 Metzler, *A Social History of Disability*, 40 and 229n33. The Latin in Metzler's
    footnote is taken from Achim Hölter, *Die Invaliden: Die vergessene Geschicite
    der Kriegskrüppel in der europäischen Literature biz zum 19 Jahrhundert*
    (Stuttgart: J.B. Metzler, 1995), 65.

81 See the various definitions of *impotentia* in du Cange et al., *Glossarium
    mediae et infimae latinitatis*, t. 4, http://ducange.enc.sorbonne.fr/
    IMPOTENTIA1 and http://ducange.enc.sorbonne.fr/IMPOTENTIA2.
    Accessed 2 July 2015.

82 Bynum, *Jesus as Mother*. On Christ's materiality see *Fragmentation and
    Redemption: Essays on the Human Body in Medieval Religion* (New York: Zone
    Books, 1992), 82 ff.

83 Leah deVun, "The Jesus Hermaphrodite: Science and Sex Difference
    in Premodern Europe," *The Journal of the History of Ideas* 69:2 (2008),
    193–218, 209.

84 As Jacqueline Murray has noted, male saints tended to be understood as
    a universalized human, rather than sexed as masculine. Where concerns
    about a saint's masculinity entered the written record, the concern tended
    to focus on controlling sexual urges. This contrasts with female saints,
    who were constantly portrayed as embodied. See Jacqueline Murray, "The
    Law of Sin That Is My Members": The Problem of Male Embodiment,"
    in *Gender and Holiness: Men, Women and Saints in Late Medieval Europe*
    (Abingdon and New York: Routledge, 2002), 9–22, 10 ff. Very little
    research has been done to date on the potential feminization of male
    saints, although Alison More's recent work on the holy men and women
    of Liège suggests that both men and women took on characteristics of
    both genders, moving from an active to a more contemplative life, before
    striving to move beyond a gendered and embodied experience through
    devotion to God. See Alison More, "Convergence, Conversion, and
    Transformation: Gender and Sanctity in Thirteenth-Century Liège," in
    *Representing Genders and Sexualities in Europe: Construction, Transformation
    and Subversion, 600–1530*, ed. Elizabeth L'Estrange and Alison More, 33–48
    (Aldershot: Ashgate, 2011).

85 Even so, most historians do not argue that Francis exhibited a feminine
    spirituality. An outlier in this respect is Catherine Mooney, who suggests
    that Francis presented himself as both a mother and a father, and in doing
    so, he might be best understood as "an androgynous figure." She points

to his *stigmata* as a feminizing feature but notes that Thomas of Celano
worked to portray even the stigmatized Francis as virile. See Catherine
Mooney, "Francis of Assisi as Mother, Father and Androgynous Figure," in
The Boswell Thesis: Essays on Christianity, Social Tolerance and Homosexuality,
ed. Matthew Kuefler, 301–32 (Chicago: University of Chicago Press, 2006).

86 "Cernebant eum a pristinis moribus alteratum et carnis maceratione
   valde confectum, et ideo totum quod agebat exinanitioni et dementiae
   imputabant." This line is exactly the same in both the VP and LTC.
   VP 1.5.11, FF 288, FA:ED 1.191, and LTC 6.17, FF 1391, FA:ED 2.78.

87 VS 2.80.114, FF 548, FA:ED 2.323.

88 AC 79, FF 1590, FA:ED 2.181, and AC 82, FF 1595, FA:ED 2.184.

89 LM 5.1, AVR 204.

90 LTC 7.22, FF 1395–6, FA:ED 2.81; VS 1.9.14, FF 457, FA:ED 2.253.

91 AC 71, FF 1576, FA:ED 173–4.

92 VP 1.19.52, FF 327, FA:ED 1.228; AC 80, FF 1590–2, FA:ED 2.1812. This
   story is also recounted in Bonaventure's *Legenda maior*: LM 6.2, FF 824–5,
   FA:ED 2.570.

93 AC 81, FF 1592–3, FA:ED 2.182–3; VS 2.94.131, FF 563, FA:ED 2.333.

94 VS 2.22.51, FF 492, FA:ED 2.281. This miracle is recounted in no other
   known source.

95 Adamson, *Food in Medieval Times*, 11–12.

96 AC 8, FF 1478–9, FA:ED 2.121–2.

97 On the centrality of Francis' eucharistic adoration to his piety, see
   Vauchez, *Francis of Assisi*, 66–67.

98 Francis of Assisi, *Epistola ad fideles I*, FAS 174–8, 176.

99 Francis of Assisi, *Epistola fideles II*, FAS 186–200, 186, esp. sentences 6–10.

100 "Debemus siquidem confiteri sacredoti omnia peccata nostra. Et
    recipiamus corpus et sanguinem Domni nostri Jesu Christi ab eo, quia
    [qui] non manducat carnem suam et non bibit sanguinem suum no potest
    introire in regnum Dei." Francis of Assisi, *Epistola ad fideles II*, 190. See
    also the English translation at FA:ED 45–51, 47.

101 "Debemus etiam ecclesias visitare frequenter et venerari clericos et
    revereri, non tantum propter eos si sint peccatores, sed propter officium
    et administrationem sanctissimi corporis et saguinis Christi, quod
    sacrificant in altari et recipiunt et aliis administrant. Et firmiter sciamus
    omnes quia nemo salvari potest, nisi per sancta verba et sanguinem
    Domini nostri Jesu Christi, que clerici dicunt, annuntiant et ministrant.
    Et ipsi soli ministrare debent non alii." Francis of Assisi, *Epitola ad fideles
    II*, FAS 190–2. FA:ED 1.49.

102 Francis of Assisi, *Epistola ad custodes I*, FAS 146, FA:ED 1.56.

103 See Francis of Assisi, *Epistola toti ordinis missa*.

104 Francis of Assisi, *Admonitions*, FAS 352–76, 352–4, FA:ED 1.128–37.

105 "Et sicut ipsi intuitu carnis sue tantum eius carnem videbant, sed
ipsum Deum esse credebant oculis spiritualibus contemplantes, sic et
nos, videntes panem et vinum oculis corporeis, videamus et credamus
firmiter, eius sanctissimum corpus et sanguinem vivum esse et verum.
Et tali modo semper est Dominus cum fidelibus suis, sicut ipse
dicit: "Ecce ego vobiscum sum usque ad consummationem saeculi."
Admonitions 1, FAS 354. See also the translation in FA:ED 1.129.

106 See, for instance, the *Epistola ad fideles I* and *II* and the *Admonitiones*.

107 "et nolo in ipsis considerare peccatum, quia Filium Dei discerno in ipsis,
et domini mei sunt." *Testamentum I*, FAS 394–404, 394. Translation taken
directly from FA:ED 1.125.

108 "Et propter hoc facio, quia nichil video corporaliter in hoc saeculo de ipso
altissimo Filio Dei, nisi sanctissimum corpus et sanctissimum sanguinem
suum, quod ipsi recipiunt et ipsi soli aliis ministrant." Francis of Assisi,
Testamentum I, FAS 394–6. See also the translation in FA:ED 1.125.

109 Bynum, *Holy Feast and Holy Fast*, loc. 1322.

110 "Omnes qui Dominum diligunt ex toto corde, ex tota anima et mente,
ex tota virtute a et diligunt proximos suos sicut se ipsos, et odio habent
corpora eorum cum viciis et peccatis." Francis of Assisi, *Epistola ad
fideles I* in FAS 174–8, 174. English translation from FA:ED 1, 41–4, 41.
The idea of the necessity of hating one's body is also found in the second
recension of this letter. "Debemus odio habere corpora nostra cum vitiis
et peccatis." Francis of Assisi, *Epitola ad fideles II*, FAS 186–200, 192.
This discussion can also be found in the *Regula non bullata*, chapter 22.
FAS 275, FA:ED 1.79.

111 This phrase is found in the fragments of the RNB found in Worcester
Cathedral Q 27. "Et castigemus corpus nostrum crucifigentes illud cum
vitiis et concupiscentiis et peccatis," in FAS 300, FA:ED 1.87.

112 RNB, chapter 22.

113 See AC 50, 79, 82, 89, 111, 117, 120. Note that his austerity in both sickness
and health is a very common trope in the *Assisi Compilation* especially.

114 "Exinde tanta se carnis maceratione afflixit, quod, sanus et infirmus,
corpori suo nimis austerus existens vix aut nunquam sibi voluit
indulgere. Propter quod, die mortus eius instante, confessus est se
multum pecasse in fratrum corpus." LTC 5.14, FF 1388, FA:ED 2.76.

115 "Si vero propter inopiam et paupertatem frater corpus suas necessitates,
[in] infirmitate et sanitate habere non potest, dum honeste et cum
humilitate fratri suo vel suo prelato illas petierit amore Dei, et sibi non
dantur, patienter sustineat amore Domini et sibi a Domino pro martyrio
imputabitur. Et quoniam fecit quod suum est, videlicet quod petiit
suam necessitatem, excusatur a peccato, etiam si corpus inde magis
infirmaretur." AC 120, FF 1690, FA:ED 2.229–30.

116 This passage is authenticated with the phrase "nos, vero, qui cum ipso
fuimus." See AC 50, FF 1524–5, FA:ED 150.

117 RNB 10, FAS 258–60, FA:ED 1.71–2. All known fragments of the RNB also
contain this exhortation.

118 "'Sed in cuiuslibet martyrii compensatione hanc infirmitatem pati vel per
tres dies molestius mihi foret, quod non pro mercedis remuneratione
loquor, sed pro sola quam ingerit molestia passionis.'" VP 2.7.107, FF 385,
FA:ED 275.

119 VS 2.165.219, FF 635–6, FA:ED 2.389.

120 On Francis' suffering as *imitatio christi* in Franciscan *lives*, see Donna
Trembinski, *"Non alter Christus*: Early Domincan Lives of St. Francis,"
Franciscan Studies 63 (2005), 69–105, 86–90.

121 "Dominus ita dedit mihi fratri Francisco incipere faciendi poenitentiam:
quia cum essem in peccatis nimis mihi videbatur amarum videre
leprosos. Et ipse Dominus conduxit me inter illos et feci misericordiam
cum illis. Et recedente me ab ipsis, id quod videbatur mihi amarum,
conversum fuit mihi in dulcedinem animi et corporis." Francis of Assisi,
Testamentum I, FAS 394, FA:ED 1.124.

122 "Deinde vero totius humilitatis sanctus amator se transtulit ad leprosos,
eratque cum eis, diligentissime serviens omnibus propter Deum, et
lavans putredinem omnem ab eis, ulcerum etiam saniem extergebat."
VP 1.7.17, FF 293, FA:ED 1.195.

123 "quia homines consueverunt abhorrere leprosos qui essent multum
plagati." AC 64, FF 1561, FA:ED 2.166.

124 This is an interesting comment, for if the narrator is correct in saying Francis
confessed to Peter Catani as minister general, the episode is relatively late
in Francis' converted life, between 1218 and 1221. And the narrator might
be correct, since this passage is authenticated with the phrase "Qui scri[p]
sit hoc, vidit et testimonium perhibuit (And he who wrote this saw it and
presents the testimony)." AC 64, FF 1563, FA:ED 2.167.

125 "Et factum est, dum sederet beatus Franciscus ad mensam cum leproso
et aliis fratribus, apposita est scutella inter ambos. Nam leprosus erat
totus vulneratus et ulceratus, et maxime digitos, cum quibus comedebat,
habebat contractos et sanguinolentos, ita ut semper, cum mitteret ipsos in
scutellam, deflueret in eam sanguis." AC 64, FF 1562–3, FA:ED 1.167.

126 Bynum, *Holy Feast and Holy Fast*, loc. 4484n166, Kindle.

127 Bynum, *Holy Feast and Holy Fast*, loc. 1313, Kindle.

128 VS 1.5.9.

129 Cusato, "Francis of Assisi, Deacon?"

130 Cusato, *La Renonciation au pouvoir chez les Freres mineurs au 13e siècle*, 147–9.

131 At one point, while Francis was suffering from a grave illness, he was
recorded as saying, "Who are these men who took my religion (my
order) and my brothers from my hands! But I will go to the general

chapter and show them what I will." See AC 44, FF 1518, FA:ED 2.146 and VS 2.141.188, FF 608–9, FA:ED 2.367. See also Cusato, *La renonciation au pouvoir*, 141–2.

132 On this see Aviad Kleinberg, *Prophets in Their Own Country* (Chicago: University of Chicago, 1992), 145–8.

133 There is some debate about the authenticity of this encyclical letter since no manuscript version of it survives. The oldest extant version was published in a *life* of St. Francis written by the German friar Wilhelm Spoelberch in 1620. That a letter was written by Elias on the occasion of Francis' death is not in dispute, as it is mentioned in several contemporary sources. That this is *the* letter is a question. On the encyclical as a forgery see Felice Accrocca, "Is the 'Encyclical Letter of Brother Elias in the Transitus of St. Francis' Apocryphal?," supplement, *Greyfriars Review*, 13 (1999), 18–64. For a discussion of the controversy and a finding that it is more or less authentic, see Solanus Benfatti, *The Five Wounds of St. Francis: A Historical and Spiritual Investigation* (Charlotte, NC: TAN Books, 2011), loc. 729–88, Kindle.

134 On this, see Spoto, *Reluctant Saint*, 192, and Jacques Dalarun, *The Stigmata of Francis of Assisi: New Studies, New Perspectives* (St. Bonaventure, NY: Franciscan Institute Publications, 2006), 19.

135 Muessig, "Signs of Salvation," 67.

136 Jantzen, *Power, Gender and Christian Mysticism*, 158–9.

Postscript: Disability as a Category of Analysis

1 Davis, *Enforcing Normalcy*, 1–49; Catherine Kudlick, "Disability History: Why We Need Another Other," *American Historical Review* 108:3 (June 2003), 763–3; Kim Nielson, "Historical Thinking and Disability Theory," *Disability Studies Quarterly* 28:3 (2008), http://dsq-sds.org/article/view/107/107, accessed 23 September 2015.

Accrocca, Felice. "Is the Encyclical Letter of Brother Elias on the *Transitus* of Saint Francis Apocryphal?" Translated by Robert Stewart. *Greyfriars Review* 13 (1999): 19–63.
– "The 'Unlettered One' and His Witness: Footnotes to a Recent Volume on the Autographs of Brother Francis and Brother Leo." Translated by E. Hagman. *Greyfriars Review* 16:3 (2002), 265–82.
Adamson, Melitta Weiss. *Food in Medieval Times*. Westport, CT: Greenwood, 2004.
Admundsen, Darrel. "Medieval Canon Law on Medical and Surgical Practice by the Clergy." *Bulletin of the History of Medicine* 52:1 (1977): 22–43.
Albana, Ken. "Fish in Renaissance Dietary Theory." In *Fish: Food from the Waters*, edited by Harlan Walker, 9–19. Oxford: Oxford Symposium, 1998.
Alexandre, Pierre. *Les séismes en Europe occidentale de 394 à 1259: Nouveau catalogue critique*. Brussels: Observatoire Royale de Belgique, 1990.
Allen, Prudence. *The Concept of Woman: The Aristotelian Revolution, 750 BC–AD 1250*. Grand Rapids, MI, and Cambridge: Eerdmans Publishing, 1985.
Allen, Shannen K., and Richard D. Semba. "The Trachoma "Menace." *History of Ophthalmology* 47:5 (September/October 2002): 500–9.
Amico, David. "Bernard of Besse: Praises of the Blessed Francis (Liber de laudibus beati Francisci)." *Franciscan Studies* 48 (1998): 213–68.
Anastasiou, Evilena, and Piers D. Mitchell. "Palaeopathology and Genes: Investigating the Genetics of Infectious Diseases in Excavated Human Skeletal Remains and Mummies from Past Populations." *Gene* 528 (2013): 33–40.
Anonymi Perusini de inceptione vel fundamento ordinis. In *Fontes Franciscana*, edited by E. Menestò and Stefano Brufani, 1298–352. Assisi: Porziuncula, 1995.
Anonymous of Perugia. In *Francis of Assisi: Early Documents*, edited by Regis J. Armstrong, J.A. Wayne Hellmann, and William J. Short, 2.34–58. 3 vols. Hyde Park, NY: New City Press, 1999–2001.

Arikha, Noga. *Passions and Tempers*. New York: Ecco, 2007.

Aristotle. *On the Generation of Animals*. Translated by Arthur Platt. eBooks@ Adelaide. http://ebooks.adelaide.edu.au/a/aristotle/generation/. University of Adelaide Library. Last updated 23 March 2013.

Assisi Compilation. In *Francis of Assisi: Early Documents*, edited by Regis J. Armstrong,, J.A. Wayne Hellmann, and William J. Short, 2.119–2.231. 3 vols. Hyde Park, NY: New City Press, 1999–2001.

Auberger, Jean-Baptiste. "A Short Note on the Autographs of Francis of Assisi." Translated by E. Hagman. *Greyfriars Review* 17:1 (2004): 1–4.

Barash, Moshe. *Blindness: The History of a Mental Image in Western Thought*. Abingdon and New York: Routledge, 2001.

The Beginning or Founding of the Order and the Deeds of Those Lesser Brothers Who Were the First Companions of Blessed Francis (The Anonymous of Perugia). In *Francis of Assisi: Early Documents*, edited by Regis J. Armstrong, J.A. Wayne Hellmann, and William J. Short, 2.30–2.59. 3 vols. Hyde Park, NY: New City Press, 1999–2001.

Benfatti, Solanus. *The Five Wounds of St. Francis: A Historical and Spiritual Investigation*. Charlotte, NC: TAN Books, 2011. Kindle.

Black, Robert. *Humanism and Education in Medieval and Renaissance Italy: Tradition and Innovation in Latin Schools from the Twelfth to the Fifteenth Century*. Cambridge: Cambridge University Press, 2001.

Blastic, Michael. "Francis and His Hagiographic Tradition." In *The Cambridge Companion to Francis of Assisi*, edited by Michael J.P. Robson, 68–83. Cambridge: Cambridge University Press, 2012.

– "Letter to the Clergy." In *The Writings of Francis of Assisi: Letters and Prayers*, edited by M. Blastic, J. Hammond and J.A.W. Hellmann, loc. 2049–164. St. Bonaventure, NY: Franciscan Institute Publications, 2011. Kindle.

– "Letter to the Entire Order." In *The Writings of Francis of Assisi: Letters and Prayers*, edited by M. Blastic, J. Hammond and J.A.W. Hellmann, loc. 2287–556. St. Bonaventure, NY: Franciscan Institute Publications, 2011. Kindle.

Bonaventure. *Legenda maior sancti Francisci*. In *Fontes Franciscana*, edited by E. Menestò and Stefano Brufani, 778–962. Assisi: Porziuncula, 1995.

– *The Major Legend of St. Francis*. In *Francis of Assisi: Early Documents*, edited by Regis J. Armstrong, J.A. Wayne Hellmann, and William J. Short, 2.526–2.650. 3 vols. Hyde Park, NY: New City Press, 1999–2001.

Bournet, Albert. *S. François d'Assise: Étude Sociale et Médicale*. Lyon: A. Storch, 1893.

Brooke, Christopher. Review of *Francis of Assisi: A New Biography*, by Augustine Thompson. *Journal of Theological Studies* 64:1 (April, 2013): 300–3.

Brooke, Rosalind. *Early Franciscan Government: Elias to Bonaventure*. Oxford: Oxford University Press, 1959.

– *The Image of St. Francis: Responses to Sainthood in the Thirteenth Century*. Cambridge: Cambridge University Press, 2006.

– "Introduction." In *Scripta Leonis, Rufini et Angeli sociorum S. Francisci: The Writings of Leo, Rufino and Angelo, Companions of St. Francis*, edited by Rosalind Brooke, 3–78. Oxford: Clarendon Press, 1970.

Brown, Peter. *The Body and Society: Men, Women and Sexual Renunciation in Early Christianity*. New York: Columbia University Press, 1988.

– "Rise and Function of the Holy Man in Late Antique Society." In *Journal of Roman Studies* 61 (1971), 80–101.

Brown, T.S. "Urban Violence in Early Medieval Italy: The Cases of Rome and Ravenna." In *Violence and Society in the Early Medieval West*, edited by Guy Halsall, 77–89. Woodbridge: Boydell, 1998.

Brundage, James. "The Teaching and Study of Canon Law in the Law Schools." In *The History of Medieval Canon Law in the Classical Period*, edited by Wilfried Hartmann and Kenneth Pennington, 98–120 Washington, DC: Catholic University of America Press, 2008.

Bullarium Franciscanum, ed. G. Sbaralea. Assisi: Edizione Porziuncula, 1759–.

Bullough, Vern L., with Gwen Whitehead Brewer. "Medieval Masculinities and Modern Interpretations: The Problem of the Pardoner." In *Conflicted Identities and Multiple Masculinities*, edited by J. Murray, 93–110. New York, Taylor and Francis, 1999.

Bultmann, Rudolf. *History of the Synoptic Tradition*. Translated by J. Marsh. Peabody, MA: Hendrickson Publishing, 1994.

Burr, David. *The Spiritual Franciscans: From Protest to Persecution in the Century after St. Francis*. Philadelphia: University of Pennsylvania Press, 2001. Kindle.

Bynum, Caroline Walker. *Fragmentation and Redemption: Essays on the Human Body in Medieval Religion*. New York: Zone Books, 1992.

– *Holy Feast and Holy Fast: The Religious Significance of Food to Medieval Women*. Berkeley: University of California Press, 1987. Kindle.

– *Jesus as Mother: Studies in the Spirituality of the High Middle Ages*. Berkeley: University of California Press, 1984.

Cadden, Joan. *Meanings of Sex Differences in the Middle Ages: Medicine, Science and Culture*. Cambridge: Cambridge University Press, 1993.

– *Nothing in Nature Is Shameful: Sodomy and Science in Late Medieval Europe*. Philadelphia: University of Pennsylvania Press, 2013.

Cadderi, Attilio. *Fra Angela da Rieti, Compagno di San Francesco*. Assisi: Frascati, 1996

Cadderi, Attilio. "Introduzione." In *Anonymous of Rieti, Actus beati Francisci in valle Reatina*, edited by A. Cadderi, 5–128. Porziuncola: Edizioni Porziuncola, 1999..

Canciarelli, Santo. *Francesco di Pietro Bernardone:Malato et santo*. Florence: Nardini, 1972.

Carney, Margaret. "The 'Letter' of Fourteen Names: Reading the 'Exhortation.'"
    In *Francis of Assisi: History, Hagiography and Hermeneutics in the Early Documents*,
    edited by J.M. Hammond, 90–104. New York: New City Press, 2004.

Carruthers, Mary. "Sweetness." *Speculum* 81:4 (October 2006): 999–1013.

Cataldo, Lisa. "Religious Experience and the Transformation of Narcissism:
    Kohutian Theory and the Life of St. Francis of Assisi." *Journal of Religion
    and Health* 46 (2007): 527–40.

Causse, Maurice. "Des sources Primatives de *La Légende des Trois Compagnons*."
    Collectanea Franciscana 68:3–4 (1998): 469–91.

Centers for Disease Control and Prevention. *Signs and Symptoms of Brucellosis.*
    http://www.cdc.gov/brucellosis/symptoms/index.html. Retrieved
    13 November 2013.

Charcot, Jean-Martin. *La foi qui guerit*. Paris: Bureaux du Progrès Medical, 1897.

Chaucer. *Canterbury Tales*. Edited by Larry D. Benson. 3rd ed. Boston: Houghton
    Mifflin, 1987.

Coakley, John. "Gender and the Authority of the Friars: The Significance of
    Holy Women for 13th Century Franciscan and Dominican Women." *Church
    History* 60:4 (December 1991): 445–60.

– *Women, Men and Spiritual Power: Female Saints and Their Male Collaborators.*
    New York: Columbia University Press, 2006.

Compilatio Assisiensis. In *Fontes Franciscana*, edited by E. Menestò and Stefano
    Brufani, 1471–691. Assisi: Porziuncula, 1995.

Constantine of Oriveto. *Legenda Sancti Dominici*, edited by D. H-C. Scheeben,
    286–352. MOPH 16. Rome: Institutum Historicum Fratrum Praedicatorum,
    1935.

Console, Renzo, and Christopher Duffin. "Peter Hispanus (ca 1215–1277) and
    the 'Treasury of the Poor.'" *Pharmaceutical Historian: British Society for the
    History of Pharmacy* 42:4 (Autumn 2012): 82–8.

Constitutiones generalis narbonensis (1260). In *Constitutiones generalis ordinis
    fratrum minorum*, edited by C. Cenci and R.G. Maillaux, 69–104. Grottoferrata:
    Editiones Collegii S. Bonaventurae, 2007.

Constitutionum praenarbonensium particulae (1239–1254). In *Constitutiones
    generalis ordinis fratrum minorum*, edited by C. Cenci and R.G. Maillaux,
    17–36. Grottaferrata: Editiones Collegii S. Bonaventurae, 2007.

Cotelle, Théodore. *Saint François d'Assise: Étude medicale*. Paris: Libr. Ch.
    Poussielgue, 1895.

Crislip, Andrew. *Thorns of the Flesh, Illness and Sanctity in Late Ancient
    Christianity*. Philadelphia: University of Pennsylvania Press, 2006.

Cunningham, Lawrence. *Francis of Assisi: Performing the Gospel Life*. Grand
    Rapids, MI: William B. Eerdmans Publishing, 2004.

Cusato, Michael. "Francis and the Franciscan Movement 1181/82–1226." In
    The Cambridge Companion to Francis of Assisi, edited by Michael J.P. Robson,
    17–33. Cambridge: Cambridge University Press, 2012.

– "Francis of Assisi, Deacon?: An Examination of the Claims of the Earliest
  Franciscan Sources, 1229–1235." In *Defenders and Critics of the Franciscan Life*,
  edited by Michael Cusato and Guy Geltner, 9–39. Leiden: Brill, 2009.
– "The Letters to the Faithful." In *The Writings of Francis of Assisi: Letters and
  Prayers*, edited by Michael Blastic et al., loc. 2567–3480. St. Bonaventure, NY:
  Franciscan Institute Publications, 2001. Kindle.
– *"La Renonciation au pouvoir chez les Frères mineurs au 13e siècle.* PhD thesis,
  Université de Paris IV, Sorbonne, January 1991.
D'Ors, Angel. "Petrus Hispanus, O.P." *Auctor Summularum, Vivarium* 35
  (1997): 21–91.
Dalarun, Jacques. *Francis of Assisi and Power.* St. Bonaventure, NY: Franciscan
  Institute Publications, 2007.
– *Francis of Assisi and the Feminine.* Translated by P. Pierce and M. Sutphin.
  St. Bonaventure, NY: Franciscan Institute Publications, 2006.
– *The Misadventure of Francis of Assisi: Towards a Historical Use of the Franciscan
  Legends.* Translated by E. Hagman. St. Bonaventure: Franciscan Institute
  Publications, 2002.
– *The Rediscovered Life of Francis of Assisi.* Translated by T. Johnson.
  St. Bonaventure, NY: Franciscan Institute Publications, 2016.
– *The Stigmata of Francis of Assisi: New Studies, New Perspectives.*
  St. Bonaventure, NY: Franciscan Institute Publications, 2006.
– "Thomas Celanensi Vita beati patris nostril Francisci (Vita brevior)
  Présentation et edition critique." *Analecta Bollandiana* 133:1 (2015): 23–86.
– *Vers une résolution de la question franciscaine: La légende ombrienne de Thomas of
  Celano.* Paris: Fayard, 2007.
Damrosch, David. *"Non alia sed aliter*: The Hermeneutics of Gender in
  Bernard of Clairvaux." In *Images of Sainthood in Medieval Europe*, edited by
  Renate Blumenfeld-Kosinski and Timea Szell, 181–95. Ithaca, NY: Cornell
  University Press, 1991.
Danziger, Kurt. *Naming the Mind: How Psychology Found Its Language.*
  Thousand Oaks, CA: Sage, 1997
Davis, Lennard J. *Enforcing Normalcy: Disability, Deafness and the Body.* London
  and New York: Verso, 1995.
De Beer, Francis, *François, que disait-on de toi.* Paris: Éditions Franciscaines,
  1977.
Decrees of the Ecumenical Councils: Nicaea to Lateran V. Edited by Normal
  Tanner. 2 vols. Washington, DC: Georgetown University Press, 1990.
Desbonnets, Théophile. *From Intuition to Institution: The Franciscans.*
  Translated by Jerry DuCharme and Paul Duggan. Chicago: Franciscan
  Herald Press, 1988.
– "La lettre à tous les fidèles de François d'Assise." In *I frati Minori e il
  Terzo Ordine: Problemi e discussioni storiografiche*, edited by Stanislao da
  Campagnola, 53–76. Todi: Accademia Tudertina, 1985.

deVun, Leah. "The Jesus Hermaphrodite: Science and Sex Difference in Premodern Europe." *Journal of the History of Ideas* 69:2 (2008): 193–218.

Di Ciaccia, Francesco. "S. Chiara 'Domina' e Jacopa dei Dettesoli 'Fratello' di S. Francesco d'Assisi." *Studi Franciscani* 79:3 (1982): 327–41.

di Fonza, Lorenzo. "*L'Anonimo Perugino* tra le fonti francescane del secolo XIII: Rapporti letterari e testo critico." *Miscellaneo Franciscana* 72 (1972): 117–483.

du Cange, Charles du Fresne, et al. *Glossarium mediae et infimae latinitatis.* Niort: L. Favre, 1883–7. Available online at http://ducange.enc.sorbonne.fr/

Eldredge, Laurence M. "The Latin Manuscripts of Beneventus Grassus' Treatise on Diseases and Injuries to the Eye." In *Beneventus Grassus' On the well-proven Art of the Eye: Pratica oculorum et De probatissima arte oculorum: Synoptic Edition and Philological Studies*, edited by A. Miranda-García and S.G. Fernández-Corugedo, 19–33. Bern: Peter Lang, 2011.

– "The Textual Tradition of Beneventus' Grassus' *De arte probatissima oculorum.*" *Studi Medievali* 34 (1993): 95–138.

– "A Thirteenth-Century Ophthalmologist, Benvenutus Grassus: His Treatise and Its Survival." *Journal of the Royal Society of Medicine* 91:1 (1998): 47–52.

Esser, Cajetan. *Origins of the Franciscan Order.* Translated by A. Daly and I. Lynch. Chicago: Franciscan Herald Press, 1970.

– "Über die Chonologie der Schriften des hl. Franziskus." *Archivum Franciscanum Historicum* 65 (1972): 20–65.

Expositio quatuor Magistrorum Super Regulam Fratrum Minorum. Edited by L. Oliger. Rome: Edizioni di Storia e Letteratura, 1950.

Fontes Franciscana. Edited by E. Menestò and Stefano Brufani. Assisi: Porziuncula, 1995.

Fortini, Arnauldo. *Francis of Assisi: A Translation of the "Nova vita di San Francesco."* Translated by Helen Moak. New York: Crossroads, 1981.

– *Nova vita di San Francesco*, 4 vol. Assisi: Edizioni Porziuncula, 1959.

Fragmenta inserta in Hugo de Digne: Expositio super Regulam fratrum minorum. Edited by David Flood. Grottaferrata: Editiones Collegii S. Bonaventurae, 1979.

Fragmenta Priscarum Constitutionum Praenarbonensium (1239). In *Constitutiones generalis ordinis fratrum minorum*, edited by C. Cenci and R.G. Maillaux, 5–12. Grottaferrata: Editiones Collegii S. Bonaventurae, 2007.

Francis of Assisi. *Epistola ad clericos I.* In *Francisci Assisiensis: Scripta.* Edited by C. Paolazzi, 140. Grottaferrata: Collegi S. Bonaventurae, 2009.

– *Epistola ad custodes II.* In *Francisci Assisiensis: Scripta.* Edited by C. Paolazzi, 142. Grottaferrata: Collegi S. Bonaventurae, 2009.

– *Epistola ad custodes I.* In *Francisci Assisiensis: Scripta.* Edited by C. Paolazzi, 146. Grottaferrata: Collegi S. Bonaventurae, 2009.

– *Epistola ad custodes II.* In *Francisci Assisiensis: Scripta.* Edited by C. Paolazzi, 154. Grottaferrata: Collegi S. Bonaventurae, 2009.

– *Epistola ad fideles I.* In *Francisci Assisiensis: Scripta.* Edited by C. Paolazzi, 174–8. Grottaferrata: Collegi S. Bonaventurae, 2009.

– *Epistola ad fideles II*. In *Francisci Assisiensis: Scripta*. Edited by C. Paolazzi, 186–200. Grottaferrata: Collegi S. Bonaventurae, 2009.

– *Epitola ad fratrem Leonem*. In *Gli Autografi di Frate Francesco e di Frate Leone*. Edited by A. Bartoli Langeli, 47–50. Turnhout: Brepols, 2000.

– *Epistola ad quendam ministrum*. In *Francisci Assisiensis: Scripta*. Edited by C. Paolazzi, 164–6. Grottaferrata: Collegi S. Bonaventurae, 2009.

– *Epistola toti ordini missa*. In *Francisci Assisiensis: Scripta*. Edited by C. Paolazzi, 210–20. Grottaferrata: Collegi S. Bonaventurae, 2009.

– *Regula bullata*. In *Francisci Assisiensis: Scripta*. Edited by C. Paolazzi, 322–8. Grottaferrata: Collegi S. Bonaventurae, 2009.

– *Regula non bullata*. In *Francisci Assisiensis: Scripta*. Edited by C. Paolazzi, 242–8. Grottaferrata: Collegi S. Bonaventurae, 2009.

– *Testamentum*. In *Francisci Assisiensis: Scripta*. Edited by C. Paolazzi, 394–404. Grottaferrata: Collegi S. Bonaventurae, 2009.

Francis of Assisi and Brother Leo. *Assisi Chartula*. In *Gli Autografi di Frate Francesco e di Frate Leone*, edited by A. Bartoli Langeli, 31–40. Turnhout: Brepols, 2000.

Freud, Sigmund, and Josef Breuer. *Studies on Hysteria*. Translated by James Strachey. Standard edition, vol. 2. London: Basic Books, 1955.

Frugoni, Chiara. *Francesco e l'invenzione delle stimmate: Una storia per parole e immagini fino a Bonaventura e Giotto*. Turin: Einaudi, 1993.

– *Francis of Assisi: A Life*. Translated by J. Bowden. New York: Continuum, 1998.

Garland-Thomson, Rosemarie. "Integrating Disability, Transforming Feminist Theory." In *Gendering Disability*, edited by Bonnie G. Smith and Beth Hutchison, 73–103. New Brunswick, NJ: Rutgers University Press, 2004.

– *Extraordinary Bodies: Figuring Physical Disability in American Culture and Literature*. New York: Columbia University Press, 1997.

Garosi, Alcide. *Siena nella storia della medicina, 1240–1555*. Florence: Olschki, 1978.

Geltner, Guy. *The Medieval Prison: A Social History*. Princeton, NJ: Princeton University Press, 2008.

– "Medieval Prisons: Between Myth and Reality, Hell and Purgatory." *History Compass* 4:2 (March 2006), 261–74.

Gerschick, Thomas J., and Adam Stephen Miller. "Gender Identities at the Crossroads of Masculinity and Physical Disability." In *Toward a New Psychology of Gender*, edited by Mary M. Gergen and Sara N. Davis, 455–75. Abingdon and New York: Routledge, 1997.

Godden, Rick, and Jonathan Hsy. "Encountering Disability in the Middle Ages." *New Medieval Literatures* 15 (2015), 314–39.

Godet-Calogeras, Jean-François. "The Autographs of Brother Francis." In *The Writings of Francis of Assisi: Letters and Prayers*, edited by Michael Blastic et al. St. Bonaventure, NY: Franciscan Institute Publications, 2011. Kindle.

– "Francis of Assisi's Resignation: An Historical and Philological Probe." In *Charisma und religiöse Gemeinschaften in Mittelalter*, edited by G. Andenna, M. Breitensten, and G. Melville, 281–300. Berlin: LIT Verlag, 2005.

Goetz, Walter. *Die Quellen zur Geschichte des heiligen Franziskus von Assisi.* Gotha: F.A. Perthes, 1904.

Goodich, Michael. "The Politics of Canonization in the Thirteenth Century: Lay and Mendicant Saints." *Church History* 44:3 (September 1975): 294–307.

Gratian. *Decretum.* Edited by A.L. Richter. Graz: Verlagsanstalt, 1959.

Grau, Engelbert. "Thomas von Celano, Leben und Werk." *Wissenschaft and Weisheit* 52 (1989): 97–120.

– "Thomas of Celano: Life and Work." Translated by Xavier John Seubert. *Greyfriars Review* 8 (1994): 177–200.

Gregory the Great. *The Letters of Gregory the Great.* Translated by John R.C. Martyn. Toronto: PIMS, 2004.

Grumett, David, and Rachel Muers. *Theology on the Menu: Asceticism, Meat and the Christian Diet.* Abingdon and New York: Routledge, 2010.

Grumett, David. "Vegetarian or Franciscan: Flexible Dietary Choices Past and Present." *Journal of the Study of Religion, Nature and Culture* 1:4 (2007): 450–67.

Grundmann, Herbert. "Die Bulle 'Quo elongati' Papst Gregor IX." *Archivum franciscum historicum* 54 (1961): 20–5.

Gualino, Lorenzo. *L'uomo d'Assisi.* Turin: Fratri Bocca, 1927.

Hacking, Ian. *Mad Travelers: Reflections on the Reality of Transient Mental Illness.* Cambridge: Harvard University Press, 2002.

– *Rewriting the Soul: Multiple Personalities and the Sciences of Memory.* Princeton, NJ: Princeton University Press 1995.

Haines, Keith. "The Death of Francis of Assisi." *Franziskanische Studien* 58 (1976): 27–46.

Hartung, E.F. "St. Francis and Medieval Medicine." *Annals of Medical History* 7 (1935): 85–91.

Haseldine, David. "Early Dominican Hagiography." *New Blackfriars* 75 (1994): 400–14.

Hawkins, Joy. "Blindness and Sanctity in Later Medieval History." *Studies in Church History* 47 (2011): 148–58.

Hellmann, Wayne. "Authority According to St. Francis: Power or Powerlessness?" In *Theology and Authority*, edited by R. Penaskovic, 24–41. Peabody, MA: Hendrickson Publishers, 1987.

Hodges, Kenneth. "Wounded Masculinity: Injury and Gender in Sir Thomas Malory's *Le Morte Darthur.*" *Studies in Philology* 106:1 (Winter 2009): 14–31.

Hollywood, Amy. *Sensible Ecstasy: Mysticism, Sexual Difference and the Demands of History.* Chicago: University of Chicago Press, 2001.

– *The Soul as Virgin Wife: Mechthild of Magdeburg, Marguerite Porete, and Meister Eckhart.* South Bend, IN: University of Notre Dame Press, 1995.

Hölter, Achim. *Die Invaliden: Die vergessene Geschicite der Kriegskrüppel in der europäischen Literatur biz zum 19 Jahrhundert.* Stuttgart: J.B. Metzler, 1995.

Hughes, Bill. "Medicine and the Aesthetic Invalidation of Disabled People." *Disability and Society* 15:4 (2000): 555–68.

Humbert of Romans. *Legenda sancta Dominici,* edited by D. H-C. Scheeben, 355–443. MOPH 16. Rome: Institutum Historicum Fratrum Praedicatorum, 1935.

Jantzen, Grace. *Power, Gender and Christian Mysticism.* Cambridge: Cambridge University Press, 1995.

John of Pecham. *Tractatus contra Kilwardly.* Edited by F. Tocco. British Society for Franciscan Studies, vol. 1. Aberdeen: Typis Academicis, 1910.

Jordan of Giano. *Chronica: Analecta Franciscana I,* 1–19. Quaracchi: Collegium S. Bonaventurae, 1885.

– *Chronicle.* In *Thirteenth Century Chronicles,* 17–77. Translated by P. Hermann. Chicago: Franciscan Herald Press, 1984.

Jordan of Saxony. *Libellus de principiis Ordinis Praedicatorum.* In *Sancti Patris Nostri Dominici,* edited by M.H. Laurent. MOPH 16, 25–88. Rome: Institutum Historicum Fratres Praedicatorum, 1935.

Karras, Robert. *The Admonitions of St. Francis: Sources and Meanings.* St. Bonaventure, NY: St. Bonaventure University Press, 1999.

Karras, Ruth Mazo. *Sexuality in Medieval Europe: Doing Unto Others.* 3rd ed. Abingdon and New York: Routledge, 2017.

Kehnel, Annette. "The Narrative Tradition of the Medieval Franciscan Friars on the British Isles: Introduction to the Sources." *Franciscan Studies* 63 (2005): 461–530.

Kelly, Henry Ansgar. "The Pardoner's Voice, Disjunctive Narrative, and Modes of Effemination." In *Speaking Images: Essays in Honor of V.A. Kolve,* edited by R. Yeager and C. Morse, 411–44. Asheville, NC: Pegasus Press, 2001.

Kelly, Kathleen Coyne. "Malory's Body Chivalric." *Arthuriana* 6:4 (Winter 1996): 52–71.

Kudlick, Catherine J. "'Disability' and 'Divorce': A Blind Parisian Cloth Merchant Contemplates His Options in 1756." In *Gendering Disability,* edited by Bonnie Smith and Beth Hutchison, 134–44. New Brunswick, NJ: Rutgers University Press, 2004.

– "Disability History: Why We Need Another Other." *The American Historical Review* 108:3 (June 2003), 763–793.

King, James R. "The Mysterious Case of the 'Mad' Rector of Bletchingdon: The Treatment of Mentally Ill Clergy in Late Thirteenth-Century England." In *Madness in Medieval Law and Custom,* edited by W. Turner, 57–80. Leiden and Boston: Brill, 2010.

Kleinberg, Aviad. *Prophets in Their Own Country.* Chicago: University of Chicago Press, 1992.

Krahmer, Shawn M. "The Virile Bride of Bernard of Clairvaux." *Church History* 69:2 (2000): 304–27.

Landau, Peter. "Gratian and the Decretum Gratiani." In *The History of Medieval Canon Law in the Classical Period: From Gratian to the Decretals of Pope Gregory IX*, edited by Wilfried Hartmann and Kenneth Pennington, 22–44. Washington, DC: Catholic University of America Press, 2008.

Langeli, Attilio Bartoli. *Gli Autografi di Frate Francesco e di Frate Leone*. Corpus Christianorum Augographa Medii Aevi V. Turnhout: Brepols 2000.

Lapsanski, Duane. "The Autographs on the *Chartula* of St. Francis of Assisi." *Archivum Franciscanum Historicum* 67 (1974): 18–37.

Legend of the Three Companions. In *Francis of Assisi: Early Documents*, edited by Regis J. Armstrong, J.A. Wayne Hellmann, and William J. Short, 2.67–2.111. 3 vols. Hyde Park, NY: New City Press, 1999–2001.

Legenda trium sociorum. In *Fontes Franciscana*, edited by E. Menestò and Stefano Brufani, 1375–446. Assisi: Porziuncula, 1995.

Leone, Massimo. *Conversion and Identity*. Abingdon and New York: Routledge, 2003.

Lindberg, David C. *A Catalogue of Medieval and Renaissance Optical Manuscripts*. Toronto: PIMS, 1975.

Lindgren, Kristen. "Bodies in Trouble: Identity, Embodiment and Disability." In *Gendering Disability*, edited by Bonnie G. Smith and Beth Hutchison, 145–65. New Brunswick, NJ: Rutgers University Press, 2004.

Little, A.G." Chronicles of the Mendicant Friars." In *Franciscan Papers, Lists and Documents*, edited by A.G. Little, 25–41. Manchester: Manchester University Press, 1943.

Lorber, Judith, and Lisa Jean Moore. *Gender and the Social Construction of Illness*. Walnut Creek, CA: Alta Mira Press, 2002.

Madden, Thomas. *Enrico Dandolo and the Rise of Venice*. Baltimore: Johns Hopkins University Press, 2003.

Manselli, Raoul. *"Nos qui cum eo fuimus": A Contribution to the Franciscan Question*. Translated by E. Hagman. Edited by Regis J. Armstrong and Ingrid Peterson. Supplement, *Greyfriars Review* 14 (2000): 1–196.

– *"Nos qui cum eo fuimus": Contributo alla questione francescana*. Rome: Istituto storico dei Cappuccini, 1980.

Mazzoni, Cristina. *Saint Hysteria: Neurosis, Mysticism and Gender in European Culture*. Ithaca, NY: Cornell University Press, 1996.

McCleery, Iona. "Opportunities for Teaching and Studying Medicine in Medieval Portugal before the Foundation of the University of Lisbon (1290)." *Dynamis* 20 (2000): 305–29.

McDonnell, Myles. *Roman Manliness: Virtus and the Roman Republic*. Cambridge: Cambridge University Press, 2006.

McLaughlin, Terence P., ed. *The Summa parisiensis on the Decretum gratiani*. Toronto: PIMS, 1952.

McMichael, Steven J. "Francis and the Encounter with the Sultan (1219)." In *The Cambridge Companion to Francis of Assisi*, edited by Michael J.P. Robson, 127–42. Cambridge: Cambridge University Press, 2012.

McNamara, Jo Ann. "The Need to Give: Suffering and Female Sanctity in the Middle Ages." In *Images of Sainthood in Medieval Europe*, edited by Renate Blumenfeld-Kosinski and Timea Szell. 199–221. Ithaca, NY: Cornell University Press, 1991.

"Medieval Clergy and Disability." Borthwick Institute for Archives, University of York. www.york.ac.uk/borthwick/holdings/guides/research-guides/disability/medieval-clergy-and-disability/. Accessed 19 February 2015.

Meirinhos, José Francisco. "Petrus Hispanus Portugalensis: Elementos para uma differençâo de autores. *Revista Española de Filosofia Medieval* 3 (1996: 51–76.

Menestò, Enrico. "A Re-reading of Francis of Assisi's 'Letter to the Faithful.'" *Greyfriars Review* 14:2 (2000): 97–110.

Menestò, Enrico, and S. Brufani. *Fontes Franciscani*. Assisi: Edizioni Porziuncula, 1996.

Metzler, Irina. *Disability in Medieval Europe: Thinking about Physical Impairment during the High Middle Ages, 1100–1400*. Abingdon and New York: Routledge, 2006.

– "Medieval Blindness and the Law". Scribd. https://www.scribd.com/document/157675720/Irina-Metzler-EN-Medieval-blindness-and-the-law-visual-impairment-in-canon-law-and-civil-jurisprudence-and-as-judicial-consequence, 1–9. Last updated 2 August 2013.

– *A Social History of Disability in the Middle Ages: Cultural Considerations of Physical Impairment*. Abingdon and New York: Routledge 2013.

Mitchell, Piers. *Medicine in the Crusades: Warfare, Wounds and the Medieval Surgeon*. Cambridge: Cambridge University Press, 2004.

Montford, Angela. "Brothers Who Have Studied Medicine: Dominican Friars in Thirteenth-Century Paris." *Social History of Medicine* 24:3 (2011): 535–53.

– "Occupational Health in the Mendicant Orders." In *The Use and Abuse of Time in Christian History*, edited by R.N. Swanson, 95–106. Studies in Church History 37. Cambridge: Cambridge University Press, 2002.

– *Health, Sickness, Medicine and the Friars in the Thirteenth and Fourteenth Centuries*. Aldershot: Ashgate, 2004.

Mooney, Brian. *Francis of Assisi and His Canticle of Brother Sun Reassessed*. New York: Palgrave-MacMillan, 2013.

Mooney, Catherine. "Francis of Assisi as Mother, Father and Androgynous Figure." In *The Boswell Thesis: Essays on Christianity, Social Tolerance and Homosexuality*, edited by Matthew Kuefler, 301–32. Chicago: University of Chicago Press, 2006.

Moorman, John. *A History of the Franciscan Order from Its Origins to the Year 1517*. Oxford: Clarendon Press, 1968.

– *The Sources for the Life of St. Francis of Assisi.* Manchester: Manchester University Press, 1940.

More, Alison. "Convergence, Conversion, and Transformation: Gender and Sanctity in Thirteenth-Century Liège." In *Representing Genders and Sexualities in Europe: Construction, Transformation and Subversion, 600–1530,* edited by Elizabeth L'Estrange and Alison More, 33–48. Aldershot: Ashgate, 2011.

Muessig, Carolyn. "Signs of Salvation: The Evolution of Stigmatic Spirituality before Francis of Assisi." *Church History* 82:1 (March 2013): 40–68.

Murray, Jacqueline. "The Law of Sin That Is My Members": The Problem of Male Embodiment." In *Gender and Holiness: Men, Women and Saints in Late Medieval Europe,* edited by Samantha Riches and Sarah Salih, 9–22. Abingdon and New York: Routledge, 2002.

Nielsen, Kim. "Historical Thinking and Disability History." *Disability Studies Quarterly* 28:3 (2008). http://dsq-sds.org/article/view/107/107.

Niermeyer, J.F. *Mediae Latinitatis Lexicon Minus: Abbreviationes et index fontium.* Leiden: Brill, 1997.

Nimmo, Duncan. *Reform and Division in the Franciscan Order: 1226–1538.* Rome: Capuchin Historical Institute, 1987.

Paolazzi, Carlo. "Le Epistole Maggiori di Frate Francesco." *Archivum Fratrum Historicum* 101 (2008): 3–154.

– "Francis and His Use of Scribes: A Puzzle to Be Solved." Translated by E. Hagman. *Greyfriars Review* 18:3 (2004): 481–97.

– "Introduzione a *Cantico do Fratre Sole.*" In *Francisci Assisiensis: Scripta,* 118–20. Grottaferrata: Collegi S. Bonaventurae, 2009.

– *Il Cantico di frate Sole.* Genoa: Marietti, 1992.

–, ed. *Francisci Assisiensis: Scripta.* Grottaferrata: Collegi S. Bonaventurae, 2009.

Parisotti, Orestes. *Quo morbo oculi sensum amisit Francescus ab Assiso.* Rome: Tipografia pontificia, 1918.

Paster, Gail Kern. "The Unbearable Coldness of Female Being: Women's Imperfection and the Humoral Economy." *English Literary Renaissance* 28:3 (1998): 416–40.

– *Humoring the Body: Emotions and the Shakespearean Stage.* Chicago: University of Chicago Press, 2004.

Pásztor, Edith. "St. Francis, Cardinal Hugolino and 'The Franciscan Question.'" Translated by P. Colbourne. *Greyfriars Review* 1:1 (Fall 1987): 1–29.

Patrologia Latina, ed. J.P. Migne. Paris: Garnier fratres, 1866–1882.

Pattenden, Miles. "The Canonization of Clare of Assisi and Early Franciscan History." *Journal of Ecclessiastical History* 59:2 (April 2008): 208–26.

Pearman, Tory Vanderventer. *Woman and Disability in Medieval Literature.* New York: Palgrave Macmillan, 2010.

Pellerini, Luigi. "Considerazioni e proposte metodologiche per una analisi delle fonti Francesane." *Laurentianum* 18 (1977): 292–13.

Perkins, Judith. *The Suffering Self: Pain and Narrative Representation in the Early Christian Era*. Abingdon and New York: Routledge, 1995.

Peter Ferrand. *Legenda sancti Dominici*, edited by D. H-C. Scheeben, 209–60. MOPH 16. Rome: Institutum Historicum Fratrum Praedicatorum, 1935.

Plouvier, L. "L'electuaire, un medicament plusieurs fois millenaire." *Bulletin-Cercle Benelux d'histoire de la pharmacie* 86 (1994): 7–21.

– "Le 'Lectuaire': Une confiture du bas Moyen Âge." In *Du Manuscrit à la Table*, edited by C. Lambert, 243–56. Montreal: Les Presses de l'Université de Montréal, 1992.

Pozzi, G. "Lo stile di San Francesco." *Italia mediovale e umanistica* 41 (2000): 7–72.

Pratesi, A. "L'autografo di San Francesco nel Duomo di Spoleto." In *San Francesco e i francescani a Spoleto*, 17–26. Spoleto: Academia Spoletina, 1984.

Prudlio, Donald. *Certain Sainthood: Canonization and the Origins of Papal Infallibility in the Medieval Church*. Ithaca, NY: Cornell University Press, 2016.

Rawcliffe, Carole. *Leprosy in Medieval England*. Woodbridge: Boydell, 2006.

– *Medicine and Society in Later Medieval England*. Stroud: Sutton Publishing, 1995.

Raymond of Peñafort. *Decretalium gregorii*. In *Decretalium Collections*, edited by A.L. Richter, 1–928. Graz: Akademische Druck-u. Verlagsanstalt, 1959.

Retief, Marno, and Rantoa Letšosa. "Models of Disability: A Brief Overview," *HTS Teologiese Studies/Theological Studies*, 74:1 (2018), 1-8.

Richards, Graham. *Putting Psychology in Its Place: An Introduction from a Critical Historical Perspective*. Abingdon and New York: Routledge, 1996.

Richardson, Tim. *Sweets: A History of Candy*. New York: Bloomsbury, 2002.

Riley, Paul V., Jr. "Francis' Assisi": Its Political and Social History, 1175–1225." *Franciscan Studies* 34 (1974): 393–424.

Robson, Michael. *The Franciscans in the Middle Ages*. Woodbridge: Boydell Press, 2006.

Robson, Michael, and Patrick Zutshi. "An Early Manuscript of the *Admonitions* of St. Francis of Assisi." *Journal of Ecclesiastical History* 62:2 (April 2011): 217–54.

Roest, Bert. *Reading the Book of History: Intellectual Contexts and Educational Functions of Franciscan Hagiography, 1226–ca 1350*. PhD diss., Groningen University, 1996.

Röhrkasten, Jens. "Authority and Obedience in the Early Franciscan Order." In *Episcopacy, Authority and Gender: Aspects of Religious Leadership in Europe, 1100–2000*, edited by Jan Wim Buisman, Marjet Derks, and Peter Raedts, 98–115. Leiden: Brill, 2015.

Ross, Ellen. "'She Wept and Cried Right Loud for Sorrow and for Pain': Suffering, the Spiritual Journey, and Women's Experience in Late Medieval Mysticism." In *Maps of Flesh and Light: The Religious Experience of Medieval Women Mystics*, edited by Ulrike Wiethaus, 45–59. Syracuse, NY: Syracuse University Press, 1993.

Rueben, Adrian. "Landmarks in Hepatology." *Hepatology* 36:3 (2002): 770–73.

242 Bibliography

Sabatier, Paul. *Life of Francis of Assisi*. Translated by L.S. Houghton. New York: Charles Scribner's Sons, 1919.

Salas-Salvadó, J., P. Casas-Agustench, and A. Salas-Huetos. "Cultural and Historical Aspects of Mediterranean Nuts with Emphasis on Their Attributed Healthy and Nutritional Properties." Supplement 1, *NMCD: Nutrition, Metabolism and Cardiovascular Diseases* 21 (2011): S1–S6.

Sassetti, Angelo. *Analecta Franciscana Reatina*. Reiti: Soc. Tip. "Giornale di Basilicata," 1926.

Sayers, Jane E. *Papal Government in England during the Pontificate of Honorius III, (1216–1227)*. Cambridge: Cambridge University Press, 1984.

Schatzlein, Joanne, and Daniel Sulmasy. "The Diagnosis of St. Francis: Evidence for Leprosy." *Franciscan Studies* 47:25 (1987): 181–217.

Schlosser, Katherine. "History of Trachoma." Special edition, *Trachoma Matters: Newsletter of the International Trachoma Initiative*. http://trachoma .org/other-resources.

Schmucki, Octavian. "The Illnesses of Francis during the Last Years of His Life." Translated by Edward Hagman. *Greyfriars Review* 13:1 (1999): 21–59.

– "St. Francis' Level of Education." Translated by P. Barrett. *Greyfriars Review* 10:2 (Winter 1996): 153–70.

– *The Stigmata of St. Francis of Assisi: A Critical Investigation in Light of Thirteenth Century Sources*. Translated by C.F. Connors. St. Bonaventure, NY: Franciscan Institute Publications, 1991.

Schroeder, H.J. *Disciplinary Decrees of the General Councils: Text, Translation and Commentary*. St. Louis: B. Herder, 1937.

Seton, Walter. "The Last Two Years of the Life of St. Francis." In *St. Francis of Assisi: Essays in Commemoration, 1226–1926*, edited by W. Seton, 219–41. London: University of London, 1926.

Shakespeare, Tom. "The Sexual Politics of Disabled Masculinity." *Sexuality and Disability* 17:1 (1999): 53–64.

Shaw, Theresa. *The Burden of the Flesh: Fasting and Sexuality in Early Christianity*. Minneapolis: Fortress Press 1998.

Shuttleworth, Russell, Nikki Wedgewood, and Nathan Wilson. "The Dilemma of Disabled Masculinity." *Men and Masculinities* 15:2 (2012): 174–94.

Sigbert of Gembloux. *Gesta abbatum Gemblacensium*, edited by G. Pentz, 523–42. *Monumenta Germaniae Historica*, Scriptores 8. Hanover: Impensis Bibliopolii Hahniani, 1848.

Singer, Julie. "Disability and the Social Body." *Postmedieval: A Journal of Medieval Cultural Studies* 3:2 (2012): 135–41.

– "Towards a Transhuman Model of Medieval Disability." *Postmedieval: A Journal of Medieval Cultural Studies* 1:1–2 (2010): 173–79.

Siraisi, Nancy. *Medieval and Early Renaissance Medicine: An Introduction to Knowledge and Practice*. Chicago: University of Chicago Press, 1990.

Smith, Roger. "The History of Psychological Categories." *Studies in History and Philosophy of Biological and Biomedical Sciences* 36:1 (March 2005): 55–94.

Speculum perfectionis (ed. Lemmens), sive Speculum perfectionis (minus). In *Fontes Franciscana,* edited by E. Menestò and Stefano Brufani, 1745-1825. Assisi: Porziuncula, 1995.

Speculum perfectionis (ed. Sabatier), sive Speculum perfectionis. In *Fontes Franciscana,* edited by E. Menestò and Stefano Brufani, 1849–2053. Assisi: Porziuncula, 1995.

Spigelman, Mark, and Eshitu Lemma. "The Use of the Polymerase Chain Reaction (PCR) to Detect *Mycobacterium tuberculosis* in Ancient Skeletons." *International Journal of Osteoarchaeology* 3:2 (1993): 137–43.

Spoto, Daniel. *Reluctant Saint: The Life of Francis of Assisi.* New York: Penguin, 2002.

"Statua generalia ordinis edita in capitulis generalibus celebratis Narbonae an 1260, Assisii an. 1279 atque Parisiis ad. 1292." Edited by M. Bihl. *Achivum franciscanum historicum* 36 (1941): 13–94 and 284–358.

Stebel, Josef. "Kulturhistorisches aus der Geschichte der Opthalmologie und Medizen. Diagnose des Augenleidens des hl. Franziskus von Assisi. Ein Beitrag zu Behandlung der Augenleiden im Hochmittelalter. Die Todesursache A. Dürers." *Klinische Monatsblätter für Augenheilkunde* 99 (1937): 252–60.

Stiker, Henri-Jacques. *A History of Disability.* Translated by William Sayers. Ann Arbor, MI: University of Michigan Press, 2002.

Sturges, Robert S. *Chaucer's Pardoner and Gender Theory: Bodies of Discourse.* New York: Palgrave, 2000.

Taylor, Hugh. *Trachoma: A Blinding Scourge from the Bronze Age to the Twenty-first Century.* East Melbourne: Centre for Eye Research Australia, 2008.

Temperini, Lino. *Francesco di Assisi: Cronistoria psicologia itinerario spirituale.* Rivoli: Neos Edizioni, 2012.

Thomas of Celano. *Tractatus de miraculis beati Francisci.* In *Fontes Franciscana,* edited by E. Menestò and Stefano Brufani, 642–755. Assisi: Porziuncula, 1995.

– *The Life of Saint Francis.* In *Francis of Assisi: Early Documents,* edited by Regis J. Armstrong, J.A. Wayne Hellmann, and William J. Short, 1.181–1.301. 3 vols. Hyde Park, NY: New City Press, 1999–2001.

– *The Remembrance of the Desire of a Soul (The Second "Life" of St. Francis).* In *Francis of Assisi: Early Documents,* edited by Regis J. Armstrong, J.A. Wayne Hellmann, and William J. Short, 2.232–2.395. 3 vols. Hyde Park, NY: New City Press, 1999–2001.

– *The Treatise on the Miracles of St. Francis.* In *Francis of Assisi: Early Documents,* edited by Regis J. Armstrong, J.A. Wayne Hellmann, and William J. Short, 2.396–2.469. 3 vols. Hyde Park, NY: New City Press, 1999–2001.

244   Bibliography

– *Vita brevior*. In "Thomas Celanensi Vita beati patris nostril Francisci (Vita brevior): Présentation et edition critique," edited by J. Dalarun. *Analecta Bollandiana* 133:1 (2015): 35–86.

– *Vita prima*. In *Fontes Franciscana*, edited by E. Menestò and Stefano Brufani, 274–425. Assisi: Porziuncula, 1995.

– *Vita secunda*. In *Fontes Franciscana*, edited by E. Menestò and Stefano Brufani, 442–641. Assisi: Porziuncula, 1995.

Thomas of Eccleston. *De adventu fratrum minorum in Angliam*. In *Analecta Franciscana I*, edited by Patres Collegii S. Bonaventurae, 217–56. Quarrachi: Typographia Collegii S. Bonaventurae, 1885.

Thomas Spalatensis. *Historia Pontificum Salonitanorum et Spolatinorum, Monumenta Germaniae Historica*, 568–98. Scriptores 29. Hanover: Impensis Bibliopolii Hahniani, 1892.

Thompson, Augustine. *Francis of Assisi: A New Biography*. Ithaca, NY: Cornell University Press, 2012.

Trembinski, Donna. *"Non alter Christus:* Early Dominican Lives of St. Francis." *Franciscan Studies* 63 (2005): 69–105.

Trexler, Richard. "The Stigmatized Body of Francis of Assisi Conceived, Processed, Disappeared." In *Frömmigkeit im Mittelalter*, edited by Klaus Schreiner, 463–97. Munich: Fink, 2002.

de Troyes, Chrétien. "Perceval." In *Arthurian Romances*, translated by William Kibler, 381–94. London: Penguin, 1991.

Urner, Carol Reilley. *The Search for Brother Iacopa: A Study on Jacopa Deo Settesoli, Friend of Francis of Assisi and His Movement*. Unpublished MA thesis. Manila University, 1980.

Vauchez, André. *Francis of Assisi: The Life and Afterlife of a Medieval Saint*. Translated by Michael Cusato. New Haven, CT: Yale University Press, 2012.

– *François d'Assise: Entre histoire et mémoire*. Paris: Fayard, 2009.

– *Sainthood in the Later Middle Ages*. Translated by J. Birrell. Cambridge: Cambridge University Press, 2005.

"Vetigia constitutionum praenarbonensium (1239–1257)." In *Constitutiones generalis ordinis fratrum minorum*, edited by C. Cenci and R.G. Maillaux, 43–63. Grottaferrata: Editiones Collegii S. Bonaventurae, 2007.

Vidier, A. "Le Trésor de la Sainte-Chapelle." *Mémoires del a Société de l'histoire de Paris et de Île-de-France* 34 (1907): 199–234.

Vincent of Beauvais. *Speculum naturale*. B. Belleri, 1624; repr. Graz: Akademischen Druck-u. Verlagsanstalt, 1967.

Vorreaux, Damian. *The Tau: A Franciscan Symbol: History, Chronology, Iconography*. Translated by M. Archer and P. Lachance. Chicago: Franciscan Herald Press, 1977.

Wadding, Luke. *Annales minorum*. Rome: Ex Typographia Ioannis Petris Collinii, 1654.

Wade, Susan. "Abbot Erluin's Blindness: The Monastic Implications of Violent Loss of Sight." In *Negotiating Community and Difference in Medieval Europe: Gender, Power, Patronage and the Authority of Religion in Latin Christendom*, edited by Katherine Allen Smith and Scott Wells, 207–22. Leiden: Brill, 2009.

Warren, Carolina. "Aging and Identity in Premodern Times." *Research on Aging* 20:1 (1998): 11–35.

Weinstein, Donald, and Rudolph M. Bell. *Saints and Society*. Chicago: University of Chicago Press, 1982.

Wells, Scott. *The Exemplary Blindness of Francis of Assisi*. In *Disability in the Middle Ages: Rehabilitations, Reconsiderations, Reverberations*, edited by J. Eyler, 67–80. Farnham: Ashgate, 2010.

Wheatley, Edward. "Blind Jews and Blind Christians: Metaphorics of Marginalization in Medieval Europe." *Exemplaria* 14:2 (2002): 351–79.

– *Stumbling Blocks before the Blind: Medieval Constructions of a Disability*. Ann Arbor: University of Michigan Press, 2010.

Whitney, Elspeth. "What's Wrong with the Pardoner: Complexion Theory, the Phlegmatic Man, and Effeminancy?" *The Chaucer Review* 45:4 (2011): 357–89.

Wickersheimer, Ernest. *Dictionnaire biographique des médecins en France au moyen âge*. Paris: Droz, 1936.

Wilson, Daniel J. "Fighting Polio Like a Man: Intersections of Masculinity, Disability and Gender." In *Gendering Disability*, edited by Bonnie G. Smith and Beth Hutchison, 119–33. New Brunswick, NJ: Rutgers University Press, 2004.

Winroth, Anders. *The Making of Gratian's* Decretum. Cambridge: University of Cambridge Press, 2000.

The Writings of Francis of Assisi: Letters and Prayers. Edited by M. Blastic et al. St. Bonaventure, NY: Franciscan Institute Publications, 2011. Kindle.

Yarom, Nitza. *Body, Blood and Sexuality: A Psychoanalytic Study of St. Francis' Stigmata and Their Historical Context*. New York: Peter Lang, 1992.

Zavalloni, Roberto. *La personalità di Francesco d'Assisi: Studio psicologico*. Padua: Edizioni Messaggero, 1991.

Zeppa, Rosario. "San Francesco's Blindness." *Journal of Paleopathology* 3:3 (1991): 133–35.

Ziegler, Joseph. *Medicine and Religion c. 1300: The Case of Arnau da Vilanova*. Oxford: Oxford Historical Monographs, 1998.

Index